FURTHER ENHANCE YOUR STUDY

Student Workbook

Spiritual growth is most effective when we study the Word at home in addition to our time at church. To encourage more interaction with Scripture, the Student Workbook includes daily devotions to study the week's lesson and passage in greater depth.

Lesson Manual Dropcard

Teachers can take advantage of the digital format of lessons provided on this Dropcard to customize lessons for their church. All fifty-two lessons from this volume are provided on the Dropcard in both Word and PDF files.

Lesson Leaves

Engage guests in their study of the week's lesson by providing a lesson leaf—a one-page sheet that contains the focus verse, lesson text, and focus thought of the lesson so guests without a Student Workbook or Lesson Manual can follow along. (One set of Adult Lesson Leaves contains five copies per lesson.)

Apostolic Handbook Series

Would you like to continue your study of Scripture beyond the lesson materials? The Apostolic Handbook Series offers eight books covering the major sections of the Bible with insights on culture, language, and history, thoroughly grounded by Apostolic writers.

VISIT WWW.PENTECOSTALPUBLISHING.COM FOR MORE DETAILS

CONTENTS

CONTENTS

You've wisely secured Apostolic teaching materials for you and the adult learners of the church.

What about your children and youth?

WORD AFLAME CURRICULUM

Versatile Apostolic Curriculum for Every Age:

Teacher Manual

Available for:

Toddler - ages 2–3

Kindergarten - ages 4–5

Beginner - grades 1–2

Primary - grades 3–4

Preteen - grades 5–6

Activity Papers

Teacher's Resource Packet

Questions? Need a sample lesson? Ready to order?

Contact a PPH curriculum specialist:

866.819.7667 | www.pentecostalpublishing.com

FALL 2019

The Living Word
SERIES

Godly Leadership

LESSON
MANUAL

Lesson Manual

© 2019 Pentecostal Publishing House • 36 Research Park Court • Weldon Spring, MO 63304
www.pentecostalpublishing.com • All rights reserved.
Manufactured in USA, September 2019, 1911911

EDITORIAL STAFF
Editor in Chief: Robin Johnston
Associate Editor, Curriculum: Lee Ann Alexander
Word Aflame Adult Editor: Jonathan McClintock

WRITERS

Ann Ahrens
James Boatman
John Moore
Carlton Coon

Gayla Baughman
Richard Davis
Chris Paris
Tom O'Daniel

CONTENTS

GODLY LEADERSHIP

by Jonathan McClintock

Looking at the bookshelves of the local big box bookstores, we see a massive number of leadership books, which seem to suggest leadership is a popular ambition among most people. It can appear everyone wants to be a leader. Perhaps one reason so many covet the idea of leadership is the recognition and honor great leaders receive, and to us as humans, recognition and honor are appealing to our flesh.

However, though many crave the recognition and honor successful leadership brings, often men and women thrust into leadership positions fail to realize their lack of internal readiness. This lack of internal readiness has produced numerous leadership tragedies, proving leadership is not something to be desired for the wrong reasons.

The Bible is replete with examples of both good and bad leadership. Men like Saul show us the dangers that come to leaders who lack patience and the ability to harness the struggles within. Examples like Samuel show us the strength it takes to exercise good leadership, even in the face of challenging circumstances.

Then examples like David show us both the good and bad side of leadership, emphasizing that even godly leaders have a human side.

It is important for us to pray for the leaders God has placed in our lives. We must pray for their strength not to fail, even when the pressures of the position try to crush their spirits, their passions, and their vision. We must pray for their faith to prevail, as they listen intently to God's voice and seek to lead us in the paths of righteousness.

Godly leadership truly is a gift from God. If you find yourself serving under a leader whose heart is sensitive to God's presence, whose mind is focused on God's plan, and whose voice consistently declares God's ways, take the time each day to thank God for your leader and cover your leader in prayer.

However, if you find yourself in a place of leadership, seek God's face daily, navigate God's Word regularly, and surrender your heart to God's purpose and plan, so you avoid the pitfalls of ungodly leaders and find yourself accurately portraying godly leadership.

LESSON MANUAL

This Lesson Manual has been developed with the goal of providing teachers numerous options to assist in preparation and delivery of each lesson.

In each lesson you will find a Focus Thought, Focus Verse, and Lesson Text that lay a foundation and give direction for the material that is to be presented. Questions are dispersed throughout the body of each lesson to provoke thought and spark discussion. We urge teachers to use these questions as a means of helping students apply each portion of the lesson.

> » *How does God being "all knowing" bring you comfort?*

STUDENT WORKBOOK

The Student Workbook has been organized in such a way that students are given the tools to not only follow the major points of each lesson but will also have a tool to further their personal discipleship and devotion throughout the week.

1. The Focus Thought, Focus Verse, and Culture Connection have been included in the Student Workbook.
2. The Lesson Outline has also been included to give the student a template to follow as the lesson is being taught. In addition, certain parts of the outline correspond with the daily discipleship prompts in the Approach section. This is designed to show what part of the lesson corresponds to the particular day's lesson text and application questions.
3. The Approach section is designed to give the student daily discipleship prompts by including portions of the lesson and application questions. The flexibility of this section allows for the student to follow along and interact during class, to become familiar with the lesson content before class, or to spend time in review during the week following class.
4. The Ask and Apply questions are presented for the purpose of helping the student contemplate the truths of Scripture and the content of the lesson. The first of the questions in each set is taken directly from the Lesson Manual, while the second question in each set is an additional prompt designed to help the student apply what is being taught.

POWERPOINTS

To access your FREE PowerPoints visit: Pentecostalpublishing.com/wappt

God Places Leaders in Our Lives

FOCUS THOUGHT

Because we often need someone to show us the way, God places leaders in our lives.

 **FOCUS VERSE**

I Samuel 3:19

And Samuel grew, and the LORD was with him, and did let none of hls words fall to the ground.

 **LESSON TEXT**

I Samuel 3:19–21

19 And Samuel grew, and the LORD was with him, and did let none of his words fall to the ground.

20 And all Israel from Dan even to Beer-sheba knew that Samuel was established to be a prophet of the LORD.

21 And the LORD appeared again in Shiloh: for the LORD revealed himself to Samuel in Shiloh by the word of the LORD.

I Samuel 7:3–6

3 And Samuel spake unto all the house of Israel, saying, If ye do return unto the LORD with all your hearts, then put away the strange gods and Ashtaroth from among you, and prepare your hearts unto the LORD, and serve him only: and he will deliver you out of the hand of the Philistines.

4 Then the children of Israel did put away Baalim and Ashtaroth, and served the LORD only.

5 And Samuel said, Gather all Israel to Mizpeh, and I will pray for you unto the LORD.

6 And they gathered together to Mizpeh, and drew water, and poured it out before the LORD, and fasted on that day, and said there, We have sinned against the LORD. And Samuel judged the children of Israel in Mizpeh.

CULTURE CONNECTION

LEADING THE BLIND

Michael Hingson was rescued during the 9/11 attack on the Twin Towers in New York in 2001. His hero was not who you would expect. In fact, she was not even human. The story of a faithful dog named Roselle, leading her blind master and others down nearly eighty flights of stairs in Twin Tower 1, is an amazing story of courage and dedication. The beautiful cream-colored Labrador was the hero, guiding them through fire and thick smoke and finally safely outside the building seconds before it collapsed.

This story is amazing and reminds us of God's care in providing a faithful dog to lead so many people to safety. Most of those people would have died were it not for Roselle, the Labrador hero. God has strategically placed people in our lives to lead us when we are wandering helplessly through life. He handpicks people who will encourage us when we are discouraged, give us sound advice when we are about to make an important decision, or cry with us when we are hurting. When God places a leader in our lives, we can rest assured, that person will help us arrive at the right place. God positions leaders in our lives at just the right time and place.

 ## OUTLINE

I. GOD SPOKE TO SAMUEL
  A. God's Voice Sounded Like Eli's Voice
  B. Speak Lord, Your Servant Is Listening

II. SAMUEL OBEYED GOD'S CALL
  A. Godly Leaders Obey God's Call
  B. Godly Leaders Lead People According to God's Word

III. AS THEIR LEADER, SAMUEL INTERCEDED FOR ISRAEL
  A. Samuel Called the People to Repentance
  B. Samuel Called Upon the Lord
  C. God Heard and Answered

IV. GODLY LEADERS ARE GOD'S GIFT TO HIS PEOPLE

CONTEMPLATING THE TOPIC

The story is told of a group of weary soldiers during the Revolutionary War who were using their last measure of strength to dig a trench in which to shelter themselves. Instead of offering to help, the leader of this ragged group of soldiers barked orders from the sidelines, threatening punishment if the work was not completed within an hour.

The soldiers and their leader barely noticed the stranger who rode past on horseback. Pausing to observe the scene, the stranger asked the leader, "Why aren't you helping these men dig the trench?" Offended, the leader responded, "Because I am in charge here. If you don't like it, get down in the trench and dig with them." Much to the surprise of all, the stranger grabbed a shovel and began digging; he stayed until the job was completed.

After taking a few moments to congratulate the men on a job well done, the stranger approached the leader and said, "If in the future you find that your exalted rank prevents you from supporting your men, notify your superiors and I will find a more permanent solution." Immediately the arrogant leader realized with whom he was speaking: General George Washington.

I. GOD SPOKE TO SAMUEL

The opening verse of I Samuel 3 reveals, "The word of the LORD was precious in those days; there was no open vision." The implication is that a direct word from God was rare, so one would likely be surprised and maybe even a little skeptical as to whether or not it was God who was actually speaking. Some Old Testament scholars believe Eli, Samuel's mentor, had never had a direct encounter with God in his lifetime. Given Samuel's young age, and the fact that the older, wiser, and well-seasoned high priest Eli had never received direct communication from God, one can understand the confusion Samuel must have felt at the repeated calls for his attention.

This original encounter with God would set the stage for the rest of Samuel's life. Time and time again, the voice of the Lord would come to Samuel while he served as the prophet to God's people. I Samuel 3:19 indicates Samuel's influence was great, and that the Lord "did let none of his words fall to the ground." None of Samuel's words were wasted or empty. His influence stretched across the nation of Israel, "from Dan even to Beer-sheba" (I Samuel 3:20), an area covering the far north of the nation, all the way to the southern border, near the Negev Desert.

A. God's Voice Sounded Like Eli's Voice

The Temple in Shiloh, where Samuel was apprenticed under the leadership of Eli, was likely a small structure and could have been no more than a well-constructed tent. Since it was not replenished throughout the night, the oil-filled lamp near the Ark of God where Samuel lay sleeping began to flicker and would soon go out.

Samuel was a young boy, and Scripture indicates in I Samuel 3:7 that Samuel "did not yet know the LORD, neither was the word of the LORD yet revealed unto him." Given his youth and inexperience, it is not surprising that when called by God, Samuel mistook the voice for that of Eli. He immediately ran to his mentor out of obedience and duty, assuming the aged man needed assistance. Samuel's trademark obedience demonstrated here would come into play many times in his future as God's prophet to Israel.

B. Speak Lord, Your Servant Is Listening

Samuel's obedience at this point in his young life is remarkable. Not only did he faithfully serve his mentor, the high priest Eli, but he willingly answered the voice of God from whom he had never heard before. As was noted in I Samuel 3:1, for many years there had rarely been a word from God, and visions had been infrequent, if at all. But Samuel had been faithfully and carefully taught about Jehovah, the God of his people. Samuel knew the history of their deliverance from Egypt and of Jehovah's powerful hand of provision in the lives of his ancestral people. Though innocent and young, Samuel chose to be obedient and to trust this great God he had yet to know for himself.

While Samuel's obedience is extraordinary, the patience and persistence of God toward Samuel demonstrated his promise to be "slow to anger" (Exodus 34:6, NIV), one of five key characteristics by which God described Himself to Abraham. God, who knows all hearts, knew Samuel was young and inexperienced and would not likely recognize His voice.

» *Think about a time in your life when you sensed God's calling or direction. Did you, like Samuel, feel incapable, too young, or too old to believe God could be calling you to a specific work for Him? Explain.*

II. SAMUEL OBEYED GOD'S CALL

After three attempts to speak to Samuel, the Lord called a fourth time. Although Eli had instructed Samuel to respond to the call with, "Speak, LORD; for thy servant heareth," Eli did not reveal to Samuel the identity of the one who called (I Samuel 3:9). Samuel's obedience was, again, remarkable as he followed the instruction of Eli. The unknown voice did not introduce Himself to Samuel, nor did He commission Samuel into the service of God as His prophet. Instead, what followed was like unto a nightmare, as God detailed the bone-chilling judgment He was about to pour out upon the house of Eli because of the blasphemy committed by his sons against God (I Samuel 2:12–17). Jehovah announced, in no uncertain terms, that this judgment upon Eli's house would be forever, and the sins committed would not be forgiven.

» *How can Samuel serve as an example to believers when it comes to obediently carrying out God's commands even when the way forward is unclear?*

A. Godly Leaders Obey God's Call

One can hardly fathom what must have been going through the heart and mind of young Samuel. Scripture states in I Samuel 3:7, "Now Samuel did not yet know the LORD, neither was the word of the LORD yet revealed unto him." Samuel did not know the Lord, nor had he ever heard His voice. Yet despite his lack of knowledge and understanding, Samuel obeyed Eli and answered as instructed. Sharing such a grim pronouncement of judgment with Eli must have been unnerving for Samuel, for Scripture states that instead of going to straight to Eli in the middle of the night, he waited until the following morning (I Samuel 3:15). Although the news was devastating, Eli knew the word was from the Lord and concluded, "It is the LORD: let him do what seemeth him good" (I Samuel 3:18).

Samuel demonstrated obedience on many levels following his initial encounter with the Lord. Although the voice of the Lord must have been unsettling given the grim pronouncement, Samuel faithfully listened with an obedient heart, ready to carry out the Lord's commands. The morning after hearing God's voice, Samuel arose and faithfully carried out his duties in the Temple, being obedient to Eli's instruction. Then when Eli inquired as to the message from the Lord, Samuel obediently shared all God had said. I Samuel 3:18 reveals, "Samuel told him every whit, and hid nothing from him."

B. Godly Leaders Lead People According to God's Word

Samuel's obedience was key to his effectiveness as a leader and prophet in Israel. His responses to God and Eli were filled with humility and respect, even though he knew God was going to pour out judgment for the sins committed by Eli's sons. Because of his obedience, Samuel came to be trustworthy, a key character trait for effective leaders. Following this initial encounter, Samuel heard God's voice and faithfully passed his words on to the people of Israel. I Samuel 3:19 speaks to the prolific nature of Samuel's prophetic work, noting that not only was God with him, but He "did let none of his words fall to the ground." None of Samuel's words were wasted, but all carried significant weight, because they were the words of God to His people.

Samuel's words were truthful and effective, and because of this, his reputation spread throughout all Israel. I Samuel 3:20 states, "All Israel from Dan even to Beersheba knew that Samuel was established to be a prophet of the LORD." The people who lived in this large geographic area came to trust Samuel as their leader and prophet because of his obedience and determination to share the true words of Jehovah with the people. Samuel did not use his position to avoid difficult or messy situations; instead he responded with the same willing heart that heard God's voice as a youth. Because the people knew Samuel had proven himself to be a trustworthy leader, he went on to play key roles in delivering God's promises and judgments to the people for the rest of his life.

» *Think about some leaders in your life who have followed God in obedience. How has their humility and servant leadership helped to shape your life?*

III. AS THEIR LEADER, SAMUEL INTERCEDED FOR ISRAEL

The opening verses of I Samuel 7 find the people of Israel lamenting. Twenty years earlier, the Ark of the Lord had been returned to the house of Abinidab after being stolen by the Philistines. The people mourned and repented over their sinful worship of the gods of the Philistines, Baal and Astaroth. Baal, the pagan god of fertility, was believed to be the son of Dagon, the false god that repeatedly fell face first before the Ark of the Lord after it had been captured by the Philistines (I Samuel 5:3). Astaroth, the goddess of love and fertility, was worshiped during many rituals throughout the land. These practices were so depraved that worship of these gods was especially abominable in the sight of the Lord. That Israel had sunken so low as to worship in such a hideous manner deeply grieved the Lord.

A. Samuel Called the People to Repentance

Samuel's plea to the people to gather in repentance was likely filled with urgency due to the grievous nature of their sins. In contrast to demands of false gods that enslaved the people, Samuel's call to repentance was filled with grace and compassion that could only come from Israel's true God. The instructions given by Samuel in I Samuel 7:3 stipulated that the people return to God "with all your hearts." This was not an outward show of repentance, but one generated from the heart. Samuel knew that unless the hearts of the people were changed, they would never turn to the Lord.

But what if the people refused to experience the "heart surgery" necessary to truly turn them away from false gods? What if they had only paid lip service to Samuel and had walked away with sinful hearts still bound to the false gods? Samuel once again demonstrated effective and godly leadership by getting to the heart of the matter with the people, both literally and figuratively. Samuel lead the people in straightforward, honest confession. Together they prayed, "We have sinned against the Lord" (I Samuel 7:6). Samuel knew that unless the people were direct and wholeheartedly honest about their sin, they would quickly backslide into the same depraved practices.

» *What specifically about Samuel's process in leading the people to repentance can be applied in our own time given the depraved nature of our world?*

B. Samuel Called Upon the Lord

In I Samuel 7:5–6, Samuel prayed for the people, essentially standing between them and the God they had so grievously disappointed and sinned against. Samuel knew from the experience of Eli's sons that God did not tolerate willful sin or any flagrant violation of His covenant with the people. Perhaps Samuel wondered if God's wrath would burn against the people, causing him to be caught in the middle. Samuel knew God's grace, faithfulness, mercy, compassion, and slowness to anger, so in humility he led the people in a prayer of repentance. As he prayed, Samuel called upon the name of the Lord, the one true God of Israel.

» *Samuel demonstrated God's compassion and mercy in his prayer for the people. How can Samuel's prayer serve as an example for our own prayers for ourselves and others?*

C. God Heard and Answered

As the people of Israel repented for their sins against Jehovah, they poured out water before the Lord and fasted together for the entire day (I Samuel 7:6). Both of these acts were symbolic of the people's sincerity and true repentance, and God responded by showing Israel favor when the Philistines attacked. I Samuel 7:8 finds the people crying out to Samuel, "Cease not to cry unto the Lord our God for us, that he will save us out of the hand of the Philistines." Here the people claimed Jehovah as "our God," another symbol of their turn from abominable sin to the one true God. They did not turn to one another; instead they looked to Samuel as the one who had been established by God to lead them.

As the Philistine army bore down upon the people of Israel, Samuel once again stood between them and the eminent danger approaching. Taking a young lamb, Samuel offered it as a burnt offering to God, and "cried unto the Lord for Israel; and the LORD heard him" (I Samuel 7:9). Samuel modeled obedience to God's commands, placing himself in harm's way instead of running away from the approaching army in order to save himself. God's response to Samuel's obedience and godly sacrificial leadership of the people was remarkable and overwhelming: "The LORD thundered with a great thunder on that day upon the Philistines, and discomfited them; and they were smitten before Israel" (I Samuel 7:10). Without Samuel's courageous and obedient leadership, the people would likely have been defeated that day.

IV. GODLY LEADERS ARE GOD'S GIFT TO HIS PEOPLE

Faithful men and women have sacrificially served and led God's people throughout history. Serving with obedience even when it could have cost their lives, these men and women became God's hands, feet, and voice to call His people to repentance and consecration. That God would partner with humans who themselves are prone to sin is remarkable, yet time and again Scripture records God doing just that. These godly leaders do not see themselves as above the people, but they come alongside the people, partnering with them as they pursue a life of holiness and separation unto God. These key characteristics of godly leadership were demonstrated throughout Samuel's life as he continued to be the prophet and judge to whom Israel looked in time of need.

▶▶▶ INTERNALIZING THE MESSAGE

Sometimes godly leaders must get their hands dirty, both literally and figuratively, as did George Washington in the opening story of this lesson. When God's people are weary from battles of everyday life, godly leaders come alongside and demonstrate God's compassion, mercy, faithfulness, and goodness. They also remind us how easily our hearts can stray from the cause to which we are called. Those Revolutionary War soldiers had all but lost hope until their great leader came along and offered a helping hand. Seeing General Washington get down in the ditch and dig alongside them helped them to find renewed strength and courage for the coming battle.

And so it goes with the leaders God places in our lives. These men and women know the weariness of battle; they know how it feels to have all but lost hope. In their faithfulness to God, they intercede, gently but firmly leading those God has placed in their care. Godly leaders "dig with the soldiers," working to advance God's kingdom while caring for His people. While it is tempting to complain when we do not understand the decisions or directions taken by leadership, we can know that those who consistently seek God's face and order their lives by God's Word will ultimately be led by His hand.

God's Plan Is Better

FOCUS THOUGHT

Though it is easy to get caught up in making our own plans, we must submit to God's plan because His plan is always better.

 FOCUS VERSES

I Samuel 8:19–20

Nevertheless the people refused to obey the voice of Samuel; and they said, Nay; but we will have a king over us; that we also may be like all the nations; and that our king may judge us, and go out before us, and fight our battles.

 LESSON TEXT

I Samuel 8:10–20

10 And Samuel told all the words of the LORD unto the people that asked of him a king.

11 And he said, This will be the manner of the king that shall reign over you: He will take your sons, and appoint them for himself, for his chariots, and to be his horsemen; and some shall run before his chariots.

12 And he will appoint him captains over thousands, and captains over fifties; and will set them to ear his ground, and to reap his harvest, and to make his instruments of war, and instruments of his chariots.

13 And he will take your daughters to be confectionaries, and to be cooks, and to be bakers.

14 And he will take your fields, and your vineyards, and your oliveyards, even the best of them, and give them to his servants.

15 And he will take the tenth of your seed, and of your vineyards, and give to his officers, and to his servants.

16 And he will take your menservants, and your maidservants, and your goodliest young men, and your asses, and put them to his work.

17 He will take the tenth of your sheep: and ye shall be his servants.

18 And ye shall cry out in that day because of your king which ye shall have chosen you; and the LORD will not hear you in that day.

19 Nevertheless the people refused to obey the voice of Samuel; and they said, Nay; but we will have a king over us;

20 That we also may be like all the nations; and that our king may judge us, and go out before us, and fight our battles.

>>> CULTURE CONNECTION

SAFETY SIGNS

There are several popular hiking trails in Arizona. However, tourists not familiar with the area often do not adequately prepare for the three-digit temperatures that scorch the trails in the middle of summer. If these hikers do not have enough water and some protection from the sun, the hike can be fatal.

It is difficult sometimes to realize that certain decisions we make could end up being the worst decisions of our lives. What do you think the individuals who did not make it safely home from their hike on an Arizona mountain would say to us if they had a chance? Maybe they would admit, "I wish I would have followed the signs." Or "I knew better, but I thought I could make it without more water." Or "I should have been more prepared." Or "I should have packed a compass."

Some poor decisions we make may not be fatal, but they can have devastating effects on our lives, causing everything to change. Many of us have often thought, If only I could go back and alter that one decision. Sadly, our lives can take on the hopeless "if only" theme.

But there is hope. God has given us His Word as a compass to help us maneuver through life on a safe course. If we will stay alert, we will notice the signs along the way that give us direction. God uses people, situations, and other experiences to warn us of impending danger. All He requires of us is to pay attention to His plan, which is clearly posted in His Word.

 OUTLINE

I. ISRAEL DEMANDED A KING
  A. To Be like Other Nations
  B. Israel Wanted Their Own Way

II. SAMUEL WARNED ISRAEL
  A. A King Will Rule over Them
  B. You Will Become His Servants

III. GOD'S PLAN IS BETTER THAN OUR PLANS
  A. God Wants to Be Our King
  B. God Wants to Give Us the Best

 CONTEMPLATING THE TOPIC

God created humans in His likeness with the ability to think and make judgments of right and wrong. All was well for some time as Adam and Eve lived in a paradise of blessing and comfort. Life was neither hard nor complicated. God's instructions were clearly understood. Of all the fruit in the Garden they were permitted to eat and enjoy, they were warned not to eat the fruit from the Tree of the Knowledge of Good and Evil.

When there were no evil influences, Adam and Eve made correct judgments. However, when Satan entered the Garden, Adam and Eve were tempted to make a decision that was against their best interest. It appeared to them to be the logical thing to do at the time. Who would not consider greater wisdom to be an advantage in life? Not realizing they were being deceived, they decided to go against God's counsel.

Beginning in the Garden of Eden unto this day, God has always provided counsel for humanity. He made us and knows what is best for us. Our advantage is to seek His counsel in all matters of life. His way is always best. His Word is true. His path is right and straight. His judgments are always better because He knows the beginning from the end.

I. ISRAEL DEMANDED A KING

From the time of Moses until the selection of Saul as the first king of the commonwealth of Israel, God's chosen system of government for Israel was that of a theocracy. In a theocracy, God is sovereign, and priests rule in the name of God. This fulfilled God's intent that Israel should become "a kingdom of priests" unto the world (Exodus 19:6). Priests and judges ruled Israel through the conquest of the Promised Land. With time—approximately five hundred years—the priesthood deteriorated into a state of selfishness. (See I Samuel 2:27–36.) Therefore, the Lord raised up prophets to speak for Him to Israel.

Samuel was the first of the kingdom prophets. As a child, he wore a linen ephod and ministered before the Lord (I Samuel 2:18). Before the lamp of God went out in the Temple, the Lord called Samuel to be a prophet (I Samuel 3:3). As Samuel grew, the Lord was with him and none of his words fell to the ground. Therefore, all the people knew he was established to be a prophet of the Lord (I Samuel 3:19–21). With the weakened priesthood and Israel's dependence on strongmen to lead them during the conquest of Canaan, Israel's hearts were turned to desire their own king.

» *Why do you think Israel rejected God's plan and desired their own king?*

A. To Be like Other Nations

Samuel traveled throughout Israel and judged Israel all the days of his life (I Samuel 7:15). But when Samuel was old and his sons walked not in the ways of the Lord, the elders of Israel gathered before Samuel in Ramah and demanded a king (I Samuel 8:4–5). It seemed logical with the aging Samuel and the growing populace, but the desire of Israel was to be like other nations.

Their reasoning was twofold: Samuel was old, and his sons walked not in his (Samuel's) ways. It mattered not that the Lord had brought Israel out of Egypt, provided for them, and protected them during the conquest of the land. Their history was that of a victorious people. As long as Samuel lived, the hand of the Lord was against the Philistines, the archenemies of Israel (I Samuel 7:13). Their peace and prosperity were linked with their keeping of the commandments and Passover. The elders had a misplaced trust. They trusted in Samuel rather than the Lord.

B. Israel Wanted Their Own Way

Samuel's heart was grieved that the elders wanted a king like other nations. When Samuel prayed unto the Lord, the Lord told him to harken to the voice of the people for they had rejected Him to reign over them (I Samuel 8:7). The pattern of this people since coming out of Egypt, even unto that day, was dependence upon strong men as leaders. It is amazing how quickly people with no strong voice of leadership can slip away in commitment and devotion to those to whom they owe so much. Israel had found other gods to worship and rejected Jehovah (I Samuel 8:8).

As Israel sought for Moses to stand in for them at Sinai, because the presence of the Lord was so overpowering, they now, hundreds of years later, sought Samuel to cry to the Lord for them when facing the Philistines (I Samuel 7:8). Too often there is dependence on others as we shirk our personal responsibilities to have our own relationship with God. When people cease to worship the true God, they always turn to the arm of flesh to supply needs that have previously been promises of the Lord. It is difficult to trust a God in whom you have no continuing relationship.

Israel wanted to select their own leader rather than depend upon the Lord. They wanted to have a king like other nations, to judge them, to go before them, and to fight their battles (I Samuel 8:20). As time unfolded and Saul was selected to be their king, their visions of a great king to fight for them in battle were not realized. When the battle with the Philistines reoccurred, Saul was not on the battlefield leading them, but he allowed David, a lad, to go to battle against the giant (I Samuel 17:37–39). Israel selected Saul, but God chose David. It was easy to see their way was not the best.

» *Discuss how easy it is to find fault with leadership when one's personal devotion is lacking.*

II. SAMUEL WARNED ISRAEL

The Lord permitted Israel to have their own way, but not without warning.

Samuel was instructed of the Lord to warn the people of the adverse effects a king would have upon them. This Samuel did in explicit detail. When people reject the Lord, they reject the Lord's counsel also. The consequences of a wrong choice can be very destructive, even when mercy and grace are present. Israel was making a wrong choice. Their rationale justified their decision. Those who counsel among themselves, rejecting divine guidance from above, are not wise. Sin is usually the cause for rejecting spiritual counsel, but not always. Lack of experience or information concerning the issue can be equally damaging. But in Samuel's case, it was the elders of the tribes who asked for a king. The key is what the Lord told Samuel: Israel had a pattern of rejecting the Lord (I Samuel 8:8).

It is amazing that God's love for Israel remained, even when they rejected the Lord's counsel. It speaks to the covenant God made with Abraham and confirmed with Moses concerning His people. God's love is firm. His covenant prevails over any faltering of the people. Consider the seven churches in the Book of Revelation. They had faults, but they were still God's church.

» *How have you seen wrong choices lead to horrible consequences?*

A. A King Will Rule over Them

Samuel warned the people: The king will take your sons for his army. He will reap his own harvest from your lands and vineyards, taking them from you. Your daughters will become his servants. He will take a tenth of your seed, your vineyards, and your sheep, and you will be his servants. And, most importantly, in that day when you will cry unto the Lord, the Lord will not hear you (I Samuel 8:10–19). Nevertheless, they refused to listen to the counsel of Samuel. When Israel chose a monarchy rather than a theocracy as their rule of government, they chose someone to rule over them rather than someone to watch over them. A king's position and perspective are horizontal in every respect. It is of human height, authority, power, vision, and intellect. The Lord's position and perspective is vertical, altogether different. He is above, with unlimited vision, wisdom, power, and authority. More importantly, He shows unselfish love and commitment to the welfare of the people. The Lord's oversight is without greed or need of personal enrichment. Plus, the guidance of love grows sweeter with time rather than the pattern of overbearing rule.

B. You Will Become His Servants

In the five-hundred-year period between Moses and King Saul, Israel had battled to possess the land. It seems logical that they must have observed the lifestyles of the nations they conquered in the conquest. Did they not observe the cruelty and servanthood of those nations and their kings? Had they forgotten the historical path to freedom from the slavery of Egypt? Does history have a way of repeating itself and enslaving us to the same bondage as our forefathers unless we choose to remain a free people?

Israel was free under the liberty God provided them to worship God and direct the affairs of their families as they desired. But with a king, Samuel warned, "Ye shall be his servants" (I Samuel 8:15–17). He shall take the best of your young and a tenth of your lands and goods. Israel was choosing to serve two masters, the God of love and the king of law. Israel's cost was to double with a tenth for the Lord and a tenth for the king. Her service was to double also, with the duty and commitment to the king's will added to the love and joy of serving God. The law of servitude is that the servant's importance diminishes in direct proportion to the rise in the king's prominence. The Spirit of the Lord is a liberating, lifting Spirit, while the law of man weighs down.

> » *What causes people to forget their freedom in Jesus Christ and fall once again under slavery to sin?*

III. GOD'S PLAN IS BETTER THAN OUR PLANS

The lesson in Eden with the first family has remained true through the ages. God's plan is better than our plans. His plan is perfect and needs no correction. His ways are right and need no repentance. His directives lead to rewards of joy and peace with prosperity and purity. Our plans are not always bad, but neither are they always right and rewarding. Joshua knew what he was calling for when he admonished Israel to choose whom they would serve. History was speaking. Joshua chose to serve the Lord rather than the well-known gods of this world (Joshua 24:15).

A. God Wants to Be Our King

God's intent for Israel was that they be a nation unlike any other. They were to be His people with His cause before them. They were to be a holy nation, a kingdom of priests (Exodus 19:6). With a kingdom, there is of necessity a king. But a holy nation, whose subjects are priests, demands a complementing holy king. Jesus is the only King who can qualify for such a position. He is the Lord of Glory, the King of kings, the only potentate who can be such a king. (See I Corinthians 2:8; Revelation 19:16; I Timothy 6:15.) In Him was no sin. He was and is holy.

The Lord Jesus wants to be our King. Israel rejected the physical Jesus as the King of the Jews, even though Pilate wrote on the cross, "JESUS OF NAZARETH THE KING OF THE JEWS" (John 19:19). Jesus was not only the King of the Jews, but He was, and is, the King of all who desire the kingdom of God. The kingdom of God was first preached by John the Baptist, the righteous forerunner of Jesus (Luke 16:16). Jesus said His kingdom was not of this world (John 18:36) and was without observation (Luke 17:20), meaning it was a spiritual kingdom not limited to the Jews. Jesus preached the kingdom of God (Luke 4:43) and sent His disciples to do the same (Luke 9:2). Upon the Resurrection, Jesus again discussed the kingdom of God with His disciples (Acts 1:3). The disciples continued to teach and preach the kingdom of God after Pentecost (Acts 8:12; Romans 14:17).

B. God Wants to Give Us the Best

The purpose of Jesus coming was to save His people from their sins and to establish a church to embody and represent the kingdom of God. He is the King; His subjects are chosen of Him and destined to be His bride. What kind of a kingdom exists where servants are heirs and joint-heirs with the king? Only a kingdom built upon the principles of love and righteousness. Servants in the kingdom of God are not there out of duty, but of love. We choose to serve the Lord as our King because He chose to become our servant first.

In the Gospels, Mark presents Jesus as the servant, Matthew as Jesus the King, Luke as Jesus the man, and John as Jesus the divine.

Heaven gave its best when Jesus was born. He was the only begotten Son of God (John 3:16), given in love for a purpose. That purpose was so we might have forgiveness of sins and life through Him—not only life, but life more abundantly. We are promised not only a better, more abundant life in this world, but also life eternal. John wrote, "In this was manifested the love of God toward us, because that God sent his only begotten Son into the world, that we might live through him. Herein is love, not that we loved God, but that he loved us, and sent his Son to be the propitiation for our sins" (I John 4:9–10).

God's plan is to give us His best. To be a servant in the kingdom of God is a privilege with many blessings, the greatest of which is eternal life. But that is not all King Jesus wants to give. He desires that we sit with Him on His throne as heirs and joint-heirs with Christ, and not only to sit with Him, but to share His glory (Romans 8:17). And because He wants to give us the best, we shall be the bride of Christ (Revelation 21:9), chosen of Him, a glorious church, without spot or wrinkle.

That he might present it to himself a glorious church, not having spot, or wrinkle, or any such thing; but that it should be holy and without blemish. (Ephesians 5:27)

» **What are some of the "best" things God wants to give us?**

▶▶▶ INTERNALIZING THE MESSAGE

In the fourth century, Jerome, famous in the Latin Vulgate, wrote a saying that is still with us today. "Good, better, best. Never let it rest. 'Til your good is better and your better is best." For us, the "good" is the experience of salvation, including the baptism of the Holy Ghost. The "better" is Heaven, by the grave or the Rapture. Paul said, "To live is Christ, and to die is gain" (Philippians 1:21). But the "best" is, as the bride of Christ, to behold the Lamb in His full glory. The Lord has reserved the best for His people. That best concluded Jesus' prayer in John 17, when He prayed that His followers would be with Him and behold His glory. It was Jesus' request that His disciples would see the end of the matter, the conclusion in Heaven when all the glory and power of God were manifest in Jesus. Jesus described it as glory given of the Father (John 17:24).

When love is glorified, it is absolutely God's best. When we see love manifest in this life, we stand in awe. Consider what it will be like to see God's love manifest in its most glorified moment in Heaven. Eye has not seen, nor has it entered into the heart of man the wonders the Lord has prepared for those who walk upright before Him (I Corinthians 2:9). His way is always best.

Impatient Leadership

FOCUS THOUGHT
Impatience can hinder the working of God's plan in our lives.

 FOCUS VERSES

I Samuel 13:13–14
   And Samuel said to Saul, Thou hast done foolishly: thou hast not kept the commandment of the LORD thy God, which he commanded thee: for now would the LORD have established thy kingdom upon Israel for ever. But now thy kingdom shall not continue: the LORD hath sought him a man after his own heart, and the LORD hath commanded him to be captain over his people, because thou hast not kept that which the LORD commanded thee.

 LESSON TEXT

I Samuel 13:7–15
   7 And some of the Hebrews went over Jordan to the land of Gad and Gilead. As for Saul, he was yet in Gilgal, and all the people followed him trembling.

   8 And he tarried seven days, according to the set time that Samuel had appointed: but Samuel came not to Gilgal; and the people were scattered from him.

   9 And Saul said, Bring hither a burnt offering to me, and peace offerings. And he offered the burnt offering.

   10 And it came to pass, that as soon as he had made an end of offering the burnt offering, behold, Samuel came; and Saul went out to meet him, that he might salute him.

   11 And Samuel said, What hast thou done? And Saul said, Because I saw that the people were scattered from me, and that thou camest not within the days appointed, and that the Philistines gathered themselves together at Michmash;

   12 Therefore said I, The Philistines will come down now upon me to Gilgal, and I have not made supplication unto the LORD: I forced myself therefore, and offered a burnt offering.

   13 And Samuel said to Saul, Thou hast done foolishly: thou hast not kept the commandment of the LORD thy God, which he commanded thee: for now would the LORD have established thy kingdom upon Israel for ever.

   14 But now thy kingdom shall not continue: the LORD hath sought him a man after his own heart, and the LORD hath commanded him to be captain over his people, because thou hast not kept that which the LORD commanded thee.

   15 And Samuel arose, and gat him up from Gilgal unto Gibeah of Benjamin. And Saul numbered the people that were present with him, about six hundred men.

CULTURE CONNECTION

TIME IS ON OUR SIDE

Mego was a purebred Pekingese dog. With long hair draped to the ground, he looked more like a mop. One day as his owner called him for dinner, he bolted into the dining area. Unfortunately, he had not counted on the slick linoleum floor, nor the corner he would have to maneuver around to get to his dog bowl. As he approached the edge of the table, he tried gallantly to make the turn. However, his little legs were running and going nowhere. The linoleum was like ice. Smack! He hit the table leg head-on with a thud. His owner ran to his rescue, relieved to see that Mego was only a little stunned. He sat back on his hind legs only a few seconds before rising once again and lumbering to his feast. As impatience hindered this poor pooch from getting his dinner on time, perhaps we are somewhat like Mego.

Why is it hard for us to remember that time is on our side? Most of us tend to rush things along when a decision or issue needs to be addressed. If we can learn to give the situation time, often the circumstance will take care of itself without our intervention. We often hear the saying, "In God's time." God is not limited to our time. He lives in eternity, where there is no time. Since God is not relegated to our time, He will always do things right on time. We can find comfort in knowing that God gave us time to buffer some of the impatience we as humans cannot resist.

 OUTLINE

I. WAR WITH THE PHILISTINES
  A. Jonathan Attacked the Philistines at Geba
  B. The Philistines Responded

II. ISRAEL COWERED IN FEAR
  A. Saul Remained at Gilgal
  B. Saul Waited for Samuel's Guidance

III. SAUL GREW IMPATIENT
  A. Saul Offered Sacrifice Instead of Samuel
  B. Samuel Rebuked Saul

IV. SAUL'S KINGDOM WILL NOT ENDURE
  A. Impatience and Disobedience Led to the Forfeiting of Saul's Kingdom
  B. A Warning to Us to Remain Patient and Faithful to God

 CONTEMPLATING THE TOPIC

Peter, Paul, and other New Testament writers brought the believers into remembrance of what Jesus had taught as a source of strength and stability for their lives. Remembering the words of Jesus builds confidence, knowing the Lord is in control of our lives and will fight our battles. Our examples are plentiful of those who attempted to subvert the ways of the Lord with their own solutions to problematic situations. But if we remember the Kingdom belongs to the Lord and we are His subjects, then our faith is placed in His directive to accomplish the task before us and not in our own ability and wisdom.

Patience is often the single most important key to success in the Christian life. Waiting on the Lord is the source of renewed strength (Psalm 27:14; 37:34). Waiting gives time for God to work; for believers to pray and meditate; for counsel to be obtained; and for the adversary to worry, reconsider, and change.

Isaiah said it best: "But they that wait upon the LORD shall renew their strength; they shall mount up with wings as eagles; they shall run, and not be weary; and they shall walk, and not faint" (Isaiah 40:31). The eagle waits for the winds to come and lift it high. Likewise, we ought to wait for the Spirit, so we may run and not be weary (escape the enemy) and walk and not faint (experience God's presence in peace).

I. WAR WITH THE PHILISTINES

Believers have archenemies: The devil, the world, and the flesh. They are as old as time. They war against our souls and will continue to do so until the Lord removes His church from this world. Paul concluded his Christian life with the declaration, "I have fought a good fight, I have finished my course, I have kept the faith" (II Timothy 4:7). For many years, Israel's archenemy was the Philistines. After five hundred years of conquest and occupying the land of promise—from the days of Joshua to the kingship of Saul—the Philistines were still present. Christians of every generation will be involved in conflict. Jesus' entire life was lived under the political influence of the Herods, yet Jesus was victorious. He overcame the world (John 16:33).

Israel repented of her sin to desire a king and asked Samuel to pray unto the Lord that they would not die (I Samuel 12:16–25). Samuel calmed their fears, reassuring them that they were God's chosen people to bear His name. Samuel further added that he would not sin by not praying for them. God's mercy was extended, and Saul reigned as king. But mercy and forgiveness did not negate the prophesy of Samuel to Israel that a king would take their children into war. Forgiveness does not always remove the consequences for sin, but it does afford the presence of God in dealing with the aftermath of sin.

A. Jonathan Attacked the Philistines at Geba

Saul was king for two years before he organized an army of men around him. Two thousand men were with Saul in Bethel and a thousand were with Jonathan, his son, in Gibeah. The rest were sent home to their tents (I Samuel 13:1–2). Saul evidently followed the pattern of kings who went forth to battle as described in David's downfall (II Samuel 11:1). Unfortunately, it was a pattern of war that was to continue throughout Saul's reign as Samuel predicted.

Jonathan took his one thousand men against the garrison of the Philistines at Geba and smote them. News of the slaughter spread quickly in both Israel and among the Philistines. Saul trumpeted the news throughout all Israel of his victory (I Samuel 13:3–4). It was the first step in Saul's downfall as a person and as king. He promoted himself over his own son, taking credit for another's accomplishments. This flaw was greatly magnified by the time the women of Israel sang their song, "Saul hath slain his thousands, and David his ten thousands" (I Samuel 18:7–8). Jealousy is as cruel as the grave (Song of Solomon 8:6).

» *Why do you think Saul promoted himself over his own son?*

B. The Philistines Responded

I Samuel 13:4 tells us the Philistines utterly abhorred Israel. "The word translated 'abomination' is not the Hebrew word generally used in the Bible. Here the word refers

21

to the fact that to the Philistines, the Israelites stank" (*Apostolic Study Bible*, note for I Samuel 13:4). Jonathan's victory over the garrison of Philistines rallied the Philistines to rise up against Israel in overwhelming numbers: "Thirty thousand chariots, and six thousand horsemen, and people as the sand" of the sea (I Samuel 13:5). Resistance to evil will certainly arise from its primary source to battle again in even greater numbers.

When Jesus resisted the initial temptation of Satan for bread, the devil took Jesus to the Temple, tempting His identity and relationship to the written Word. Lastly, Satan offered Jesus all the kingdoms of the world. (See Matthew 4:3–9.) If there is something that can cause a believer to sin, the devil will present it. The strength of truth is the believer's resistance to temptation and sin. The Word in you is greater than the world around you. "Resist the devil, and he will flee from you" (James 4:7).

The Philistine forces far exceeded those of King Saul. A crushing defeat seemed imminent for Israel, except for the favor of Israel's God. Israel's victories against overwhelming odds were always because of divine favor rather than military genius. Believers will experience a flood of resistance when confronting evil, but the name of the Lord is a strong tower into which the righteous can run and be safe (Proverbs 18:10). Even Legion's thousands of devils were no match for Jesus' words (Mark 5:1–13).

II. ISRAEL COWERED IN FEAR

Israel's rejoicing over the victory of Jonathan was short-lived. The victory of one battle does not make a victory of war. Evil rallies itself when confronted, as did the Philistines. They gathered themselves together to fight (I Samuel 13:5). Israel cowered under the massive force of the Philistines against them. They hid in the rocks and hills, in caves and thickets. Some even fled to the eastern side of Jordan in their distress (I Samuel 13:6–7). Fear has torment (I John 4:18), especially in impossible, life-threating situations. Israel's cry for a king two years earlier had not brought with it the security and peace of mind Israel needed for this battle. The will of the flesh seems strong when it is not facing overpowering adversaries or temptations. But when the enemy comes in like a flood, the Spirit of God is the only secure standard against it (Isaiah 59:19).

» *What are some of the adversaries and temptations we face in our day?*

A. Saul Remained at Gilgal

King Saul was not on the frontlines facing the enemy. With the Philistine army advancing and the Hebrew people fleeing, King Saul remained at Gilgal with his committed followers. But "all the people followed him trembling" (I Samuel 13:7). The people's trust before had been in the protective presence of God under the spiritual leadership of God's inspired judges, priests, and prophets. Now Saul, the new king, their giant—being head and shoulders above all others—was not leading in the battle. Saul remained at Gilgal. The psalmist said it well: "It is better to trust in the LORD than to put confidence in man." (See Psalm 118:5–9.)

22

B. Saul Waited for Samuel's Guidance

Saul tarried seven days, waiting in Gilgal for Samuel to come (I Samuel 13:8). Saul was king, but Samuel was still the spiritual leader of Israel. Samuel's voice was still the one God honored. Samuel's confidence was in God, not the forces accumulated by Saul for battle. To Saul's credit, he waited for Samuel at Gilgal as he was instructed to do. It is never wrong to wait for the presence of spiritual people in times of difficulty. When one comes with a word from the Lord, great confidence is secured, for the word of the Lord is true, sure, steadfast, trustworthy, and strengthening. Saul needed that word of the Lord from Samuel before Saul entered the battle. He needed the assurance of God being with them in order to gain the victory. So he waited.

III. SAUL GREW IMPATIENT

Waiting is sometimes a difficult task, especially when you are the leader and those looking to you for leadership are becoming concerned for their own well-being. One of the traits of being a strong leader is having the courage to make difficult decisions and knowing when to proceed cautiously. Some see indecisiveness as being equated with weakness, even incompetence and cowardice. Saul and the people needed assurance from God to proceed.

Saul felt the pressure from the people to make a decision to go into battle. But in his heart and because of his experience, he needed to hear the voice of Samuel more. Therefore, he waited seven days for Samuel. Possibly one of the most difficult tasks a leader must perform is that of encouraging people's faith and confidence while waiting on God. God's timing is perfect. But our patience is subject to pressure. Saul grew impatient with Samuel's arrival. And in his impatience as a leader, he made a wrong decision.

A. Saul Offered Sacrifice Instead of Samuel

Saul knew what was needed to win the battle. Victory would come, not by might or strength, but by the hand of the Lord. Saul decided to make supplication unto the Lord with burnt offerings and peace offerings (I Samuel 13:9–12). The burnt offerings were for sin, and the peace offerings were for thanksgiving. This sacrificial offering was what Samuel was to facilitate when he arrived. But Saul, in his impatience, stepped into the place of Samuel and offered what he knew Samuel would offer.

The gifts and callings of God are of His choosing. The Lord sets up kings; He appoints and anoints. He chooses the part each of us is to play in the Kingdom and gives each position authority. The church is a body with many members. We are not all eyes or ears, but each plays an important part within the body for good (I Corinthians 12:12–25). When one part tries to operate in the place of another, confusion results. The church is a building fitly framed together for the glory of God (Ephesians 2:20–22).

In Heaven and Earth, God has established a leadership structure for families, society, and the church. With that structure comes authority. With authority comes responsibility. Lucifer, while in Heaven, stepped out of his place. The result was failure and judgment. Satan later tempted Jesus' patience by offering Him the kingdoms of this world to be His immediately, rather than waiting for them through the will and plan of God (Luke 4:4–7). As God judged the angels who stepped out of their place, so judgment will fall upon those who disregard the ways of the Lord. Impatience has its consequences. But patience has its reward.

> *Why are actions taken outside of authority damaging to those who rebel?*

B. Samuel Rebuked Saul

When Samuel arrived, Saul went out to meet Samuel and give him the respect he merited as the prophet of God. Samuel had arrived soon after the offerings were finished. Rather than greeting Saul warmly, Samuel questioned him, "What hast thou done?" (I Samuel 13:11). Sensing Samuel's displeasure, Saul attempted to defend his actions with three points: the people were scattering, Samuel was late, and the Philistines were coming. Saul's error in judgment was blamed on the people, the prophet, and the Philistines. His final justification was that he forced himself to do it, implying he did not want to do it but felt he had to offer the sacrifices (I Samuel 13:12).

Samuel rebuked Saul, saying he had done foolishly. But this was more than a foolish act. Saul had disobeyed a specific command of God. "Thou hast not kept the commandment of the LORD thy God, which he commanded thee" (I Samuel 13:13). Impatience will become sin if it causes one to disobey the Lord. Saul was not only out of place, but he also was disobedient to the Lord. Even doing good things becomes sin if it is disobedience.

IV. SAUL'S KINGDOM WILL NOT ENDURE

Samuel's judgment was placed upon Saul that very day. Saul's kingdom would not continue. It was the will of God that the kingdom of Saul be established forever, but sin canceled God's desire. The same was true in the Garden of Eden. Adam and Eve would have lived forever had they not sinned. But sin has consequences that result in death. Saul's kingdom was to become David's kingdom. The covenants of God are everlasting, but the rewards of leadership are subject to the leader's obedience and faithfulness.

A. Impatience and Disobedience Led to the Forfeiting of Saul's Kingdom

Saul's character flaws emerged with his position as king. Saul did not appear to have any flaws in character before he became king. But position, power, and responsibility under pressure will bring out the best or worst in a person's character. Saul's humble nature changed over time. He went from a timid soul, hiding among the stuff (I Samuel 10:22), to a tyrant king, willing to kill anyone threating his throne. What caused this?

While there were probably many little things in Saul's life that lead to his destruction, the two most imposing were those of impatience and disobedience. When impatience toward God's anointed causes us to step out of place, it leads to other sins of even greater consequence. Luke 21:19 states: "In your patience possess ye your souls." The context of this verse is that of betrayal, adversity, and testing. Patience is your safety and strength. Trials and tests are ever before Christian believers. But God is faithful; we must just trust in His word and be patient.

Disobedience separates us from the blessings of God. All the promises God has intended for us can be forfeited with disobedience. Saul's disobedience was a pattern, not a single mistake. It was not accompanied with true repentance. Unfortunately, there is no record of Saul's repentance to Samuel's rebuke. Samuel left Gilgal and Saul went to war with a heavy heart.

» *How can a wrong motive for an improper act be more damaging than the act itself?*

B. A Warning to Us to Remain Patient and Faithful to God

The Bible is full of direct commands and examples of the need for patience in our lives. Saul's example is a warning to us to be patient in matters of the Kingdom and to be faithful in matters of obedience. God's kingdom and church will prevail and be triumphant. It is predestined to succeed. However, faithfulness is a long-term commitment to the purpose of Christ Jesus. The work of His church will be accomplished His way, by His people. Faithfulness is the rewarded virtue of believers, and patience is the vehicle employed to accomplish the task. The Lord's welcoming greeting to those entering Heaven will be: "Well done, thou good and faithful servant: thou hast been faithful over a few things, I will make thee ruler over many things: enter thou into the joy of thy lord" (Matthew 25:21).

» *What role does remembrance play in remaining patient and faithful?*

▶▶▶ INTERNALIZING THE MESSAGE

If our prayers are not answered immediately, we must learn to pray again and again until the answer comes. Paul wrote that if we have hope, then we wait with patience for it to come to pass (Romans 8:25). But in the following verse Paul told us the Spirit helps our infirmities, making intercession for us (Romans 8:26). The secret to obtaining the promises of God that we hope for is having patience and being faithful. We must watch, pray, and wait.

And in God's good time, it will come to pass. Patience in prayer is faith in action. The formula for blessing is found in Mark 11:24: "What things soever ye desire, when ye pray, believe that ye receive them." Patient prayer filters desire so faith can bring it to pass. Patience and obedience are essential.

We are admonished to seek first the kingdom of God and His righteousness, and the things we need will be added unto us. For it is the Lord's desire and pleasure to give us the Kingdom. (See Luke 12:31–32.) The Lord's good pleasure for King Saul was that his kingdom would last forever. The Lord's good pleasure for each of us is that we be a part of the everlasting kingdom of God. We must have patience and remain faithful, and we will see what the Lord has in store.

The Heart of a Leader

FOCUS THOUGHT

God chooses leaders, not based on how they look, but according to what is in the leader's heart.

 FOCUS VERSE

I Samuel 16:7

But the LORD said unto Samuel, Look not on his countenance, or on the height of his stature; because I have refused him: for the LORD seeth not as man seeth; for man looketh on the outward appearance, but the LORD looketh on the heart.

 LESSON TEXT

I Samuel 16:1–7, 11–13

1 And the LORD said unto Samuel, How long wilt thou mourn for Saul, seeing I have rejected him from reigning over Israel? fill thine horn with oil, and go, I will send thee to Jesse the Beth-lehemite: for I have provided me a king among his sons.

2 And Samuel said, How can I go? if Saul hear it, he will kill me. And the LORD said, Take an heifer with thee, and say, I am come to sacrifice to the LORD.

3 And call Jesse to the sacrifice, and I will shew thee what thou shalt do: and thou shalt anoint unto me him whom I name unto thee.

4 And Samuel did that which the LORD spake, and came to Beth-lehem. And the elders of the town trembled at his coming, and said, Comest thou peaceably?

5 And he said, Peaceably: I am come to sacrifice unto the LORD: sanctify yourselves, and come with me to the sacrifice. And he sanctified Jesse and his sons, and called them to the sacrifice.

6 And it came to pass, when they were come, that he looked on Eliab, and said, Surely the LORD's anointed is before him.

7 But the LORD said unto Samuel, Look not on his countenance, or on the height of his stature; because I have refused him: for the LORD seeth not as man seeth; for man looketh on the outward appearance, but the LORD looketh on the heart.

. . . . .

11 And Samuel said unto Jesse, Are here all thy children? And he said, There remaineth yet the youngest, and, behold, he keepeth the sheep. And Samuel said unto Jesse, Send and fetch him: for we will not sit down till he come hither.

12 And he sent, and brought him in. Now he was ruddy, and withal of a beautiful countenance, and goodly to look to. And the LORD said, Arise, anoint him: for this is he.

13 Then Samuel took the horn of oil, and anointed him in the midst of his brethren: and the Spirit of the LORD came upon David from that day forward. So Samuel rose up, and went to Ramah.

CULTURE CONNECTION

MERCIFUL MARINES

Smoke came pouring out of a building in Washington, D.C. The cause of the fire was unknown, but many of the residents were helpless to escape. The Marine barracks was only a short distance away. Marines stationed there saw the smoke, and about one hundred soldiers came running to the rescue. With their assistance, the fire department and paramedics were able to rescue all the residents, treat them for injuries, and shelter them safely until their loved ones arrived (www.foxnews.com).

This untimely event was probably not on the soldiers' agenda that day, but to them it was imperative to help these people. The burning building was a residence for senior citizens, and all the people the Marines helped that day were elderly. However, the age of those in need did not matter to the Marines. People were in need, and the Marines were there to help.

When God is looking for someone to lead, we would expect Him to choose from the elite. He could pick from the most handsome, the strongest, or the most intelligent. But when God is looking for leaders, it does not matter how old, how smart, or what the person's background is. God looks for the precious commodity of availability, and He equips those who are willing to serve.

 ## OUTLINE

I. GOD SENT SAMUEL TO ANOINT A NEW KING
    A. Jesse's House in Bethlehem
    B. Sacrifice and Consecration

II. GOD LOOKS ON THE HEART
    A. None of the First Seven Sons Were Chosen
    B. Are These All of Your Sons?

III. DAVID WAS CALLED TO THE HOUSE
    A. This Is the One
    B. David Was Anointed

IV. GOD VALUES WHAT IS IN YOUR HEART

 ## CONTEMPLATING THE TOPIC

Martin Luther King Jr. was killed at the age of thirty-nine. According to the autopsy report, he had the heart of a sixty-year-old man. Doctors believed his heart had aged due to the significant stress caused by his work as the prominent leader of the civil rights movement. While his physical heart was in poor shape, his spiritual heart was stronger than ever. His resilience in the face of consistent political pressure and frequent physical harm was demonstrated in his final speech given the night before his death. He stated, "Only when it is dark enough can you see the stars." Within twenty-four hours of uttering these words, the man was gone, and his movement saw its darkest hour. Yet his words would carry on and inspire others to take up the mantle and lead the movement forward. This is simply one statement of many spoken by this iconic leader, demonstrating his passion and understanding that leaders must be strong of heart, even in the face of their own demise.

A leader's heart cannot waiver or falter from the path ahead. When others lose heart, a leader's heart is encouraged because a leader sees the end result, or even more, a leader sees the glory that will be given to God. When other's hearts fail them because of fear, a leader's heart will be strengthened in the fire of the trial. Leaders realize the power of God is on their side.

I. GOD SENT SAMUEL TO ANOINT A NEW KING

As a leader, especially in a spiritual capacity, the task of removing someone you lead from a prominent position can be extremely stressful. This can be an emotionally turbulent event for the leader due to the time invested mentoring and grooming the individual, and this can also cause a feeling of personal failure within the heart of the leader at that individual's shortcoming. Even more, there is the difficult task of finding a suitable replacement during a period when the leader may experience some insecurity based on the previous poor choice of a candidate. Samuel certainly experienced all of this as he faced the difficult task of separating himself from Saul and seeking his replacement.

The situation Samuel faced was challenging. Although Samuel may have been angry and disappointed at Saul's disobedience to the command of the Lord, Samuel must have felt some responsibility for failing to influence the king. Additionally, the disheartened Samuel had to be stirred out of his depression by God. The Lord stated in I Samuel 16:1, "How long wilt thou mourn for Saul, seeing I have rejected him from reigning over Israel? fill thine horn with oil, and go, I will send thee to Jesse the Bethlehemite: for I have provided me a king among his sons."

The idea that Samuel mourned Saul as though he had died demonstrates the level of depression Samuel suffered. Only when God stirred him was he able to see that God was in control and had a plan. Like many of us in our time of suffering and loss, Samuel had to trust in the Lord completely. He had to trust God to help him work past his insecurities and move forward to anoint the next king.

A. Jesse's House in Bethlehem

God chose the next king from the house of Jesse in Bethlehem. We can attest that his family was favored by God as his great-grandfather, Boaz, a man from the tribe of Judah, married Ruth, a Moabitess who turned away from the ungodly ways of her people and embraced the God of the children of Israel. After finding favor with God, Ruth bore a son, Obed. The inclusion of a Gentile woman into the tribe of Judah and the prophecy concerning this lineage is given in Ruth 4:14–15: "And the women said unto Naomi, Blessed be the LORD, which hath not left thee this day without a kinsman, that his name may be famous in Israel. And he shall be unto thee a restorer of thy life, and a nourisher of thine old age: for thy daughter in law, which loveth thee, which is better to thee than seven sons, hath born him." Later Obed would have a son named Jesse. The background of this family demonstrates faithfulness to God and shows that the family had favor with God. This was significant not only to the son of Jesse being anointed king, but it proved significant to all the prophecies of the Messiah coming from the lineage of Jesse, and eventually the Messiah's birth in Bethlehem.

» *Do we find favor with God when we choose to follow His plan over our own ambitions? Explain.*

B. Sacrifice and Consecration

Samuel had concerns that if Saul discovered his intent to anoint a new king, Saul would try to kill Samuel. Samuel was in Ramah, but the route to Bethlehem would take him through Gibeah. A prophet, or seer, traveling through the land would draw attention, and should word of it get to Saul, it might arouse his suspicion. But God provided Samuel with a legitimate reason for his visit to Bethlehem by telling him, "Take an heifer with thee, and say, I am come to sacrifice to the LORD. And call Jesse to the sacrifice, and I will shew thee what thou shalt do: and thou shalt anoint unto me him whom I name unto thee" (I Samuel 16:2–3). Because the house of God had not yet been established in Jerusalem, the place of sacrifice could be set up in any town of the prophet's choosing. By inviting Jesse and his family to the sacrifice, this would also conceal the additional intent of the prophet. Offering a sacrifice was not simply a cover-up; making a sacrifice to God before anointing a king would have been part of the process. Sacrifices were offered for many reasons under the Mosaic law, so offering a sacrifice alone would not have been cause for suspicion. With God's perfect plan in place, Samuel went forward in faith to execute God's command to anoint a new king.

II. GOD LOOKS ON THE HEART

An old expression says, "Beauty is in the eye of the beholder." Human beings are an interesting species in that we are visually stimulated. We are quick to size up an individual's abilities, intelligence, and many other attributes simply by that person's appearance. Marketing firms have paid millions of dollars to research the various ways to visually stimulate people in order to sell their products. Every day we are inundated with visual cues that give us direction, cause us to think on certain things, or simply voice an idea to provoke thought on a given subject. Billboards are still widely used as a powerful marketing tool. Some studies say we humans receive almost 90 percent of our information visually. Perhaps this is why we are quick to judge things by what we see. Another old expression says, "You can't judge a book by its cover."

Samuel was displeased when the elders of Israel approached him asking for a king. Unfortunately, his sons were described as dishonest, taking bribes and perverting justice. Samuel could not dispute what had become obvious to all the people, so he petitioned God on behalf of the people for a king. God chose Saul only to grant the people their choice. Saul is described in the Bible as a handsome man, taller than the other men. Samuel must have been impressed, as were others. The people had asked for a king, and Saul certainly looked the part.

A. None of the First Seven Sons Were Chosen

When Samuel arrived in Bethlehem, the elders of the town trembled at his coming, even asking if he had come in peace. Samuel assured them he had come in peace, desiring to offer a sacrifice to the Lord. He instructed them to sanctify themselves and to go with him to the sacrifice. Samuel invited Jesse and his sons to the sacrifice, taking the opportunity to consecrate them. As each son passed by, Samuel began to assess each of them. The first of the sons to catch his eye was Eliab, whose name means "God is my father." Samuel declared that Eliab must be the one. God quickly corrected Samuel, giving him a refined guideline, "Look not on his countenance, or on the height of his stature; because I have refused him: for the LORD seeth not as man seeth; for man looketh on the outward appearance, but the LORD looketh on the heart" (I Samuel 16:7).

Samuel began using spiritual discernment to assess the remaining six sons as they passed by. When Samuel viewed the last son, he realized God had not chosen any of them. Samuel had thought the first son he had seen was surely the chosen one; however, God had chosen David to be king.

» *How often do we make important decisions or choices based on our instincts rather than relying on direction from God? Explain.*

B. Are These All of Your Sons?

When Samuel had seen the last of Jesse's sons, he quickly sensed something was wrong. He had worked and walked with God for years. Had he missed something? He told Jesse the Lord had not chosen any of the sons who were present. In an instant, godly wisdom presented a question in Samuel's mind. He asked Jesse if all his sons were present. Jesse stated that the youngest son was not present; he was tending to sheep.

When artists put their work out on display, only the pieces that are complete will be available to the viewing public. Unfinished work is not usually placed on display unless it is the intent of the artist to demonstrate the process of creation. Jesse put his most mature sons on display for Samuel to view. Since David was the youngest, his duty was to care for the flock while his brothers tended to other business. The idea that all seven of the older siblings would be passed over in favor of the youngest was simply not business as usual. However, God does not always conduct business as usual. Jesse did not exclude David out of shame, but this was simply tradition. Typically, within the families of this era, the greatest responsibility and blessings fell to the eldest son. When the time would come, the father would pass on the inheritance to the eldest son, who in turn would care for the rest of the family. However, if Samuel had requested that Jesse bring all his sons, David should have been included, regardless of tradition.

» *Do people ever hold things back from God because they feel the things may be irrelevant? How can this hinder the plan of God in our lives?*

III. DAVID WAS CALLED TO THE HOUSE

In the southeastern part of the United States, the expression "called to the house" is not synonymous with good things. Typically it means there is trouble at home.

30

Depending on the situation, it will either encourage the individual to hurry home or cause the individual to move at a glacial pace. Either way, the need to return home after being summoned by the aforementioned phrase does not bode well for the individual.

Samuel instructed Jesse to send someone to get David and have him brought before Samuel. Likely whoever went to retrieve David from the fields stated his father had summoned him at the command of the prophet. An obedient son would only need to know his father alone had summoned him to be motivated to move swiftly. This assumption is based on the cultural norms of the time, when parents were held with the highest regard. When David arrived, the Bible describes him as being ruddy, or red in the face. This could indicate he returned to his father's house from the fields with great haste.

A. This Is the One

We have all made major decisions in our lives, like purchasing a home or car, or electing to accept or decline a promotion. These decisions end up making a significant impact on our lives. There is no way to compare the aforementioned scenarios to making a spiritual decision, yet we all know that something within us told us, "This is the right one." Without a doubt, we knew which decision was the one. When we maintain a strong relationship with God, the Holy Spirit becomes our inner voice, directing our paths, even for what may seem like trivial decisions.

Samuel had arrived in Bethlehem, made his sacrifice, and had assessed the seven sons of Jesse who were presented to him. When Samuel finished and realized none of them were the one God had sent him to anoint, he discovered there was another son who was not present. Jesse sent for David. Once David arrived, Samuel heard the voice of God stating, "This is the one."

» *What difference would it make in our choices if we focused on hearing from God every day?*

B. David Was Anointed

Samuel heard God command him to take the oil and anoint the future king. The Scripture tells us Samuel took the horn of oil and anointed David in the midst of his brothers, "and the Spirit of the LORD came upon David from that day forward" (I Samuel 16:13).

Whenever a leader passes authority to another, it is imperative it be done in a manner that validates the person's authority over others. Samuel did not have to anoint David in front of his brothers, yet this display was not insignificant. Years ago, a pastor in a local church began to travel frequently. During the church service prior to each departure, he would let the congregation know he would be gone and would announce the name of the person who would be in charge during his absence. This was a normal occurrence in that church for many years. Many did not see the relevance at the time, but years later, a younger pastor took over the church. Over time he began to lose many of the subordinate leaders within the church without understanding why. One day a well-respected elder pulled him aside and stated the importance of publicly naming or anointing those to whom he delegates his authority, in order to remove all doubt and argument over who is in charge.

IV. GOD VALUES WHAT IS IN YOUR HEART

The heart is where the essence of a human being is stored. Jesus explained in Matthew 15:18–19, "But those things which proceed out of the mouth come forth from the heart; and they defile the man. For out of the heart proceed evil thoughts, murders, adulteries, fornications, thefts, false witness, blasphemies." This is not to say that everything we say or think is purely evil. In other words, the evil things we harbor in our hearts will come out of our mouths and will be seen by our actions at some point. Thus we ought to pray as the psalmist prayed, "Create in me a clean heart, O God; and renew a right spirit within me" (Psalm 51:10). We must surrender our carnal nature to the Spirit of God and allow Him to change our hearts.

The spiritual leader's prayer life must be strong. Leaders cannot rest upon past achievements, nor can they quit at every crisis or failure. Only when a leader's heart is strong in the Lord can a leader be bold as a lion. God considers the heart because true repentance begins there. Words can be used to deceive. Lengthy, righteous-sounding prayer does not fool God. Psalm 19:14 states best what our daily desire should be, "Let the words of my mouth, and the meditation of my heart, be acceptable in thy sight."

> » *Do you seek to purify your heart in the presence of God through prayer every day?*
> *Explain.*

▶▶▶ INTERNALIZING THE MESSAGE

Vince Lombardi is credited for the famous quote, "Leaders are made, they are not born." Though it may seem the great leaders throughout history have been born with something special that others do not have, each person is born with different gifts and must learn to develop those gifts to their fullest potential. It is in the development process that great leaders emerge. One commonality among great leaders is they usually have at least one mentor who greatly influenced them during the development process. Jesus demonstrated through His mentorship of the disciples how important it is to develop strong future leaders. Throughout the Bible we see individuals from different eras and circumstances failing or succeeding on one common factor: the condition of their relationship with God. Only when we maintain a strong relationship with Jesus will we have a strengthened heart to endure any trial we may encounter.

Leadership and Submission

FOCUS THOUGHT

Because godly leaders want what is best for God's kingdom, they recognize the importance of submission.

 FOCUS VERSE

I Samuel 20:4

Then said Jonathan unto David, Whatsoever thy soul desireth, I will even do it for thee.

 LESSON TEXT

I Samuel 18:1–4

1 And it came to pass, when he had made an end of speaking unto Saul, that the soul of Jonathan was knit with the soul of David, and Jonathan loved him as his own soul.

2 And Saul took him that day, and would let him go no more home to his father's house.

3 Then Jonathan and David made a covenant, because he loved him as his own soul.

4 And Jonathan stripped himself of the robe that was upon him, and gave it to David, and his garments, even to his sword, and to his bow, and to his girdle.

I Samuel 19:4–6

4 And Jonathan spake good of David unto Saul his father, and said unto him, Let not the king sin against his servant, against David; because he hath not sinned against thee, and because his works have been to thee-ward very good:

5 For he did put his life in his hand, and slew the Philistine, and the Lord wrought a great salvation for all Israel: thou sawest it, and didst rejoice: wherefore then wilt thou sin against innocent blood, to slay David without a cause?

6 And Saul hearkened unto the voice of Jonathan: and Saul sware, As the Lord liveth, he shall not be slain.

I Samuel 20:1–4

1 And David fled from Naioth in Ramah, and came and said before Jonathan, What have I done? what is mine iniquity? and what is my sin before thy father, that he seeketh my life?

2 And he said unto him, God forbid; thou shalt not die: behold, my father will do nothing either great or small, but that he will shew it me: and why should my father hide this thing from me? it is not so.

3 And David sware moreover, and said, Thy father certainly knoweth that I have found grace in thine eyes; and he saith, Let not Jonathan know this, lest he be grieved: but truly as the Lord liveth, and as thy soul liveth, there is but a step between me and death.

4 Then said Jonathan unto David, Whatsoever thy soul desireth, I will even do it for thee.

CULTURE CONNECTION

SAFETY OF SUBMISSION

Charles Spurgeon once said, "It is, perhaps, one of the hardest struggles of the Christian life to learn this sentence, 'Not unto us, not unto us, but unto Thy name be glory'" (www.christianquotes.info).

Driving the freeway during rush hour can be hazardous. People are either in a hurry going home after a hard day or anxious to get to work to clock in on time. Whether it is morning or evening, the commute can seem like unbelievable craziness. However, there are some rules that help if those on the road will comply. Comply is a good word for obeying traffic laws. If everyone would obey the traffic signs, rush hour would be much easier to navigate. However, there is always that one car—the one that tailgates the slow vehicle, switches lanes unsafely, and swerves across all four lanes to the exit from the High Occupancy Vehicle (HOV) lane.

As we travel the highway of life, it seems there are always those who disregard the road signs in God's Word. When believers choose to comply—submitting to God's Word—it makes a drastic impact not only on them but also on all those with whom they come in contact. Submission is not a bad word. It is a preferred pathway in life, allowing God to take control of our vehicle, so to speak, and surrendering our own way to His. Charles Spurgeon was right. Surrendering is hard for most of us, but if we can grasp the magnitude of glory that God receives through our submission, we would gladly comply.

 ### OUTLINE

I. JONATHAN HONORED DAVID
   A. Their Covenant
   B. Jonathan Gave David His Armor

II. JONATHAN INTERCEDED FOR DAVID
   A. Saul Wanted to Kill David
   B. Saul Listened to Jonathan

III. JONATHAN PROTECTED DAVID
   A. Saul's Anger Was Kindled against David
   B. Jonathan Warned David

IV. EVEN LEADERS ARE TO SUBMIT TO AND HONOR OTHER LEADERS

 ### CONTEMPLATING THE TOPIC

The principles expressed by the words leadership and submission are not always clearly understood. Those who submit are led by someone to accomplish significant things.

Some time back, a successful businessman spoke of a difficult decision he had to make. His daughter had grown up around the business. Upon completion of her education, he hired her. The expectation was for her to prepare and eventually lead the company.

Things did not go well. She assumed her family connection had elevated her, and she would not submit to authority. In an attempt to correct things, the father talked with his daughter. Nothing helped. Soon, other employees who were wonderful workers began to resign.

The father eventually had to fire his own daughter. She thought was above submission. This was not the case. We all have someone to whom we must submit. Unfortunately, some do not understand this. Such people will not yield to authority. In God's will, no connection—family or otherwise—gives us a guarantee. Leadership and the authority and influence that go with it cannot be presumed. First of all, leadership must be God's will. Even when God's will is accomplished, there remains a process for gaining trust.

There is an extreme contrast between David's experiences with Saul and his experiences with Saul's son Jonathan. David had been anointed to be the next king of Israel. I Samuel 18:1–4 presents the beginning of the relationship between David and Jonathan.

Jonathan quickly became one of David's greatest supporters. However, Saul saw David as a threat and an enemy. Jonathan submitted to David as the future king. Saul, the current king, did everything in his power to destroy the future king.

Submission is the opposite of stubborn self-will. Submission requires us to stop protecting our own ambitions. At times a respectful mutual submission is called for. Leadership and submission can be complex.

People who have gained influence must know how to distinguish between their own ambitions and God's will. Jonathan was a successful warrior. He was well thought of in Israel. Jonathan succeeded in yielding any ambition he may have had. He promoted and defended David.

One era of leadership will eventually transition to another. Today's leadership that was birthed yesterday may have difficulty yielding to the leadership of tomorrow that was birthed today. Saul was yesterday's leadership. David was the leadership of tomorrow.

Presumptions can be made regarding the future. What if the thing we presume is not God's will? This happened with David and Jonathan.

» *During the reign of Saul, his son Jonathan played an important role. What do you remember about some of Jonathan's exploits?*

I. JONATHAN HONORED DAVID

Jonathan's response to David perfectly portrays a leader submitting to God's authority and to the leadership of another. Jonathan was a prince of Israel. His father was King Saul. Jonathan had repeatedly acquitted himself well in battle against the Philistines (I Samuel 13:3; 14:1–14). Jonathan was not an unproven novice and was well thought of by his peers.

David and Jonathan became acquainted shortly after David defeated Goliath. David's victory over Goliath (I Samuel 17) was the start of David's becoming famous. I Samuel 17 ends with Saul in a conversation with David about the recent victory.

At Saul's insistence, David did not return to caring for his flock of sheep or to his father's home. Instead, David became a resident of Saul's palace. Jonathan and David were in the palace together, and these two successful men became fast friends.

I Samuel 18:1 says, "The soul of Jonathan was knit with the soul of David." The Hebrew word translated *knit* is often translated by the English words *conspired* or *bound*.

A. Their Covenant

As a result of their being knit together, Jonathan and David made a covenant. The Bible does not give us the specifics of their covenant, but the biblical word *covenant* was not used casually. A covenant denoted a formal and legally binding declaration of benefits to be given by one party to another. There may or may not be conditions attached. It is clear that there was a serious and significant agreement between Jonathan and David.

B. Jonathan Gave David His Armor

Jonathan's behavior in finalizing the covenant shows Jonathan's commitment to his friend David. Jonathan stripped himself of his robe and garments and gave them to David (I Samuel 18:4). Jonathan was a prince—a king's son. If Israel's royal family was like most, a prince likely dressed in clothes that were better than average. Jonathan's princely robes likely identified him as someone important.

David had arrived straight from the sheepfold to the conflict with Goliath. After the contest with Goliath, David moved into the palace. The clothing of a shepherd would have been out of place in the royal palace. Jonathan's gift to David had meaning. From early on, Jonathan began to care for and provide for David in a practical way.

Because of their covenant, Jonathan gave David his sword, bow, and girdle. Remember, David overcame Goliath with a sling and stone. As a shepherd, David had not needed a sword. Going forward, Saul wanted David to do battle with Israel's enemies. David needed the things Jonathan provided. Jonathan's submission to this relationship meant he positioned David to succeed in what Saul was going to ask David to do. There is no indication that Saul took any steps to equip David for the next things David was to do.

Jonathan's behavior shows no jealousy or insecurity. While we do not know if Jonathan was aware David had been anointed as the future king, Jonathan certainly knew David was highly regarded by the people of Israel. To do as Jonathan did and serve someone else who is highly regarded by others requires a person to be secure and confident. David had the courage to conquer, and Jonathan made weapons available for David to do battle.

The same cannot be said of King Saul. Saul was angry when the women of Israel sang, "Saul hath slain his thousands, and David his ten thousands" (I Samuel 18:7–9). Insecure people cannot celebrate their own successes if someone else is perceived as having accomplished more. From the day Saul heard the women sing of David's success, Saul was jealous. He began putting David into perilous situations.

Jonathan celebrated and participated in David's ascendancy and success. In contrast, Saul was threatened by David's success and popularity and began treating David as an enemy.

» *Why do some people feel threatened by other people's success?*

II. JONATHAN INTERCEDED FOR DAVID

A. Saul Wanted to Kill David

Saul became progressively more afraid of the influence David was gaining. In spite of Saul recognizing God's hand on David's life, Saul became David's enemy continually (I Samuel 18:28–29). As Saul became steadily more angry, David did not retaliate against Saul. Instead, David continued to serve Saul and Israel well.

Saul's behavior was that of a leader who was more concerned about himself than the continued success of those he was leading. Saul was trying to eliminate a man who had been effective on behalf of Israel. Saul's motive in this was his own insecurity and jealousy.

David's lack of reaction to Saul's jealousy modeled a proper response to someone who is jealous. Eventually Saul's jealousy became so pointed that he told all his servants to kill David. When this happened, Jonathan warned David of Saul's plan and suggested that David escape.

B. Saul Listened to Jonathan

Jonathan's covenant with David caused Jonathan to send David into hiding. Jonathan then approached Saul on David's behalf. He reminded Saul that David's work on Saul's behalf had been good. Jonathan went so far as to indict his father for the desire to slay "innocent blood" (I Samuel 19:5). Saul listened to Jonathan's defense of his friend and allowed David to return to the palace. For a time, things seemed better.

Jonathan's behavior showed just how much he cared for his friend. Regardless of how popular David was, Jonathan did not want his friend to suffer harm. Saul was Jonathan's father, but at no time did Jonathan defend Saul's actions or attitude. Instead, Jonathan tried to correct Saul's behavior. Regardless of our relationship to a person, we must defend those who cannot defend themselves. Instead of entering into Saul's folly, Jonathan acted as a protector and advocate on behalf of David.

Leaders who are in development need influential people to protect them and advocate on their behalf. Jonathan was protecting a valuable relationship. He was also protecting a valuable warrior for the nation of Israel.

» *Can you recall a time when someone spoke up on your behalf? Did this person protect you from someone else's harshness or take some action that expanded your opportunities? Explain.*

III. JONATHAN PROTECTED DAVID

A. Saul's Anger Was Kindled against David

Saul's respite from his anger toward David was brief. Some time later, David again led Israel's army in defeating the Philistines. When David returned from battle, Saul was soon overcome by an evil spirit. As a result, Saul repeatedly tried to kill David.

On one occasion Saul threw a spear at David. Saul was so resentful of David that he asked his daughter Michal, who was also David's wife, to conspire against her husband. Michal did not obey her father; instead she helped David to escape.

From this point forward, the relationship between Saul and David never returned to anything near normal. Saul became consumed with jealously over David's success and popularity. Saul also saw David as a threat to Saul's family continuing to occupy the throne of Israel (I Samuel 20:31).

By this point, Saul no longer had the favor of God. Perhaps he began to realize his leadership had seen its best days. Yet Saul was not ready to prepare a future king—unless, perhaps that king were to be his son.

Saul wanted Israel to remain under his family's control. But because of the prophet Samuel's words to him, Saul had to know there would be no dynasty. However, with stubborn jealousy, Saul did everything he could to hinder the ascendancy of David.

What a difference between the behavior of Saul and that of Jonathan. Saul was primarily interested in defending his place and position. Meanwhile, Jonathan was interested in protecting and supporting his friend David.

B. Jonathan Warned David

I Samuel 20 details Jonathan's final efforts to protect David. Jonathan knew how angry his father had become and that David was much at risk. So these two men came up with a plan.

One evening at dinner, Saul noticed David was missing. Jonathan spoke up and tried to explain David's absence. Saul was irate and warned Jonathan that as long as David lived, Jonathan would not be king. However, Jonathan was not bothered by that reality because he had already submitted to the reality of God's hand and anointing being on David. In contrast, Saul had not.

Saul's words fueled his own anger. Just as he had thrown a javelin at David, he now threw one at his own son (I Samuel 20:33). Saul was out of control. From that day forward, Saul spent more time and energy trying to kill David than in strengthening the nation of Israel. What a tragic way for Saul to use his time, energy, and influence.

Jonathan now knew the extent of Saul's anger. Jonathan had never been blatantly disloyal to his father, but he had always kept the interests of Israel and David ahead of his own self-interest. Jonathan had chosen to support and express loyalty to David at a time when Jonathan's own ascendancy to the throne may have seemed near. Jonathan was remarkable and unusual. He was a leader who could also effectively follow. Jonathan was willing to submit.

Saul's insecurity, jealousy, and fear of David would not allow him to let David have any normal position of influence in Israel. After David's escape to the wilderness, his initial followers were a motley crew. Due to Saul's insecurity, David went from life in the palace to being a vagabond in the wilderness. David went from doing battle for the expansion and securing of the nation of Israel to hiding for his life. Money, time, energy, and resources better used for other purposes were spent trying to destroy David.

One insecure leader who could not submit to an inevitable future sent David to flight. Even Jonathan could not fully protect David from Saul, but Jonathan did all within his power to declare his support. He recognized the hand of God was on David and that the future of the kingdom lay in David's hands. Jonathan never seemed to struggle with the idea of submitting to David as a future leader.

> » *Why do you think some people struggle with the idea of submission? Why do you think Jonathan did not have that struggle?*

IV. EVEN LEADERS ARE TO SUBMIT TO AND HONOR OTHER LEADERS

Jonathan, Saul, and David were all men of influence. Saul used his influence to threaten and limit David. Jonathan used his position to protect and advocate on David's behalf. From the time the women sang of David having slain his ten thousands, Saul could not find it in himself to give honor to David.

All leaders should give honor and respect to others who lead. Saul was threatened by the arriving generation. While Jonathan displayed no behavior indicating he felt entitled to be the next king of Israel. Jonathan submitted to God's will and partnered with David in David's successes.

> » *In what areas of life do people seem to have the most difficultly submitting to someone else?*

▶▶▶ INTERNALIZING THE MESSAGE

One of Saul's ongoing challenges was his resistance to authority. He would not yield to the oversight of Samuel, the same man who had anointed him king. Saul failed to understand that leaders cannot lead effectively without an authority above them. Even people in positions of great influence have corporate boards overseeing their efforts. Saul behaved as though there was no authority beyond himself. He would no longer listen to Samuel and had lost patience with Jonathan.

Saul had become an authority unto himself. The Bible calls on all followers to submit to godly leadership. Kings, priests, and prophets had an authority to which they submitted. We are to submit one to another.

In submitting we must remember: "But God is the judge: he putteth down one, and setteth up another" (Psalm 75:7). Trusting God's process and yielding to His plan are not always easy. Truly John the Baptist's sentiment more accurately captures the attitude of submission: "He must increase, but I must decrease" (John 3:30).

Leadership and Respect

FOCUS THOUGHT

Though it is often easy to be critical of leadership, we must instead choose to be respectful of the leaders God has placed in our lives.

 FOCUS VERSE

I Samuel 26:23

The LORD render to every man his righteousness and his faithfulness: for the LORD delivered thee into my hand to day, but I would not stretch forth mine hand against the LORD's anointed.

 LESSON TEXT

I Samuel 24:5–7

5 And it came to pass afterward, that David's heart smote him, because he had cut off Saul's skirt.

6 And he said unto his men, The LORD forbid that I should do this thing unto my master, the LORD's anointed, to stretch forth mine hand against him, seeing he is the anointed of the LORD.

7 So David stayed his servants with these words, and suffered them not to rise against Saul. But Saul rose up out of the cave, and went on his way.

I Samuel 26:7–12, 23–24

7 So David and Abishai came to the people by night: and, behold, Saul lay sleeping within the trench, and his spear stuck in the ground at his bolster: but Abner and the people lay round about him.

8 Then said Abishai to David, God hath delivered thine enemy into thine hand this day: now therefore let me smite him, I pray thee, with the spear even to the earth at once, and I will not smite him the second time.

9 And David said to Abishai, Destroy him not: for who can stretch forth his hand against the LORD's anointed, and be guiltless?

10 David said furthermore, As the LORD liveth, the LORD shall smite him; or his day shall come to die; or he shall descend into battle, and perish.

11 The LORD forbid that I should stretch forth mine hand against the LORD's anointed: but, I pray thee, take thou now the spear that is at his bolster, and the cruse of water, and let us go.

12 So David took the spear and the cruse of water from Saul's bolster; and they gat them away, and no man saw it, nor knew it, neither awaked: for they were all asleep; because a deep sleep from the LORD was fallen upon them.

. . . . . .

23 The LORD render to every man his righteousness and his faithfulness: for the LORD delivered thee into my hand to day, but I would not stretch forth mine hand against the LORD's anointed.

24 And, behold, as thy life was much set by this day in mine eyes, so let my life be much set by in the eyes of the LORD, and let him deliver me out of all tribulation.

CULTURE CONNECTION

PUBLIC PRAISE

Tim Tebow, former National Football League quarterback, is the youngest of five children. His parents were missionaries in the Philippines when he was born. He grew up in a Christian family that instilled the values and belief system that often surfaced in the media. His respect for God would often be exhibited when he would drop to one knee in prayer—head resting on one hand—before each game. This gesture became a signature pose called Tebowing. Even though Tim was widely criticized, Tebowing became a cultural phenomenon during the 2011 football season (www.biography.com).

It is amazing how a simple gesture like prayerful respect made an impact on millions of people. We do not realize the affect we have on this world when we take our relationship with God to a public level. Praying in public can be intimidating, but when we push past the feelings of embarrassment and bow our heads and talk to God, it impacts those around us. When a crisis arises, calling out to God comes without a second thought of who will be judging us. As born-again believers, we should consider stepping out into the front lines and becoming leaders in the public display of respect for God. We could make a lasting impact on our world by living out our faith intentionally in public places.

OUTLINE

I. DAVID SPARED SAUL'S LIFE
A. Saul Rested in a Cave
B. David Cut Off a Piece of Saul's Robe

II. DAVID SPARED SAUL'S LIFE AGAIN
A. Saul Was Asleep
B. David Took Saul's Spear and Jug of Water

III. DAVID REFUSED TO HARM THE LORD'S ANOINTED
A. Respect Those in Authority and Leadership
B. Trust God's Plan and Timing

CONTEMPLATING THE TOPIC

A pastor was building a significant church building. The decision to proceed with the project had been made by the church trustees and then the entire congregation. A loan was secured, and the project began. Some months into the project, the banker to whom the project had been assigned contacted the pastor.

The banker was concerned. The secretary-treasurer of the church had visited the banker to communicate to her that he saw no way for the church to ever repay the loan. As can be expected, that pastor was frustrated and angry. When the pastor met with the banker, all of the banker's concerns were addressed.

The secretary-treasurer of that church had not shown proper respect to his pastor, the church's trustees, or the decision of the church body itself. That gentleman's lack of respect temporarily cast the church in a bad light in the local business community.

The pastor met with the secretary-treasurer to address the matter. The secretary-treasurer could not justify acting as he had. Even if the concern was viable, his first responsibility was to speak with his pastor. He did not show respect to the leader in his life, and his act embarrassed his pastor.

When the meeting ended, the secretary-treasurer tendered his resignation. The wise pastor would not accept it. In all matters, except this one, the man had served well. The pastor told him, "What has happened is between me, you, and the church's banker. It will stay that way."

That pastor demonstrated more respect than what he had been given, and the secretary-treasurer became one of the pastor's most devoted supporters.

Three observations relative to respect, influence, and leadership can be drawn from this story:

1. The behaviors of the two men offer a sharp contrast. One was respectful; the other was not. The pastor extended respect to a man who some might say did not deserve respect.
2. Being respected is not certain, even when a leader makes good decisions. In this instance, the pastor who had a made a decision in concert with the church body was not respected.
3. Being respectful to other leaders is a choice. The secretary-treasurer made a mistake, but his pastor chose to treat him with respect.

▶▶▶ SEARCHING THE SCRIPTURES

In this lesson we will continue to consider the relationship between Saul and David. David's behavior toward Saul was exemplary. He gave us the perfect example of how to be respectful, even in times of difficulty.

On the other hand, Saul's interactions with David demonstrate the exact opposite. The interactions between Saul and David must have been difficult for Saul. David was in ascendancy while Saul was in decline. Regardless, David deserved better treatment than what he received from Saul.

Our Scripture text recounts for us two specific experiences between Saul and David. Saul had returned from battling the Philistines. David had been nothing but an asset to King Saul. But Saul saw David as a threat based on David's popularity with the people.

David had fled Saul's palace and took up residence in the scraggy rocks of southern Palestine. When Saul heard where David was, he selected three thousand chosen men to join him in finding and destroying David. Saul took his best warriors to address a rather minor internal matter, even as Israel was surrounded by nations ready to go to war.

With this action, Saul started down a path of publicly treating David with disrespect. Saul's concern over David's popularity had existed for a time, but as long as Saul was addressing an external enemy, David was left alone.

When Saul was no longer at war with the Philistines, he chose to do battle with David, a man who was also an Israelite. It seems people who are not busy with advancing and expanding the kingdom of God are those who most often attack those in the church. These people seem to easily show disrespect toward others.

I. DAVID SPARED SAUL'S LIFE

A. Saul Rested in a Cave

Though Saul did not know it, he happened upon David's hiding place. Saul had chosen that exact location as a camp. Taking extreme caution, David and his men shrank back against the dark walls of the cave. Likely, David's band of men breathed a sigh of relief when Saul and others near him went to sleep. In whispered conversation they encouraged David to end the struggle. Their thoughts were, *Saul is right here at our hands. Kill him and be done with it.*

> **What should we do when people close to us give us wrong advice?**

B. David Cut Off a Piece of Saul's Robe

David would have none of this. Instead, he cut a piece off Saul's robe. This bit of cloth would later be used to confirm David had been in that cave. Almost immediately, David regretted having treated Saul in this manner. David's dismay at having disrespected King Saul by cutting away a piece of garment is touching.

In a world where disrespect is an accepted norm, a rebirth of David's attitude would be great progress. David's inclination was to protect the leader of his nation, who he understood to be God's anointed leader. When others in David's company wanted to destroy Saul, David rose to Saul's defense. David's respect for Saul as the anointed king of Israel stirred him to protect a man who was trying to kill him. The default setting of David's life was to be respectful toward others. How wonderful it would be if we had the same default.

Most acts of disrespect toward others—including those in leadership—is verbal. The disrespect may come in the form of gossip, innuendos, or words that cast aspersions and raise doubt. David chose to use different words. After having cut the cloth from Saul's garment, David told his men:

> The LORD forbid that I should do this thing unto my master, the LORD'S anointed, to stretch forth mine hand against him, seeing he is the anointed of the LORD. So David stayed his servants with these words. (I Samuel 24:6–7)

David's words of respect for Saul include the phrases "my master" and "the anointed of the Lord." Though in duress, David still spoke of Saul with respect. Instead of adding fuel to the men's resentment, David's words of respect "stayed his servants."

> **Respect is usually communicated by the way we speak of someone else. You cannot respect someone and at the same time be speaking ill of that person. When have you seen others go out of their way to declare their respect for another person?**

David's respect was not limited to quiet deference, nor was his respect empty words. David did not speak with respect while at the same time turning his back while someone else damaged "the LORD'S anointed." Those who truly respect their leader actively defend their leader when their leader is at risk. An active expression of respect often stops the assassination of a good man's character.

II. DAVID SPARED SAUL'S LIFE AGAIN

A. Saul Was Asleep

A bit later, another opportunity arose for David to harm Saul. Saul had incessantly pursued David. The stress of Saul's relentless pressure would have worn on any man. Men under such pressure often respond by lashing out.

Saul and his men were again asleep in their encampment. David and Abishai—a warrior loyal to David—slipped into Saul's camp. Abishai saw this as an opportunity to bring Saul's pressure to an end. Again David's respect was seen. He did not allow Abishai to kill Saul. David's explanation of why he would not seize the opportunity is telling: "Who can stretch forth his hand against the LORD's anointed" (I Samuel 26:9).

Saul being "the LORD's anointed" was significant to David. Saul and David had both been anointed by the prophet Samuel, but it was not Samuel's anointing of which David spoke. Rather, the respect was established in Saul being "the LORD's anointed."

David's restraint of Abishai seems counterintuitive. Saul's kingdom was nearing an end. Saul's last years had been difficult. Saul had made many mistakes. And now, Saul was attempting to destroy David, a man who had been a hero to Israel. Abishai probably thought Saul needed to die for the good of Israel. David was warning Abishai that killing Saul would be wrong even if Saul's death proved beneficial to Israel.

A person seldom goes wrong extending respect to another. By contrast, disrespect toward another person—even someone who seems to deserve little respect—will often result in unintended consequences.

David's final statement on the matter was an expression of confidence in his God. He did not know how Saul would perish, but perish he would. David left the matter in God's hands.

» *Why is it difficult at times to be patient and leave matters in God's hands?*

B. David Took Saul's Spear and Jug of Water

As David and Abishai left Saul's encampment, they took Saul's spear and a jug of water. When David called back to Saul letting him know of his visit to the camp, David held up the spear and cruse. He had not harmed Saul, nor had he harmed Saul's possessions.

David asserted his expected outcome: "And, behold, as thy life was much set by this day in mine eyes, so let my life be much set by in the eyes of the LORD" (I Samuel 26:24).

David asked God to value him as David had valued Saul, and it seemed to work in exactly that way. Those who are respectful toward others are held in high value by God.

» *Why do you think God chooses to honor those who show respect to leadership?*

III. DAVID REFUSED TO HARM THE LORD'S ANOINTED

A. Respect Those in Authority and Leadership

David is a tremendous biblical example for us when it comes to respecting those in authority and leadership. If Saul would have handled the situation in a godly manner, he would have extended respect to David. Those in authority and leadership are to also respect the people they lead. Saul did not do this. He made David an enemy when David much preferred to be his friend.

» **Why is it important for leaders to show respect to those they lead? What are some ways they can do this?**

B. Trust God's Plan and Timing

David's respect for Saul was grounded in David's own sense of security. He knew who he was. David knew an anointing was on his life. David chose to trust God's plan rather than institute his own. When we choose to operate by our own time and schedule, we will likely wreak havoc on the plan God would like to establish in our lives.

▶▶▶ INTERNALIZING THE MESSAGE

God has a plan for each one of us. He does not always inform us of life's stops or starts. Travel time from one stop to the next is often an unknown. Still He has a plan. Someone secure in God having a plan does not feel the need to disrespect others.

Like David's men, we can become impatient. However, respect for others and for the Lord means we allow Him to determine the fullness of time.

To respect another person is never a mistake. If any person had a "right" to be vengeful, David was that person. Instead, David chose to express respect toward a man who was showing him none. Track the outcome—David's way worked best. Respect those who lead you. Respect those who serve alongside you. Do the difficult thing and show respect for people who demonstrate no respect for you.

Respect simply works. Those who respect win.

Leadership and Peacemaking

FOCUS THOUGHT

In difficult times family leaders must step forward and make peace in their homes.

 FOCUS VERSES

I Samuel 25:33–34 (NKJV)

And blessed is your advice and blessed are you, because you have kept me this day from coming to bloodshed and from avenging myself with my own hand. For indeed, as the Lord God of Israel lives, who has kept me back from hurting you, unless you had hurried and come to meet me, surely by morning light no males would have been left to Nabal!

 LESSON TEXT

I Samuel 25:23–28, 32–34 (NKJV)

23 Now when Abigail saw David, she dismounted quickly from the donkey, fell on her face before David, and bowed down to the ground.

24 So she fell at his feet and said: "On me, my lord, on me let this iniquity be! And please let your maidservant speak in your ears, and hear the words of your maidservant.

25 Please, let not my lord regard this scoundrel Nabal. For as his name is, so is he: Nabal is his name, and folly is with him! But I, your maidservant, did not see the young men of my lord whom you sent.

26 Now therefore, my lord, as the Lord lives and as your soul lives, since the Lord has held you back from coming to bloodshed and from avenging yourself with your own hand, now then, let your enemies and those who seek harm for my lord be as Nabal.

27 And now this present which your maidservant has brought to my lord, let it be given to the young men who follow my lord.

28 Please forgive the trespass of your maidservant. For the Lord will certainly make for my lord an enduring house, because my lord fights the battles of the Lord, and evil is not found in you throughout your days.

. . . . .

32 Then David said to Abigail: "Blessed is the Lord God of Israel, who sent you this day to meet me!

33 And blessed is your advice and blessed are you, because you have kept me this day from coming to bloodshed and from avenging myself with my own hand.

34 For indeed, as the Lord God of Israel lives, who has kept me back from hurting you, unless you had hurried and come to meet me, surely by morning light no males would have been left to Nabal!"

⫸⫸ CULTURE CONNECTION

PRIZE FOR PEACE

The Nobel Peace Prize is among the world's most prestigious awards. Several presidents of the United States have been awarded this honor in the past: Theodore Roosevelt, Woodrow Wilson, Jimmy Carter, and Barack Obama. It was originally intended for "those who, during the preceding year, shall have conferred the greatest benefit on mankind" (www.nobelpeaceprize.org). The peace prize is selected by the Norwegian Nobel Committee and awarded on December 10 each year. Other Nobel prizes awarded that day include prizes for physics, chemistry, literature, and medicine or physiology.

Our spiritual leaders may not be nominated for the Nobel Peace Prize, but many would qualify. They work relentlessly toward peace in our communities and churches. Through biblical teaching, they give hope to the hopeless. Through their unselfish giving, they serve the less fortunate. To those who think conflict and chaos is their destiny, they offer a transforming relationship with the Prince of Peace. The Nobel Peace Prize is a treasured honor, but more important is the spiritual work godly leaders do on a weekly basis. We can be assured that the reward in Heaven to these brave men and women will supersede the honor of the Nobel Peace Prize.

⫸⫸ OUTLINE

I. DAVID PROTECTED NABAL'S SHEEP
A. David Asked for Payment
B. Nabal Refused and Disrespected David

II. DAVID AND HIS MEN DETERMINED TO KILL NABAL
A. Nabal's Servants Warned Abigail
B. Abigail Prepared a Peace Offering

III. ABIGAIL MADE PEACE WITH DAVID
A. David Changed His Mind
B. Abigail Saved Her Household by Making Peace with David
C. God Killed Nabal

IV. GODLY LEADERS MAKE PEACEMAKING A PRIORITY

⫸⫸ CONTEMPLATING THE TOPIC

As we teach truth to our children—passing it down from generation to generation—God's purpose becomes a fortress of strength and truth against the devil's strategy. We must do everything in our power to keep our families strong, unified, and grounded in truth. Every family experiences ups and downs, trials and hard times. Sometimes one member's crisis can thrust a family into a downward spiral and make it difficult to regain a clear focus. Drug use, alcohol, financial crisis, and even packed schedules can disrupt a family's routine. Emotions can run high and everyone in the family can be affected by one member's crisis. Since the family is a unit, the effect of one person's struggle in the family is felt by all. We do indeed feel each other's pain. When one hurts, the whole family is affected. Similar to an injured animal that is being cornered, those who are hurting often attack those closest to them. A crisis often destroys peace in the home. When this occurs the leader of the home must use wisdom and compassion and exercise a lot of patience. A godly family leader can step in and bring peace in the midst of chaos, defusing the intent of the enemy to divide and bringing unity back into the family.

God has enabled a leader in each family. It may be a mother or a father; it could even be a grandparent. Whatever the dynamics of the family, there is someone God has empowered to be the leader. The wisdom and love of a leader can guide a family in times of crisis. When confusion, chaos, and problems bring unrest into the home, a wise and prayerful leader can bring back peace and rest.

The unrest in our society threatens the tranquility of our homes. The only real relief we can hope for comes from God. God can bring peace in a world filled with war and unrest. His peace is so evident when others observe it, they are amazed and cannot explain its existence. "And the peace of God, which passeth all understanding, shall keep your hearts and minds through Christ Jesus" (Philippians 4:7). This prevalent peace of God is what stabilizes the hearts and minds of His children. God's appointed leader in the family must guide the family back to the real peace of God while living in the midst of all the chaos in the world.

Our lesson is more about Abigail than her unwise husband Nabal. It seems Abigail realized the severity of the situation more than her foolish husband, thus motivating her into action.

Nabal rebuffed David's soldiers and shamed them for suggesting that they had provided protection for Nabal's property. Upon hearing this, David gathered his men to go and annihilate Nabal's family household. Abigail met the vengeance seekers with humility and apologies. She made an effort to appease David's men by presenting them gifts. With wisdom Abigail presented peace offerings while interceding for her loved ones' safety. She rose to the challenge of leadership when her husband failed to understand the situation or act to prevent pending destruction.

⟫⟫⟫ SEARCHING THE SCRIPTURES

I. DAVID PROTECTED NABAL'S SHEEP

Nabal was a wealthy man. He owned one thousand goats and three thousand sheep. Evidently Nabal's wealth had a negative effect on his character. He became hard to get along with, becoming arrogant and cantankerous. Even his servants were aware of his moody, mean ways. David's army had kept watch while Nabal's servants were herding his sheep. As night approached, David's soldiers kept a watch on the shepherds and assured their safety. Nabal had not asked David's men to look out for his shepherds or his sheep; they did this as a courtesy to the man who owned the land near their camping place.

A. David Asked for Payment

For a time all was well with Nabal's shepherds. David's men and Nabal's household enjoyed a mutually peaceful and friendly relationship. The conflict in this story arose during the time of harvest. Sheepshearing season was a time of celebration. It was also a time of reaping and gathering. David sent some men, requesting they participate in this celebration with Nabal's household and reminding Nabal of the service David and his men had given by protecting Nabal's shepherds and sheep while they were in the fields. David did not ask for money or payment; he merely asked Nabal to share his provisions with David's men. David simply asked for a gesture of gratitude for the service his men had shown Nabal's shepherds.

B. Nabal Refused and Disrespected David

But the unexpected happened. An ungrateful Nabal showed selfish ambition and arrogance rather than reciprocating respectfully in a manner of integrity. Nabal stormed in fury, "Who is this David? . . . Why should I take my bread and water, and the meat I have slaughtered for my shearers, and give it to men coming from who knows where?" (I Samuel 25:10–11, NIV).

II. DAVID AND HIS MEN DETERMINED TO KILL NABAL

When David's men came back and told him what Nabal had said, David was ready to go to war. He called on his men to arm themselves and march for battle against the household of Nabal.

A. Nabal's Servants Warned Abigail

In the meantime, a servant had overheard the encounter between Nabal and David's men and rushed to inform Abigail. The servant told Abagail how Nabal had disrespected David and his men by refusing to offer any provisions to them. Instead, Nabal had screamed insults at them. The servant provided Abigail the backstory so she would also know how much David's men had done for them while they had tended their sheep near Carmel, near where David's army was camped. David's men had been a wall of protection each night for the men and their sheep. Thus the servant implored Abigail to do something. Knowing the strength of David's men, this servant feared they might come and kill everyone in Nabal's household, all because of Nabal's rude and unreasonable behavior.

B. Abigail Prepared a Peace Offering

Abigail sprang into action. Without telling Nabal her intentions, she extravagantly prepared wine, meat, cakes, and other delicious delicacies as a peace offering for David and his men. No price was too high to save her household from destruction. She loaded donkeys with provisions and sent servants ahead with the gifts. Abigail had insight into the situation because of a faithful servant. She was able to see that the outcome could be devastating to the household of Nabal. However foolish and evil Nabal was, he was her husband and she was a part of that family. God gave her wisdom to act on behalf of her family. In the midst of chaos, Abigail had inspiration and insight to bring about a peaceful resolution.

At the beginning of this account, Scripture expresses the difference of temperament between Nabal and Abigail. "She was a woman of good understanding, and of a beautiful countenance: but the man was churlish and evil in his doings" (I Samuel 25:3). Left unchecked, Nabal would have destroyed everything for which he had worked. His wicked ways were destined to catch up with him, but thankfully he had a wise wife, Abigail, who stepped up as a leader and brought peace.

III. ABIGAIL MADE PEACE WITH DAVID

Abigail's attitude and expediency were vital to the successful resolution of her plight and the salvation of her household. Nabal had angered David with his arrogant and disrespectful rebuff. David was prepared to utterly wipe out the house of Nabal. As David thundered forward in the direction of Nabal's house, he saw something in the distance. Many donkeys laden down with gifts had the effect Abigail intended. As David and his men contemplated the meaning of the provisions, David saw Abigail in the distance coming toward him. Abigail moved closer to David's approaching army. She dismounted from her animal and bowed herself to the ground in reverence and obeisance to the man who had been anointed king. Abigail had heard of David's victories. She was knowledgeable of his exploits and God's blessings upon him (I Samuel 25:30).

A. David Changed His Mind

Abigail pleaded for mercy and asked David to overlook the actions of her foolish husband, Nabal. As Abigail launched into her appeal for peace, David's heart was softened by this wise, resourceful, and humble woman. He could see she had come with gifts of great expense. She risked her own life to save the lives of her household and a wicked, selfish husband. David acknowledged her wisdom in coming out to meet his army and assured her that had she not come, not only Nabal, but every male in the household would have been killed. David let Abigail know that her cunning plan and humble approach were instrumental in changing his mind.

» *Why was it so important for Abigail to put her life on the line for her family?*

B. Abigail Saved Her Household by Making Peace with David

On Abigail's journey back home, no doubt she rejoiced with relief as she thought of her sons. Her children may have been among those David had vowed to kill. Perhaps she thought of her servants' sons and husbands. Abigail put her life on the line, but it was worth the risk for it saved many lives in her household. Through her leadership and intervention, she secured peace for her family and her household was saved.

The incentive to keep peace in the family brings about its own reward. Small children in the home, who are depending on the provision of their parents, are great reasons to build peace in the family. Today is the best time to start. We cannot wait until a crisis appears; we must prepare today so crisis does not catch us off guard. Abigail's quick and timely response suggests she knew this day would come. She was prepared. It did not take her long to prepare the peace offering she needed to assuage the anger of David.

» *What are some ways we can promote peace in our communities, workplaces, and homes?*

C. God Killed Nabal

Nabal eventually reaped the reward of his evil sowing. As Abigail arrived home, she found Nabal in the middle of a feast, drinking and eating with excessive indulgence. He was very drunk, so she saved her story of how she averted the near catastrophe of destruction by David's army until the next morning. When that time came and the alcohol had worn off, Abigail told Nabal about her encounter with David. Immediately Nabal collapsed from a stroke and lay paralyzed on his bed for ten days before God finally took his life.

The consequence of ignoring our place as leader in the family may not reap the verdict of death today, but eventually the outcome will be meted out. As leaders of our families, we must make every effort to keep peace and provide safety in our homes. The fact that God pronounced a guilty verdict of death on Nabal shows how serious his actions were to God. God requires humility and integrity from the leaders of the home. Compare the sacrificial actions of Abigail to the trivial response of a selfish Nabal, partying while his family was in eminent danger.

» *Why do you think Nabal's actions warranted death?*

IV. GODLY LEADERS MAKE PEACEMAKING A PRIORITY

Unfortunately, Nabal fell short of the leadership his family needed. However, God was not to be outdone by a man who would not fulfill his role of leadership. God prepared the heart of Abigail to step in and fulfill the purpose of God in Nabal's family. Her choices and priorities were pleasing to God, which was opposite of Nabal's evil ways.

Our hope is that political leaders would have peace and security high on their list of priorities. Unfortunately, some prioritize political gain over peace. However, in these troubling times, we should adopt the attitude of Abigail. She was driven by God to be an ambassador of peace.

As stated in the Culture Connection, several United States presidents have won the Nobel Peace Prize over the years. Now, whether or not we identify these men as godly, God has the power to guide our leaders into a peaceful agenda. However, this will only happen if we are diligent to pray for our leaders as we face an uncertain future. We should ask God for God-fearing men and women to rise to leadership in our government. Peacemaking is a priority with godly leaders.

» *What would the world today be like if our leaders cultivated peace?*

▶▶▶ INTERNALIZING THE MESSAGE

Each afternoon, a young girl would go to a pastor's home, not to play with the children, but just to sit on the couch. The pastor's wife would ask if the young girl needed anything. Her answer was always simply, "No." The pastor's wife let the girl know that if she needed to talk, the pastor's wife would stop what she was doing and sit down and listen. The young girl said there was no need; she was comfortable just sitting alone in the living room. After a while the young girl would leave. This went on for several days. Finally one day the pastor's wife sat down with the girl and asked why she came to the house just to sit. The young girl replied, "I love to sit here because I feel peace in this house."

Our Christian homes should be a refuge for anyone who comes in. They should be a place of peace in our world of war and destruction. When we make peace a priority, everyone around us will feel the repercussions of something so amazing, it is beyond understanding. (See Philippians 4:7.) God's Word is clear concerning our pursuit of peace. "Depart from evil, and do good; seek peace, and pursue it" (Psalm 34:14).

God has a plan for our lives that includes peace. "The LORD will give strength unto his people; the LORD will bless his people with peace" (Psalm 29:11). This Scripture shows us that peace is a blessing from the Lord. For each leader of the family, peace should be a priority. Our homes should be a place of refuge and peace because that is what God wants for us. "But the meek shall inherit the earth; and shall delight themselves in the abundance of peace" (Psalm 37:11). *Meek* means "enduring injury with patience and without resentment; submissive; not violent or strong" (Merriam-Webster Dictionary). Those with a meek spirit are the ones who inherit the earth. In other words, they are the ones who will experience success and fulfillment in this life.

Employers, supervisors, and corporate leaders who cultivate a peaceful environment in the workplace will receive dividends far beyond the confines of the corporation. A peaceful atmosphere in the workplace will reach beyond the walls of the company and extend into the homes of the workers. Coming home after a hard day at work is hard enough without the complications of conflict, manipulation, and harsh treatment also being a part of the day. Leaders have the choice to be meek or overpowering. The meek shall inherit the earth, and they are given an abundance of peace. Leaders exemplify peace by their actions. Overpowering, territorial leaders can make life miserable for everyone, including themselves. The misery of working in an environment void of peace is excruciating. Conflict and hostility surface where peace is absent. The super-charged, negative energy in a peace-deprived environment is obvious to those who come into close proximity. On the opposite side, people can feel and sense peace when it is present.

Jesus is the Prince of Peace. (See Isaiah 9:6.) He brings peace in the midst of turbulence. He speaks peace to the troubled heart. Peace is our reward as a benefit of our personal relationship with the Prince of Peace. There is nothing more precious than peace in the home, workplace, and community. As Christians, we should be the ones to cultivate peace.

Leadership and Grace

FOCUS THOUGHT

Godly leaders demonstrate the importance of keeping covenants and showing grace to those they lead.

 FOCUS VERSE

II Samuel 9:1

   And David said, Is there yet any that is left of the house of Saul, that I may shew him kindness for Jonathan's sake?

 LESSON TEXT

II Samuel 4:4

   4 And Jonathan, Saul's son, had a son that was lame of his feet. He was five years old when the tidings came of Saul and Jonathan out of Jezreel, and his nurse took him up, and fled: and it came to pass, as she made haste to flee, that he fell, and became lame. And his name was Mephibosheth.

II Samuel 9:1–7

   1 And David said, Is there yet any that is left of the house of Saul, that I may shew him kindness for Jonathan's sake?

   2 And there was of the house of Saul a servant whose name was Ziba. And when they had called him unto David, the king said unto him, Art thou Ziba? And he said, Thy servant is he.

   3 And the king said, Is there not yet any of the house of Saul, that I may shew the kindness of God unto him? And Ziba said unto the king, Jonathan hath yet a son, which is lame on his feet.

   4 And the king said unto him, Where is he? And Ziba said unto the king, Behold, he is in the house of Machir, the son of Ammiel, in Lo-debar.

   5 Then king David sent, and fetched him out of the house of Machir, the son of Ammiel, from Lo-debar.

   6 Now when Mephibosheth, the son of Jonathan, the son of Saul, was come unto David, he fell on his face, and did reverence. And David said, Mephibosheth. And he answered, Behold thy servant!

   7 And David said unto him, Fear not: for I will surely shew thee kindness for Jonathan thy father's sake, and will restore thee all the land of Saul thy father; and thou shalt eat bread at my table continually.

CULTURE CONNECTION

SPILLED TEA

It was a long-awaited visit to her parents' home, so understandably this young mother wanted everything to go perfectly. Her two small children were usually well-behaved, and she was proud to present them to her parents. During the visit, as her little boy was sitting at the table, he insisted his tea be in a glass rather than the usual sippy cup. Against her better judgment, she gave him a glass, but only half full, so if there were an accident, it would only be half the mess. Sure enough, as he was raising the glass, it slipped from his hand and crashed to the floor.

Tea went everywhere. The young mother went running toward him and yelling at the same time. "Why didn't you hold onto it? What's the matter with you? Always use two hands!" The little boy began to sob as the ranting continued. She frantically tried to sop up the tea stains from the carpet. Suddenly, a still small voice got her attention. God seemed to say, "I've never scolded you when you dropped a glass. I've only lovingly cleaned up your mess and held you in My arms as you cried."

She immediately stopped what she was doing, got up, and took her son in her arms. As she consoled her little one, she raised her head to Heaven and thanked God for His mercy and grace during all the times she made mistakes. She purposed in her heart from that moment forward to choose mercy over judgment when dealing with anyone in her charge.

OUTLINE

I. DAVID REMEMBERED HIS COVENANT WITH JONATHAN

    A. Ziba

    B. Mephibosheth

II. DAVID CALLED FOR MEPHIBOSHETH

    A. Saul's Land Returned

    B. Seated at the King's Table

III. DAVID SHOWED GRACE

    A. Godly Leaders Keep Covenants and Promises

    B. Godly Leaders Are Gracious

CONTEMPLATING THE TOPIC

The story of David and Mephibosheth has its beginning in David's friendship with Mephibosheth's father, Jonathan. Over time an intense loyalty developed between David and Jonathan. Their relationship was deeper than the typical connection between best friends; they were more like brothers. By all rights, Jonathan, being the firstborn of King Saul, should have been the successor to the throne of Israel. However, God rejected Saul for his rebellion and chose David and his descendants to rule instead. There was no indication in Scripture that Jonathan was jealous of David. If anything, Jonathan seemed to be at peace with the workings of God despite his unreasonable father.

I. DAVID REMEMBERED HIS COVENANT WITH JONATHAN

With his gifted musical talent, David had opportunities to be in the palace whenever he was called upon to soothe the disturbed spirit of King Saul. Many times David even sat at the table with royalty and was treated as part of the royal entourage. When Saul threatened to kill David, Jonathan, Saul's son, was the one who warned him. Jonathan advised David to avoid the palace for his father was intent on David's destruction. Saul's jealous rage failed to tarnish the relationship between Jonathan and David. They were like brothers, and no one could break that bond. Jonathan's loyalty and love for David transcended any selfish thought of whose right it was to become king.

After two separate attempts on his life, David was warned by Jonathan to leave the palace and never come back. David began his life as a fugitive, fleeing the palace and living on the run. Before he left, however, he had one last encounter with Jonathan in which they made a covenant. (See I Samuel 20:14–19.)

David's respect for the man God had anointed to be king transcended the hatred and jealousy Saul showed toward him. David respected the anointing of God's man even while Saul hunted him down. When he had opportunities to kill Saul, David chose mercy. Out of these acts of compassion, Saul was moved to ask David for a promise and David made an oath with Saul.

So it was, when David had finished speaking these words to Saul, that Saul said, "Is this your voice, my son David?" And Saul lifted up his voice and wept. Then he said to David: "You are more righteous than I; for you have rewarded me with good, whereas I have rewarded you with evil. And you have shown this day how you have dealt well with me; for when the LORD delivered me into your hand, you did not kill me. For if a man finds his enemy, will he let him get away safely? Therefore may the LORD reward you with good for what you have done to me this day. And now I know indeed that you shall surely be king, and that the kingdom of Israel shall be established in your hand. Therefore swear now to me by the LORD that you will not cut off my descendants after me, and that you will not destroy my name from my father's house." So David swore to Saul. And Saul went home, but David and his men went up to the stronghold. (I Samuel 24:16–22, NKJV)

» *Why do you think David made this oath to Saul after all Saul had done to David?*

A. Ziba

Ziba was a servant in the house of Saul. Being the residence of a former king, this was probably a large and lavish compound. When Saul was killed in battle, everything changed for Ziba.

Ishbosheth became king over Israel after his father (Saul) and brothers died in battle on Mount Gilboa. It is not clear if Ishbosheth resided in the same location as Saul, but the land and houses were referred to as Saul's household. After Ishbosheth, the last living son of Saul was killed, the tribes of Israel approached David and asked him to become their king. David had been king of Judah for the last seven-and-a-half years, so now Judah and the tribes of Israel were reunited under the rule of King David.

King David became ruler under the direction of God and was careful to obey all of God's commands. Ziba no doubt watched as David carefully set faithful men in leadership positions. (See II Samuel 8:15–18.) Perhaps while reflecting on these faithful men, David began to wonder who among Saul's relatives were still alive and a part of his kingdom. He contacted Ziba, knowing he was a servant in Saul's household, and asked him if there was anyone living to whom he could show kindness for Jonathan's sake. We do not know for sure, but it may have been possible that Ziba was already employed by Saul when David frequented the palace and sat at the king's table. (See I Samuel 20:27.) Nevertheless, David remembered the oath between him and his dearest friend, who had been killed in battle along with Saul (I Samuel 31:1–5). Upon inquiry, David learned of Mephibosheth, Jonathan's son.

After David's invitation and inclusion of Mephibosheth into David's household, he appointed Ziba to be Mephibosheth's servant. Ziba, his fifteen sons, and twenty servants were commissioned to farm the land and bring in the crops, so every need of Mephibosheth would be provided for (II Samuel 9:9–10). David also appointed Mephibosheth to be the master of all the people in Ziba's household. Ziba was no longer called the servant of Saul's household. He and his family and servants were to serve Mephibosheth.

B. Mephibosheth

Mephibosheth was just a child when news of the deaths of Saul and Jonathan was proclaimed. In her haste to flee, Mephibosheth's nurse dropped him and he became crippled (II Samuel 4:4). Mephibosheth grew up in another man's house in the land of Lo-debar (II Samuel 9:4). We do not know how old Mephibosheth was when he was taken to David, but he was old enough to have a son. (See II Samuel 9:12.)

Mephibosheth thought David intended to kill him. His fears were warranted because many times when a king ascended to the throne, he would order all those who were related to the prior regime be slain. Perhaps this fear caused Mephibosheth to be content to live the life of a pauper in another man's house rather than claim the land of his father and grandfather. His first response to David shows Mephibosheth must have had no knowledge of the covenant David had made with his father. He fell on his face and reverenced David with the highest form of surrender (II Samuel 9:6). Mephibosheth called himself a dead dog to the mighty King David (II Samuel 9:8). Mephibosheth feared for his life, but he had no cause to be afraid. David had made an oath to Mephibosheth's father, Jonathan, and this was the day David would honor that oath.

» **Do you think people take oaths as seriously today as they did in David's time? Explain.**

II. DAVID CALLED FOR MEPHIBOSHETH

Never in his wildest dreams did Mephibosheth think he would end up back in a palace, eating at the king's table, but that is what David offered his best friend's son. When King David called for him, Mephibosheth came before the throne with humility and reverence, falling on his face and declaring his servitude to David. David could see the fear in this man, and David assured Mephibosheth he had no need to be afraid. David let Mephibosheth know his grandfather's land would be restored to him, and he was welcome to eat at the king's table every day.

A. Saul's Land Returned

In fulfillment of his oath to Jonathan, David restored Mephibosheth's inheritance. It is significant that David restored Saul's land to Mephibosheth because this was the heritage of his father and grandfather. For Mephibosheth, the restoration of Saul's land was a recovery of honor and acceptance. David reaffirmed the covenant he had made with Jonathan, and Mephibosheth knew he was welcome in the house of David to live in peace.

B. Seated at the King's Table

To be given a seat at the king's table was a tremendous honor. Those who surrounded the king in the closest proximity of his daily meals were those he trusted most. The significance of sitting at the king's table was made quite clear when David told Ziba his intentions for Mephibosheth (II Samuel 9:11).

The honor of sitting at the king's table was one of family inclusion. This was a bold statement that Mephibosheth would be as welcome as any of David's sons.

One day we will sit at the table of King Jesus. "And he saith unto me, Write, Blessed are they which are called unto the marriage supper of the Lamb" (Revelation 19:9). What an honor it will be to sit with Jesus in one of the most intimate family settings. The Lord has assured us we will be His sons and daughters. "Wherefore come out from among them, and be ye separate, saith the Lord, and touch not the unclean thing; and I will receive you, and will be a Father unto you, and ye shall be my sons and daughters, saith the Lord Almighty" (II Corinthians 6:17–18). When we show our resolve to be His, by separating ourselves from the world and unto Him, He embraces us as His children and He becomes our Father. There is no better relationship to share with God Almighty.

III. DAVID SHOWED GRACE

It has often been quoted, "Mercy is not getting what we deserve; grace is getting what we do not deserve." Throughout his life, David experienced a lack of mercy on the part of Saul. It seems when David began to trust him, Saul would go into one of his rages and take it out on David. It all began when Saul threw a spear at David, one of his most loyal men and his armor bearer. It did not matter how loyal David was to Saul or how hard David tried to prove himself, it seemed mercy was always just out of reach. Saul was more intent upon soothing his jealousy than in showing a little mercy to a man worthy of Justice. Perhaps that is what inspired David to search for the family of Jonathan. The greatest act of mercy that David experienced from the family of Saul had come from Jonathan. He showed grace and mercy toward David when Saul lacked both. The friendship between David and Jonathan was a gift. They loved each other as their own souls (I Samuel 18:3). Their relationship was more comparable to twin brothers than friends. This amazing relationship taught them both the beauty of grace. Jonathan learned to embrace grace when he was over-looked as the next heir to the throne. David learned grace when Jonathan spared his life and put his own life in jeopardy to keep David safe from Saul's angry abuse (I Samuel 20:30–33).

David assured Mephibosheth that he was in the presence of a man who had been shown mercy and grace and would now reciprocate the same to him. David extended kindness toward Mephibosheth on behalf of his father, Jonathan.

» *Keeping an oath between two living people is honorable, but what does it say about David's honor when he kept his oath to Jonathan even after his death?*

A. Godly Leaders Keep Covenants and Promises

As we study the life of David, we can see he made many mistakes. However, he valued the covenant he made with Jonathan. It is important as godly leaders to honor promises and keep covenants. Leaders should pay their bills. An invoice is a document stating the promise between a business and a customer. When we agree to pay a bill, we should be diligent and prompt to repay the debt. It does not take long to put a black mark on our testimony of Jesus Christ if we are consistently late on our payments and reluctant to pay our bills. We should do all we can to keep our word and guard our testimony.

» *Do you think it is honorable and necessary to pay off all your debt and become debt free?*

David was mindful of the promises he made to God and was careful to follow God's statutes and laws. When David made a mistake, he was quick to repent and ask God for forgiveness. After David committed adultery with Bathsheba and caused her husband to be slain in battle, he prayed, "Create in me a clean heart, O God; and renew a right spirit within me. Cast me not away from thy presence; and take not thy holy spirit from me. Restore unto me the joy of thy salvation; and uphold me with thy free spirit" (Psalm 51:10–12). When we sin we have the same hope for restoration. If we will look to the Word of God, we will find direction back to Him.

Through the power of repentance, we can be forgiven and restored. Our God is merciful and full of grace. We would all be lost and without hope if it were not for the grace of God. How much more should we show grace to others when we have been given so much ourselves. As we have learned from David's life, a godly leader who has experienced the mercy and grace of God should generously offer it to others.

B. Godly Leaders Are Gracious

A person who is gracious is also kind and courteous. These are the qualities we see in David's treatment of Mephibosheth. Perhaps David remembered the kindness of Jonathan. Whatever it was that motivated David to seek Jonathan's descendants, the gesture was truly gracious, and David is remembered for his kind, gentle spirit toward Mephibosheth.

Remembering where God brought us from is a good place to study grace. We have all sinned and come short of the glory of God (Romans 3:23). No one is exempt because we were born into a broken world. "In sin did my mother conceive me" (Psalm 51:5). When God extends His grace toward us, it is our only hope. His grace is truly amazing, and we all have access to it. God is not restrictive about who receives this grace. It is available to all who will embrace it. Godly leaders will afford the same blessings on others. David's grace made him a great leader. In times of trouble, his gracious attitude drew people toward him—people who trusted him and believed in him as their leader. If we are gracious with others, we will gain trust and loyalty.

> » *How hard is it to show grace to someone who is unworthy? Is this not what David did to Saul? Explain.*

▶▶▶ INTERNALIZING THE MESSAGE

An old children's song says, "Be kind to one another. Be kind to one and all. Be kind to one another, and God will bless your heart." Being kind to others is exhibiting graciousness. When we are gracious toward others, it has its rewards. Gracious people find others are drawn to them. When we show kindness to others, it initiates reciprocal treatment. It is an example of what it means to "pay it forward." When one shows kindness to another, it makes the other want to show kindness to someone else. Graciousness is contagious.

As David felt committed to his oath to Jonathan, we should honor commitments and covenants we make with others. When we honor a commitment, it shows those around us how important it is to keep a promise. Keeping commitments or covenants cultivates trust in those with whom we make those promises. If people are true to their word, they are people of integrity. Others see virtue in them and know they can feel safe, being assured that what they see is what they get.

Leadership and God's Blessings

FOCUS THOUGHT
Godly leaders treasure God's presence and understand His presence is a blessing in their lives.

 FOCUS VERSE

I Chronicles 13:14
And the ark of God remained with the family of Obed-edom in his house three months. And the LORD blessed the house of Obed-edom, and all that he had.

 LESSON TEXT

I Chronicles 13:7–14
7 And they carried the ark of God in a new cart out of the house of Abinadab: and Uzza and Ahio drave the cart.

8 And David and all Israel played before God with all their might, and with singing, and with harps, and with psalteries, and with timbrels, and with cymbals, and with trumpets.

9 And when they came unto the threshingfloor of Chidon, Uzza put forth his hand to hold the ark; for the oxen stumbled.

10 And the anger of the LORD was kindled against Uzza, and he smote him, because he put his hand to the ark: and there he died before God.

11 And David was displeased, because the LORD had made a breach upon Uzza: wherefore that place is called Perez-uzza to this day.

12 And David was afraid of God that day, saying, How shall I bring the ark of God home to me?

13 So David brought not the ark home to himself to the city of David, but carried it aside into the house of Obed-edom the Gittite.

14 And the ark of God remained with the family of Obed-edom in his house three months. And the LORD blessed the house of Obed-edom, and all that he had.

I Chronicles 15:25–28
25 So David, and the elders of Israel, and the captains over thousands, went to bring up the ark of the covenant of the LORD out of the house of Obed-edom with joy.

26 And it came to pass, when God helped the Levites that bare the ark of the covenant of the LORD, that they offered seven bullocks and seven rams.

27 And David was clothed with a robe of fine linen, and all the Levites that bare the ark, and the singers, and Chenaniah the master of the song with the singers: David also had upon him an ephod of linen.

28 Thus all Israel brought up the ark of the covenant of the LORD with shouting, and with sound of the cornet, and with trumpets, and with cymbals, making a noise with psalteries and harps.

⨠⨠ CULTURE CONNECTION

NO LESS THAN EVERYTHING

On July 24, 1874, Oswald Chambers was born in Scotland. He was involved in a Bible Training College in London and served as a chaplain to British Commonwealth troops in Egypt during World War I. He died at the early age of forty-three from complications of an appendectomy. His wife, Bitty, transcribed her shorthand of his sermons and notes. From those come one of the most widely read devotionals, *My Utmost for His Highest*. The devotional was published in the United States in 1934, seventeen years after his death. One of his famous quotes was: "Shut out every other consideration and keep yourself before God for this one thing only—'My Utmost for His Highest.' I am determined to be absolutely and entirely for Him and for Him alone" (www.utmost.org).

Many people still use the daily devotional *My Utmost for His Highest*. Chambers has been quoted in sermons and speeches for many years. His message is clear and concise: "Give God everything; He deserves it." As we treasure the presence of God in our lives, each day we become more aware of His presence. As we offer our lives a living praise to Him, He showers us with love, direction, and a deepening relationship. Yes, we certainly need to be reminded that the best we can give to our powerful, amazing, and merciful God is our everything.

⨠⨠ OUTLINE

I. DAVID DESIRED TO BRING THE ARK BACK TO JERUSALEM
   A. Used Wrong Method
   B. Uzzah Died

II. ARK WAS LEFT WITH OBED-EDOM FOR THREE MONTHS
   A. Obed-Edom Was Blessed Because of the Ark
   B. We Are Blessed When We Live with God's Presence

III. DAVID HEARD OF OBED-EDOM'S BLESSINGS
   A. Prepared to Bring the Ark Home
   B. Worship and Sacrifice during the Journey Home

IV. GOD BLESSES THOSE WHO TREAT HIS PRESENCE WITH RESPECT

⨠⨠ CONTEMPLATING THE TOPIC

Spending time with those we love is one of the best ways to communicate our love and appreciation for them. Someone once suggested, "T-i-m-e is how you spell love to a child." That is also true for adults. Perhaps nothing is more important in a relationship than spending quality time together.

It is difficult to comprehend God's desire to have a relationship with sinful humans, but He has taken incredible measures to make redemption possible so that we may experience and enjoy His divine presence. In His foreknowledge, God knew when He created humanity that we would fall into sin, but still He created us, already having a plan for human redemption (I Peter 1:19–20). Through salvation we can experience His presence and draw spiritual strength and power for each day.

Charles Stanley commented, "We can be tired, weary and emotionally distraught, but after spending time alone with God, we find that He injects into our bodies energy, power and strength" (www.brainyquote.com).

The Tabernacle in the Wilderness contained significant lessons for all people who would have a relationship with the one true God. The people of Israel moved this portable place of worship everywhere they journeyed on their way from Egypt to the Promised Land.

First was the outer court. In this area was the brazen altar, which could be a model for the place of repentance, and the brazen laver, where natural cleansing took place and it could be seen as a foreshadow of water baptism. From the outer court, the priest entered into the Holy Place, which contained the table of shewbread, the golden candlesticks, and the altar of incense. Finally, on the other side of a great veil, or curtain, was the Holy of Holies. Inside this special place was the Ark of the Covenant. Only the high priest entered this room once a year on the Day of Atonement. This Holy of Holies and the Ark of the Covenant represented the divine presence of the Almighty.

It was no accident that when Jesus Christ died on the cross, the earth shook and the heavy veil was torn from top to bottom, opening the way into the Holy of Holies. This symbolized that all people everywhere could now access the holy presence of God.

It seems always to have been God's desire to have an intimate relationship with humanity. From the earliest days of life in the Garden, God appeared to have an ongoing relationship with His newly created people. Further, when one considers the extent to which God went to provide human redemption after the Fall, it seems safe to conclude God was determined to have a relationship with redeemed individuals. Consequently, it would seem that for a person to seek to live in God's divine presence would be the greatest possible source of human blessing. It is no wonder then that David desired to return to Jerusalem the piece of the Tabernacle furniture that represented the presence of the Almighty.

I. DAVID DESIRED TO BRING THE ARK BACK TO JERUSALEM

The story of the sad saga of the capture of the Ark of the Covenant began when many of God's people lost their respect for God, the house of God, and the things of God. They gave lip service to God while continuing to live lifestyles that failed to reflect honor and respect for God. For instance, consider what God told Samuel about Eli the priest and his sons. "For I have told him that I will judge his house for ever for the iniquity which he knoweth; because his sons made themselves vile, and he restrained them not" (I Samuel 3:13). As a result of this prevailing attitude toward God and righteousness, God and holy things became only tools to utilize whenever one fell into trouble.

After losing a terrible battle to the Philistines, the people decided to take the Ark of the Covenant with them into battle (I Samuel 4:1–3). They wrongly presumed the Ark would be their key to victory on the battlefield. They lost not only that battle with the Philistines, but they also lost the Ark (I Samuel 4:10–11). God brought judgment upon the nation by allowing their loss in battle, their loss of the Ark, and the death of the wicked sons of Eli—Hophni and Phineas—who were slain in the battle. Thus began seven months that the Ark remained in the possession of the enemies of Israel (I Samuel 6:1).

A. Used Wrong Method

It would be difficult to fault David's desire to return the Ark to its rightful home in Jerusalem. It was a holy artifact that was rich with spiritual heritage and significance to the people of Israel. However, doing the right thing is never enough; one also must do what is right in the way that is right. David learned this lesson the hard way. Symbolic of the lack of respect that led to Israel losing the Ark to their enemies in the first place, David and his people failed to discover the proper way for handling the Ark of the Covenant.

B. Uzzah Died

As they began to move the Ark out of the house of Abinadab, the oxen stumbled and Uzzah reached out to steady the Ark with his hand. Not understanding the proper protocol for carrying and handling the Ark, Uzzah kindled God's anger and was struck dead.

> At the threshing floor of Kidon the oxen drawing the cart on which the ark rested stumbled and evidently rocked the ark. Uzzah reached out his hand to steady it. This was a serious ritual offense since only authorized persons, the Levites, were to carry the tabernacle and all its furnishings. The wrath of the Lord flared forth against Uzzah, and he died. (J. A. Thompson, The New American Commentary: 1, 2 Chronicles)

» *Does God's judgment of Uzzah seem extreme? Why?*

Matthew Henry made a worthy observation regarding this tragedy:

> Let the sin of Uzzah warn us all to take heed of presumption, rashness, and irreverence, in dealing about holy things (v. 9), and not to think that a good intention will justify a bad action. In our communion with God we must carefully watch over our own hearts, lest familiarity breed contempt, and we think God is in any way beholden to us. (Matthew Henry's Commentary on the Whole Bible: Complete and Unabridged in One Volume)

II. ARK WAS LEFT WITH OBED-EDOM FOR THREE MONTHS

At this sudden turn of events, David was bewildered and fearful of God because of God's judgment. I Chronicles 13:12 records his perplexity: "And David was afraid of God that day, saying, How shall I bring the ark of God home to me?"

David recognized the seriousness of the situation and determined to leave the Ark at the home of Obed-Edom the Gittite. There it remained for three months while David inquired as to the proper way to get the Ark back to Jerusalem.

A. Obed-Edom Was Blessed Because of the Ark

It was unfortunate that Uzzah died in the process of trying to move the Ark improperly; however, the three-month interlude opened a door of understanding into the value and blessing of holy things, especially the value and blessing of God's divine presence.

> *A proper attitude toward the things of God brings blessing while a cavalier spirit brings divine displeasure. (Eugene H. Merrill,* The Bible Knowledge Commentary*)*

We can only imagine the blessings experienced by Obed-Edom and his household, for Scripture does not enlighten us as to the exact nature of those blessings. The Scriptures only note that his house was blessed "and all that he had" (I Chronicles 13:14). Still, to imagine God blessing us in all our actions and in all our possessions is an inspiring thought. How wonderful is the blessing of God!

B. We Are Blessed When We Live with God's Presence

When we recognize that the Ark symbolized the presence of God, and we consider the blessings that came to Obed-Edom and his house, the truth is clear: God's presence brings great blessing to those who live in fellowship with Him. What a blessing it is to walk in the power of Christ's holy presence, knowing He will never leave us or forsake us. David described this blessing as "fulness of joy" and "pleasures for evermore" (Psalm 16:11). Peter described it as "joy unspeakable and full of glory" (I Peter 1:8).

In his book *The Pursuit of God*, A. W. Tozer observes, "God dwells in His creation and is everywhere indivisibly present in all His works. This is boldly taught by prophet and apostle and is accepted by Christian theology generally. That is, it appears in the books, but for some reason it has not sunk into the average Christian's heart so as to become a part of his believing self. . . . He is transcendent above all His works even while He is immanent within them. What now does the divine immanence mean in direct Christian experience? It means simply that God is here. Wherever we are, God is here. There is no place, there can be no place, where He is not."

The omnipresence of God is an absolute and undeniable biblical truth; however, humans must desire His presence and become sensitive to Him in order to experience the blessing of His presence. When we become in tune with His divine presence, only then can we fully recognize it, appreciate it, and benefit from it.

» **What practices could we develop to become more sensitive to the abiding presence of God?**

Whatever was the extent of the blessings experienced by Obed-Edom, news of his blessings reached all the way to David in Jerusalem, prompting him to finish the task of transporting the Ark back home.

III. DAVID HEARD OF OBED-EDOM'S BLESSINGS

A. Prepared to Bring the Ark Home

David would not make the same mistake twice. Upon his return to Jerusalem, he began to inquire and research the proper way for transporting the Ark of the Covenant. David began to prepare "a place for the ark of God," and he also "pitched for it a tent" (I Chronicles 15:1). The extent to which he went in making appropriate preparations in advance of the Ark's return reflected his leadership toward cultivating a renewed attitude of respect in Israel for holy things. As the leader, David would cause holy respect to take root in the hearts of all the people, so they would have a healthy fear of God and His house.

David discovered the proper way to carry the Ark—only the Levites were to carry it, and they would use poles, which would be placed through the rings at each corner. Further, David recruited all Israel to go and accompany the return of the Ark home to Jerusalem with great praise and worship unto the Lord.

David led the Levites and priests by instructing them to sanctify themselves in preparation for the task. He further told them to organize the people who would be the accompanying singers and musicians. These individuals would lead the joyful worship of the Lord as the caravan journeyed back to Jerusalem.

B. Worship and Sacrifice during the Journey Home

A multitude of singers and musicians accompanied the Ark on its journey home. What a joyful sound they all must have made as they celebrated this great day of the return of the Ark.

> *And it came to pass, when God helped the Levites that bare the ark of the covenant of the LORD, that they offered seven bullocks and seven rams. And David was clothed with a robe of fine linen, and all the Levites that bare the ark, and the singers, and Chenaniah the master of the song with the singers: David also had upon him an ephod of linen. Thus all Israel brought up the ark of the covenant of the LORD with shouting, and with sound of the cornet, and with trumpets, and with cymbals, making a noise with psalteries and harps. And it came to pass, as the ark of the covenant of the LORD came to the city of David, that Michal the daughter of Saul looking out at a window saw king David dancing and playing: and she despised him in her heart. (I Chronicles 15:26–29)*

» **What lesson should we learn from Michal's reaction to David's dancing as they carried the Ark home?**

IV. GOD BLESSES THOSE WHO TREAT HIS PRESENCE WITH RESPECT

Finally the Ark had come home. The Israelites had learned their lesson well. Their initial lack of respect for something very holy had caused them to lose the Ark to their enemy, the Philistines. Even as they were trying the first time to return the Ark to Jerusalem, they failed to exhibit the proper measure of respect for a holy thing of God. They failed to learn what God required, and their disrespectful ignorance cost Uzzah his life.

» **How important is proper respect for God in the life of a believer?**

After witnessing the wrath of God and then taking the time to learn what was necessary for handling the Ark of the Lord properly, the Israelites began to approach, treat, and handle it with the utmost respect. The Ark deserved their respect, for it represented the presence of the Almighty.

As they carried the Ark home to Jerusalem, they experienced the great blessing of God as they worshiped Him from their hearts, sacrificed unto Him, and handled with respect the symbol of His presence.

〉〉〉 INTERNALIZING THE MESSAGE

Our world needs a revival of respect. First of all, people should have a basic sense of respect for others and for their property. A revival of respect would eliminate road rage, physical and verbal assaults, burglaries, and vandalism. It would cause people to look at others with appreciation and honor even though they might be very different from them culturally and philosophically. We do not have to agree on every topic in order to extend fundamental respect to others. What a blessing it would be to witness the positive effects of civility between individuals of differing ideologies and cultures and to see people extending basic human respect to one another.

> In his book Blink, Malcolm Gladwell writes about a relationship expert who was able to predict the potential success of a couple's marriage based on their interaction with one another. What was it he looked for that indicated a marriage was headed for trouble? Contempt! If one treated the other with contempt, the relationship was usually doomed to fail. Now, insincerity and flattery don't work. For a person to feel valued [he or she] must know you genuinely value them. To feel respected, [he or she] must know you genuinely respect them. When we devalue others we start treating them like objects, not people. (https://www.preaching.com/sermon-illustrations/illustration-relationships-respect)

Secondly, and even more importantly, we need a revival of respect for God and for the things of God. A revival of spiritual respect would cause us to approach and treat the house of God reverently and respectfully. It would create an increased measure of trust between members of the body of Christ. It would cause us to think twice before speaking angrily and without courtesy toward a brother or sister in Christ. It would cause us to avoid and reject gossip. It would lead us to come to worship services with an attitude of praise and jubilation for the goodness of God rather than with complaints, criticisms, and long sour faces.

If only we could recognize fully what a blessing it is to enjoy the presence of God daily in our lives, that He actually abides within us by His Holy Spirit. It was lack of respect and lack of showing due diligence that caused the people of Israel to lose the Ark of the Covenant. What we could lose today due to a lack of respect is far greater than a symbol of God's presence. We could lose His presence in our lives, and that is a risk too great to bear. Let us respect God, the family of God, and all the holy things of God. Let us walk in the presence of God with great joy and lead others to enjoy His presence as well.

Leadership and God's Voice

FOCUS THOUGHT

God often chooses to speak through the leadership He raises up.

 FOCUS VERSE

II Samuel 7:5

Go and tell my servant David, Thus saith the LORD, Shalt thou build me an house for me to dwell in?

 LESSON TEXT

I Chronicles 17:3–15

3 And it came to pass the same night, that the word of God came to Nathan, saying,

4 Go and tell David my servant, Thus saith the LORD, Thou shalt not build me an house to dwell in:

5 For I have not dwelt in an house since the day that I brought up Israel unto this day; but have gone from tent to tent, and from one tabernacle to another.

6 Wheresoever I have walked with all Israel, spake I a word to any of the judges of Israel, whom I commanded to feed my people, saying, Why have ye not built me an house of cedars?

7 Now therefore thus shalt thou say unto my servant David, Thus saith the LORD of hosts, I took thee from the sheepcote, even from following the sheep, that thou shouldest be ruler over my people Israel:

8 And I have been with thee whithersoever thou hast walked, and have cut off all thine enemies from before thee, and have made thee a name like the name of the great men that are in the earth.

9 Also I will ordain a place for my people Israel, and will plant them, and they shall dwell in their place, and shall be moved no more; neither shall the children of wickedness waste them any more, as at the beginning,

10 And since the time that I commanded judges to be over my people Israel. Moreover I will subdue all thine enemies. Furthermore I tell thee that the LORD will build thee an house.

11 And it shall come to pass, when thy days be expired that thou must go to be with thy fathers, that I will raise up thy seed after thee, which shall be of thy sons; and I will establish his kingdom.

12 He shall build me an house, and I will stablish his throne for ever.

13 I will be his father, and he shall be my son: and I will not take my mercy away from him, as I took it from him that was before thee:

14 But I will settle him in mine house and in my kingdom for ever: and his throne shall be established for evermore.

15 According to all these words, and according to all this vision, so did Nathan speak unto David.

CULTURE CONNECTION

EVEN AS CHILDREN

Nona Freeman was eleven years old when she received the Holy Ghost. According to her book *Everything Is Gonna Be All Right*, she was flat on her back as she spoke in tongues. She also received a vision from God that she was preaching in an African language. Over the next eight years, Nona's dreams were often about Africa, revealing the call to the mission field in her heart. At age nineteen Nona answered the compelling call of God on her life. She married E. L. "Bug" Freeman, and the two eventually became missionaries to Africa, ministering there for forty-one years. In 1989 the Freemans returned to minister to the churches in America. For ten years they followed the instructions of the Lord and ministered greatly to the churches. Nona wrote over twenty books, and after her husband passed away, she traveled extensively, ministering to men and women everywhere she went. The fulfillment of her calling spanned a lifetime. God outlined every detail in her childhood until He took her home on December 26, 2009.

There are many accounts of God's call on children's hearts, leading them into a life of commitment. Sunday school ministry is vital to the future of the church. We never know who is sitting in our classroom or congregation. As children give their lives to God, we will eventually see many of them become missionaries, pastors, teachers, and evangelists, answering the call of God on their lives.

OUTLINE

I. DAVID WANTED TO BUILD A HOUSE FOR THE ARK

II. GOD SPOKE TO NATHAN, THE PROPHET

III. NATHAN INSTRUCTED DAVID CONCERNING WHAT GOD SAID

IV. DAVID RESPONDED IN WORSHIP TO GOD

   A. David Listened to Nathan

   B. We Look to Our Pastor for Instruction from God

CONTEMPLATING THE TOPIC

For centuries people believed that Aristotle was right when he said that the heavier an object, the faster it would fall to earth. Aristotle was regarded as the greatest thinker of all time, and surely he would not be wrong. Anyone, of course, could have taken two objects, one heavy and one light, and dropped them from a great height to see whether or not the heavier object landed first. But no one did until nearly 2,000 years after Aristotle's death. In 1589 A.D. Galileo summoned learned professors to the base of the Leaning Tower of Pisa. Then he went to the top and pushed off a ten-pound and a one-pound weight. Both landed at the same instant. The power of belief was so strong, however, that the professors denied their eyesight. They continued to say Aristotle was right. (www.bible.org)

God has put in place certain laws, both natural and spiritual, and they govern many aspects of life. For instance, one is the natural law of gravity. Inventors have worked for centuries to create methods and systems to assist a person in countering gravity, and many of those inventions, such as aircraft, have improved human life. Despite the good accomplished by many of these inventions, however, humanity still must contend with the basic law of gravity, which remains firmly intact.

Another law of life is a spiritual law that establishes the structures of authority. To ignore the laws of authority in life is to invite trouble at best and catastrophe at worst. "The powers that be are ordained of God. Whosoever therefore resisteth the power, resisteth the ordinance of God: and they that resist shall receive to themselves damnation" (Romans 13:1–2).

The person who desires to accomplish anything positive in life is wise to understand authority and work through the appropriate authority structures. For example, before commencing a major renovation project in Jerusalem, Nehemiah sought the approval of the king (Nehemiah 2:5). The king had the authority to make or break the success of Nehemiah's undertaking.

God ordained authority in this world to bring order and to avoid the chaos that would ensue by every person doing what is right in his own eyes. Consequently, God ordains spiritual leaders among His people, and God speaks to His leaders. It is important that believers work in tandem with and submission to those in authority over them, for God often speaks first to those in leadership.

There are several ways God speaks His will to us. God's Word, the Holy Bible, is a supreme channel through which He speaks. His Word is forever established and unchangeable, and it reflects His basic will for humanity. Further, God speaks to us through our prayers, devotions, and moments of meditation. He also speaks to us through His leaders who operate with authority under God's sovereignty.

I. DAVID WANTED TO BUILD A HOUSE FOR THE ARK

David had an expressed desire to build a house for God. David felt badly that he lived in a fine "house of cedars" while God's presence was still symbolically headquartered in a tent (I Chronicles 17:1). Without question, David's passion for building a house for God was unassailable; it was an expression of deep love and respect for the Sovereign of the universe. David even began his respectful campaign with the complete favor and backing of the man of God in his life, Nathan the prophet (I Chronicles 17:2). However, God had another plan regarding David's desire. Consequently, God spoke to Nathan, the figure of authority in David's life.

> *Why do you think God spoke to David through Nathan the prophet instead of speaking directly to David?*

II. GOD SPOKE TO NATHAN, THE PROPHET

After speaking with David positively regarding David's desire to build a house for God, Nathan retired to his place of abode for the night. Interestingly, God spoke vividly to Nathan that night regarding David's plan. "And it came to pass the same night, that the word of God came to Nathan, saying, Go and tell David my servant, Thus saith the LORD, Thou shalt not build me an house to dwell in" (I Chronicles 17:3–4). God left no room for doubt about the matter: David was not to build a dwelling place for God. We learn more later regarding God's conclusion about David's plan:

> Then David the king stood up upon his feet, and said, Hear me, my brethren, and my people: As for me, I had in mine heart to build an house of rest for the ark of the covenant of the LORD, and for the footstool of our God, and had made ready for the building: but God said unto me, Thou shalt not build an house for my name, because thou hast been a man of war, and hast shed blood. (I Chronicles 28:2–3)

Whether God personally gave David more details regarding God's will later or whether that detail came through Nathan the prophet, we do not know for certain. But God made clear the reason for His decision: David had been a man of war and he had shed blood—the blood of those created in the image of God. God determined that David's son Solomon would be the one to build a house for Him (I Chronicles 28:6).

We should not be surprised at God choosing to speak to and work through His authorized leaders as He did with Nathan the prophet for David. God established authority for a reason—to bring order and avoid the chaos created by people doing according to their own ideas and opinions. God spoke clearly to Nathan, and it was Nathan's responsibility under God to take to David the word of the Lord.

III. NATHAN INSTRUCTED DAVID CONCERNING WHAT GOD SAID

Nathan delivered to David the words given to him by the Lord. Nathan was responsible to do nothing less, and he would be accountable directly to God for his faithfulness to deliver God's message. Nathan did as the Lord instructed him and took the message that undoubtedly was disappointing to the king.

> » *David was the king and could have taken his disappointment out on the prophet, possibly even having him killed as other kings before him had killed their subjects. What would be your concerns if charged with taking a negative spiritual message to a person of political authority and power?*

Pastors and other spiritual authorities are accountable to God for providing spiritual leadership in our lives. It is not always easy for them to preach the messages God gives them, but they must be faithful to the one who anoints them to preach. At times they are probably quite uncomfortable giving counsel to those they lead, especially counsel they know is not what the individuals want to hear. However, if they neglect to obey the Lord in their spiritual duties, they will have to answer to Him.

We ought to uphold our spiritual leaders and pray for them faithfully. We cannot comprehend the burden they bear for our spiritual well-being. Further, listening to and receiving their spiritual direction is for our eternal good.

> Obey them that have the rule over you, and submit yourselves: for they watch for your souls, as they that must give account, that they may do it with joy, and not with grief: for that is unprofitable for you. (Hebrews 13:17)

IV. DAVID RESPONDED IN WORSHIP TO GOD

David responded to God's message to him through the prophet Nathan with contrition, humility, gratitude, and sincere worship from his heart. (See I Chronicles 17:16–27.) Surely David must have been disappointed. The great heartfelt desire he had for building a house for the Lord had been dashed by the very one for whom he desired to build it. He could have been angry, insulted, and even vengeful toward God and the man of God, but instead he humbly accepted God's declaration to him. With sincere gratitude he worshiped the name of the Lord and celebrated the fact that his son would one day accomplish David's dream of building a great house for God.

There is another important fact that accompanied David's response to the word of God delivered to him. While he accepted the pronouncement that he would not be allowed to build God a house, he recognized, nonetheless, there were actions he could take toward the fulfilment of his vision. He began to acquire and stockpile the building materials that would one day be required for building the Temple. (See I Chronicles 28–29.)

» *Even though David would not be allowed to build the Temple, what did his actions in collecting building materials for the Temple say about his attitude toward God and authority?*

A. David Listened to Nathan

Not only did David respond with worship unto the Lord at the news delivered by Nathan, but he also listened to Nathan's pronouncements. David accepted the words of the prophet in his life, and he obeyed the words he received as being directly from God. Obedience is the best response to the authorities in our lives, even when we do not understand the reasons behind their instructions.

> *Neil Marten, a member of the British Parliament, was once giving a group of his constituents a guided tour of the Houses of Parliament. During the course of the visit, the group happened to meet Lord Hailsham, then lord chancellor, wearing all the regalia of his office. Hailsham recognized Marten among the group and cried, "Neil!" Not daring to question or disobey the "command," the entire band of visitors promptly fell to their knees! (sermoncentral.com)*

David's predecessor, Saul, learned the lesson of disobedience the hard way. Samuel the prophet instructed Saul to go up against the Amalekites and utterly destroy them, sparing not a man, woman, child, animal, or possession. He was to destroy it all. Unfortunately, Saul disobeyed and spared Agag as well as the best of the flocks (I Samuel 15:9). God gave to Samuel a word of judgment against Saul: "And Samuel said, Hath the LORD as great delight in burnt offerings and sacrifices, as in obeying the voice of the LORD? Behold, to obey is better than sacrifice, and to hearken than the fat of rams" (I Samuel 15:22). God rejected Saul from being king over Israel, and ultimately, Saul suffered a miserable death on the battlefield.

Believers should understand the lessons learned from the holy Scriptures. They must not fail to recognize the importance of obeying those who are in authority over them and heeding their spiritual instructions. It is a dangerous thing to ignore or disobey the guidance of our pastors and spiritual leaders.

B. We Look to Our Pastor for Instruction from God

God has given us pastors to watch for our souls (Hebrews 13:17). In the North American culture of our modern world, many people have developed an independent spirit that resists correction and instruction from anyone. They think they are "their own person," and they owe no allegiance to anyone above them. It is a dangerous culture that encourages individuals to "look out for number one" and heed the advice and counsel of none.

We ought to recognize the invaluable benefit God has provided us through the structures of authority. Authority is for our benefit and protection. True, pastors are human and like us they can fall prey to temptation and fail God. But unless their instruction directly contradicts the Word of God, we are accountable to heed their counsel and respect their guidance in our lives.

Jesus gave us a profound illustration of the benefit of authority, which is for our good. A Roman centurion came to Jesus desiring Him to heal his servant who was suffering at home. During this request, Jesus perceived this centurion possessed an exceptional understanding of authority.

The Greek word used here for centurion was *hekatontarchēs*, which means "Roman officer, a centurion, commander of a military unit of 100 soldiers" [James Swanson, Dictionary of Biblical Languages with Semantic Domains: Greek (New Testament)].

> *And Jesus saith unto him, I will come and heal him. The centurion answered and said, Lord, I am not worthy that thou shouldest come under my roof: but speak the word only, and my servant shall be healed. For I am a man under authority, having soldiers under me: and I say to this man, Go, and he goeth; and to another, Come, and he cometh; and to my servant, Do this, and he doeth it. When Jesus heard it, he marvelled, and said to them that followed, Verily I say unto you, I have not found so great faith, no, not in Israel. (Matthew 8:7–10)*

Jesus recognized the centurion's amazing grasp on the value of authority. Notice the centurion did not boast of being a man of authority, but that he was a man under authority. In other words, the only thing that gave him authority over others was that he himself was subject to the authority that was in place over him.

The structure of authority functions like a protective shield or umbrella over every person. Ultimately, God's sovereign authority watches over all people. Under that shield of God's protection are levels of authority, each of which bears certain responsibilities. As people submit to God's authority over them, they are able to bear responsibility for accurately guiding the ones who labor under their authority. Authority is not a club to threaten others, but an umbrella to shield and protect them.

In the case of pastors, God protects and guides them as they protect, guide, and counsel those under their authority. Pastors are responsible to hear from God and equally responsible to share God's words with those who look to them for leadership. Pastors must give an account; consequently, they should lead with compassion, care, and love for those under their care. They are not to act as ogres of repression but as loving and caring protectors, and they will answer to God for how they carry out this responsibility. Peter wrote, "Feed the flock of God which is among you, taking the oversight thereof, not by constraint, but willingly; not for filthy lucre, but of a ready mind; neither as being lords over God's heritage, but being ensamples to the flock. And when the chief Shepherd shall appear, ye shall receive a crown of glory that fadeth not away" (I Peter 5:2–4).

» *What are some of the best leadership qualities your pastor possesses?*

⫸ INTERNALIZING THE MESSAGE

Why would a person under the guise of independence ignore the warnings and admonitions of a spiritual leader whose responsibility is to guide, protect, and lead that person to a saved and prosperous life on earth and eternity in Heaven? How foolish it is to ignore sound spiritual admonition!

> *In Addison, Wisconsin, a sixteen-year-old boy, to his own hurt, ignored the warning mechanisms at a train-track crossing. In the Saturday, April 28, 2018, edition of the website of ABC's 12WISN, staff writers related the incident: "A 16-year old Hartford boy was injured in a train accident Saturday afternoon. The Washington County Sheriff's Office says the teen drove across the tracks on Aurora Road in the Township of Addison, despite the warning bells and flashing lights. The crossing did not have gates. The train hit the back of the driver's side, causing the car to spin and hit a signal bungalow near the tracks. Rescuers extricated the 16-year old from the car. He was sent to Children's Hospital for treatment." (www.wisn.com)*

It seems so reckless for a person to ignore natural warning signs and risk his life and health, but many people ignore the spiritual warnings and admonitions of those in authority over them. We ought to heed the words of our pastors and spiritual leaders. They care for our souls, and they will give an account to God for their leadership given to us. Further, we will give an account to God for how we treated our spiritual authorities and our responses to their leadership in our lives.

Leadership and Unselfish Servanthood

FOCUS THOUGHT

When godly leaders in our lives face difficulty, we are to serve them unselfishly.

 FOCUS VERSE

II Samuel 19:32

Now Barzillai was a very aged man, even fourscore years old: and he had provided the king of sustenance while he lay at Mahanaim; for he was a very great man.

 LESSON TEXT

II Samuel 17:27–29

27 And it came to pass, when David was come to Mahanaim, that Shobi the son of Nahash of Rabbah of the children of Ammon, and Machir the son of Ammiel of Lo-debar, and Barzillai the Gileadite of Rogelim,

28 Brought beds, and basons, and earthen vessels, and wheat, and barley, and flour, and parched corn, and beans, and lentiles, and parched pulse,

29 And honey, and butter, and sheep, and cheese of kine, for David, and for the people that were with him, to eat: for they said, The people is hungry, and weary, and thirsty, in the wilderness.

II Samuel 19:31–32

31 And Barzillai the Gileadite came down from Rogelim, and went over Jordan with the king, to conduct him over Jordan.

32 Now Barzillai was a very aged man, even fourscore years old: and he had provided the king of sustenance while he lay at Mahanaim; for he was a very great man.

CULTURE CONNECTION

IN THE MIDST OF THE STORM

Michael was a category four hurricane that hit the Florida Panhandle on October 10, 2018. Recorded as the most powerful hurricane to hit the continental United States in over fifty years, with winds of up to 155 miles per hour, the devastating aftermath was shocking. Media outlets released pictures of slabs of concrete where homes once stood; trees and lumber were scattered like toothpicks. After being downgraded to a tropical storm category, Michael wormed its way up the coast causing destruction in Alabama, Georgia, and the Carolinas, leaving many homes without power and under water. Thousands of National Guard troops, law enforcement officers, and rescue teams worked tirelessly rescuing people and looking for survivors.

When catastrophe strikes, it is comforting to see how people rally to help each other. In the same way the National Guard and other rescue operations rushed to help the people caught in the storm, we should also respond to those caught in the storm of temptation and spiritual destruction. We may not have all the answers, but being there when others need us shows the compassion God desires each of us to have for one another.

 OUTLINE

I. ABSALOM USURPED THE THRONE
  A. David Fled from Jerusalem
  B. Absalom Plotted to Kill David
  C. David Was Warned
  D. Absalom's Death

II. BARZILLAI SERVED AND PROVIDED FOR KING DAVID
  A. Served the King during a Difficult Time
  B. David Wanted to Honor Barzillai
  C. Barzillai Wanted Nothing in Return

CONTEMPLATING THE TOPIC

People in the Bible often seem perfect. Yes, we know their flaws, but we see them as larger-than-life figures who did the impossible through their faith in God. Determined to serve the Lord, they pressed on past every pain and every obstacle. As a result, many became members of what we call the Hall of Faith in Hebrews 11. We often take these champions of faith and place them on pedestals because they are shining examples of what God wants us to be. We desire to emulate them. Because they inspire us, we aspire to be like them.

We also search for godly examples to follow at church. We look to pastors, pastors' spouses, other ministers, and faithful saints of God. In some way we know they are human just like everyone else, but most of the time we marvel at their ministry and giftings as we observe their good works. When they face a difficult situation, we realize these men and women are truly human. They can be hurt, and they may have difficulty recovering from their wounds.

During their times of difficulty, we desire to help them, but we feel unsure of what to do. We want to be there for them because they were there for us, but how can we help? Perhaps we need to realize our own value to the kingdom of God in order to assist them. Today's lesson shows how the great and powerful King David received help in his time of need.

As a warrior, David was heroic. He had great resolve and accomplished many wonderful things for God and the kingdom of Israel. The Lord had anointed David and made him king over all of Israel. Gone were the days of running from Saul. David finally sat on the throne, having seen God fulfill the prophecy He had given to Samuel long before.

Despite his successes, David had many failures. In one such instance, he found himself in a dark place, and he needed help. Some of the people closest to him betrayed him. Others remained devoted to him despite his dire circumstances. They served the king as warriors, spies, and advisors. These celebrated individuals were part of David's entourage. They were part of the king's court.

Another man who was not part of David's court also rose to help David in one of the most difficult periods in the king's life. Despite his advanced age, Barzillai provided for King David after he lost his kingdom and perhaps thought he might not retain the throne. We too must help leaders in times of crisis. No matter our current situation, we must come to their aid. We must be stalwart and loyal, providing the support they need in troubling times.

I. ABSALOM USURPED THE THRONE

King David faced some troubling times when his son Absalom usurped the throne. The father and son had already experienced disagreement and alienation. At one point Absalom had fled the kingdom and lived in exile. Soon David would find himself in temporary exile, living outside of the kingdom God promised to give him and that he had battled to win.

David must have felt shocked and betrayed when he heard the news of Absalom's coup. David had so many great hopes for his son. He had named his son *Absalom*, which means "father of peace." The naming reveals that David hoped to defeat all his enemies and give the land rest so his son Absalom could reign in peace and prosperity. Now the "father of peace" had transformed into the son of destruction, usurping the throne of his father.

Despite Absalom's treachery, King David was not without blame. One of David's other sons, Amnon, had raped Absalom's sister, Tamar. The king had not responded with justice. He should have punished Amnon. Instead the king allowed Amnon to continue living his life as though nothing had happened. A furious Absalom quelled his anger to avoid acting in haste and passion. The rage, however, seethed beneath the surface as Absalom plotted to kill his half-brother Amnon and avenge his sister's rape.

When Absalom finally acted and King David heard the news, David feared all his sons were dead. Absalom had only given the green light to kill Amnon, but the seeds of destruction were sown in Absalom's heart. Absalom fled and lived in exile for many years until he was allowed to return home.

» *Why does family betrayal seem to hurt us worse than any other type of betrayal?*

Despite being home, Absalom and his father did not repair their broken relationship. The prince remained banished from court. Once again Absalom bided his time. Finally he decided to take his rage out on Joab's fields. He knew that burning Joab's crops would get the attention of his father's general. Joab responded by convincing the king to restore Absalom's status in the kingdom. Finally it seemed this father and son had made peace with each other.

Rather than rejoicing in his restoration, the cold and calculating Absalom plotted his biggest move yet. He stood at the gates of the city, acting as judge to win the hearts of the people. He told them his father the king would not listen to them, but he would hear them. Although many might criticize Absalom for his actions, his words show he did not want the loyal subjects of the kingdom to be treated like his sister Tamar. Amnon had almost gotten away with the rape of Tamar, but Absalom had intervened. Justice would not be denied the innocent in Israel. Absalom would not be denied his chance at kingship. His machinations set in motion a plot that won him the favor of the people and looked as if it would win him the throne. The banished and wounded prince was on his way to becoming king. The betrayed and weakened King David needed allies.

A. David Fled from Jerusalem

David had no choice but to flee the capital city of Jerusalem, the place he had won in battle and where he hoped to build a Temple to the Lord. The banished king soon found himself reliving his days on the run. He hid in the wilderness just as he had done to escape the wrath of his father-in-law Saul. This time he found himself seeking shelter from his vengeful son Absalom.

To add insult to injury, David encountered Shimei, a man of the house of Saul, who threw stones at David and cursed him: "Come out, come out, thou bloody man, and thou man of Belial: the LORD hath returned upon thee all the blood of the house of Saul, in whose stead thou hast reigned; and the LORD hath delivered the kingdom into the hand of Absalom thy son: and, behold, thou art taken in thy mischief, because thou art a bloody man" (II Samuel 16:7–8). One of David's men, Abishai, offered to kill Shimei for his insolence. David refused. He told Abishai, "Behold, my son, which came forth of my bowels, seeketh my life: how much more now may this Benjamite do it? let him alone, and let him curse; for the LORD hath bidden him. It may be that the LORD will look on mine affliction, and that the LORD will requite me good for his cursing this day" (II Samuel 16:11–12). These verses reveal David had hope, but he would need the Lord and his friends to come to his rescue and provide the support he so desperately needed.

» *What are the most effective ways we can help our leaders?*

B. Absalom Plotted to Kill David

David needed the help of his friend Hushai to overcome a plot that threatened to lead to the king's death. Absalom sought to gather his troops and pursue David in order to have a successful coup. And Ahithophel counseled the would-be king to do just that. Like Shimei, Ahithophel had a grudge against David because Ahithophel was Bathsheba's grandfather (II Samuel 11:3, 23:34). David's sin with Bathsheba had not only led to his son acting against him, but David had made an enemy of his advisor, Ahithophel.

In contrast, Hushai remained loyal to David. He would be needed to overcome the wise counsel of Ahithophel. Hushai wanted to leave with David, but the king had asked him not to flee with everyone else. Along with the priests Zadok and Abiathar, Hushai had returned to Jerusalem to assist David behind enemy lines. David told Hushai, "If thou passest on with me, then thou shalt be a burden unto me: but if thou return to the city, and say unto Absalom, I will be thy servant, O king; as I have been thy father's servant hitherto, so will I now also be thy servant: then mayest thou for me defeat the counsel of Ahithophel" (II Samuel 15:33–34).

Defeating the counsel of Ahithophel would be a tall order. II Samuel 16:23 states, "And the counsel of Ahithophel, which he counselled in those days, was as if a man had enquired at the oracle of God: so was all the counsel of Ahithophel both with David and with Absalom."

Nevertheless, Hushai challenged the advice of Ahithophel.

Ahithophel advised Absalom to pursue David and win the battle. The counsel seemed good to Absalom and his advisors. Hushai countered by telling Absalom of his father's military prowess and stealth in the wilderness. Hushai made a convincing argument in his description of David: "And he also that is valiant, whose heart is as the heart of a lion, shall utterly melt: for all Israel knoweth that thy father is a mighty man, and they which be with him are valiant men" (II Samuel 17:10). Hushai's argument won the day because "the LORD had appointed to defeat the good counsel of Ahithophel, to the intent that the LORD might bring evil upon Absalom" (II Samuel 17:14).

C. David Was Warned

The loyalty and cleverness of Abishai bought David much-needed time. Hushai spoke to Jonathan and Ahimaaz, the sons of the high priests Abiathar and Zadok. Hushai told them to warn David not to remain in the wilderness. The two men fled Jerusalem to inform the king, but they narrowly escaped discovery. Providentially, David's network of spies delivered the needed information. David and his troops crossed the Jordan River in order to survive, regroup, and create a plan to defeat Absalom.

David must have felt his life had completely regressed, not just personally, but on a national scale. Personally, David had lost the throne. On a larger scale, Israel's anointed king found himself going over the Jordan River, headed in the wrong direction. Joshua had once led the people across the Jordan River. The Lord had parted the waters, and God had given Israel victory after victory. David had taken up the warrior's sword and the mantle of leadership to continue Joshua's mission. Now David found himself losing all the progress he had gained. Sadly, his next loss would be even greater.

» *Our leaders have often won great victories, but they sometimes face challenging times. In their time of trouble, how can we remind them of all the good they have done?*

D. Absalom's Death

Back in Jerusalem Absalom had lost valuable time because he had heeded the advice of David's spy, Hushai, instead of listening to the wise counsel of Ahithophel. This decision would cost him his life. Absalom entered the battle. While riding on a mule, Absalom's long hair got caught in the branches of a tree. Joab seized the opportunity to kill Absalom and put an end to the unrest in the kingdom.

Meanwhile David waited for news of the battle. Informed of the name of an approaching messenger, David hoped he would bring a positive report. David received good news from him. David's men had emerged victorious. Unfortunately, another messenger brought the sad news of Absalom's death. Despite all the evil Absalom had caused, the king still greatly loved his son. "And the king was much moved, and went up to the chamber over the gate, and wept: and as he went, thus he said, O my son Absalom, my son, my son Absalom! Would God I had died for thee, O Absalom, my son, my son!" (II Samuel 18:33).

The king had been brought to a place even lower than losing the throne. He had lost his son. He mourned not only the loss of his boy, but also for what might have been. Absalom could have risen after David's death to become the new king. He could have lived up to his name as the "father of peace." He would not have to fight battles and have blood on his hands because his father would have already defeated all of Israel's enemies. These hopes died with Absalom and left the king in despair.

II. BARZILLAI SERVED AND PROVIDED FOR KING DAVID

David experienced one of the most difficult times of his life when Absalom usurped power and ultimately died. David discovered he had loyal friends and enemies who held grudges. While he could rely on Abishai, Hushai, and the priests Abiathar and Zadok, as well as their sons, he found himself being cursed by Shimei and betrayed by Ahithophel. Even though Joab won the battle to restore the kingdom, David was perplexed because his seemingly loyal general had killed his son Absalom. Even Mephibosheth, the lame son of Jonathan whom David had given a place at his table, fell under David's suspicion. Mephibosheth did not flee with David, and the king suspected treachery when he returned (II Samuel 19:24–30).

Mephibosheth's servant had told the king that Mephibosheth had slandered David. Mephibosheth tried to plead his case with the king. His appearance seemed to reveal his loyalty because he "had neither dressed his feet, nor trimmed his beard, nor washed his clothes, from the day the king departed until the day he came again in peace" (II Samuel 19:24). Perhaps due to all the betrayals he had faced, King David did not believe him. He gave some of Mephibosheth's land to his servant.

Despite all the real and perhaps imagined betrayals, David still had friends. In the midst of all David's heartache, another friend arose to stand in the gap for the king and lift him up. The octogenarian Barzillai came to help David over the Jordan River and return him to his rightful place. The older man had proven to be a key ally. He had provided sustenance during David's exile from Jerusalem.

A. Served the King during a Difficult Time

As an eighty-year-old man, Barzillai could have felt he had little to contribute. He was not a young, spry warrior. He could not serve as a spy for David like others. He had not defeated the counsel of the wise Ahithophel like Hushai. Yet Barzillai played an important role during David's time of trouble. He was there for David.

Barzillai provided David and his men with what they needed. Barzillai chose loyalty over betrayal. He chose faithfulness over falseness. He chose to lift up a man instead of kicking him when he was down.

B. David Wanted to Honor Barzillai

The king appreciated Barzillai's loyalty and faithfulness. David wanted to return the older gentleman's kindness by hosting him and feeding him in Jerusalem. David's desire to honor others showed he appreciated those who had helped him during the dark days of Absalom's coup. David not only respected Barzillai for the wisdom of his age, but he respected him for his willingness to risk his life for the sake of the kingdom. Had the battle gone differently, Barzillai could have faced death by Absalom for aiding and abetting the enemy. Now Barzillai faced an interesting situation: the most powerful man in the land felt indebted to him and wanted to reward him.

> » *Sometimes supporting our leaders may come at personal risk. We may be tempted to avoid conflict. How can we be loyal even when it might cost us?*

C. Barzillai Wanted Nothing in Return

Faithful Barzillai did not want to accept the reward for himself. He told David of his failing eyesight, deteriorating hearing, and inability to taste food. He had risen above these limitations to help the king. Even though he refused the king's reward, he acted honorably by showing the next generation how to be loyal to the Lord's anointed.

Instead of accompanying the king back to Jerusalem and eating at the king's table, Barzillai told David to take his servant Chimham and reward him. Chimham had likely proven faithful to Barzillai just as Barzillai had shown loyalty to David. Now Chimham would reap the rewards of this steadfastness. In honoring Chimham, Barzillai taught the next generation to honor leadership.

> » *How can we teach the next generation to show respect and honor to leadership?*

⟫⟫ INTERNALIZING THE MESSAGE

The pastor of a small church always reached out to families in need. He visited saints in the hospital, checked on shut-ins, and assisted families with funeral preparations. His daughter watched him tirelessly minister to the saints. She admired her father for consistently helping others in their times of need. With her father's good example and the family's commitment to the Lord, she should have felt positive about the church.

And she did for quite some time—that is, until a death occurred in her family. Perhaps greater than the absence of the loved one was the absence of church members. They showed no compassion or even concern. Perhaps greater than the grief of loss was the hurt caused by the apathetic. They never appeared on the doorstep with a casserole or even a card. The girl was stunned.

The pastor's daughter felt as though all her father's good works had returned void. Worse yet, the church members had not only failed to do what was good and decent, but they had failed to follow the pastor's fine example.

If only this sad story were the product of a writer's imagination. Sadly, the story is true, and the daughter's commitment to the Lord is not secure. This church fell well short of godly expectations and even failed to live up to the standards of most communities. Although very hurt, the pastor was not to blame. He had done his best. He had sowed kindness that he would not reap—at least in this life.

In contrast, David was reaping a harvest of heartache, and he was to blame for his awful choices. In the story of David and Barzillai, we see a flawed king fleeing the terrible situation he had created. Some, like Shimei, would choose to kick the king when he was down. Barzillai, however, remembered all the good David had accomplished for Israel.

Barzillai remembered the lone shepherd boy who had stood up against the giant, so Barzillai stood with David when others would not. Barzillai remembered the man who had refused to kill Saul in spite of multiple opportunities to end his life, so Barzillai refused to add to the king's anguish. He most likely knew of David's sin with Bathsheba, but he chose not to bring more darkness into David's life. Instead, he arose as a shining beacon of help in the midst of David's trouble.

Barzillai knew that sometimes good leaders face difficult situations. In these times, they need respite rather than spite. Those who have lent a helping hand need the hand of friendship extended to them. Those who have given words of encouragement need a kind word and a pat on the back.

The church should rise up and support godly leaders. Like David, some of them may have trouble with their children. Congregations should recognize the humanity of their pastors and their families. Such issues should not be used as an occasion to the flesh.

The church should follow Barzillai's fine example and recognize the good even in the midst of the problematic. Churches that have received words of encouragement through good teaching and preaching should speak hope and life to their pastors and their families. Churches that have benefited from the prayers of praying men and women of God should make intercession for their leaders. Most importantly, churches should not wait for a time of crisis to recognize the sacrifices and contributions of their leaders. Godly pastors and their families should be supported and encouraged at all times.

Leadership and Transition

FOCUS THOUGHT

When godly leaders face transition, they can trust God to unfold His will and give clear direction.

 FOCUS VERSE

I Kings 1:35

Then ye shall come up after him, that he may come and sit upon my throne; for he shall be king in my stead: and I have appointed him to be ruler over Israel and over Judah.

⟩⟩⟩ LESSON TEXT

I Kings 1:28–40

28 Then king David answered and said, Call me Bath-sheba. And she came into the king's presence, and stood before the king.

29 And the king sware, and said, As the LORD liveth, that hath redeemed my soul out of all distress,

30 Even as I sware unto thee by the LORD God of Israel, saying, Assuredly Solomon thy son shall reign after me, and he shall sit upon my throne in my stead; even so will I certainly do this day.

31 Then Bath-sheba bowed with her face to the earth, and did reverence to the king, and said, Let my lord king David live for ever.

32 And king David said, Call me Zadok the priest, and Nathan the prophet, and Benaiah the son of Jehoiada. And they came before the king.

33 The king also said unto them, Take with you the servants of your lord, and cause Solomon my son to ride upon mine own mule, and bring him down to Gihon:

34 And let Zadok the priest and Nathan the prophet anoint him there king over Israel: and blow ye with the trumpet, and say, God save king Solomon.

35 Then ye shall come up after him, that he may come and sit upon my throne; for he shall be king in my stead: and I have appointed him to be ruler over Israel and over Judah.

36 And Benaiah the son of Jehoiada answered the king, and said, Amen: the LORD God of my lord the king say so too.

37 As the LORD hath been with my lord the king, even so be he with Solomon, and make his throne greater than the throne of my lord king David.

38 So Zadok the priest, and Nathan the prophet, and Benaiah the son of Jehoiada, and the Cherethites, and the Pelethites, went down, and caused Solomon to ride upon king David's mule, and brought him to Gihon.

39 And Zadok the priest took an horn of oil out of the tabernacle, and anointed Solomon. And they blew the trumpet; and all the people said, God save king Solomon.

40 And all the people came up after him, and the people piped with pipes, and rejoiced with great joy, so that the earth rent with the sound of them.

RELENTLESS RESCUE

In the summer of 2018, twelve teenage soccer players were on an outing with their coach. They were exploring the caves in Thailand. However, as they hiked farther and farther into the caves, they discovered the waters were rising and found themselves trapped. News outlets around the world covered the dramatic situation. Concern escalated due to the location of the cave. "Divers involved in the rescue described treacherous conditions, with fast-moving shallow water passing through very narrow passages" (www.cnn.com).

As the waters began to rise due to rain, the amount of air in the cave became a concern for the boys. The only way out was to dive. Expert divers reached the boys and began teaching them how to use scuba gear. It was a harrowing experience. Only a few at a time could dive single file with an experienced diver. At one point, rescuers held the oxygen tanks ahead of the boys so they could maneuver through tight, submerged passageways. Through the unrelenting efforts of the rescue mission and expert divers, every one of the boys were safely rescued after two weeks of being trapped in the cave.

It would be interesting to know what the soccer coach was feeling. Situations may rise where leaders do not have answers. They must be patient and trust God to give them direction or send others to come alongside to help in the time of need.

▶▶▶ OUTLINE

I. ADONIJAH DECLARED HIMSELF KING

II. NATHAN SPOKE UP
- A. Nathan Warned Bathsheba
- B. Bathsheba Spoke to David
- C. Nathan Counseled David

III. WE MUST SEEK GOD'S WILL DURING TRANSITION
- A. David Declared Solomon King
- B. A Clear Voice of Direction Is Needed during Transition

▶▶▶ CONTEMPLATING THE TOPIC

Some children grew up playing with Batman toys, pretending to fight crime in the Batmobile. They also read about the adventures of Batman and wondered who would take up the mantle of Batman once Bruce Wayne decided to hang up his tights. No matter who anyone suggested to replace Wayne, there was a real sense that no one else could truly be Batman. Even if someone tried, that person would always live in the shadow of the original Batman.

Although this line of thinking comes from a fictional universe, sometimes the story is all too real in leadership transitions. Many senior pastors have served faithfully for years. They have dedicated babies, baptized those same children, and officiated the weddings of their now grown parishioners.

A pastor's life is entwined in the lives of church members. They worship together and fellowship together. They share tears and laughter. They participate in trips to camp meetings and trips for camping, hunting, and fishing. The church may have its ups and downs, but the pastor and the pastor's family remain constant and faithful.

As pastors age, church members continue to honor them and remember the good times. At times they may be surprised to see their aging pastor preaching just as spryly as a younger person. Elder pastors still feel the anointing of the Lord, but the same voice that speaks powerful sermons into the heart of the aging pastor may begin to prepare the pastor for a transition. Neither the church nor the pastor may truly feel ready, but change must occur because there is a time and a season for everything.

I. ADONIJAH DECLARED HIMSELF KING

As David entered the final stages of his life, his son Adonijah prepared to become the new king. After the deaths of his brothers Amnon and Absalom, he viewed himself as the rightful heir to the throne. He shrewdly sought out political connections to support his claim to the throne by garnering the support of David's general Joab and the high priest Abiathar. Adonijah, however, did not have the support of everyone in the kingdom. Most importantly, God had not sanctioned his rule as king.

II. NATHAN SPOKE UP

Before the situation could get completely out of control, the prophet Nathan sprang into action. As a young prophet, Nathan had found himself confronting David about his sin with Bathsheba. Although David had sinned, the prophet still recognized David as the rightful king. When Nathan had rebuked David for his adultery with Bathsheba, Nathan likely had no idea that David and Bathsheba would one day have a son whom God would choose to sit on the throne. The situation seemed impossible, but the Lord chose to honor His covenant with David despite the king's failures. As David neared death, Nathan needed to speak to the king to ensure a proper succession.

» *How has God remained faithful to you in spite of your sin and mistakes?*

A. Nathan Warned Bathsheba

The wise and clever prophet Nathan did not immediately seek an audience with the king. In his previous dealings with David, he had learned to be shrewd. Rather than directly confronting the king about his sin with Bathsheba, Nathan had told the king a parable that smote his heart and led to his repentance. Now Nathan focused his attention on getting Bathsheba to speak to the king. She had the king's ear and needed to act in order to preserve her life and the life of her son Solomon.

B. Bathsheba Spoke to David

Once Adonijah became king, Bathsheba and Nathan feared the new monarch would wipe out anyone else with a claim to the throne. Solomon and Bathsheba would be at the top of the hit list. With the life of her son at stake and her own life in jeopardy, Bathsheba approached King David.

She reminded her husband of the promise he had made to her, "My lord, thou swarest by the LORD thy God unto thine handmaid, saying, Assuredly Solomon thy son shall reign after me, and he shall sit upon my throne. And now, behold, Adonijah reigneth; and now, my lord the king, thou knowest it not: and he hath slain oxen and fat cattle and sheep in abundance, and hath called all the sons of the king, and Abiathar the priest, and Joab the captain of the host: but Solomon thy servant hath he not called" (I Kings 1:17–19). She pleaded with the king to help him realize the seriousness of the situation, "And thou, my lord, O king, the eyes of all Israel are upon thee, that thou shouldest tell them who shall sit on the throne of my lord the king after him. Otherwise it shall come to pass, when my lord the king shall sleep with his fathers, that I and my son Solomon shall be counted offenders" (I Kings 1:20–21).

> *How can we exercise wisdom in the midst of transition?*

C. Nathan Counseled David

Perhaps worried about the king's advanced years and memory, Bathsheba and Nathan planned for the prophet to come in afterward and confirm the words of the first lady of Israel. Nathan appeared on the scene and questioned whether the actions of Adonijah coincided with the king's wishes.

Nathan also recognized the political nature of the situation and gathered allies. Although Adonijah had the support of Joab and the priest Abiathar, Solomon had the support of the military leader Benaiah and the other priest Zadok.

The shrewd prophet did not tell the king what to do. He did not even make the same case for Solomon that Bathsheba had made. Rather, Nathan asked the king a pointed question, "Is this thing done by my lord the king, and thou hast not shewed it unto thy servant, who should sit on the throne of my lord the king after him?" (I Kings 1:27). By behaving wisely, Nathan gave David time to consider the situation and not feel unduly pressured.

As a result, David recalled Bathsheba and reaffirmed his promise that Solomon would be king. "As the LORD liveth, that hath redeemed my soul out of all distress, even as I sware unto thee by the LORD God of Israel, saying, Assuredly Solomon thy son shall reign after me, and he shall sit upon my throne in my stead; even so will I certainly do this day" (I Kings 1:29–30). God had once promised David that one of his descendants would always sit on the throne of Israel. The promise was not in doubt, but the specifics were in question.

> *We may sometimes know the overall plan of God, but we may not know the specifics. How can we trust God to fill in the details that make up the big picture?*

III. WE MUST SEEK GOD'S WILL DURING TRANSITION

The will of God may sometimes seem obvious. We may look at a situation and want to proclaim we have found the will of God. However, Scripture tells us we must prove the will of God (Romans 12:1–2), and we must "prove all things" (I Thessalonians 5:21). Transitions require us to go the extra mile.

To many outside observers, Adonijah may have appeared the logical choice to be king. He likely had some gifts that would have helped him rule the kingdom. He could certainly look to the good parts of his father's life and emulate them. The Lord, however, had not chosen Adonijah to be king.

The situation brings to mind David's own journey to the throne. The people had desired Saul due to his stature. As a man head and shoulders above the rest of the people, Saul should have fought the giant Goliath. Instead, a young, unheralded shepherd boy had providentially arrived on the scene to steal the Philistines' thunder and a victory for Israel. The underdog David triumphed.

God not only gave David victory, but He also bestowed His anointing on David. When Samuel wanted to anoint one of the older brothers of David, the Lord helped the prophet see things in a different light. The Lord told Samuel, "Look not on his countenance, or on the height of his stature; because I have refused him: for the LORD seeth not as man seeth; for man looketh on the outward appearance, but the LORD looketh on the heart" (I Samuel 16:7). The Lord's proclamation forever changed the way people should view godly leaders.

Some members of David's own entourage did not understand the will of God. David's general Joab supported Adonijah's claim to the throne. He likely felt as though he was backing a winner who would allow him to continue to lead the military and retain power. His failure to bolster Solomon's claim to the throne would ultimately lead to his death at the hands of Benaiah, the new general.

The priest Abiathar also backed Adonijah. Even though he was a man of God, Abiathar did not truly know the will of God. Perhaps he relied on political instincts instead of seeking to fully understand the plan of God. His desire to remain in his position as priest in the new king's court may have clouded his judgment. In the end, his failure to recognize Solomon as the rightful heir led to the dissolution of his ministry. He had shared the priesthood with Zadok. During Solomon's reign, Zadok became the sole priest in Israel when King Solomon banished Abiathar to his family estate.

» *What advice would you give to a church transitioning from one pastor to another?*

A. David Declared Solomon King

The supporters of Solomon knew the will of God. King David heeded the advice of Nathan and Bathsheba. David prepared to declare Solomon king, but he knew he would need to strengthen Solomon's tenuous hold on the throne by surrounding him with loyal supporters. He called on the prophet Nathan, the warrior Benaiah, and the priest Zadok to solidify Solomon's claim to the throne. These men prepared to faithfully serve the new king just as they had served his father.

They took Solomon and set him on David's mule as a sign of his enthronement. Together the prophet Nathan and the priest Zadok anointed Solomon as king over all Israel. This show of unity by the ministry of the priest and prophet would help to quell the opinions of any naysayers who spoke against King Solomon or who even considered supporting Adonijah.

Benaiah would reinforce Solomon's kingship by giving him the backing of the military. This support would be crucial since David's general Joab had the respect of the troops. Benaiah, however, had his own claims to fame that showed his military prowess: II Samuel 23:20–21 declares, "And Benaiah the son of Jehoiada, the son of a valiant man, of Kabzeel, who had done many acts, he slew two lionlike men of Moab: he went down also and slew a lion in the midst of a pit in time of snow: and he slew an Egyptian, a goodly man: and the Egyptian had a spear in his hand; but he went down to him with a staff, and plucked the spear out of the Egyptian's hand, and slew him with his own spear." Although lesser known in Scripture than Joab, Benaiah proved to be more than capable of leading the military for a young king.

Benaiah also showed the importance of honoring and respecting the elder king while being excited about the prospects of the new king. When King David proclaimed that Solomon would succeed him as the king of Israel, Benaiah stated, "Amen: the LORD God of my lord the king say so too. As the LORD hath been with my lord the king, even so be he with Solomon, and make his throne greater than the throne of my lord king David" (I Kings 1:36–37).

David's chosen group of leaders blew the trumpet and declared Solomon king. The people shouted, "God save king Solomon" (I Kings 1:39). Indeed the Lord had saved both King Solomon and the nation of Israel from the wrong king.

Meanwhile those attending Adonijah's feast heard the commotion. Their revelry soon turned to panic as the would-be king recognized he had failed in his attempt to seize power. Adonijah's supporters quickly extricated themselves from the party, but they would not be able to remove themselves from the sticky situation they had created by backing the wrong son of David. Their lives and positions were in jeopardy.

Meanwhile the faithful supporters of both the new and the old king looked to the future while honoring the past. I Kings 1:47 records, "And moreover the king's servants came to bless our lord king David, saying, God make the name of Solomon better than thy name, and make his throne greater than thy throne. And the king bowed himself upon the bed." In the midst of the transition, King David was not forgotten. The people blessed him. Yet the king likely felt happier about the fact that his son could be greater than he was. He had fought many wars to bring the peace that Solomon would reap. In fact, David had chosen the name Absalom for one of his sons because it meant "father of peace." Although Absalom had betrayed his father and brought war to the house of David, the elder king felt confident in Solomon's ability to achieve a lasting peace in the land.

David felt grateful to the Lord. He said, "Blessed be the LORD God of Israel, which hath given one to sit on my throne this day, mine eyes even seeing it" (I Kings 1:48). David would not get to build the Temple, but he would get to see a man rise to the throne who would finally fulfill his dreams.

» *How can we show support for leadership both new and old?*

B. A Clear Voice of Direction Is Needed during Transition

The story of Adonijah's failed attempt to seize power and Solomon's ultimate rise to the throne of Israel reveals the importance of seeking the will of God during times of transition. Not everyone involved in the situation completely knew what should happen. Men of God found themselves on opposite sides. The priest Abiathar favored Adonijah, while the priest Zadok backed Solomon.

The entire kingdom had to rely on the strategic actions of the prophet Nathan. Although most known for confronting David after his sin with Bathsheba, Nathan's role in ensuring a successful continuity in the house of David should be celebrated. This man of God deserves respect for being what his nation needed during a time of great possibility.

Churches that find themselves in pastoral transitions may need to seek the advice of outside counsel. District officials, wise elders, and even trusted friends of the church can be counted on to provide much-needed perspective, prayer, fasting, and unbiased advice during times of transition.

Young leaders and even seasoned leaders who aspire to pastor a church need the support that can only come from godly counsel. As they seek to change careers or move from one church to another, the stakes are high. Every party involved desires the will of God. Yet many opinions and ideas will come into play. It is only human to speculate, to hope, and to dream. In the end, however, the will of God must be done. Souls are at stake.

In considering the events that took place in Israel, some readers may need to be reminded that Solomon had yet to pray for and be granted the wisdom that made him famous. As a young man about to embark on a new journey of leadership, Solomon faced mixed emotions. He cared for his aged and ailing father. He felt the sting of the rivalry with Adonijah. Thankfully, Solomon could rely on the wise counsel of Nathan as well as the support of Benaiah and Zadok. Perhaps most importantly, Solomon could rely on his mother to speak on his behalf. Families have an important role to play during transitions, and Bathsheba helped make the transition go more smoothly.

Solomon would soon face many great challenges as he presided over the kingdom of Israel. He would fulfill the dreams of his father by building the Temple. He would maintain peace in the land. In the end, Solomon would not be a perfect ruler, but no one could deny God had chosen him to lead Israel. His supporters had put great care into his transition. The rest was up to him.

⟫⟫⟫ INTERNALIZING THE MESSAGE

Transitions can prove difficult, even in the kingdom of God. Churches put a great deal of trust in pastors, and many leaders have served faithfully for many years. The new pastor, no matter how talented or anointed, often faces an uphill battle in gaining acceptance. Family members of the former pastor may remain at the church. Even though the family attempts to manage the situation, the transition may feel like a loss, which may turn into grief. Hurt feelings may give way to anger and misunderstanding.

Sometimes these feelings may lead church members to defect. In one such situation, church members participated in an annual Saturday evening spring banquet, but they did not return to church the next day. They chose to quit attending that church after the celebration and never return. While many of them may have felt justified in leaving the church because they had disagreements with the new pastor, they failed to realize the impact they had on their fellow church members. Those who showed up the next Sunday morning not only saw a few more empty pews, but they also felt as though those friendships had dissolved overnight. Those who decided to continue attending the church felt torn between being loyal to the church and the pastor and being loyal to their friends. In some cases, converts will see friends, mentors, and spiritual leaders leaving to join a new church. They will feel conflicted. Should they stay or should they go?

This scenario reflects a sad reality, particularly for members of Generation X. Some of them saw several church splits. Members of this generation who heeded the call to ministry often sought pastorates of their own. They left steady jobs and the safety and comfort of their own home churches in order to assume the mantle of pastor. These new pastors often served under a senior pastor or a bishop who had called them to be united in ministry. Unfortunately, many of these transitions did not work out.

Not every situation ended in disaster, however. Some transitions worked quite well. The passing of the baton proved most effective when senior pastors had prepared themselves financially, spiritually, and emotionally for retirement or the office of the bishop. They also avoided any hint of nepotism. Their successors acted with humility and respect, honoring the former pastor while recognizing the need to move the church in new and positive directions. The change also required churches to be accepting of new pastors, appreciating the work of the former pastor while giving the new pastor the opportunity to make changes and press forward—even if the new pastor did things differently.

As long as a new pastor stays true to the Apostolic message, churches should support the ministry of the pastor. Church members should be on guard for those who might try to sow discord during transition. They should also be aware of their own personal feelings. Sometimes a connection to the previous pastor might lead church members to have difficulty fully trusting the new pastor. They should realize trust can take time to build. Nevertheless, the church should give the new pastor the benefit of the doubt and consistently pray for the will of God.

Many churches spend a great deal of time in prayer and fasting as a pastoral election nears. Some churches may believe the work of prayer is done once the new pastor is elected. The reality is that prayer and fasting should continue. Church members should partner with the new pastor in prayer. They should seek to build up the new pastor. They should recognize that differing styles of leadership and personality are not grounds for rejecting a new pastor. In fact, God may have chosen the new pastor "for such a time as this." While the former pastor ministered successfully in his or her era, a new style might be necessary to guide the church into a positive future.

Leadership and Prayer

FOCUS THOUGHT

A godly leader is a person of prayer who regularly calls on the Lord in worship and intercession.

 FOCUS VERSE

I Chronicles 29:10

Wherefore David blessed the LORD before all the congregation: and David said, Blessed be thou, LORD God of Israel our father, for ever and ever.

 LESSON TEXT

I Chronicles 29:10–19

10 Wherefore David blessed the LORD before all the congregation: and David said, Blessed be thou, LORD God of Israel our father, for ever and ever.

11 Thine, O LORD, is the greatness, and the power, and the glory, and the victory, and the majesty: for all that is in the heaven and in the earth is thine; thine is the kingdom, O LORD, and thou art exalted as head above all.

12 Both riches and honour come of thee, and thou reignest over all; and in thine hand is power and might; and in thine hand it is to make great, and to give strength unto all.

13 Now therefore, our God, we thank thee, and praise thy glorious name.

14 But who am I, and what is my people, that we should be able to offer so willingly after this sort? for all things come of thee, and of thine own have we given thee.

15 For we are strangers before thee, and sojourners, as were all our fathers: our days on the earth are as a shadow, and there is none abiding.

16 O LORD our God, all this store that we have prepared to build thee an house for thine holy name cometh of thine hand, and is all thine own.

17 I know also, my God, that thou triest the heart, and hast pleasure in uprightness. As for me, in the uprightness of mine heart I have willingly offered all these things: and now have I seen with joy thy people, which are present here, to offer willingly unto thee.

18 O LORD God of Abraham, Isaac, and of Israel, our fathers, keep this for ever in the imagination of the thoughts of the heart of thy people, and prepare their heart unto thee:

19 And give unto Solomon my son a perfect heart, to keep thy commandments, thy testimonies, and thy statutes, and to do all these things, and to build the palace, for the which I have made provision.

CULTURE CONNECTION

TEACH THE CHILDREN

At the UPCI General Conference in 2018, General Superintendent David K. Bernard was scheduled to preach to the constituency on the final night. Before he began his sermon, he requested his family come up to the platform, lay hands on him, and pray. It was a moving and precious sight. Although he had done this at other General Conferences, this time it was different. One of his grandchildren stood apart from the group to the left. She was a picture of grace with her little hands together and her head bowed, praying for God's anointing on her beloved grandfather. This was not only special because it was a leader's grandchild, but also because someone had taken the time to teach this little girl how to pray. She was prepared, she was sincere, and she was engaged.

Children catch more of what they see exemplified than what they hear. We should not be afraid to let our children and grandchildren see us interceding in the Spirit. We should take the time to guide them in prayers of their own and encourage them to participate in altar services and prayer meetings. As we make prayer a part of our lives, we pass that legacy down to those we lead.

 OUTLINE

I. DAVID PRAISED GOD

    A. God's Greatness

    B. God's Blessings

II. DAVID PRAYED FOR THE PEOPLE

III. DAVID PRAYED FOR SOLOMON

IV. LEADERS MUST PRAY FOR THOSE THEY LEAD

CONTEMPLATING THE TOPIC

True Christians strive to be Christ-like. Jesus supplies Christians with the ultimate role model for emulation. Christian leaders should set an example to their followers by their diligence in following Jesus' model and Jesus' modeled prayer. As God manifested in the flesh (I Timothy 3:16), Jesus was fully God and fully man. As a human, Jesus prayed to the Father. His prayers provide more than just an example for us, they teach us an important lesson. Leaders need to pray regularly and fervently.

Jesus' prayers inspired His disciples to beseech Him to teach them to pray, "And it came to pass, that, as he was praying in a certain place, when he ceased, one of his disciples said unto him, Lord, teach us to pray, as John also taught his disciples" (Luke 11:1). Jesus responded with what is commonly known as the Lord's Prayer. It is important here to note two things about prayer. First, Jesus prayed in public and His disciples witnessed His prayer life. Second, John the Baptist also taught his disciples to pray. Spiritual leaders not only pray, but they also teach their followers to pray.

I. DAVID PRAISED GOD

David wrote approximately half of the Book of Psalms. The psalms in the first half of the book are mostly Davidic, with those in the last half remaining either anonymous or ascribed to various authors including David. David believed His God to be worthy of praise (Psalm 18:3) and desired for others to join with him in exalting the Lord: "O magnify the LORD with me, and let us exalt his name together" (Psalm 34:3).

David's passion for praising and worshiping God motivated him to desire to build a Temple for the Lord. David felt convicted that the Ark of the Covenant still dwelt in a tent since its return to Jerusalem. First Chronicles 13:1–16:6 provides a record of David facilitating the Ark returning to Jerusalem. In I Chronicles 16:7–36, David sang a song of praise to God before beginning preparation to build the Temple (chapter 22). However, God denied David permission to construct the Temple: "But God said unto me, Thou shalt not build an house for my name, because thou hast been a man of war, and hast shed blood" (I Chronicles 28:3). God informed David that his son Solomon, David's successor as king, should construct the Temple. Despite David's likely disappointment, he continued his efforts of collecting the materials to build the Temple. David's labor allowed Solomon to construct a magnificent house for the Lord that history identifies as Solomon's Temple. David followed his successful collection efforts with a prayer before the people, recorded in our lesson's Scripture text. Our focus verse highlights David blessing the Lord as he commenced his prayer, "Wherefore David blessed the LORD before all the congregation: and David said, Blessed be thou, LORD God of Israel our father, for ever and ever" (I Chronicles 29:10).

» *Do you ever read the psalms out loud as a way of praising God? If so, do you have a favorite? Explain.*

Note that David's efforts for the kingdom of God flourished even though God refused his desire for involvement. Likewise, David's prayers and blessing of the Lord in prayer continued. Too many people fail to give their best efforts in working for God unless they get to choose the position in which He uses them. David's collection of materials enabled Solomon to erect the beautiful Temple he built, yet history does not refer to it as the Temple of David and Solomon. In the kingdom of God, a lot of people get credit for successes made possible by the labors of the myriad of people who remain nameless. Many people experience someone else getting credit for their hard work and must remind themselves that God knows, God is a debtor to no man, and they did not do it to get the credit. Often that requires some quality prayer time.

In his book *Good to Great*, Jim Collins, a former faculty member at Stanford University Graduate School of Business, speaks of high-level (Level Five) leaders of successful companies that transformed from being good companies to great companies. His research consistently identified the leaders of these companies as people with personal humility, who kept their egos under control. These exemplary leaders considered the success of the company as paramount and their getting the credit as irrelevant. Endeavoring to set up their successors for success further characterizes Level Five leaders.

David envisioned the Temple, a house built for the glory of God, and viewed his getting the credit as immaterial. He set up Solomon for success and supplied a biblical example of a Level Five leader. David realized all the praise and glory belonged to God. As stated in the conclusion of the Lord's Prayer, "For thine is the kingdom, and the power, and the glory, for ever. Amen" (Matthew 6:13).

A. God's Greatness

David portrayed his acute awareness of God's awesomeness throughout the psalms he penned. He extolled, "For the LORD Most High is awesome; He is a great King over all the earth" (Psalm 47:2, NKJV). The lyrics "our God is an awesome God" from the contemporary song by Rich Mullins echoes David's awareness. David further proclaimed the unfathomableness of God's greatness: "Great is the LORD, and greatly to be praised; and his greatness is unsearchable" (Psalm 145:3).

While God's greatness may be unfathomable, it behooves Christians to consider the nature of God nevertheless. God's attributes include being omnipresent (present everywhere), omnipotent (all powerful), omniscient (all knowing), eternal (timeless), and immutable (unchangeable). Contemplating these truths inspires faith. When the challenges of everyday life become daunting, we need to understand like Paul, "For I know whom I have believed, and am persuaded that he is able to keep that which I have committed unto him against that day" (II Timothy 1:12).

In East Africa, Christian Kiswahili speakers often say, *"Mungu anajua,"* which literally translates, "God knows." This utterance of faith encompasses a strong element of understanding of God's greatness. God not only knows, but He also remains in charge with everything under control. These Christians truly believe Him to be "head above all" (I Chronicles 29:11). David knew it, he acknowledged it, he included it in his prayer, and Scripture records it for our edification. In His omniscience God knows all things, and in His omnipotence He has it under control.

» *Does understanding that God knows everything give you comfort? Explain.*

B. God's Blessings

David set an example for the people of God by giving generously of his own wealth for the building of the Temple (I Chronicles 29:3). The Israelites responded by giving generously themselves: "Then the people rejoiced, for that they offered willingly, because with perfect heart they offered willingly to the LORD: and David the king also rejoiced with great joy" (I Chronicles 29:9). This statement immediately precedes and potentially inspires David's prayer. Yet, while David rejoiced at the giving of the people, his prayer acknowledged that all he and the Israelites gave always belonged to God. He linked together God's greatness and His blessings: "Both riches and honour come of thee, and thou reignest over all; and in thine hand is power and might; and in thine hand it is to make great, and to give strength unto all" (I Chronicles 29:12). Serving a great God results in blessings, and we must remind ourselves of the origin of our blessings.

» *How has God blessed you recently?*

As we contemplate more about God's awesomeness, one way of better comprehending His greatness flows from studying the names of God found in Scripture. (See *The Oneness of God* by David K. Bernard.) One Old Testament name for God, Jehovah, appears in several compound forms. For example, Jehovah-Jireh comes from Abraham's experience on Mount Moriah when he, at the direction of God, prepared to sacrifice his son, Isaac. God stopped him and supplied a ram to be sacrificed in Isaac's place (Genesis 22:14). *Jehovah-Jireh* literally means "God sees" and speaks of God supplying the needs of His people. No matter what situation we face, God knows, God sees, and God supplies. God not only supplied what the people of Israel needed for themselves but also provided them with the extra needed to build a house for the Lord. David's prayer acknowledged that God's blessing enabled them to give willingly: "But who am I, and who are my people, That we should be able to offer so willingly as this? For all things come from You, And of Your own we have given You" (I Chronicles 29:14, NKJV).

Unfortunately, some misunderstand the nature of giving to the kingdom of God. Paying of tithes and giving of offerings signifies a privilege we enjoy because of God's blessings. We return to Him that with which He has blessed us. When we return tithes and offerings to Him, He continues to bless us, enabling us to continue to give. David's prayer reminds us that even though God gives blessings to us, what we have still belongs to Him: "O LORD our God, all this store that we have prepared to build thee an house for thine holy name cometh of thine hand, and is all thine own" (I Chronicles 29:16). A conservative talk show host claims to have "talent on loan from God." Without confirming or denying that claim, we need to realize that whatever God blesses us with still belongs to Him. However God blesses us, whether with riches, honor, recognition, or just the strength to carry on (I Chronicles 29:12), we need to respond with thankfulness (I Chronicles 29:13), realizing that when we delight ourselves in the Lord, He gives us the desires of our hearts (Psalm 37:4).

Never let Satan deceive you into thinking you cannot afford to give. Contrary to what seems logical, you will receive more by giving. Read the story of the widow of Zarephath in I Kings 17:8–16. It may appear she could not afford to give bread to the prophet, but rather she could not afford not to give him bread. Jesus taught His disciples not to worry about food, drink, or clothing: "But seek ye first the kingdom of God, and his righteousness; and all these things shall be added unto you" (Matthew 6:33). David's prayer acknowledged that God receives pleasure from

94

His people giving willingly and with integrity (I Chronicles 29:17). A pleased Father blesses His children.

II. DAVID PRAYED FOR THE PEOPLE

David's wisdom as a leader caused him to realize the significance of the response of the people in giving willingly and generously for the building of the Temple. He understood that "where your treasure is, there will your heart be also" (Matthew 6:21). Wise spiritual leaders encourage their followers to give to the kingdom of God of their finances and time because it not only indicates their commitment to the things of God but also helps to cement it. Jesus admonished us not to put our treasures in the temporary things of this earth but into heavenly things with eternal significance (Matthew 6:19–20).

Social science research shows that doing an act of kindness for someone endears that person to you. Logic says, if you want to get someone to like you, do a favor for that person. However, getting that person to do a favor for you may prove more effective. We might pray, "God, help me love You more so I can do more for You." However, if we really want to love Him more, doing more for Him may facilitate our loving Him more.

David's prayer asked God to preserve in the thoughts and hearts of His people the willingness to give generously to God's kingdom: "And now have I seen with joy thy people, which are present here, to offer willingly unto thee. O LORD God of Abraham, Isaac, and of Israel, our fathers, keep this for ever in the imagination of the thoughts of the heart of thy people, and prepare their heart unto thee" (I Chronicles 29:17–18). David desired for the people of Israel to remain with their hearts fixed on the God of their fathers and understood that their willingness to give to God was linked to their loyalty to Him. While all humanity chooses or rejects salvation for themselves, God's work in our lives contributes to our spiritual well-being (John 6:44; Philippians 2:13).

Our giving to the kingdom of God is not the only indicator of our spiritual wellness, but when we slack off in our giving, it indicates we are lukewarm (or worse) to the things of God. When spiritual leaders admonish us to give willingly to support the work of God, Satan would like us to think they are just after our money. We need to understand that concern for our souls spurs them to encourage us to give. Spiritual leaders, like David, pray that their followers will be faithful givers to God's kingdom.

III. DAVID PRAYED FOR SOLOMON

After praying for the Israelites, David prayed for his son and successor, Solomon. Good leaders understand there is no success without a successor. The successor's success reflects well on the predecessor. Wise leaders develop understudies. Servant leaders not only enjoy developing others but also receive pleasure from seeing others succeed. While in the business world it may not be normative to pray for your successor, spiritual leaders help set up successors for success through their prayers. David besought God to give Solomon a perfect heart so he would be loyal to the things of God. David prayed for Solomon's faithful obedience to the Word and direction of God. David prayed God would enable Solomon to build the Temple for which David had made provision (I Chronicles 29:19). David knew Solomon's success depended upon God's enabling.

When a leader passes the baton of leadership to a successor, it can be difficult to turn loose of the baton. However, the leader must. The successor cannot win the race while dragging the predecessor behind. Ideally a relationship between predecessor and successor exists, allowing for mentoring and coaching, which often includes cheering from the sidelines. Certainly, prayer is always in order.

> *Why is it important for a former leader to let go when the new leader is in place?*

IV. LEADERS MUST PRAY FOR THOSE THEY LEAD

Organizations identify competencies they desire in potential candidates for hiring. These competencies vary depending upon positions and circumstances. Prayer qualifies as an essential competency for a spiritual leader. Success or failure as a leader often hinges on a leader's prayer life, "The effectual fervent prayer of a righteous man availeth much" (James 5:16). No matter how proficient a leader is in other areas, when a spiritual leader's prayer life fails, that person's leadership will fail. Therefore, a leader must diligently guard against becoming too busy to pray. In Acts 6, when the Grecians complained to the apostles because their widows were not being properly cared for, the apostles appointed deacons to take care of that need, "But we will give ourselves continually to prayer, and to the ministry of the word" (Acts 6:4). Followers must occupy a high level of priority on a leader's prayer list.

> *Why is prayer such an important component in the life of a spiritual leader?*

>>> INTERNALIZING THE MESSAGE

Just as David prayed for his successor, Solomon, and his followers, Jesus loved and prayed for His followers. Jesus informed Peter of Satan's desire to have him and sift him like wheat (Luke 22:31). Jesus then encouraged Peter by telling him, "I have prayed for thee" (Luke 22:32). However, Jesus knew Satan desired to destroy all His disciples and they all needed God's protection. John records the High Priestly prayer of Jesus: "I pray for them: I pray not for the world, but for them which thou hast given me; for they are thine" (John 17:9). Today in the world in which we live, Satan still targets born-again Christians, and they need the prayers of their spiritual leaders to help sustain them. Protection and strength come through the prayers of spiritual leaders. Spiritual leaders who fail to pray for their followers are guilty of negligence. Thank God for Christ-like spiritual leaders who pray for their followers.

WINTER 2019–2020

The Living Word

SERIES

Enduring Faith

LESSON
MANUAL

Lesson Manual

© 2019 Pentecostal Publishing House • 36 Research Park Court • Weldon Spring, MO 63304
www.pentecostalpublishing.com • All rights reserved.
Manufactured in USA, December 2019, 1922011

EDITORIAL STAFF
Editor in Chief: Robin Johnston
Associate Editor, Curriculum: Lee Ann Alexander
Word Aflame Adult Editor: Jonathan McClintock

WRITERS
Daniel Segraves
Scott Graham
Talmadge French
L J Harry
Jonathan Mohr
Robert Gilstrap
Daniel Koren

CONTENTS

All Scripture quotations are taken from the King James Version unless otherwise noted.

Scripture quotations marked (AMP) are taken from the Amplified Bible, Copyright © 1954, 1958, 1962, 1964, 1965, 1987 by The Lockman Foundation. Used by permission.

Scripture quotations marked (ESV) are from The Holy Bible, English Standard Version® (ESV®), copyright 2001 by Crossway, a publishing ministry of Good News Publishers. Used by permission. All rights reserved.

Scripture quotations marked "NKJV™" are taken from the New King James Version®. Copyright © 1982 by Thomas Nelson, Inc. Used by permission. All rights reserved.

Scripture quotations marked (NLT) are taken from the Holy Bible, New Living Translation, copyright© 1996, 2004, 2007. Used by permission of Tyndale House Publishers, Inc., Carol Stream, Illinois 60188. All rights reserved.

Scripture quotations marked (NIV) are taken from the HOLY BIBLE, NEW INTERNATIONAL VERSION®. NIV®. Copyright© 1973, 1978, 1984 by International Bible Society. Used by permission of Zondervan. All rights reserved.

ENDURING FAITH

by Jonathan McClintock

Faith may be seen as a strictly religious concept to most, but even those who claim to have no religious affiliation operate their lives on some basis of faith. Dictionary.com offers its first two definitions for faith as "confidence or trust in a person or thing; belief that is not based on proof."

On a daily basis, non-religious people place faith in people and things. They place faith in their cars and faith in their family. They operate on a certain level of faith as they drive down a two-lane road, trusting the oncoming vehicle will stay in its lane.

Even atheists operate with a certain level of faith. They would like to tell us life on our planet came from one tiny organism, though they cannot tell us where that organism originated. They would like to say they have proof, but they are actually operating on a foundation of faith.

Our belief in Creation is founded on faith. Yes, we stand firmly on God's Word as the proof we need, but none of us were there when God said, "Let there be light." But we are OK admitting our lives are firmly planted on a foundation of faith because our personal experience with the Creator is all the proof we need.

The Christian life is built first and foremost on a foundation of faith. To come to God, we must have faith. To experience salvation, we must have faith. And to endure to the end, ultimately securing our eternal prize in Heaven, we must have faith.

However, where we place our faith will ultimately determine how long our faith will endure. When we place our faith in temporal things, vacillating human philosophies, or dangerous deceptions, our faith will fall apart. But when our faith is rooted and grounded in Jesus Christ, we can be confident we will not be disappointed in the end.

God is calling us to have enduring faith—faith that will last the test of time. No matter the trial, the test, or the temptation, if we will cling to our faith, God will come through; He will never fail.

LESSON MANUAL

This Lesson Manual has been developed with the goal of providing teachers numerous options to assist in preparation and delivery of each lesson.

In each lesson you will find a Focus Thought, Focus Verse, and Lesson Text that lay a foundation and give direction for the material that is to be presented. Questions are dispersed throughout the body of each lesson to provoke thought and spark discussion. We urge teachers to use these questions as a means of helping students apply each portion of the lesson.

> » *How does God being "all knowing" bring you comfort?*

STUDENT WORKBOOK

The Student Workbook has been organized in such a way that students are given the tools to not only follow the major points of each lesson but will also have a tool to further their personal discipleship and devotion throughout the week.

1. The Focus Thought, Focus Verse, and Culture Connection have been included in the Student Workbook.
2. The Lesson Outline has also been included to give the student a template to follow as the lesson is being taught. In addition, certain parts of the outline correspond with the daily discipleship prompts in the Approach section. This is designed to show what part of the lesson corresponds to the particular day's lesson text and application questions.
3. The Approach section is designed to give the student daily discipleship prompts by including portions of the lesson and application questions. The flexibility of this section allows for the student to follow along and interact during class, to become familiar with the lesson content before class, or to spend time in review during the week following class.
4. The Ask and Apply questions are presented for the purpose of helping the student contemplate the truths of Scripture and the content of the lesson. The first of the questions in each set is taken directly from the Lesson Manual, while the second question in each set is an additional prompt designed to help the student apply what is being taught.

POWERPOINTS

To access your FREE PowerPoints visit: Pentecostalpublishing.com/wappt

The Better Plan

FOCUS THOUGHT
Because Adam's plan failed to cover his sin, God instituted a better plan for our salvation.

 FOCUS VERSE

Hebrews 1:3
Who being the brightness of his glory, and the express image of his person, and upholding all things by the word of his power, when he had by himself purged our sins, sat down on the right hand of the Majesty on high.

 LESSON TEXT

Hebrews 1:1–8
1 God, who at sundry times and in divers manners spake in time past unto the fathers by the prophets,

2 hath in these last days spoken unto us by his Son, whom he hath appointed heir of all things, by whom also he made the worlds;

3 who being the brightness of his glory, and the express image of his person, and upholding all things by the word of his power, when he had by himself purged our sins, sat down on the right hand of the Majesty on high;

4 Being made so much better than the angels, as he hath by inheritance obtained a more excellent name than they.

5 For unto which of the angels said he at any time, Thou art my Son, this day have I begotten thee? And again, I will be to him a Father, and he shall be to me a Son?

6 And again, when he bringeth in the firstbegotten into the world, he saith, And let all the angels of God worship him.

7 And of the angels he saith, Who maketh his angels spirits, and his ministers a flame of fire.

8 But unto the Son he saith, Thy throne, O God, is for ever and ever: a scepter of righteousness is the scepter of thy kingdom.

Luke 1:30–33
30 And the angel said unto her, Fear not, Mary: for thou hast found favour with God.

31 And, behold, thou shalt conceive in thy womb, and bring forth a son, and shalt call his name JESUS.

32 He shall be great, and shall be called the Son of the Highest: and the Lord God shall give unto him the throne of his father David:

33 And he shall reign over the house of Jacob for ever; and of his kingdom there shall be no end.

CULTURE CONNECTION

YOUR SECRET IS SAFE WITH—OH, WAIT!

In recent elections, James O'Keefe became a name Americans mentioned because of his work with *Project Veritas*—an undercover journalistic sting operation. He and his people plant cameras and microphones in places or on persons, unknown to their target. The undercover journalists get a politically significant person to open up about what the candidate really believes or to spill juicy details of what is going on behind the scenes. While O'Keefe's efforts have turned some red with anger, others appear to be overjoyed with his revealing investigations.

The whole idea of a hidden camera capturing one's deepest darkest secrets seems unsettling. Humans have secrets they do not want others knowing. As much as we are curious about and interested in the secrets of others, we double down security on our own closeted skeletons. Somehow in perfecting this lifestyle of hide-and-seek, humanity has overlooked the hidden camera from above.

On the flip side, knowing the secrets of others can become burdensome. According to a study of 237 participants, if one must keep a friend's secret from other mutual friends with whom he or she has frequent contact, the levels of stress and emotional weight increase greatly (Susan Krauss Whitbourne, Ph.D., "Dangerous Confessions," *Psychology Today* November 3, 2018). It seems the thing we seek could be our own undoing.

The only safe secret-keeper is the Lord. Those who turn from sin have their secrets safe with Him. However, those who continue to hide it will be exposed.

 ## OUTLINE

I. ADAM SINNED AND NEEDED A SAVIOR
A. Sin Brought Shame
B. Sin Caused Adam and Eve to Hide from God
C. We Have All Sinned and Are in Need of a Savior

II. ADAM'S PLAN WAS TO COVER HIS OWN SIN
A. Fig Leaves
B. The Skin of an Animal
C. We Try to Cover Our Own Sin

III. GOD HAD A BETTER PLAN
A. The Offspring of Woman—the Messiah—Would Crush Satan's Head
B. God Became Flesh
C. His Blood Has the Power to Cover Our Sin

CONTEMPLATING THE TOPIC

The perfect crime. That's how crime seemed to begin for humanity. We usually think of it as sin, but some dictionaries offer the word *sin* as a synonym for "crime." So, for now, let's use the word *crime*, since we cannot wrap our minds around the notion of a "perfect sin."

Here they were. Who would ever know? Sure, God had told him not to eat of this tree. But where was God? He did not usually visit until the cool of the evening, so they could probably get away with it. The snake wouldn't tell . . . he was in on it with them.

The tree was beautiful, and it was clear its fruit was good to eat. Besides, who would not want to be like God, having the power to make their own decisions?

Just one bite, and she knew she had to share this experience with her husband. He accepted her offer, and everything suddenly changed.

Nothing was perfect anymore.

We knew it. There is no such thing as a perfect crime, just as there is no perfect sin.

Their sin found them out, as it always does. (See Numbers 32:23.)

I. ADAM SINNED AND NEEDED A SAVIOR

Eve was not yet created when God said to Adam, "Of every tree of the garden thou mayest freely eat: But of the tree of the knowledge of good and evil, thou shalt not eat of it: for in the day that thou eatest thereof thou shalt surely die" (Genesis 2:16–17). So why did Eve say to the serpent, "We may eat of the fruit of the trees of the garden: But of the fruit of the tree which is in the midst of the garden, God hath said, Ye shall not eat of it, neither shall ye touch it, lest ye die"? (Genesis 3:2–3).

Where did "neither shall ye touch it" come from?

Apparently, Adam failed to accurately communicate God's command to Eve. What she said may sound close enough, but we learn elsewhere that God's words are not to be amended. Whether we add to them or subtract from them, they are no longer His words. (See Deuteronomy 4:2; Proverbs 30:6; Revelation 22:18–19.)

Adding to God's words does not strengthen them; it corrupts them. To do so gives the serpent a clue we really do not know what God said and sets us up for further deception; our own *Ye shall not surely die* (Genesis 3:4).

Another indication of Adam's failure is that he was with Eve during this episode of temptation, did nothing to help her resist, and shared in her sin (Genesis 3:6). Adam placed the blame for his sin first on Eve, then on God Himself (Genesis 3:12). Paul read Genesis correctly: "By one man sin entered into the world, and death by sin; and so death passed upon all men, for that all have sinned" (Romans 5:12).

Paul wrote, "And Adam was not deceived, but the woman being deceived was in the transgression" (I Timothy 2:14). Eve was deceived. Those who are deceived are convinced they are doing the right thing. Because she was deceived, Eve fell into transgression. But Adam sinned purposefully, intentionally, and knowingly. He did not fall into it, and he was not deceived. He knew full well what he was doing was rebellion against God with dreadful consequences, but he did it anyway.

> *What is the significance of the fact that sin was introduced into the world by Adam, not Eve?*

A. Sin Brought Shame

There were four immediate consequences of the sin committed by Adam and Eve: (1) Shame (Genesis 3:7); (2) Spiritual alienation (Genesis 3:8); (3) Fear (Genesis 3:10); and (4) Blame (Genesis 3:12–13).

When people are ashamed, they tend to cower and hide. They may do this literally—as did Adam and Eve—by fleeing from those they love most. More commonly, they simply withdraw into themselves, becoming distant and uncommunicative. Shame leads to spiritual alienation from God and other people. This kind of alienation produces fear that results in blame. Those who blame God for their sins effectively cut themselves off from the grace of God.

B. Sin Caused Adam and Eve to Hide from God

In order to grasp the meaning of God's warning to Adam, "In the day that thou eatest thereof thou shalt surely die" (Genesis 2:17), it is necessary to explore the biblical meaning of death. Death involves some kind of separation. We can gain immediate insight from James 2:26: "For as the body without the spirit is dead, so faith without works is dead also." When our material part—the body—is separated from our immaterial part—the soul/spirit—we are dead. This does not mean we no longer exist. It means our material part is no longer animated. Similarly, we were "dead in trespasses and sins" (Ephesians 2:1) before we experienced the new birth. This is the kind of death to which God referred in His warning to Adam.

God did not create people to die. He created them to live forever. That is why He placed the Tree of Life in the midst of the Garden of Eden (Genesis 2:9). When Adam and Eve ate instead from the Tree of the Knowledge of Good and Evil, they experienced the death of which God had warned: separation from fellowship with God. The reason for their newfound fear of God, which drove them to hide from Him, was that they were now dead in sin. They still existed, but in a spiritually lifeless state. There is no evidence that Adam or Eve repented, and there can be no spiritual life where there is no repentance. Thus, they were expelled from the Garden with its life-giving tree (Genesis 3:22–24).

» *In what way is spiritual death different from physical death?*

C. We Have All Sinned and Are in Need of a Savior

Paul spent most of the first three chapters of Romans explaining why all people are sinners in need of a Savior. First, he addressed the situation with Gentiles in Romans 1:18–32. These were people who had no Scripture to read. Their revelation consisted only of creation, conscience, and perhaps what had been communicated to them by their ancestors. (See Romans 1:18–20, 32; 2:9–12, 14–16.) Then, Paul included Jews in his assessment of universal sinfulness. (See Romans 2:1–13, 16–29; 3:1–22.) After providing abundant support for this claim, he declared, "For all have sinned, and come short of the glory of God" (Romans 3:23).

II. ADAM'S PLAN WAS TO COVER HIS OWN SIN

A. Fig Leaves

How quickly Adam and Eve transitioned from their shameless pre–Fall nakedness to their failed attempt to conceal their sin with fig leaves! (See Genesis 2:25; 3:7.) Why fig leaves? Perhaps the reason is that fig leaves are the largest in Canaan (John H. Walton, *Bible Background Commentary*). If so, maybe this gave Adam and Eve the quickest way to attempt to deal with their sin. A fig leaf can grow more than a foot wide. However, there is no quick, easy solution to the sin problem.

B. The Skin of an Animal

In an apparent move toward offering spiritual recovery for Adam and Eve, the LORD God replaced their fig leaves with "coats of skin." (See Genesis 3:21.) Covering more than a loincloth, the tunic was for common wear and work, reaching to the knees (James A. Swanson, *Dictionary of Biblical Languages*).

It is often noted that an animal needed to be slaughtered to provide this covering in anticipation of the death of Jesus Christ for the sins of the world. (See I John 2:2.) This is probably the case, since Jesus declared Moses wrote about Him and that everything written concerning Him in the Law, the prophets, and the psalms must be fulfilled. (See John 5:46–47; Luke 24:27, 32, 44–45.)

But the choice of the Hebrew *kutonet* (tunic) may also imply the transition from the peaceful, shameless, somewhat effortless life Adam and Eve enjoyed in Eden before their sin, to the life under the curses that followed. Life before sin involved tending the Garden (Genesis 2:15), but it was a weed-free task requiring minimal exertion. Now, in this common work garb that masked God's likeness and glory (I Corinthians 11:7), Adam would toil with sweat over thorns and thistles until he returned to the very ground from which he was taken. (See Genesis 3:17–19.)

C. We Try to Cover Our Own Sin

The first thing we should do following an episode of sin is often the last thing we actually do. First, we should confess our sin to God. Instead, we make doomed attempts to conceal our sin from God and others. In this, we have Adam and Eve for our models, followed by such copies as Cain, Achan, and a long list of biblical sinners. The warning Moses gave to Reuben and Gad is relevant to all: if we disobey God, we may be sure our sin will find us out (Numbers 32:23).

» *What kind of things do we do in an effort to hide our sins?*

III. GOD HAD A BETTER PLAN

A. The Offspring of Woman—the Messiah—Would Crush Satan's Head

When it comes to dealing with the sin problem, there is something far better than fig leaves. To the serpent, God said, "I will put enmity between thee and the woman, and between thy seed and her seed; it shall bruise thy head, and thou shalt bruise his heel" (Genesis 3:15).

This early prophecy of the coming Messiah includes three distinct phrases. Each must be considered carefully to avoid misinterpretation. First: *I will put enmity between thee and the woman.* From that time forward, there would be enmity between a human being, Eve, and a member of the animal kingdom; the serpent that had been an instrument of Satan to tempt her.

Second: *I will put enmity between . . . thy seed and her seed*. The enmity introduced between the serpent and Eve would be expanded to include their descendants (i.e., snakes and human beings). In Eden, up until this time, there had been no enmity between people and animals.

Third: *It shall bruise thy head, and thou shalt bruise his heel*. The focus shifted from the enmity between the serpent and Eve, and from the serpent's descendants and Eve's offspring, to the enmity between a specific male descendant of Eve and the serpent himself. The pronoun translated *it* is masculine singular, which is why many translations render it *he*.

Allusions to this messianic prophecy are found elsewhere in Scripture. For example, Psalm 91:11–13 recognized even by Satan as a prophecy of the coming Messiah, reads, "For he shall give his angels charge over thee, to keep thee in all thy ways. They shall bear thee up in their hands, lest thou dash thy foot against a stone. Thou shalt tread upon the lion and adder: the young lion and the dragon shalt thou trample under feet." (See Matthew 4:6; Luke 4:10–11.) In His words to the serpent in Genesis 3:15, God said of the seed of the woman, "He shall bruise thy head." Psalm 91:13 expands on this statement. The *adder* is a serpent and *dragon* is also a symbol of Satan (Revelation 20:2), as is lion (I Peter 5:8). Satan's error in quoting from Psalm 91 was not to think this text was about the Messiah; it was to think God's hand can be forced.

The prophesied enmity between the serpent and Eve's descendant would result in death for both, but the Messiah, the seed of the woman, would rise from the dead (Hebrews 2:14–17; I John 3:8).

For Satan, there would be no resurrection. His eternal destiny is to be cast into the lake of fire and brimstone, where he will be tormented day and night forever and ever (Revelation 20:10).

B. God Became Flesh

How could a descendant of Eve crush the head of Satan? First, this promise indicated Eve's offspring would be human. Second, He could not be merely human, or He would be unable to destroy Satan. But how could Eve's descendant be more than human? Paul recognized this as a mystery solved by the Incarnation (I Timothy 3:16).

Since the Subject of this verse was manifest in the flesh (i.e., human existence), He was a descendant of Eve. Because He was God, He was qualified to rule the realm of creation, which takes in angels, including fallen angels like Satan, as well as reptiles appropriated by Satan for his purposes, as in Eden.

C. His Blood Has the Power to Cover Our Sin

By Himself, Jesus purged our sins. He needed no help from us nor from angels. The ultimate purpose for the incarnation was "to seek and to save that which was lost" (Luke 19:10). The Cross was God's final answer to the sin problem, the means by which the barrier between God and man was removed (Hebrews 10:12, 14).

Any suggestion that something in addition to the blood of Jesus is required to deal with man's sin is heresy of the worst sort. The atoning virtue of the blood of Jesus is limitless precisely because His death was of infinite value. This is so because in His death He was not just a man, but God manifest in the flesh. Had He been just a sinless man, His death could perhaps have atoned for one other person. But since He was truly God, His death was "the propitiation for our sins, and not for ours only but also for the whole world" (I John 2:2, NKJV).

After Jesus purged our sins, He "sat down at the right hand of the Majesty on high" (Hebrews 1:3, NKJV). The term *right hand* in Scripture is often a metaphor for power and authority. When the Bible speaks of "the right hand of God" (e.g., Acts 2:33), it refers to the ultimate power and authority. The point is He who suffered the humiliation of assuming solidarity with His creation now occupies the supreme position of exaltation (Philippians 2:5–9). In that position, He is due the homage of all creation (Philippians 2:10–11).

Concerning the phrase "the right hand of the Majesty on high," F.F. Bruce comments,

> That no literal location is intended was as well understood by Christians in the apostolic age as it is by us: they knew that God has no physical right hand or material throne where the ascended Christ sits beside Him; to them the language denoted the exaltation and supremacy of Christ as it does to us.

The statement that Jesus *sat down* would have been significant to the original readers of Hebrews, for they were acquainted with priests who never sat, for there was no end to the sacrifices they offered. (See Hebrews 10:11–12.)

» *How many comparisons can you draw between Adam's failed plan to deal with sin and God's successful plan?*

⟫⟫ INTERNALIZING THE MESSAGE

What will you do about your sins? Do you acknowledge you have sinned? (See Romans 3:23; I John 1:10.) Do you have your own version of fig leaves? How is that working for you?

The only way we can have peace with God is to deal with our sins God's way. Otherwise we will hear His voice in the garden of our life and learn of His disappointment with our excuses. The consequence of our actions will be *Paradise Lost*.

The Better High Priest

FOCUS THOUGHT

As our High Priest, Jesus made it possible for us to boldly approach Him.

 FOCUS VERSE

Hebrews 4:16

Let us therefore come boldly unto the throne of grace, that we may obtain mercy, and find grace to help in time of need.

 LESSON TEXT

Hebrews 4:14–16

14 Seeing then that we have a great high priest, that is passed into the heavens, Jesus the Son of God, let us hold fast our profession.

15 For we have not an high priest which cannot be touched with the feeling of our infirmities; but was in all points tempted like as we are, yet without sin.

16 Let us therefore come boldly unto the throne of grace, that we may obtain mercy, and find grace to help in time of need.

Numbers 18:1–7

1 And the LORD said unto Aaron, Thou and thy sons and thy father's house with thee shall bear the iniquity of the sanctuary: and thou and thy sons with thee shall bear the iniquity of your priesthood.

2 And thy brethren also of the tribe of Levi, the tribe of thy father, bring thou with thee, that they may be joined unto thee, and minister unto thee: but thou and thy sons with thee shall minister before the tabernacle of witness.

3 And they shall keep thy charge, and the charge of all the tabernacle: only they shall not come nigh the vessels of the sanctuary and the altar, that neither they, nor ye also, die.

4 And they shall be joined unto thee, and keep the charge of the tabernacle of the congregation, for all the service of the tabernacle: and a stranger shall not come nigh unto you.

5 And ye shall keep the charge of the sanctuary, and the charge of the altar: that there be no wrath any more upon the children of Israel.

6 And I, behold, I have taken your brethren the Levites from among the children of Israel: to you they are given as a gift for the LORD, to do the service of the tabernacle of the congregation.

7 Therefore thou and thy sons with thee shall keep your priest's office for every thing of the altar, and within the vail; and ye shall serve: I have given your priest's office unto you as a service of gift: and the stranger that cometh nigh shall be put to death.

I HAVE AN INSIDE CONTACT

A young teen child of a president now lives inside the executive residence. Barron Trump can claim special access to the most powerful man in the world because of one thing: belonging. Yes, this child—like the two daughters of the previous president—has special treatment in life because of his dad's place in society. A child might represent this connection as simply as, "I can go in his office and talk to him because he is mine."

Occasionally, one gets those moments of belonging where an uncle allows backstage access to a big event or a cousin gives a complementary meal at her restaurant. Belonging is a big deal today in a world where relationships are fractured. Migrants who settle in a strange land often become attached to others who speak their mother tongue, came from their homeland, or feel otherwise incompatible with the world around them. They may stick closely to each other simply because of that sense of belonging.

Prior to Jesus Christ, we had no human representation in Heaven. Then, the one on the throne stepped into time on earth and joined us in our humanity. When He died and rose from the dead, Jesus ascended high above everything else—but He never let go of His humanity. He belongs to us because He is like us. We have a High Priest and King—the person in the most important role in the universe belongs to us!

>>> **OUTLINE**

I. THE HIGH PRIEST APPROACHED GOD FOR THE PEOPLE
   A. The Priests and Levites Served in the Tabernacle
   B. The High Priest Went Behind the Veil Once a Year
   C. Others Were Not Allowed to Approach God Without Seeing Death

II. JESUS IS OUR HIGH PRIEST
   A. He Was Touched with the Feelings of Our Infirmities
   B. He Was Tempted in All Points as We Are

III. GOD WANTS US TO COME TO HIM
   A. Veil of the Temple Was Torn
   B. Boldly Approach the Throne of Grace
   C. We Can Come at Any Time

>>> **CONTEMPLATING THE TOPIC**

The writer offered us great hope in Hebrews 4:16. But how, after failing and falling into sin, can we "come boldly unto the throne of grace"? It seems hard to fathom God would encourage such an attitude after the committal of such egregious acts. Perhaps sacrifice would seem more in order. Maybe even severe punishment so the offender learns his or her lesson. But instead of sacrifice or sudden punishment, God invites us to boldly approach His throne.

"How is it that we should approach boldly? Because now it is a throne of Grace, not a throne of Judgment. Therefore boldly, that we may obtain mercy, even such as we are seeking. If thou approach now thou wilt receive both grace and mercy, for thou approachest in due season" (*The Homilies On The Epistle To The Hebrews*, St. Chrysostom)

Yes, there is coming a day of judgment for those who have not found grace, but now is the season of grace where God invites us to come and find mercy and pardon for our sins. We need not fear Him, but approach in humble boldness; with confidence in His promises but in reverence of His holiness.

I. THE HIGH PRIEST APPROACHED GOD FOR THE PEOPLE

In contrast to the relatively free access qualified priests had into the Holy Place, the Most Holy Place in the Tabernacle could be entered only by the high priest, and he could enter it only once each year, on the Day of Atonement. (See Hebrews 9:7; Leviticus 16.)

After the high priest concluded the ceremony in the Most Holy Place, he returned to the Holy Place and sprinkled some of the blood of the bull and goat on the Altar of Incense. (See Leviticus 16:18.) When this annual ceremony was being conducted, no other priest could enter the Tabernacle. (See Leviticus 16:17.) Since the events of the Day of Atonement were symbolic of a far greater reality (Hebrews 9:9)—the ultimate and final atonement provided by Christ (Hebrews 9:11–15)—the restriction of both the Holy Place and the Most Holy Place to the high priest alone may represent the exclusivity of Christ's sacrifice. No one else participated in it. True cleansing from sin is provided not by the work of Christ Jesus and someone else, but by His work alone.

Two aspects of the good news of the gospel are pertinent here: (1) Since He was sinless, Christ did not need to offer a sacrifice for Himself (Hebrews 4:15; 7:26–27); (2) the blood of Jesus atones not just for sins committed in ignorance, but for all sins, even those committed deliberately (Hebrews 9:26; John 1:29; I John 2:2). His sacrifice is thus immeasurably superior to even that of the Day of Atonement. There can be no limit to the efficacy of Christ's blood, for His death was of infinite value.

A. The Priests and Levites Served in the Tabernacle

Under the Law of Moses, Aaron and his male descendants were to serve as priests. Aaron was from the tribe of Levi. The rest of the male offspring of Levi would fill other functions in the Tabernacle. (See Leviticus 6; Numbers 2–3; 18:1–7.)

In other accounts, the Lord is seen speaking both to Moses and Aaron about the duties of priests. Why is it that in Numbers 18:1–7, the Lord spoke to Aaron alone about the priesthood, with Moses appearing for the first time in this chapter in verse 25 with the Lord's instructions for the Levites?

> *The answer perhaps lies in the author's desire to tell us something about the role of Moses as leader of God's people. His role is not limited to the work of a priest. Aaron is shown here assuming most of that responsibility. . . it appears that the role of Moses was becoming more distinct from the office of priest. Thus the writer attempts to show that Moses' role as mediator of the covenant, already well established throughout these narratives, was not merely a priestly one. There is a concern to show that he also functioned in the role of prophet as well as king, two themes that . . . receive further development in the book of Deuteronomy (Deuteronomy 18:15; 33:5). Hence as the picture of Moses develops within the Pentateuch, it more closely resembles the future messianic ruler, who is anticipated in the Pentateuch as a prophet, a priest, and a king (John H. Sailhamer, The Pentateuch as Narrative).*

14

In view of the New Testament's emphasis on the Messiah, Jesus Christ, as the major theme of the Hebrew Scriptures, it is appropriate to read the Old Testament in a prayerful attempt to discover and further develop that theme. (See John 5:39, 46–47; Luke 24:25, 27, 44–45.)

B. The High Priest Went Behind the Veil Once a Year

In contrast to the relatively free access qualified priests had into the Holy Place, the Most Holy Place in the Tabernacle could be entered only by the high priest, and he could enter it only once each year, on the Day of Atonement. (See Leviticus 16; Hebrews 9:7.) The reference to the high priest's solitary entrance into the Most Holy Place once a year should be understood as referring to one day a year, for he actually entered at least twice on the Day of Atonement. It was required that he bring blood with him as he entered. First, he had to sprinkle the blood of a bull upon the mercy seat to make atonement for himself and the members of his house. (See Leviticus 16:3, 6, 11, 14.) Then, after exiting the Most Holy Place, he had to kill a goat and reenter the Most Holy Place to sprinkle its blood on the mercy seat for the sins of the people. (See Leviticus 16:15–16.) He may have entered three times, with the first being to put in place the "censer full of burning coals" on which incense burned to obscure the mercy seat from his vision (Leviticus 16:12–13). Jewish tradition suggests there were four entries into the Most Holy Place, with the final one being to retrieve the equipment first taken in for the burning of incense at the beginning of the ceremony.

» **Why was it necessary for the mercy seat to be obscured from the high priest's vision by burning incense?**

C. Others Were Not Allowed to Approach God Without Seeing Death

Levites, who were not descendants of Aaron, were assigned non-priestly duties in relation to the Tabernacle, but they were not to come near the altar and the furnishings of the Tabernacle on penalty of death. (See Numbers 18:2–4.) This reflects the prohibition on the Israelites ascending Sinai after their initial refusal to do so.

After God called Moses to deliver the Israelites from Egypt, He said, "Certainly I will be with thee; and this shall be a token unto thee, that I have sent thee: When thou hast brought forth the people out of Egypt, ye shall serve God upon this mountain" (Exodus 3:12). The word translated "ye" is in the second person plural form, referring not only to Moses but to all who came out of Egypt. Accurate translations include "all of you will worship me on this mountain" (NIRV) and "you and they will serve God on this mountain" (NET). Of course, the old English "ye" also represents the second person plural, whereas "thou" is used for the second person singular. The point is that God wanted all the people to join Moses in an intimate relationship with Him on the mountain. This did not happen.

A close reading of Exodus 19 indicates that God wanted something better for Israel than what transpired at Sinai. First, God wanted to establish a faith covenant with His people.

Believe is faith language. But what resulted at Sinai as a consequence of the people's refusal to worship God on the mountain was not a faith covenant: "And the law is not of faith: but, the man that doeth them shall live in them" (Galatians 3:12).

Second, God wanted to make of Israel a nation of priests (Exodus 19:6).

Had this happened, the people of Israel would all have been privileged to enter into an intimate relationship with God. Instead, Israel became a nation with priests, only one of whom could enter the Most Holy Place one day each year. This promise was finally fulfilled in the church. (See I Peter 2:9.)

Third, as seen in Exodus 3:12, God invited all of those delivered from Egypt to worship Him on the mountain. This they refused. Many are used to reading Exodus 19:12 as a prohibition against going up the mountain. The prohibition was, however, only to give the people time to sanctify themselves in preparation for a personal visitation from the LORD on the third day on Mount Sinai (Exodus 19:10–11). Note that the KJV italicizes the words *that* ye and *not* in Exodus 19:12, because they do not appear in the Hebrew text.

After the third day, there would be a long trumpet blast, after which the people were to climb the mountain (Exodus 19:13).

When the LORD descended on Sinai, the people responded in fear rather than faith. They did not go up into the mountain but stood at its foot (Exodus 19:17; Deuteronomy 4:11; 5:5). This resulted in a second warning from the LORD permitting only Moses and Aaron to ascend the mountain. Had the Israelites obeyed the command to worship God on Sinai, they would have avoided the disastrous episode with the golden calf (Exodus 32). (See Hebrews 12:18–24.)

» *How can fear lead to disobedience?*

II. JESUS IS OUR HIGH PRIEST

The New Covenant was administered by Jesus, the "great High Priest." (See Hebrews 4:14.) The use of the word "great" (Greek, *mega*) with "High Priest" emphasizes His superiority to the high priests of the Mosaic Covenant.

The great High Priest is Jesus the Son of God. The term "Son of God" requires the incarnation. (See Luke 1:35.) It is by His genuine and complete humanity that Jesus can function as High Priest, for an integral part of what it means to be a High Priest is to stand in solidarity with those the priest represents. (See Hebrews 2:14–18; 4:15; 5:7–10.)

A. He Was Touched with the Feelings of Our Infirmities

In the Incarnation, the deity of Jesus did not override, obscure, or overwhelm His humanity. It did not prevent Him from sympathizing with our infirmities (Hebrews 4:15). As Gregory of Nazianzus observed, "The unassumed is the unhealed." If there were any aspect of existence inherent to humanity Jesus did not experience, that part of human existence would not have been redeemed. It should be noted, however, that sin is not inherent to human existence. Neither Adam nor Eve experienced sin before the Fall, but they were both fully human. Sin is a mar on human existence, not an essential part of it. Jesus was spared this mar by the miracle of virgin conception. He was the last Adam (I Corinthians 15:45).

B. He Was Tempted in All Points as We Are

Neither did the Incarnation prevent Jesus from being "tempted like as we are." Though Jesus did not sin, He was genuinely tempted and is thus able to identify with us in our temptations. (See Hebrews 2:18.) The high priests under the Mosaic Covenant were also tempted, of course, but they succumbed to temptation just as do all human beings. (See Hebrews 5:1–3.) Since Jesus experienced temptation, but successfully resisted it, He is superior to the high priests in the Aaronic lineage.

III. GOD WANTS US TO COME TO HIM

A. Veil of the Temple Was Torn

The tearing of the veil which separated the Holy Place from the Most Holy Place in the Temple at the moment of Jesus' death (Matthew 27:51; Mark 15:38; Luke 23:45) demonstrated the termination of the Old Covenant and the establishment of the reality of which it was merely a shadow. (See Hebrews 9:1–8; 10:19–22.) This was a dramatic and undeniable signal that the Law of Moses had come to an end. It was a divine signal, for the veil was torn from top to bottom without human intervention. According to Jewish tradition, the veil was four inches thick and was so strong it could not be torn by teams of oxen pulling in opposite directions.

The veil was apparently a symbol of the genuine humanity of the Messiah (Hebrews 10:19–20). His death on the Cross dealt with the sin problem so completely and finally that it removed the barrier between God and man and made a way for all men to come directly into the presence of God.

» *Are you convinced that the Law of Moses is no longer in effect? Explain.*

B. Boldly Approach the Throne of Grace

Jesus' identification with humanity in temptation enables Him to be so thoroughly sympathetic to our plight that we can approach the throne of grace boldly. We do not timidly approach a God who is distant and unaware of the real struggles we face. In Jesus, we have a God who willingly became so completely one of us that He recognizes the legitimacy of our weaknesses and gladly extends mercy and grace to us in our time of need. (See Philippians 2:5–8.) The term "throne of grace" indicates that God, who sits on the throne, is characterized by grace in His relationship with His children. "Grace" is translated from the Greek *charitos*, from *charis*, which essentially indicates that the favor given is free. This is the origin of the common definition of grace as the unmerited favor of God. It is significant in this regard that "the law was given by Moses, but grace and truth came by Jesus Christ" (John 1:17). The grace of God was also extended to men prior to the coming of Jesus (Genesis 6:8; Exodus 33:12–13, 16–17), but grace is the fundamental characteristic of the New Covenant, not law.

Since, in simplest terms, grace is the unmerited favor of God, mercy has to do with the clemency connected with the actual forgiveness of sins. When believers boldly approach the throne of grace, they find what they need most: A God who refuses to give them the condemnation they so richly deserve. He does not, however, merely overlook or ignore sin, He extends His free favor and forgiveness based on the atonement. His righteous judgment has been satisfied by the blood of Jesus; now He can relate to people of faith as those whose sins have been dealt with "through the offering of the body of Jesus Christ once for all" (10:10).

»   *What is the difference between mercy and grace?*

C. We Can Come at Any Time

Jesus stands ever ready, at any "time of need," to offer grace and mercy.

The boldness with which believers can approach the throne of God stands in stark contrast with the hesitancy and reluctance traditionally associated with the high priest's approach to the holiest place on the annual Day of Atonement. This is made possible by the fact that, under the New Covenant, believers approach based on the blood of Jesus (Hebrews 10:19), which has completely and permanently satisfied the righteous judgment of God against sin.

»   *When you approach God in prayer, do you come to Him with a sense of shame and fear, or do you come with confidence that He is waiting to extend mercy and grace? Explain.*

▶▶▶ INTERNALIZING THE MESSAGE

Many people struggle with feelings of inadequacy, inferiority, and guilt. But should this be so? Does not this lesson's text give us reason to reject this sort of self-rejection?

Jesus Christ, the great High Priest, sympathizes with our weaknesses and knows what it means to be tempted. When we stand before God, we will stand before someone who knows what it means to be a human being. His priestly work for us enables us to be bold in our approach to God. Because of His redemptive work for us on the Cross, we should not approach Him with reluctance, as if His sacrifice was somehow inferior and less than what was needed. This would be an insult to His supreme sacrifice.

Mercy and grace are readily available to us at any time of need. To truly honor Him, we must act as He invites us to, going before His throne as our only source of what we desperately need.

18

The Better Sacrifice

FOCUS THOUGHT

Because the sacrifices in the Tabernacle could not remove sin, Jesus offered Himself as the better sacrifice.

 FOCUS VERSE

Hebrews 9:28

So Christ was once offered to bear the sins of many; and unto them that look for him shall he appear the second time without sin unto salvation.

 LESSON TEXT

Hebrews 9:22–28

22 And almost all things are by the law purged with blood; and without shedding of blood is no remission.

23 It was therefore necessary that the pattern of things in the heavens should be purified with these; but the heavenly things themselves with better sacrifices than these.

24 For Christ is not entered into the holy places made with hands, which are the figures of the true; but into heaven itself, now to appear in the presence of God for us:

25 Nor yet that he should offer himself often, as the high priest entereth into the holy place every year with blood of others;

26 For then must he often have suffered since the foundation of the world: but now once in the end of the world hath he appeared to put away sin by the sacrifice of himself.

27 And as it is appointed unto men once to die, but after this the judgment:

28 So Christ was once offered to bear the sins of many; and unto them that look for him shall he appear the second time without sin unto salvation.

Hebrews 10:11–14

11 And every priest standeth daily ministering and offering oftentimes the same sacrifices, which can never take away sins.

12 But this man, after he had offered one sacrifice for sins for ever, sat down on the right hand of God;

13 From henceforth expecting till his enemies be made his footstool.

14 For by one offering he hath perfected for ever them that are sanctified.

John 1:29

29 The next day John seeth Jesus coming unto him, and saith, Behold the Lamb of God, which taketh away the sin of the world.

PERMANENTLY STAINED OR DANGEROUSLY CLEAN?

First-worlders have become obsessed with teeth that are cleaner than clean. A variety of products have emerged on the markets which promise to bleach, bombard, un-stain, or coat one's teeth so that a brilliant smile beams them up to success. While a visibly enhanced image seems desirable, product makers have found many of their potential customers recoiling at the long-term results of such products and procedures.

Compounds in teeth whiteners and even top-shelf toothpastes may contain chemicals shown to be harmful and carcinogenic. To an educated customer-base, such hazards create a dichotomy between the impulse for a super-clean image and the trending desire for a pure, organic, holistic body. Consumers now struggle to find effective personal care items that truly take care of their whole person.

Likewise, many today use flawed attempts to deal with sin. The stain of sin cannot be hidden by psychology, drugs, or extreme sports. Religious tradition, community activism, or pleasure-seeking may damage much more than they cover up.

When it comes to the stains of sin, one does not have to choose image over internals. The only cleaning agent in the universe that does not create collateral damage is the blood of Jesus Christ. Yes, blood—which can stain cloth badly. Only the Creator of the universe could take something that would ordinarily cause a stain and use it to remove what no other earthly product can: sin-stains. Jesus makes the dirtiest heart whiter than snow.

And that is something to smile about.

⟫⟫ OUTLINE

I. THE HIGH PRIEST OFFERED SACRIFICES FOR THE PEOPLE

  A. Blood of Bulls and Goats

  B. Once a Year Took the Blood Behind the Veil

  C. Never Removed the Sin

II. JESUS CAME TO DIE FOR OUR SINS

  A. Jesus Was the Better Sacrifice

  B. His Blood Remits Sin Completely

⟫⟫ CONTEMPLATING THE TOPIC

In Hebrews 9:25, Christ is said to have offered Himself. In Hebrews 9:28, it is said that He "was offered." This emphasis no doubt arises from the fact that the author has the great atonement passage of Isaiah 53 in mind that focuses on the Messiah as being made an offering for sin (Isaiah 53:10).

Since Jesus fully bore the penalty of sin Himself, there is no penalty left for human beings to bear, if they will put their trust in His work on their behalf.

Since Jesus dealt with finality with the sin problem on the Cross, His second appearance to those who eagerly wait for Him will be "apart from sin, for salvation" (NKJV).

Christ's second appearance will be "to those who eagerly wait for Him" (NKJV). This is in perfect harmony with the teaching of Paul concerning the rapture of the church (I Thessalonians 4:13–18). It will be an appearance only to believers, not to the world at large. Three times Paul used the same Greek word, which is here translated "eagerly wait" (NKJV), in reference to the second appearance of Christ to believers. (See I Corinthians 1:7; Galatians 5:5; Philippians 3:20.)

I. THE HIGH PRIEST OFFERED SACRIFICES FOR THE PEOPLE

Since the Levitical high priest was himself a sinner, he was required to offer sacrifices for his own sins, as well as for the sins of those whom he represented. (See Hebrews 5:3; 9:7.) Leviticus 16:6 and 11 explains that before Aaron could offer a sacrifice for the sins of the people, he first had to offer a sacrifice for himself and for his family. In this, Jesus was unlike the Levitical priesthood. Since He was without sin, he had no need to offer a sacrifice for Himself. (See Hebrews 7:26–27.)

A. Blood of Bulls and Goats

The Tabernacle and all its rituals were "symbolic for the present time" (NKJV), meaning the time during which the first covenant was in force (Hebrews 9:9). (See also Hebrews 10:1; Colossians 2:16–17.) With the coming of the New Covenant, this covenant of symbols has served its purpose (Hebrews 8:13). The gifts and sacrifices (see Hebrews 5:1) offered under the Law of Moses were incapable of making him "who performed the service perfect in regard to the conscience" (NKJV). (See Hebrews 9:9.) Those ritual offerings provided no assurance of right standing with God. Since the blood of bulls and goats did not take away sin (Hebrews 10:4) but merely served to remind Israel of their sinfulness (Hebrews 10:3), the sacrifices left the people of Israel with a troubled conscience. This does not mean that no one under the Law ever enjoyed a clear conscience, but that a clear conscience was not obtained by the sacrificial rituals. For those during the era of the Law, a clear conscience with God was gained by faith in God, just as it is today. (See Hebrews 11:1–2, 6, 39.)

» *How many rituals associated with the Law of Moses can you think of that were symbols fulfilled in the New Covenant?*

B. Once a Year Took the Blood Behind the Veil

The high priest entered the Most Holy Place in the Tabernacle only on the annual Day of Atonement. (See Leviticus 16.) He was required to sprinkle the blood of a bull upon the mercy seat to make atonement for himself and the members of his house and to sprinkle the blood of a goat on the mercy seat for the sins of the people. (See Leviticus 16:15–16; Hebrews 9:7.) The sacrifices on the Day of Atonement were for all sins that had not been dealt with previously throughout the year by other sacrifices.

C. Never Removed the Sin

What the Holy Spirit intended to signify by the rituals of the Day of Atonement is that the way into the true "holiest of all was not yet made manifest, while as the first tabernacle was yet standing" (Hebrews 9:8). As dramatic as the events of the Day of Atonement were, they were mere symbols of a greater reality. (See Hebrews 9:24.) The ceremonies served to illustrate, not how simple and easy it was to gain access into the immediate presence of God, but how difficult it was. There was nothing about the Day of Atonement that suggested to the people of Israel that they too could enjoy intimate fellowship with God. Instead, the rituals were frightening and exclusive. The high priest entered the Most Holy Place at the risk of his own death. Jewish tradition indicates that the prayer of the high priest when he exited the Most Holy Place was intentionally short "lest he put Israel in terror" (Leon Morris, *The Expositor's Bible Commentary*). When he survived the last ritual and the day was over, he invited his friends to a feast in celebration.

According to an ancient legend, when the High Priest entered the Most Holy Place on the Day of Atonement, a rope was tied around his ankle, so his body could be removed from before the Ark of the Covenant in case of his death. Scripture says nothing about this but gives strict commandments as to how the High Priest was to be dressed. We can be sure God would not tolerate deviation from His instructions. The presence of a rope would itself had been cause for death.

The phrase "while the first tabernacle was still standing" (Hebrews 9:8) further supports the claim of Hebrews that the Tabernacle associated with the Law of Moses was a thing of the past. (See Hebrews 8:13; 9:1.) At the time Hebrews was written, the Tabernacle was no longer standing. It had, of course, been replaced by the Temple, but the author is not interested in the Temple still standing in Jerusalem as he wrote. It would soon be destroyed. He is interested in the original intent and function of Tabernacle worship as prescribed by Moses under the first covenant and its comparison to New Covenant worship as prescribed by Jesus.

»   *What was the original purpose for tabernacle worship?*

The sacrificial rituals of the Law of Moses were external; they did not deal with the needs of the inner man. They pertained to "meats and drinks, and divers washings, and carnal ordinances" (Hebrews 9:10). (See Hebrews 13:9.) Leviticus 11 details the laws concerning clean and unclean foods. There were also regulations concerning acceptable drinks in a variety of circumstances (Leviticus 10:8–9; 11:33–38; Numbers 6:2–3). Commandments were given which governed ceremonial washings to effect ritual cleansing (Exodus 30:20; Leviticus 15:4–27; 17:15–16; Numbers 19:7–13).

All these regulations, and others like them included in the Law of Moses, were "carnal." (See Hebrews 7:16.) The word *carnal* (*sarx*, often translated *flesh*) does not refer in this case to that which pertains to the sin nature. It means, rather, that the rituals of the Law were external, pertaining to the outer man rather than the inner man.

In a telling statement supporting the previous declarations concerning the termination of the Law of Moses with the coming of Messiah, Hebrews declares that all of the ordinances of the Law were imposed "until the time of reformation" (Hebrews 9:10). A more literal translation of the Greek text at this point indicates they were in force until the time of "setting things right" or "straight." Contextually, this time of "reformation" has to do with the establishment of the New Covenant (Hebrews 8:13; 9:11–15). This New Covenant pertains to the inner man by providing a conscience that is cleansed (Hebrews 9:14), giving full assurance of one's right standing with God.

Since the figurative rituals of the Law of Moses did not actually take away sins (Hebrews 10:4), it is sometimes said they "rolled sin ahead." This phrase is not found in Scripture, and it is probably not the best way to describe the situation with sin before the coming of Christ. A more satisfactory biblical solution is found in Romans 3:25: "Whom God hath set forth to be a propitiation through faith in his blood, to declare his righteousness for the remission of sins that are past, through the forbearance of God." Since those living during the era of the Old Covenant could not be justified by doing the works of the Law of Moses (Romans 3:20–21), God "passed over the sins that were previously committed" (Romans 3:25, NKJV). He did this in anticipation of the atonement which would be provided by the death of Jesus. The words "declare" or "set forth" contrast the public death of Jesus with the hidden rituals associated with the mercy seat in the Most Holy place.

» *Since the sacrifices of the Law of Moses did not deal with the sin problem, how were people saved before the coming of Christ?*

II. JESUS CAME TO DIE FOR OUR SINS

The Old Testament prophecies anticipated that the coming Messiah would deal with the sin problem by bearing the sins of humanity. For example, Isaiah declared He would be "an offering for sin," He would "bear . . . iniquities," and "he bare the sin of many" (Isaiah 53:10–12). This is how the New Testament understands the doctrine commonly called "atonement." (See I Corinthians 15:3; Colossians 1:22; I Peter 2:24.) John the Baptist announced, "Behold the Lamb of God, which taketh away the sin of the world" (John 1:29).

A. Jesus Was the Better Sacrifice

To this point, the Book of Hebrews alludes to the inferiority and inadequacy of the sacrifices offered under the Law of Moses (Hebrews 9:12–14, 23), but in Hebrews 10:1 it moves to a clear emphasis on the superiority of Christ's sacrifice. All the sacrifices associated with the Law were mere shadows in which God took no pleasure. They were unable to take away sins. What all those sacrifices from the construction of the Tabernacle in about 1400 BC to the destruction of the Temple in AD 70 could not accomplish even when added together, the death of Christ accomplished in a moment of time, once and for all.

Hebrews 10:1 shows the purpose and limitation of the Law of Moses. The Law was never intended to be an end in itself. It was a mere "shadow of good things to come," incapable of perfecting those who approached God on the basis of its sacrifices.

The "good things to come" refer contextually to the provisions of the New Covenant found in Christ Jesus. (See Hebrews 10:10, 14, 16–23.) The Law offered only a "shadow" (Greek, *skia*) of these things. *Skia* appears in Hebrews 8:5 together with *hypodeigma* to describe the manner in which the ministry associated with the Aaronic priesthood was a "copy and shadow of the heavenly things" (NKJV). In

Colossians 2:17, Paul used *skia* to categorize the dietary laws, the feast days, the new moons and the sabbaths of the Law as shadows "of things to come." In contrast to these shadows, the "substance is of Christ."

Since the Law was made up of shadows, and every sacrifice was merely a representation of something good to come, those sacrifices, though offered year after year, could never make perfect those who approached God by means of them. The word "perfect" (Greek, *teleiosai*) does not refer to sinless perfection. It is defined in Hebrews 10:2 as freedom from consciousness of sins. That is, since the sacrifices themselves were only shadows incapable of taking away sins (Hebrews 10:4), they were not able to produce a clear conscience. Even after the high priest approached the Most Holy Place and executed the elaborate rituals of the Day of Atonement flawlessly, neither he nor the people of Israel had a sense of release from sin. Instead, they were simply reminded again that they were sinful people (Hebrews 10:3).

The inability of the sacrifices of the Law to deal with the sin problem is seen in that they had to be offered again and again. If those sacrifices had been sufficient to remove sin, it would not have been necessary to repeat them. They did not purify the worshipers; those who offered the sacrifices were left with a lingering consciousness of sins.

Here, by implication, is seen a marvelous consequence of the sacrifice of Christ. Since His sacrifice—in contrast to the sacrifices of the Law—was efficacious, it purifies those who approach God through Christ Jesus and leaves them with no more consciousness of sins. Because His blood does remit sin, we can "draw near with a true heart in full assurance of faith" (Hebrews 10:22).

» *Can you draw parallels between the symbolic content of the Law of Moses and the fulfillment found in the New Covenant? Explain.*

B. His Blood Remits Sin Completely

The one sacrifice of Christ was sufficient. (See Hebrews 9:25–28; 10:10, 14.) When a sacrifice is offered that can perfect those who approach God on its basis, there is no need for any further sacrifice. At that point, sacrifices can cease to be offered. (See Hebrews 10:18.)

The sacrifices associated with the Law of Moses served as annual reminders of the sinfulness of the people (Hebrews 10:3). Since the word translated "remembrance" (Greek, *anamnesis*) is used in the New Testament only here and in the establishment of the Lord's Supper (Luke 22:19; I Corinthians 11:24–25), the implication is strong for a connection between the two. Just as the sacrifices of the Law continually reminded the people of Israel of their sinfulness, so the bread and cup of the Lord's Supper continually remind believers of the New Covenant established in Christ's blood and of the cleansing from sin thereby provided.

The word translated "take away" in Hebrews 10:4 (Greek, *aphaireo*) is a strong one. It is used to describe the way Peter cut off the ear of the high priest's servant

(Luke 22:50) and the way the reproach of Elizabeth's barrenness was taken away when she conceived (Luke 1:25). The New Covenant implication is that the offering of the body of Christ was able to do what the blood of bulls and goats could not do: The blood of Jesus took away sins as decisively as Peter's sword sliced off a man's ear and as Elizabeth's conception eradicated her reproach.

» *Why is it important for us to be reminded of our sinfulness and the power of Jesus' sacrifice through the practice of the Lord's Supper?*

⟩⟩⟩ INTERNALIZING THE MESSAGE

Are you completely confident that your sins have been dealt with by Christ's sacrifice? Are you sure God no longer remembers your sins and iniquities? Is your conscience clear?

Even with the good news that Christ died for our sins and that His blood remits sin completely, some who have obeyed the gospel nevertheless fear, upon reading Hebrews 10:26–31, that they are not saved. This need not be.

The context of these verses in Hebrews shows that the willful sin warned against is defection from Jesus Christ and His New Covenant to the dead works of the Law. (See Hebrews 6:4–6; 8:6–13; 10:9, 16–17, 20, 29, 32, 35, 39.) The phrase "there remaineth no more sacrifice for sins" signifies that no other sacrifice can atone for the sins of those who reject Jesus' sacrifice. (See Hebrews 10:26.) Those who turn away from the provisions of the New Covenant are without any resource to deal with the problem of sin. The word translated "sin" (*hamartanō*) is a present (continuous) active participle, describing not a one-time sin, or even an occasional sin, but continual, persistent sin. This warning is not against the struggles with faith that all Christians experience, or even an occasional lapse of faith, but against an ongoing rejection of Jesus—outside of whom there exists no other source of salvation.

To trample under foot the Son of God (Hebrews 10:29) is to (1) reject Him as the promised Messiah, (2) deny His deity, and (3) refuse the Atonement.

Those who have placed their faith exclusively in Jesus Christ and who have obeyed the gospel message need have no fear about the loss of their salvation.

> *"But we are not of them who draw back unto perdition; but of them that believe to the saving of the soul." (Hebrews 10:39)*

The Better News

FOCUS THOUGHT

Because we were in need of hope, God gave us good news.

 FOCUS VERSE

Hebrews 1:8

But unto the Son he saith, Thy throne, O God, is for ever and ever: a scepter of righteousness is the scepter of thy kingdom.

 LESSON TEXT

Isaiah 7:14

14 Therefore the Lord himself shall give you a sign; Behold, a virgin shall conceive, and bear a son, and shall call his name Immanuel.

Isaiah 9:6

6 For unto us a child is born, unto us a son is given: and the government shall be upon his shoulder: and his name shall be called Wonderful, Counseller, The mighty God, The everlasting Father, The Prince of Peace.

Matthew 1:18–23

18 Now the birth of Jesus Christ was on this wise: When as his mother Mary was espoused to Joseph, before they came together, she was found with child of the Holy Ghost.

19 Then Joseph her husband, being a just man, and not willing to make her a publick example, was minded to put her away privily.

20 But while he thought on these things, behold, the angel of the Lord appeared unto him in a dream, saying, Joseph, thou son of David, fear not to take unto thee Mary thy wife: for that which is conceived in her is of the Holy Ghost.

21 And she shall bring forth a son, and thou shalt call his name JESUS: for he shall save his people from their sins.

22 Now all this was done, that it might be fulfilled which was spoken of the Lord by the prophet, saying,

23 Behold, a virgin shall be with child, and shall bring forth a son, and they shall call his name Emmanuel, which being interpreted is, God with us.

Luke 2:10–11

10 And the angel said unto them, Fear not: for, behold, I bring you good tidings of great joy, which shall be to all people.

11 For unto you is born this day in the city of David a Saviour, which is Christ the Lord.

THE GOOD KIND OF VIRAL

A generation ago, people avoided anything viral—it meant staying in bed, taking medicine, or missing fun stuff. Computer viruses then added another shade of unlikeability to the term "viral." Suddenly, a digital-native generation has jumped onto the scene of human history using the word "viral" as a positive thing—a different use than ever before.

Teens around the country hope to video something with their phones that will go viral. They want their YouTube channel, Instagram following, or other social media venue to "blow up" with followers or attention. Young adults make decent livings today by continuing to produce content that goes viral, driving ad revenue and sponsors to keep them in the game.

Jesus did not come to buy up TV ads and billboard space. He came with a message that would go viral. An effective viral video does not make people smile or frown—it causes them to cry or laugh. The more dramatic the response—anger, compassion, happiness—the more viewers will share it.

The gospel ("good news") has often been presented so badly some people hardly shrug. Jesus made people jumping-with-joy happy or ready-to-kill-Him angry. The gospel is powerful. Those with a dynamic experience with Jesus have a story to tell that others want to hear and share themselves. If one lacks an emotionally grabbing story, they must do like a viral marketer: take a risk. Step out in faith for Jesus—you too can "go viral" for Him like Isaiah, Joseph, and Mary.

>>> **OUTLINE**

I. THE PROPHETS FORETOLD OF HIS COMING
A. Micah
B. Isaiah

II. THE ANGELS ANNOUNCED HIS COMING
A. Good News of Great Joy
B. A Savior Is Born

III. WE PREACH THE GOOD NEWS OF THE GOSPEL
A. Jesus Died
B. Jesus Was Buried
C. Jesus Rose Again

IV. IT IS THE GOSPEL THAT SAVES US

>>> **CONTEMPLATING THE TOPIC**

The New Testament quotes, paraphrases, and alludes to the Old Testament some eight hundred times. Many of these references are messianic in nature; they foretell in some way the coming Messiah. The most frequently referenced Old Testament book is Psalms, which is referred to some two hundred times in the New Testament. This lesson's focus verse is one of those. Psalm 45:6 is quoted in Hebrews 1:8. Hebrews 1:9 also quotes Psalm 45:7.

The good news is "according to the scriptures," that is, the Old Testament (I Corinthians 15:3-4). And a major part of that good news is found in the Book of Psalms, a collection of writings largely intended to communicate the promise and hope of the coming Messiah.

I. THE PROPHETS FORETOLD OF HIS COMING

The Hebrew Scriptures are rich in their messianic content. The law, the prophets, and the psalms include profound anticipation of the coming of Messiah, Jesus Christ. (See Luke 24:25–26, 32, 44–49.) Some of these prophecies may seem somewhat obscure, but by the end of the Hebrew canon, a clear theme emerged. A genuine human being would enter the world scene, a descendant of Adam, Abraham, and David, who would at the same time be the Son of God. He would come to deal once and for all with the sin problem that had plagued humanity since Eden. (See Genesis 3:16; 49:8–12; Numbers 24:8–9, 17; Deuteronomy 18:15–19; II Samuel 7:12–16; Psalm 2; 22; Isaiah 7:14; 9:6; 11:1–10; 53; Daniel 9:24–26; Zechariah 6:11–13.)

A. Micah

Micah, a prophet to Judah in the eighth century BC, wrote,

> But thou, Beth-lehem Ephratah, though thou be little among the thousands of Judah, yet out of thee shall he come forth unto me that is to be ruler in Israel; whose goings forth have been from old, from everlasting. (Micah 5:2)

This is not the first time Ephratah is mentioned in Scripture. When Boaz, David's great-grandfather, finalized his plan to marry Ruth, a woman of Moab, the witnesses said,

> The Lord make the woman that is come into thine house like Rachel and like Leah, which two did build the house of Israel: and do thou worthily in Ephratah, and be famous in Beth-lehem: And let thy house be like the house of Pharez, whom Tamar bare unto Judah, of the seed which the Lord shall give thee of this young woman. (Ruth 4:11–12)

Just six verses later, a short biography begins tracing the ancestry of Judah—the messianic lineage—from Pharez to David, through Boaz; making Ruth David's Moabite great-grandmother. (See Ruth 4:18–22.) Due to his marriage to Ruth, Boaz would "prosper in Ephrathah and be famous in Bethlehem" (Ruth 4:11, NKJV).

A statement that at first seems quite curious appears in Psalm 132:6–7:

> Lo, we heard of it at Ephratah: we found it in the fields of the wood. We will go into his tabernacles: we will worship at his footstool.

In today's vernacular, Ephratah was the suburb or area immediately outside Bethlehem. In these environs the shepherds, in the fields of the wood, heard the glorious news of the birth of their Savior, Christ the Lord. (See Luke 2:11.) They went to His "tabernacle" (Psalm 132: 7, NKJV) or "sanctuary" (NLT), a manger, where they worshiped Him.

With Christ's first coming, detailed prophecy was fulfilled. Through His birth, Boaz prospered and was made famous in Bethlehem Ephratah. Bethlehem, the house of bread and the City of David, provided the point of entry into the created realm for the Messiah, Jesus Christ, the Bread of Life.

» **What comes to mind when you hear Jesus is the Bread of Life?**

B. Isaiah

How could Matthew claim a prophecy given to Ahaz nearly eight hundred years earlier was fulfilled in the conception of Jesus, in the womb of the virgin Mary? How could the birth of Jesus be a sign to Ahaz, who had been dead for centuries? Questions like these have caused some to deny the accuracy of Matthew's statement. But a closer look at Isaiah's prophecy removes this problem. Although it is true God offered a personal sign to Ahaz—a sign that would be meaningful to him in connection with God's promise—that Judah would not be conquered by the coalition between Israel and Syria. When Ahaz refused the offer, the LORD turned His attention from Ahaz as an individual to the house of David at large. This can be seen in that following the refusal of Ahaz to request a divine sign, the next words of the LORD are, "Hear ye now, O house of David!" (Isaiah 7:13). Ahaz was a descendant of David, but he was not the only descendant of David. The term "house of David" included all of David's descendants. The expansion of the promise beyond Ahaz is also seen in the statement, "Therefore the LORD himself shall give you a sign" (Isaiah 7:14). The Hebrew word translated "you" is plural, indicating that this sign is not for Ahaz alone; it is for the entire house of David. This sign is that a virgin would conceive and bear a Son; the Son's name would be called Immanuel, which, as Matthew pointed out, means "God with us."

Some who reject Matthew's interpretation of this prophecy point out that the Hebrew word *almah*, often translated "virgin," may refer simply to a young woman of marriageable age. But besides the fact a young unmarried woman was assumed to be a virgin in ancient Israel, we would have to ask what kind of a sign it would be for a young woman to have a son. It is evident from the context in Isaiah that the sign is miraculous; it is not something so common as to happen daily and without divine intervention. In response to this objection, it is quite significant that when Matthew quoted Isaiah 7:14, he followed the Septuagint, a Greek translation of the Hebrew text which was done in the third century BC and which is used in the majority of places where the New Testament quotes from the Old Testament. Since the New Testament is inspired equally with the Old Testament, we accept these quotations from the Septuagint as accurately representing the meaning of the Hebrew text. In the case of Isaiah 7:14, the Septuagint translates the Hebrew *almah* with the Greek *parthenos*, which focuses on virginity. As Matthew indicates, the fact that this Son would be conceived of a virgin makes this a truly miraculous sign. The Son was conceived of the Holy Spirit.

29

Isaiah 7 is not the only place in the book where we find a prophecy of a Son who would be of the house of David but who would be far more than a mere human. Isalah also gave this startling prophecy: "For unto us a child is born, unto us a son is given; and the government shall be upon his shoulder: and his name shall be called Wonderful, Counseller, The mighty God, The everlasting Father, The Prince of Peace. Of the increase of his government and peace there shall be no end, upon the throne of David, and upon his kingdom, to order it, and to establish it with judgment and with justice from henceforth even for ever. The zeal of the LORD of hosts will perform this" (Isaiah 9:6–7). When we read these words, we think immediately of Gabriel's announcement to Mary (Luke 1:31–33). In both Isaiah and Luke, a Son is in view. He is identified by a specific name. He is a descendant of David. He will rule on David's throne. His kingdom will endure forever.

» *In addition to the Scriptures we have looked at in Isaiah, how many other Old Testament Scriptures can you think of that prophesy of the coming Messiah?*

II. THE ANGELS ANNOUNCED HIS COMING

A. Good News of Great Joy

As we saw in Psalm 132:6, the words, "Lo, we heard of it at Ephratah: we found it in the fields of the wood" seem to anticipate the visit of the angel of the Lord to the shepherds who were "abiding in the field, keeping watch over their flock by night" (Luke 2:8).

The Messiah would come from Ephrathah and, as Psalm 132 looks ahead to the fulfillment of the Davidic Covenant, it connects that fulfillment with Ephrathah, that is, with Bethlehem. The statement, "We found it in the fields of the woods" brings to mind Luke's record that the shepherds, the poor among Israel (Psalm 132:15) were the first to discover and worship the Messiah. It was here in the fields that an angel of the Lord told them the good news of a Savior, Christ the Lord, born in the city of David, Bethlehem (Luke 2:9–12).

Under the Old Covenant, the Ark was God's dwelling place. Under the New Covenant, God "tabernacles" or dwells among us in the Incarnation. The word translated "dwelt" in John 1:14 is *eskēnōsen*, which includes the meaning "to abide or dwell in a tabernacle or tent." As sacred as it was, the Ark of the Covenant was merely a shadow or type of the presence of God that would take up residence among human beings in the person of Jesus Christ. (See Hebrews 9:1–10; 10:1–25; 12:24.)

In a very real sense, when the shepherds found Jesus in Bethlehem-Ephrathah lying in a manger, they went into His tabernacle and worshipped at His footstool (Psalm 132:7). Because of the fulfillment of the Davidic Covenant, God's priests are clothed with righteousness and His saints shout for joy (Psalm 132:9, 16).

B. A Savior Is Born

The message of the angel of the Lord to the shepherds included these joyous words: "For unto you is born this day in the city of David a Saviour, which is Christ the Lord" (Luke 2:11). Although the word "Saviour" does not appear in Matthew, the same angel who spoke to the shepherds appeared to Joseph in a dream with words that also identified Jesus as the Savior (Matthew 1:21).

The name *Jesus*, transliterated from the Greek *Iēsous*, means "Yahweh-Savior" (or "Jehovah-Savior). It can also be translated "Yahweh will save" and "Yahweh is Savior." The first two letters of the name, *Iē*, are transliterated from the Hebrew Yah, an abbreviation for Yahweh. This abbreviation, rendered by the KJV as *JAH*, appears in Psalm 68:4. *Yahweh* is the third person singular form of the Hebrew "to be" verb. It means "he is," or "he will be." The first person singular form of this verb is used in Exodus 3:14 where God identified Himself as "I AM." The last four letters of the Greek form of the Messiah's name, *sous*, are translated from a form of the Hebrew *yasha*, which refers to salvation or deliverance. Thus, the name Jesus literally means "He is Savior" or "He will save." This identifies Jesus as the Savior. Many people in various language groups of the world have received some form of the name "Jesus," but the Savior is the only person ever to receive this name by divine appointment, because only He is the Savior of the world.

The word "Savior" appears twenty-four times in the New Testament. In eight cases, God is identified as Savior. (See Luke 1:47; I Timothy 1:1; 2:3; 4:10; Titus 1:3; 2:10; 3:4; Jude 1:25.) In fourteen references, the Savior is identified as Jesus or Christ. (See Luke 2:11; John 4:42; Acts 5:31; 13:23; Ephesians 5:23; Philippians 3:20; II Timothy 1:10; Titus 1:4; 2:13; 3:6; II Peter 1:1, 11; 2:20; 3:18.) In one case each, the Savior is referred to as Lord (II Peter 3:18) and Son (I John 4:14).

The King James Version of II Peter 1:1 presents an interesting reading, since several verses identify the Savior as God, while most refer to the Savior as Jesus or Christ.

"Simon Peter, a servant and an apostle of Jesus Christ, to them that have obtained like precious faith with us through the righteousness of God and our Saviour Jesus Christ."

Most translations follow the Greek text with more precision. For example, "Simon Peter, a bondservant and apostle of Jesus Christ, to those who have obtained like precious faith with us by the righteousness of our God and Savior Jesus Christ" (NKJV).

God is our Savior. Jesus Christ is our Savior. Since Jesus is God, there is no contradiction in any of these verses. For there to be any contradiction, there would have to be verses with readings like *God is not our Savior*, or *Jesus is not our Savior*, or *Jesus is not God*. Such readings do not exist.

III. WE PREACH THE GOOD NEWS OF THE GOSPEL

Some people question the content of the gospel, but Paul explained it clearly. He wrote, "Moreover, brethren, I declare unto you the gospel which I preached unto you, which also ye have received, and wherein ye stand; by which also ye are saved, if ye keep in memory what I preached unto you, unless ye have believed in vain" (I Corinthians 15:1–2). As we keep reading, we discover the gospel, which means "good news," consists of three truths that first appeared in the Old Testament.

A. Jesus Died

The first aspect of the gospel is that Christ died for our sins. This is good news, because it means the sin problem has been solved.

It is important to remember the gospel was first found in the "scripture," a reference here to the Hebrew Scriptures, the Old Testament. This underscores New Testament statements concerning the fact the Old Testament is a Christ-centered document. (See John 5:39, 46–47; Luke 24:27, 32, 44–47.)

The death of the Messiah for our sins is a theme running throughout the Hebrew Scriptures, for the entire sacrificial system of the Law of Moses was a figure (*parabolē*) of the sacrifice of Christ on His cross. (See Hebrews 9:9–14; 10:1–14.) As translated by the NKJV, the sacrificial system "was symbolic" (Hebrews 9:9). In addition, the prophets foretold the death of the Messiah as an offering for sin. (See, i.e., Isaiah 53:10–12).

B. Jesus Was Buried

The burial of Jesus was proof of His death. He did not merely faint or swoon as a result of his intense suffering. The Scriptures anticipated His burial (Isaiah 53:8–9).

Precise fulfillment of the prophecy that He would be buried with the rich is seen in that "there came a rich man of Arimathæa, named Joseph, who also himself was Jesus' disciple: He went to Pilate, and begged the body of Jesus. . . . And laid it in his own new tomb, which he had hewn out in the rock" (Matthew 27:57–58, 60).

C. Jesus Rose Again

On the Day of Pentecost, Peter quoted Psalm 16:8–11 to affirm the resurrection of Jesus from the dead (Acts 2:25–28). Jesus Himself referred to Jonah's experience in the whale's belly as a sign of His own death, burial, and resurrection (Matthew 12:38–41).

The resurrection of Jesus is good news for us, because it is a guarantee of the resurrection of all those who belong to Him (I Corinthians 15:12–23, 49–54). Our blessed hope is the "glorious appearing of our great God and Savior Jesus Christ" (Titus 2:13).

» *Sometimes the gospel is referred to as the death, burial, and resurrection of Christ. Why is it better to always include the phrase "according to the Scriptures"?*

IV. IT IS THE GOSPEL THAT SAVES US

It is important to know the content of the gospel. Paul, who gave us that content in a concise statement showing how the gospel is rooted in Old Testament prophecy, wrote, "For I am not ashamed of the gospel of Christ: for it is the power of God unto salvation to every one that believeth; to the Jew first, and also to the Greek" (Romans 1:16).

The gospel is not something to which we merely give mental assent. It is something we obey (II Thessalonians 1:8). The Christian life begins when we place our faith in Jesus Christ for salvation (I Corinthians 15:1–2). It continues when genuine faith leads us to ongoing conformity to the image of Jesus Christ (Romans 8:29). This involves repentance and baptism in the name of Jesus Christ, as Peter pointed out on Pentecost (Acts 2:38). Repentant faith and baptism effect the remission of sin and secure the promise of the Holy Spirit, the sign of which is the miracle of speaking in a language never learned. (See Acts 2:4–11; 10:44–48; 19:1–6 and also Romans 6:1–6; Galatians 3:26–27; Colossians 2:11–14; I Peter 3:21.)

» *Why does genuine faith result in obedience?*

>>> INTERNALIZING THE MESSAGE

As shocking as it may be to say, the Law of Moses was not good news. Paul described it as the "ministry of death" and the "ministry of condemnation" which was passing away (II Corinthians 3:7–9, NKJV). It had "a shadow of the good things to come, and not the very image of the things," and it could never perfect those who followed it (Hebrews 10:1–10, NKJV).

A significant portion of the New Testament is taken up with comparing and contrasting the Old Covenant—the Law of Moses—and the New Covenant. This began early in the Gospels (John 1:17), continued in Acts (Acts 13:39; 15), and had a high profile in Paul's letters *and* Hebrews.

The gospel is good news—news of rescue, deliverance, hope, salvation, and eternal life in the presence of Jesus (Philippians 1:19–23).

How do you relate to God? Are you hoping someday to measure up enough by your good works that you will be counted worthy of salvation? Or have you embraced the good news that salvation is a free gift of God enjoyed by those who have believed on Jesus and who have followed His invitation to be identified with Him in His death, burial, and resurrection?

God Responds to Faith

FOCUS THOUGHT

When we put our faith in Him, God responds to our faith.

 FOCUS VERSE

Hebrews 11:6

But without faith it is impossible to please him: for he that cometh to God must believe that he is, and that he is a rewarder of them that diligently seek him.

 LESSON TEXT

Hebrews 11:1–14

1 Now faith is the substance of things hoped for, the evidence of things not seen.

2 For by it the elders obtained a good report.

3 Through faith we understand that the worlds were framed by the word of God, so that things which are seen were not made of things which do appear.

4 By faith Abel offered unto God a more excellent sacrifice than Cain, by which he obtained witness that he was righteous, God testifying of his gifts: and by it he being dead yet speaketh.

5 By faith Enoch was translated that he should not see death; and was not found, because God had translated him: for before his translation he had this testimony, that he pleased God.

6 But without faith it is impossible to please him: for he that cometh to God must believe that he is, and that he is a rewarder of them that diligently seek him.

7 By faith Noah, being warned of God of things not seen as yet, moved with fear, prepared an ark to the saving of his house; by the which he condemned the world, and became heir of the righteousness which is by faith.

8 By faith Abraham, when he was called to go out into a place which he should after receive for an inheritance, obeyed; and he went out, not knowing whither he went.

9 By faith he sojourned in the land of promise, as in a strange country, dwelling in tabernacles with Isaac and Jacob, the heirs with him of the same promise:

10 For he looked for a city which hath foundations, whose builder and maker is God.

11 Through faith also Sara herself received strength to conceive seed, and was delivered of a child when she was past age, because she judged him faithful who had promised.

12 Therefore sprang there even of one, and him as good as dead, so many as the stars of the sky in multitude, and as the sand which is by the sea shore innumerable.

13 These all died in faith, not having received the promises, but having seen them afar off, and were persuaded of them, and embraced them, and confessed that they were strangers and pilgrims on the earth.

14 For they that say such things declare plainly that they seek a country.

LAUNCH INTO THE UNKNOWN

An energetic young man went from a single-parent home to doing missionary work in an undisclosed location. In his young adulthood, the Lord spoke to him about going to China. It seemed like an impossible dream to go into a nation that was closed to the gospel and that still works to destroy the message of Jesus and His followers.

As this man grew in his walk with the Lord, he began to minister in various churches. Through faith, prayer, and fasting, the Lord showed up in powerful ways, healing and transforming lives. One year at the UPCI General Conference, this young man prayed that he would come in contact with a certain, mighty missionary from the continent of Asia. This young man wanted confirmation as to whether or not he should go into China. The missionary couple he wanted to meet led a powerful church and disciple-training school in their own nation on that continent.

At that conference, a friend of the young minister suddenly brought the missionary couple over to meet the aspiring missionary. The young preacher was shocked and overwhelmed to see this was actually playing out as he had prayed. Not only did the experienced missionaries invite the young man, they confirmed his calling and later brought him onto their team, giving him experience with multiple nationalities for years before releasing him into the dangerous world of a closed country. Like Abraham, a child of God must accept the Lord's vision for one's life by faith, letting Him work out the details.

>>> OUTLINE

I. GOD CALLED ABRAHAM

A. No Clear Destination

B. Told to Leave His Family Behind

II. ABRAHAM WENT BY FAITH

A. Left Ur

B. Went Looking for a City

III. GOD RESPONDED TO ABRAHAM AND SARAH'S FAITH

A. They Were Both Beyond Child-Bearing Age

B. Abraham and Sarah Had Struggles with Their Faith

C. God Gave Them the Promised Child, Isaac

IV. GOD RESPONDS TO OUR FAITH

>>> CONTEMPLATING THE TOPIC

There are certain things in nature that just naturally attract one another. Bring the North pole of one magnet into proximity with the South pole of another, and the result is universally consistent. One need not be a trained scientist nor even understand why it occurs to observe this powerful response. The one will draw the other without exception.

Offer the root of a plant a source of water somewhere in the soil nearby, and that root will grow purposefully in that direction. It will work around obstacles and barriers to reach the water. Why? It is attracted to it.

God is not to be compared with an inanimate magnet nor an insentient plant root, but He has bound Himself by some spiritual principles which are just as consistent as these glimpses from nature. One of these foundational elements of His nature is this: God is attracted to faith. One need not be a theologian nor even understand exactly why this is so to benefit from this truth. In every situation, in every era, and for every person, God will respond to faith. It is an immutable part of who He is.

I. GOD CALLED ABRAHAM

It must have been an amazing moment when the voice of a God he did not know spoke distinctly to Abraham. He lived, after all, in a pagan land in which idolatry was the norm. The statues and images he had worshipped heretofore had certainly never spoken to him because they lacked life and the ability to do so. The idea of hearing the voice of a "god" was undoubtedly more than Abraham could grasp.

And yet it happened! And it happened with such striking clarity that Abraham was compelled to obey. "Now the LORD had said unto Abram, Get thee out of thy country, and from thy kindred, and from thy father's house, unto a land that I will shew thee" (Genesis 12:1). This was not a random event. God did not arbitrarily select a person from the city of Ur to be the one to hear His voice. He chose Abraham by design. This was a specific moment with specific requirements featuring specific promises to a specific man. Abraham was divinely called by God Himself, and the instructions were anything but easy ones.

A. No Clear Destination

Abraham was told to depart from his homeland and to set out to find a city, but there was no more information given than that. God did not inform Abraham about which way to go, how far to travel, nor how to know when he had arrived. In today's world, we are prone to type our destination into a smart phone or a GPS system before ever leaving our driveway. Even if such had been available to Abraham, he had been given no information about what destination to input.

There are times in our lives when we feel somewhat similar in our confusion. During times of storms and trials, we often do not know which way to go. We are uncertain about how long the journey of this trial will last. We are not even certain how to know when we have traversed far enough in it. What is the end game? Where will this lead? Abraham teaches us that God sometimes requires our faith to compel us to action even when we do not have all the answers. We are given an instruction without clear details. What we lack in particulars, we must supplement with faith!

> » *Think of a time when God gave you instructions without all the specifics. How did you handle that? How would you handle it better today?*

B. Told to Leave His Family Behind

It was not enough that God asked him to depart from his homeland, God further required Abraham to leave his family behind. The journey he would take was to be a solitary one. He could not depend on the comfort or companionship of those with whom he had previously resided. This trip was to be made after leaving his kindred behind.

One might speculate about the reasons for this. Perhaps God knew these others, not having experienced His voice as had Abraham, would quickly revert to their old, idolatrous ways. Perhaps He knew Abraham would never fully trust Him if he had family members to depend on. Perhaps He desired Abraham's focus not be divided. Whatever the reason, this additional requirement only made Abraham's decision to obey that much more difficult.

But then God is not primarily interested in our ease. He calls us to faith demonstrated by obedience despite the difficulties generated by His words. There will be a challenge in pursuing God's will wholly because His ways and our ways are nearly always contrary to one another. But His ways lead inexorably to the land of which He promised.

> *Has your obedience to God ever separated you from someone you cared about? What lessons did you learn from that experience?*

II. ABRAHAM WENT BY FAITH

The most astounding thing about this Scriptural introduction to Abraham is not that God called him and asked a hard thing of him, but it is found in Abraham's response to the voice of a God whom he had just heard for the very first time. "So Abraham departed, as the LORD had spoken unto him . . ." (Genesis 12:4). We read of no hesitation. Abraham offered no debate or counterproposal to God. He simply loaded up his household and departed.

This was a supreme demonstration of faith, for nothing else would have allowed him to respond in that fashion. Faith is always exhibited in such obedience. Faith is more than simply mental assent to what God has spoken; faith is the active decision to do what He has said. Thus, when Abraham left Ur of the Chaldees, he qualified himself for inclusion in the great chapter of faith found in Hebrews 11. "By faith Abraham, when he was called to go out into a place which he should after receive for an inheritance, obeyed; and he went out, not knowing whither he went" (Hebrews 11:8).

A. Left Ur

We can be reasonably sure that Abraham's friends and family could not understand why Abraham was leaving. Can you imagine how his explanation must have sounded to these idolaters? "God spoke to you and told you to leave? Why? How long will you be gone?" Abraham had no answers to such questions, but he did have a commandment to go. And so he did, walking away from everything that was comfortable and safe.

Faith in God will often take us outside our comfortable surroundings into a land which is marked by questions and uncertainties. We will generally be required to follow God's leading on a faith journey which will take us to new places spiritually. And the unfamiliar can be frightening. Abraham dwelled "in a strange country." (See Hebrews 11:9.) Faith demanded that he trade his comfortable surroundings for a progression of indeterminate tomorrows, while his only security was the voice of a God he barely knew.

B. Went Looking for a City

Even more strange to those he left was Abraham's answer to the question on most lips. "Where are you going?" Abraham could but shrug, smile, and attempt to explain that God had simply told him to seek a city whose foundation was built by God Himself. And so he did. "For he looked for a city which hath foundations, whose builder and maker is God" (Hebrews 11:10).

Our quest is like unto his. We, too, are ultimately looking for entrance to a city which God alone has built. "And I John saw the holy city, new Jerusalem, coming down from God out of heaven, prepared as a bride adorned for her husband" (Revelation 21:2). But even between now and our arrival in our ultimate home, we are seekers here below as well. We seek His favor. We seek His face. We seek Him. We desire that every day spent in this wilderness we traverse brings us ever closer to the one who called us in the first place. The faith by which Abraham sought a city is the same faith by which we seek the builder of that city.

» *What are you currently seeking from God? Do you feel any closer to it than when you started? What do you think is the key to continuing to pursue it?*

III. GOD REPONDED TO ABRAHAM AND SARAH'S FAITH

The commandment of God to Abraham was accompanied by some wonderful promises:

> *And I will make of thee a great nation, and I will bless thee, and make thy name great; and thou shalt be a blessing: And I will bless them that bless thee, and curse him that curseth thee: and in thee shall all families of the earth be blessed. (Genesis 12:2–3)*

When Abraham and his immediate family left Ur behind, this active demonstration of his faith secured the fulfillment of these promises. There remained no question as to his becoming a great nation nor of God's blessing in his life, because he had demonstrated his faith in God. God always responds to faith!

A. They Were Both Beyond Child-Bearing Age

The journey to seeing their family become a great nation seemed longer than the one from Ur to their yet unknown physical destination. Abraham and Sarah were both biologically and physiologically incapable of producing the work God had promised. A child? At their age? This was quite simply medically impossible. Not merely unlikely, but impossible!

It is commonly true that God's promises do not just seem unlikely, but impossible. They counter logic, nature, and facts. Faith is not bound by such things, but instead accounts God's words as more important than anything else one can observe. Our senses attempt to tell us what is true in the world governed by natural laws. Our faith tells us what is true in the realm governed by His word. Abraham and Sarah's bodies might have denied the possibilities of family expansion, but faith demanded they believe something different no matter how hard that might be.

B. Abraham and Sarah Had Struggles with Their Faith

Faith is easy to exercise in the abstract, but in the concrete details of life it can be harder to employ. When God said He would make a great nation through Abraham, it was no doubt difficult to imagine, but Abraham must have believed God would do something outside the norm to bring it to pass. Perhaps he would adopt a son. Perhaps God would simply create one. Whatever might be, it was easier to grasp than these words. "And God said unto Abraham, As for Sarai thy wife, thou shalt not call her name Sarai, but Sarah shall her name be. And I will bless her, and give thee a son also of her: yea, I will bless her, and she shall be a mother of nations; kings of people shall be of her" (Genesis 17:15–16).

When God explained to Abraham his specific plans for the birth of a son, the reaction from these promise recipients was not exemplary. "Then Abraham fell upon his face, and laughed, and said in his heart, Shall a child be born unto him that is an hundred years old? and shall Sarah, that is ninety years old, bear?" (Genesis 17:17). "Therefore Sarah laughed within herself, saying, After I am waxed old shall I have pleasure, my lord being old also? (Genesis 18:12).

It is somewhat comforting that even the "father of the faithful" struggled to believe God's plan, because we often do likewise. We can clearly read what God's Word promises, and yet we have difficulty understanding how such glorious things can happen. We fall into the same trap as Abraham of trying to explain the "how" of God's promises rather than simply accept the reality of them. If God has spoken it, we do not have to figure out how he will carry out His words. When doubts try to trouble our minds, we should simply remind ourselves of this truth:

> *God is not a man, that he should lie; neither the son of man, that he should repent: hath he said, and shall he not do it? Or hath he spoken, and shall he not make it good? (Numbers 23:19)*

God understands our frame and knows just how difficult it can be for our human minds to accept a promise of the miraculous. He does not reject us for our struggles in this area, but He does call us consistently to believe Him. Doing so has great reward!

» *Consider a long-standing prayer request you have had. Have you been guilty of trying to figure out "how" God will answer? Explain.*

C. God Gave Them the Promised Child, Isaac

God gently confronted the lapse in Abraham and Sarah's faith and strengthened it by reaffirming His ability and by reiterating His promise to them. "Is any thing too hard for the LORD? At the time appointed I will return unto thee, according to the time of life, and Sarah shall have a son" (Genesis 18:14).

This word apparently renewed their trust in God, for just as God had said, Sarah did indeed conceive a son! "And the LORD visited Sarah as he had said, and the LORD did unto Sarah as he had spoken. For Sarah conceived, and bare Abraham a son in his old age, at the set time of which God had spoken to him" (Genesis 21:1–2).

Every aspect of God's promise to Abraham and Sarah was fulfilled. The son came just as God said and just when God promised. Though they were relatively new In their relationship with this God who had introduced himself back in Ur, they now had tangible proof that His word is always dependable. Each time the baby cried, Isaac was announcing to his parents the faithfulness of God. When one examines Abraham's life, this event seems to have helped him round the corner in trusting the voice of God, even to the point that when God tested him some time later, he took his precious son to the top of Mt. Moriah to offer Isaac to the Lord. (See Genesis 22:1–14.) Abraham's faith produced the fulfillment of God's promise, and God's fulfillment of this promise further established Abraham's faith.

» *What is something God has done for you that dramatically increased your faith?*

IV. GOD RESPONDS TO OUR FAITH

What was true of Abraham and Sarah is also true for us. God responds to faith! He responds to our trust in Him which is the "evidence of things not seen!" (See Hebrews 11:1.) This fact is clearly established throughout Scripture (Hebrews 11:6; James 1:6–7; Mark 11:22–23). We will allow its voice to speak to us to confirm this truth.

In that God responds to faith which is shown through obedience, how can you demonstrate your faith to God more clearly this week in order to see God respond in your life?

▶▶▶ INTERNALIZING THE MESSAGE

Every one of us faces situations in life which require our faith. We encounter difficulties, challenges, battles, and struggles. To navigate such times, it is mandatory that we live a life of faith. Faith is to be the essence of our spiritual existence, for the prophet Habakkuk recorded, ". . . but the just shall live by his faith" (Habakkuk 2:4). When we live guided and comforted by faith, the journey is a much more pleasant one.

There is an old story about a traveler in the early days of United States western expansion who came to the mighty Mississippi River. Upon encountering that vast waterway, he was dismayed to realize there was no bridge by which to cross it. Fortunately for him, it was winter, and the intense cold had sheeted the great river over with ice. The path looked good on the surface, but the traveler was afraid to trust himself to it, not knowing how thick it really was.

Finally, with infinite caution, he crept on his hands and knees and managed to get halfway over. And then he heard it. Singing! Yes, he heard singing coming ever closer from behind him. Cautiously and gingerly he turned. And there, out of the dusk, came another traveler, singing with great joy and gusto. He was driving a four-horse load of coal over the ice. Two travelers on the same journey, one scared and one singing.

Such is the effect of faith. It stills our fears, knowing that beyond our sight is the strength we need. For when we demonstrate faith by our obedience to God, He always responds by fulfilling exactly what He has promised.

40

Enduring Faith

FOCUS THOUGHT
To survive the trials of life, we must have enduring faith.

 FOCUS VERSE

Hebrews 12:2
Looking unto Jesus the author and finisher of our faith; who for the joy that was set before him endured the cross, despising the shame, and is set down at the right hand of the throne of God.

>>> LESSON TEXT

Hebrews 12:1–3
1 Wherefore seeing we also are compassed about with so great a cloud of witnesses, let us lay aside every weight, and the sin which doth so easily beset us, and let us run with patience the race that is set before us,

2 Looking unto Jesus the author and finisher of our faith; who for the joy that was set before him endured the cross, despising the shame, and is set down at the right hand of the throne of God.

3 For consider him that endured such contradiction of sinners against himself, lest ye be wearied and faint in your minds.

II Kings 4:18–21, 32–37
18 And when the child was grown, it fell on a day, that he went out to his father to the reapers.

19 And he said unto his father, My head, my head. And he said to a lad, Carry him to his mother.

20 And when he had taken him, and brought him to his mother, he sat on her knees till noon, and then died.

21 And she went up, and laid him on the bed of the man of God, and shut the door upon him, and went out.

. . . . .

32 And when Elisha was come into the house, behold, the child was dead, and laid upon his bed.

33 He went in therefore, and shut the door upon them twain, and prayed unto the LORD.

34 And he went up, and lay upon the child, and put his mouth upon his mouth, and his eyes upon his eyes, and his hands upon his hands: and he stretched himself upon the child; and the flesh of the child waxed warm.

35 Then he returned, and walked in the house to and fro; and went up, and stretched himself upon him: and the child sneezed seven times, and the child opened his eyes.

36 And he called Gehazi, and said, Call this Shunammite. So he called her. And when she was come in unto him, he said, Take up thy son.

37 Then she went in, and fell at his feet, and bowed herself to the ground, and took up her son, and went out.

CULTURE CONNECTION

NOTHING TO BE DEPRESSED ABOUT

Everyone can be bought for a price, they say. However, Turner could not. At least his "price" would have to have been much more than 4.3 million dollars. That is how much money he turned down to hang onto what he valued much more than cash: a family in the faith. Many believers would struggle at the thought of saying no to free money.

During the 1930's, anyone hearing word that they were heir to a multimillion-dollar legacy would have quickly done whatever it took to receive their prize. Turner and his wife Flora, however, took the matter to prayer. Receiving the inheritance was contingent on moving to England. This prayerful mother and father, though needing a financial boost for their many children, searched first to see if a body of believers could be found in that area. They did not want to raise a family without the influence of an apostolic church.

The search was unsuccessful. Rather than risk the souls of his children by taking them away from the godly church family he had at home, Turner declined the offer. One need not pity this family. Multiple generations later, nearly every one of Turner and Flora Gleason's 150 descendants are in the Truth. From this family have flowed teachers, preachers, Bible college presidents, district superintendents, missionaries, evangelists, and faithful believers, including Stan Gleason, Assistant General Superintendent in the UPCI. What is better than being a Great-Depression-era tycoon? Being patriarch to a family that will live forever.

OUTLINE

I. THE SHUNAMMITE WOMAN AND HER HUSBAND BUILT A ROOM FOR ELISHA
   A. She Wanted to Take Care of the Prophet
   B. She Wanted Him to Stay with Them When He Came to Town

II. THE SHUNAMMITE WOMAN WAS UNABLE TO HAVE A CHILD
   A. Her Faith Remained in God and His Miracle-Working Power
   B. She Stayed Faithful Though Her Desires Were Not Rewarded
   C. The Prophet Asked What She Desired

III. GOD GAVE HER A SON
   A. Elisha Prophesied Over Her
   B. God Honored Her Enduring Faith by Giving Her a Son

IV. JESUS ENDURED THE CROSS TO SAVE US

V. GOD CALLS US TO ENDURE OUR TRIALS BY FAITH

CONTEMPLATING THE TOPIC

Clearly faith is needed at all times during our walk with God, because we cannot please Him without it (Hebrews 11:6). But faith that lasts is particularly important during times of adversity. It is meant to be the anchor for our vessel during stormy seasons at sea. If our faith is only operative in good times, then we have little hope of long-term spiritual survival.

The prophet Jeremiah addressed this truth: "If thou hast run with the footmen, and they have wearied thee, then how canst thou contend with horses? and if in the land of peace, wherein thou trustedst, they wearied thee, then how wilt thou do in the swelling of Jordan?" (Jeremiah 12:5). If our faith cannot last in good times, then it certainly will fail us when needed most. Faith that endures must be the intention of the man who is focused on eternity.

From his life observations, Solomon wrote that the swiftest man does not always win the race, and the strongest man is not always triumphant in battle (Ecclesiastes 9:11). But Jesus explained the key to victorious living. "He that endureth to the end shall be saved" (Matthew 10:22).

I. THE SHUNAMMITE WOMAN AND HER HUSBAND BUILT A ROOM FOR ELISHA

God's prophets to Israel in the Old Testament were often itinerate in their ministry. While they may have had a home city from which they traveled, God's mission frequently compelled them to traverse the Holy Land to carry out His work. Elisha was one such man, and his journeys would with some regularity take him to the city of Shunem, a small village belonging to the tribe of Issachar and located near the Jezreel Valley.

In that hamlet resided a devout couple who had a genuine love for God and his kingdom. They demonstrated this love in a tangible way, as all true love must be shown, for abstract love is not truly love. This couple decided that Elijah needed a place to utilize as his own when he passed by their home, so they set about a construction process to that end. They built a "little chamber" on the wall of their house and furnished it for Elisha's comfort. It became the prophet's practice to turn into their home each time he passed through Shunem. (See II Kings 4:8–10.)

A. She Wanted to Take Care of the Prophet

The genesis of this idea for housing Elisha during his stays came from the heart of this unnamed lady. She conveyed her desire to her husband, and he joined with her in this project. Though their generosity was rewarded, it is important to note that the gesture of kindness in constructing the chamber was an act of altruism. It stemmed simply from their desire to care for God's messenger in their lives.

Such a desire is always found in those who love and honor the Lord. Anyone who professes a loyalty to Christ will also have a deeply seated desire to be a blessing to His messengers. No, preachers are not some special category of Christians who are better than others. And no, they should not demand nor expect special treatment from other members of the body of Christ. Still, it is entirely appropriate and even beneficial for those who are consistently blessed by preaching to desire to return that blessing in tangible ways.

» *What are some specific ways your pastor is a blessing in your life? Purpose to write your pastor a note this week expressing your gratitude.*

B. She Wanted Him to Stay with Them When He Came to Town

One commendable attitude this woman in the Biblical account had was that she was determined Elisha would be their guest. Of all the homes in which he could stay, her desire was that he come to theirs. Her passion is clearly seen in the Biblical narrative. "And it fell on a day, that Elisha passed to Shunem, where was a great woman; and she constrained him to eat bread" (II Kings 4:8). It was not a passive wish; hers was a consuming desire. She "constrained" him to come to her home. One can envision her running from her home to meet the man of God as he passed by and physically drawing him into their home. She was unmoved by what others thought; she was desperate for a visit from Elisha.

This account is particularly instructive when one considers that Elisha's name means "God is Salvation." Though this lady was a "great" woman, she did not in any fashion sit idly by in some expectation that "God is Salvation" would come to see her, and neither can we. We must also be driven by a passionate desire to commune with God. What others may or may not do to connect with Him is generally inconsequential. What will we do? How hungry are we? Are we willing to ensure that if "God is Salvation" abides in anyone's home, it will be ours?

II. THE SHUNAMMITE WOMAN WAS UNABLE TO HAVE A CHILD

Woven deeply into the creative nature of women is the desire to nurture a child. Because of that longing, having to deal with childlessness is a most difficult and personally painful trial. The Shunammite woman had known this sting for years, and the ache in her soul was accentuated every time she observed a mother and child. She desperately wanted to know that same joy.

A. Her Faith Remained in God and His Miracle-Working Power

This lady had undoubtedly poured out her heart's desire to God regularly through the years. Yet despite her heartfelt pleas to God, she had seemed to receive nothing in reply from Heaven but silence. Such circumstances have the capacity to irreparably damage one's faith. When God's reply to our deepest desire is either "no" or "wait," we begin to hear Hell's whisper that God cannot be trusted.

Instead, this lady of Shunem chose to remain faithful to God in spite of her ongoing disappointment. That she had conquered the temptation for bitterness can be seen in her ready response to the visit of the prophet. She did not project any anger toward God on His servant. Rather with open arms she embraced the opportunity to do good to God's work by caring for His messenger. She continued to believe in the miraculous as had been consistently displayed in Elisha's ministry.

» *Have you ever been angry at God? Describe the situation and how you overcame.*

B. She Stayed Faithful Though Her Desires Were Not Rewarded

Her faithfulness when the prophet arrived in Shunem was merely a reflection of her life before that time. Elisha's presence did not produce faithfulness in her; it merely revealed it. Through each long, childless year, the Shunammite woman continued to be faithful. Although her heart was torn with every announcement of a happy couple's impending birth, still she remained faithful though her arms were empty.

The true measure of our faith is not found in answered prayers, but in unanswered ones. When our deepest desires go unfulfilled, then the mettle of our trust in God is revealed. Will we be faithful? Will we be worshippers? Will we remain confident both in God's ability and in His goodness? The ancient witness of a disappointed but faithful witness in Shunem calls us to our best.

C. The Prophet Asked What She Desired

In response to her generosity, Elisha inquired of this good lady what she might want. We cannot be sure what prompted her response, or perhaps more accurately her lack of one. In that moment she did not choose to reveal to the prophet her deepest desire. Perhaps she considered that a sacred conversation to be held with God alone.

While there is merit to that perspective in our lives, still in general we should never be ashamed or embarrassed to express our righteous desires to God. In fact, we are instructed to do so. "Be careful for nothing; but in every thing by prayer and supplication with thanksgiving let your requests be made known unto God" (Philippians 4:6).

Clearly God already knows our hearts, and He does not need us to express our desires so He can finally become aware of them. Expressing our petitions to Him is not for His benefit, but ours. When we give voice to our requests, we engage our faith in a tangible way. We express our confidence in God by asking, even when the request has been previously presented. Importunity is not demonstrating a lack of faith. It is the evidence of our faith's continued viability. For if we did not believe in God, we would not continue to ask, seek, or knock. Presenting our longstanding requests to God is the proof of our faithfulness!

» *Why do you believe we are sometimes hesitant to express our deepest desires to God?*

III. GOD GAVE HER A SON

A. Elisha Prophesied Over Her

When the Shunammite did not express any specific request to him, Elisha asked his servant, Gehazi, what might be done for her. Gehazi explained her childless condition, and accordingly Elisha summoned her again. He spoke with prophetic authority, "About this season, according to the time of life, thou shalt embrace a son" (II Kings 4:16).

It is fascinating to note that when this direct word from God came to her, her faith wavered for perhaps the first time. Her response was not, "Thank you, Prophet! I receive your word!" No, instead she actually gave voice to her doubt. "And she said, Nay, my lord, thou man of God, do not lie unto thine handmaid" (II King 4:16).

Experience teaches us that quite often the moment of our faith's greatest trial is at the verge of the answer coming. It is somewhat easier to believe in God's purpose in the cloudy waters of "someday" than it is to accept the fulfillment of His plan in the tumultuous "now!" When we approach the point of our miracle, we should make a focused effort to continue to express faith when the fear of further disappointment lures us to doubt.

» *Do you believe our faith is often tested the most just before the answer to our prayers comes? Explain.*

B. God Honored Her Enduring Faith by Giving Her a Son

The great news of this passage is that God evidently gave more credence to her years of faith than to her moment of doubt. Her womb was not opened because of her rousing faith in this moment, for she had none. Instead, the promised child arrived because of her resilient faith over the years. Thankfully God responds more to faith that exhibits endurance than excitement.

It is far easier to have a "faith moment" in a powerful Sunday church service than to have a "faith life" on mundane Mondays. God desires our faith to endure as did this lady's. She had known so much heartbreak that it finally overwhelmed her when the prophet presented God's promise. She verbalized doubt. But thankfully when that occurred, God reached into the reservoir of her consistent, faithful prayers and service to Him for years, and responded to that faith to bring about her miracle. When we remain faithful in the face of temporarily unanswered prayers, we are stockpiling faith against a day God has chosen for our deliverance, even if our faith wavers at that moment. Enduring faith speaks up then!

» *Discuss the difference between faith in a moment and faithfulness over a lifetime.*

IV. JESUS ENDURED THE CROSS TO SAVE US

The man, Christ Jesus, hung on a cross not for moments, but for hours. With every labored breath He had both the knowledge that He was not suffering for anything He had done and the ability to end it with one cry to the angels. (See Matthew 26:53.) And yet, when the six hours were over, Jesus was able to utter His great, victorious declaration. "When Jesus therefore had received the vinegar, he said, It is finished: and he bowed his head, and gave up the ghost" (John 19:30).

This was a most agonizing trial of His faith. The Bible is quite clear that the experience on Calvary was something He had to endure (Hebrews 12:2). It is completely understandable that in the midst of this ordeal, as a man His flesh cried out, "And about the ninth hour Jesus cried with a loud voice, saying, Eli, Eli, lama sabachthani? that is to say, My God, my God, why hast thou forsaken me?" (Matthew 27:46). For the first time He felt Heaven's rejection and the shame of sin. And He could have ended it with one word!

Yet, in that moment, Christ demonstrated for us the power of enduring faith. Amid His agony, He kept His focus on the results and rewards to be achieved if He simply remained faithful.

V. GOD CALLS US TO ENDURE OUR TRIALS BY FAITH

While the clear majority of us will likely never face an execution like Jesus did, we all will have our faith tried by life's circumstances. These times are rarely anticipated, never enjoyable, and always painful. But they are also consistently beneficial to our eternal purpose. "That the trial of your faith, being much more precious than of gold that perisheth, though it be tried with fire, might be found unto praise and honour and glory at the appearing of Jesus Christ" (I Peter 1:7).

The way we will not only survive these times of adversity but also thrive in them is if we have faith that endures. We cannot allow our trust and confidence in God to be determined or defined by the particular path we are walking during any one season of life. What happens in this realm is not what matters. For what is our faith readying us? "For our light affliction, which is but for a moment, worketh for us a far more exceeding and eternal weight of glory" (II Corinthians 4:17).

▶▶▶ INTERNALIZING THE MESSAGE

In many real senses, we are far removed from the lady of Shunem. We live in a different time. We face different challenges. We are in a new covenant with God, living on this side of Calvary.

And yet, in many ways, the human experience is the same. We know the sting of prayer that appears to be unanswered. We face the daunting challenge of remaining faithful when the voice of our flesh calls for the contrary. In their book titled *Children at Risk*, Dr. James Dobson and Gary Bauer illustrate victory over this challenge beautifully.

"One of the most tragic events during the Reagan Presidency was the Sunday morning terrorist bombing of the Marine barracks in Beirut, in which hundreds of Americans were killed or wounded as they slept. Many of us can still recall the terrible scenes as the dazed survivors worked to dig out their trapped brothers from beneath the rubble.

"A few days after the tragedy, I recall coming across an extraordinary story. Marine Corps Commandant Paul X Kelly visited some of the wounded survivors then in a Frankfurt, Germany, hospital. Among them was Corporal Jeffrey Lee Nashton, severely wounded in the incident. Nashton had so many tubes running in and out of his body that a witness said he looked more like a machine than a man; yet he survived.

"As Kelly neared him, Nashton, struggling to move and racked with pain, motioned for a piece of paper and a pen. He wrote a brief note and passed it back to the Commandant. On the slip of paper were but two words—"Semper Fi," the Latin motto of the Marines meaning *forever faithful*."

When our battle is over and our commander receives us, may we have that same testimony. Through all our wounds and scars, when we finish our race, may our enduring faith shout our declaration as well: *Forever faithful*! And then forever home!

Faithful in Correction

FOCUS THOUGHT

If we remain faithful to God in the difficult times of trials and correction, as the result God will bring the spiritual perfection we need into our lives and make us righteous.

 FOCUS VERSE

Hebrews 12:11

Now no chastening for the present seemeth to be joyous, but grievous: nevertheless afterward it yieldeth the peaceable fruit of righteousness unto them which are exercised thereby.

 LESSON TEXT

Hebrews 12:5–11

5 And ye have forgotten the exhortation which speaketh unto you as unto children, My son, despise not thou the chastening of the Lord, nor faint when thou art rebuked of him:

6 For whom the Lord loveth he chasteneth, and scourgeth every son whom he receiveth.

7 If ye endure chastening, God dealeth with you as with sons; for what son is he whom the father chasteneth not?

8 But if ye be without chastisement, whereof all are partakers, then are ye bastards, and not sons.

9 Furthermore we have had fathers of our flesh which corrected us, and we gave them reverence: shall we not much rather be in subjection unto the Father of spirits, and live?

10 For they verily for a few days chastened us after their own pleasure; but he for our profit, that we might be partakers of his holiness.

11 Now no chastening for the present seemeth to be joyous, but grievous: nevertheless afterward it yieldeth the peaceable fruit of righteousness unto them which are exercised thereby.

WHEN REJECTED, LOVE

Asia Bibi (Aasiya Noreen) knows what it is like to stand for Jesus in a hostile country. In Pakistan, this woman was sentenced to death for speaking against the Islamic faith. As a wife and mother, her family was thrown into panic when she was imprisoned by her government many years ago. When the justice system ruled in her favor and acquitted her for insufficient evidence, Asia's haters became violent, threatening the lawyers, judges, and her family with death.

Jonah also knew what it was like to reach out to a hateful people. While such hostile countries exist around the globe, people of faith in America have always enjoyed the freedom to share their faith with others. At least, the America of a generation ago was tolerant to Christianity. Now, a new generation has arisen from the womb of Hollywood, nursed on the bottle of humanistic education. Western society grows increasingly hostile to the message and work of Jesus Christ.

How should Asia respond to her haters? What does one learn from Jonah and his angry reaction to the Lord sparing Ninevah? The Lord cares about people—even the ones who hurt His children. In a world where homosexual rhetoric, destructive policies, and godless motives are applauded, a person of purity swims against a stream of filth. While a believer will become incensed at times when observing the outrageous beliefs and behaviors in society, one must keep the mission and the method in focus: love them to Jesus.

>>> **OUTLINE**

I. JONAH RAN FROM GOD'S CALL
   A. He Took a Ship to Tarshish in Disobedience
   B. He Was Confronted with an Inescapable Storm

II. JONAH KNEW GOD WAS TRYING TO CORRECT HIM
   A. He Was Thrown Overboard
   B. He Repented in the Belly of the Fish and Was Spit Out on Dry Ground
   C. He Obeyed the Lord and Went to Nineveh to Preach

III. GOD'S CORRECTION HELPS US BECOME RIGHTEOUS
   A. The Lord Disciplines Those He Loves
   B. His Correction Is That We May Partake in His Holiness
   C. His Correction Is That We May Yield the Fruit of Righteousness

>>> **CONTEMPLATING THE TOPIC**

One of the most difficult experiences a person can face is that of working through the difficulties of the treatment, trial, and loss involved in the severe illness of a child.

Twenty-five years ago, at a time when medical advancements in the treatment of childhood blood cancers had not reached the levels they have today, an Apostolic family was suddenly facing the tragic diagnosis of their two-year-old son Jonathan. The young boy had developed childhood leukemia. An oral chemotherapy regimen was only experimental, so the young boy was placed on intravenous infusions over many months. The cancer took its toll as did the chemo's severe, debilitating side effects.

Yet in the midst of uncertainty and suffering came numerous testimonies of the miraculous hand of God in their difficult circumstance. In a fallen world of sickness and pain they witnessed the supernatural power of God in their lives in ways they had never experienced before.

Over many months of treatment and life-threatening emergencies, the dangerous reoccurrence of septic shock, painful needles, spinals, a most memorable life lesson was working in Jonathan's family. The Spirit of the Lord had drawn them repeatedly to Romans 8:28: "And we know that all things work together for good to them that love God, to them who are the called according to his purpose."

We live in a world of sin and its consequences as we await earth's final redemption. Whether we require correction for individual failings or experience the umbrella of the impact of the curse of sin upon one and all, learning the lessons of faith from the Father is an essential aspect of living a whole and holy life in this world. Bad actions require righteous correction, just as surely as bad things do happen to good people. Our trials, therefore, do not necessarily mean God's disfavor, or the lack of faith. Jesus Himself died upon an old rugged cross, yet He was in perfect favor of a righteous God. The greatest lesson of righteousness begins with the comprehension that we not resist heavenly correction, nor its will in our lives, but rather that we recognize "all things work together" in God's purposes.

The lesson, put in another way, is that God is good. Jonathan's family was experiencing that truth, just as every saint discovers God's graciousness through the difficulties and lessons of life. It is, of course, human to wonder and ask why, to seek God for the help and healing God alone can bring. It is not reasonable to blame God, any more than it is a parent's fault that correction and learning are essential in the life of their child. On one occasion in Jonathan's struggle, well into his treatment, at an extremely weakened and critical point, the healing touch of God brought a miraculous turn around, a dramatic intervention, obvious to family and doctors alike. The unsaved grandfather was so moved by it that he went to church and was filled with the Holy Ghost! Through it all, to God be the glory, and to this day, Jonathan is a cancer survivor.

God is God and we are not. Human nature demands we experience the lessons of divine discipline and truth in order to grow spiritually and become all the will of God intends. We must pray as our Lord, "nevertheless not my will, but thine be done" (Luke 22:42). Both deliverance and the supernatural power to go through the circumstances can be powerful and meaningful lessons. God is good in all of life's ups and downs. "He maketh his sun to rise on the evil and on the good, and sendeth rain on the just and on the unjust" (Matthew 5:45).

I. JONAH RAN FROM GOD'S CALL

In many ways the story of Jonah is the story of the world; it is fleeing the will of God. The world mistakenly demands that it can and must make its own way. In the case of Jonah, though, God had a strong confidence in the prophet's ultimate response. He was headed in the opposite direction from the divine will of God. But thank God for second chances. Through divine intervention God drew Jonah back into righteousness and back to a supernatural and righteous ministry.

What he learned on that dark sea that stormy night impacted Jonah's ministry more than anything he would ever again confront. He had taken an about-face and benefited from the Lord's chastening in a powerful way. He then turned around an entire city, in one of the most amazing transformations in history. In order to impact Nineveh the Lord needed to impact the man of God. In our sinful, wayward world, we face an unfortunate battle of wills in which many have miscalculated it being easier to run from God than to receive the discipline and will of God into their lives. Our generation does not need just any preaching, but it requires the transformed preaching of a Jonah.

A. He Took a Ship to Tarshish in Disobedience

As our focus scripture, Hebrews 12:11, points out, the lessons which bring us back into favor with God are often grievous, that is, they are painful. The prophet Jonah learned all too well that the will of God is not always easy, but he must not take it lightly. In Jonah 1, the prophet hoped to escape "the presence of the Lord" (Jonah 1:3) by running away to the distant Spanish port of Tarshish, only to discover that it is impossible to outrun God.

The writer of Hebrews (12:6,8) quotes from the Psalms to demonstrate and counter this tendency within sinful human nature to recoil from essential discipline, from the will of God, and especially from spiritual and transformative inward lessons of the heart. It is as fruitless as it is futile to blame God for life's difficulties and essential discipline, as though they are unwelcome distractions. Rather, says Psalm 94:12: "Blessed is the man whom thou chastenest, O Lord, and teachest him out of thy law." The man most illustrative of this divine outcome is Job, who received in his darkest hour the word of encouragement not to "despise," or take lightly, the instructive discipline or life lessons of God himself (Hebrews 12:5–6; Job 5:17). You will recall Job became one of the world's great survivors.

The heart that loves the Lord loves to be taught the disciplines of His Word. Then Hebrews 12:8 takes it even further by referring to Psalm 73:14: "For all the day long have I been plagued, and chastened every morning." In the context of the psalm, this is the cry of the heart for answers in times of difficulty. *Why me? Why not others?* The ultimate question is whether or not the Lord see us and knows what we are going through. *What is God's purpose?*

When a young father tucked his four-year-old daughter into bed that evening—after the burial of his wife, her mother—he slept close beside her in the next bed, watching over her with concern. Suddenly, out of the darkness, she asked, "Are you there?" The father assured her that he was. After a moment of pause the daughter added: "Is your face turned in this direction?" What the psalmist wants to know is that God is there in such times.

» *What Scripture verses have helped you not to run from the will of God in times of difficulty and testing?*

51

B. He Was Confronted with an Inescapable Storm

When the prophet Jonah rebelled against the difficulty of facing the evils of the city of Nineveh and sailed to Tarshish, he then faced the inescapable storm of God's discipline. He went from the pan into the fire. The truth is that God is inescapable. What is most critical for all people of God to know is that God has a purpose for their lives. When that is known, the child of God runs toward it, not away from it. The contrary course is certain shipwreck.

Judas, for example, should not have been anywhere near the garden the night of Jesus' betrayal, yet he had already set his own contrary course in his life which ended in tragic wreckage. Ananias and Sapphira should not have even thought about lying to the Holy Ghost regarding the measly sum from the sale of their possessions. But they, too, were going in the wrong direction. Peter clarified that it was "in thine own power" (Acts 5:4) to have done the right thing, but they chose the opposite course and paid the awful price.

II. JONAH KNEW GOD WAS TRYING TO CORRECT HIM

The world, too, like Jonah, is going in the wrong direction. Jonah knew better because he was a man of God. Yet he persisted in his course. To reject, deny, and run from the will of God is precisely the path of an unbelieving world, but certainly not the prophet. The world says, God cannot tell me to go to Nineveh or anywhere else. But Jonah knew better than that. He knew the storm itself was God's intervention and somehow his only hope of righteous correction. What an intervention of the ages it would turn out to be!

» *Why do you think people run from the will of God?*

A. He Was Thrown Overboard

The prophet was about to change forever. Even after Jonah informed them that he was running from the God who had sent the raging storm, the crew attempted to get him to shore, but failed (Jonah 1:13). The one who refused to offer up his life for Nineveh, now sacrificed himself for the fated crew: "cast me forth into the sea" (Jonah 1:12). We are, in fact, never more like the Creator than when we trust Him and offer ourselves in surrender to His will. The crew was out of options when they cast Jonah overboard, but God was not.

» *Why is it sometimes difficult to get people to change and respond to God's will?*

B. He Repented in the Belly of the Fish and Was Spit Out on Dry Ground

As God's plan unfolds, symbolic parallels emerge with the "great fish" which was prepared to swallow him up (Jonah 1:17). For example, as though they all were on the verge of shipwreck, the pagan crew lightened the ship and prayed, "every man unto his god," but the prophet of the true God was "fast asleep" (1:5). This parallels a so-called ministry which is fast asleep as a world in need faces mighty destructive forces. On the other hand, Jesus Christ our sinless Savior took the sins of the whole world upon Himself and willingly surrendered to the three days and three nights of death, burial, and resurrection. He reversed forever the hopelessness of mankind's chaotic fall from grace.

It is here that we see the culmination of the truth of our focus text regarding the Lord's correction (Hebrews 12:11): "Afterward it yieldeth the peaceable fruit of righteousness unto them which are exercised thereby." Jonah had been faithless, disobedient, and astray from God's holiness. Nevertheless, God "had prepared a great fish to swallow up Jonah" (Jonah 1:17). The Hebrew word manah indicates that the divine design, arrangement, and planning necessary to accomplish the task was ready and waiting. The prophet found himself in a divine discomfort of the Lord's discipline which quickly turned his heart to prayer. He cried out in such a praise of deliverance—while still deep below the surface of the waters—that God delivered him from the depths. The fish spit Jonah out upon the "dry land" (Jonah 2:1–2, 9–10).

» *How can Jonah's experience of the supernatural amidst chastisement encourage us?*

C. He Obeyed the Lord and Went to Nineveh to Preach

Nineveh became the recipient of the good news of God's mercy because of the persistent discipline of the Lord toward His servant Jonah. "I will sing of the mercies of the Lord forever: with my mouth will I make known thy faithfulness to all generations" (Psalm 89:1). An appropriate scriptural parallel for Jonah's finale is Romans 10:14: "How then shall they call on him in whom they have not believed? And how shall they believe in him of whom they have not heard? And how shall they hear without a preacher?"

III. GOD'S CORRECTION HELPS US BECOME RIGHTEOUS

A. The Lord Disciplines Those He Loves

"For whom the Lord loveth he chasteneth, and scourgeth every son whom he receiveth" (Hebrews 12:6). The writer of Hebrews is affirming that discipline is the loving responsibility of a father to those within his loving care. (See Psalm 94:12.) Fathers, indeed, gain respect precisely because they instill meaningful discipline in the lives of their children.

Consider also that the Book of Hebrews was written at a time of severe trial for those who had left Judaism to follow Christ, so much so that some were on verge of turning back. The fact of their difficulties, nonetheless, did not mean God did not love them, but the opposite. It meant they were certainly His children whom He truly loved and trusted. Through it all, we, like these early believers, are being strengthened by it all, for surely the Father of all Creation knows what is best for us. His face is turned in our direction however dark the night.

B. His Correction Is That We May Partake in His Holiness

Our positive response to God's discipline is essential: "Shall we not much rather be in subjection unto the Father of spirits, and live?" (Hebrews 12:9). Earthly fathers may have limited knowledge of what is best for us, but not our heavenly Father. His plan for our ultimate good is that we share in his holiness: "that we might be partakers of his holiness, …. without which no man shall see the Lord" (Hebrews 12:10, 14). If we want to *live*, it is essential that we accept a rephrased slant on this major theme of Hebrews: "You cannot go back now!" Only the gospel has the power to give us life.

C. His Correction Is That We May Yield the Fruit of Righteousness

The discipline of the Lord in the heart of the child of God brings a welcome and needed corrective afterward. The original Greek literally means that it *repays* you (*yieldeth*) as its result. The result is framed in the language of exercise, "unto them which are exercised thereby" (Hebrews 12:11), that is, those experiencing the Lord's wise and loving correction are *strengthened*. Scripture warns us not to reject or be upset at God's will and correction: "My son, despise not the chastening of the Lord; neither be weary of his correction" (Proverbs 3:11).

» *In what ways have you been strengthened by the Lord's discipline in your own life?*

▶▶▶ INTERNALIZING THE MESSAGE

With faith in the goodness of God, all believers must be prepared to patiently run the race that lies before them, for God has determined its course and we are in it come what may! The race is not to the one who starts well but fails to persevere due to hinderances. The race is to the one who recovers the original intensity of purpose, shakes off the hindering mindset, and regains the confidence in God to win (Hebrews 12:1; 10:32–34; 2:1; 3:17; 4:11;10:35, 39). A song of encouragement rightly puts trust in the Lord: "In the good times praise his Name! In the bad times, do the same!" "In every thing give thanks: for this is the will of God in Christ Jesus concerning you" (I Thessalonians 5:18).

Showing Our Faith

FOCUS THOUGHT

God places his favor upon those who live out their faith.

 **FOCUS VERSE**

Hebrews 13:16

But to do good and to communicate forget not: for with such sacrifices God is well pleased.

 **LESSON TEXT**

Hebrews 11:7, 13

7 By faith Noah, being warned of God of things not seen as yet, moved with fear, prepared an ark to the saving of his house; by the which he condemned the world, and became heir of the righteousness which is by faith.

. . . . .

13 These all died in faith, not having received the promises, but having seen them afar off, and were persuaded of them, and embraced them, and confessed that they were strangers and pilgrims on the earth.

RUN WITH FAVOR

Are you ready to "run with favor"? Americans are still accepting the term "Uber" as a daily-usage word and adjusting to the role this business plays in so many lives today. Meanwhile, a new company has emerged to put on uber sneakers, so to speak. "Favor" is a personal-assistant service in many cities around the nation, delivering "tacos, groceries, dry cleaning" and just about anything else (description from favordelivery.com).

While playing on the concepts of doing someone a favor and finding favor with others, this company has filled a gap in society. Rather than viewing favor-running as a part-time opportunity to get some cash ahead for your vacation this year, perhaps favor-running should be a way of life. Noah found favor with God. He was able to move forward in doing a nearly impossible task simply because he knew he had the favor of the Lord on his life and work.

Believers today are called to run with grace (favor) before the Lord. The apostle Paul desired to rejoice in the presence of the Lord as one having run a meaningful race, not falling into disfavor (Philippians 2:16). Likewise, the believer is to find favor with those outside the Kingdom. If a person can put on a blue T-shirt and drive all over town running with Favor in exchange for tips, surely a child of God can run with the favor of the Lord in all he or she does.

⟫⟫ OUTLINE

I. GOD DECIDED TO DESTROY ALL LIVING THINGS

  A. Wickedness on the Earth

  B. But Noah Found God's Favor

II. GOD CALLED NOAH TO BUILD AN ARK

  A. He Was Ridiculed by Others

  B. Noah Built the Ark by Faith

III. GOD PLACED HIS FAVOR ON NOAH WHEN HE LIVED OUT HIS FAITH

  A. Noah and His Family Were Saved

  B. God Made a Covenant with Noah

IV. GOD PLACES HIS FAVOR ON US WHEN WE LIVE OUT OUR FAITH

  A. We Must Do What Is Good and Right

  B. God Is Pleased with Those Who Do What He Has Asked

⟫⟫ CONTEMPLATING THE TOPIC

A name in American patriotism which has come to be associated with the very word *loyalty*, and embodies the favor of an entire nation, is that of twenty–one-year-old Revolutionary War soldier Nathan Hale. After graduating Yale in 1773, he became a school teacher in his native state of Connecticut, only to close the little one room school house in New London when he joined the continental army in 1776. To this day that building is proudly preserved to the honor of Hale's actions, and to an event considered one of the greatest moments in all American patriotism. It was deemed an amazing act of selfless service in the inaugural dawn of the newly emerging nation. What kind of favor would instill Hale's heroics into the national consciousness in such a way that it remains alive two hundred and fifty years later?

In September 1776, Nathan Hale, in serious and urgent service to his nation and to General George Washington, was captured and hanged by the invading British army. What the young man represented, though, was far more than the sum of his actions that day, resulting in an indelible bestowal of favor rarely seen.

The story of his capture and heroic death spread instantly, a rallying cry for endurance, not merely because of his actions, but because of the way he offered his life for his country. He requested a Bible and a clergyman but was refused. He then bravely faced his executioners with these departing words: "I only regret that I have but one life to lose for my country!"

Not surprisingly, therefore, statues have been erected in his name and stamps issued in his honor and with his image. Nathan Hale remains the official "state hero" of Connecticut. But just as dramatic, symbolic favor can be rendered as the result of actions, so the converse can mark unworthy actions, such as those of the man who symbolizes treason more than any other, Benedict Arnold. Interestingly, it was Benjamin Tallmadge, Hale's college classmate, who revealed the betrayal of Arnold's 1780 intended surrender of West Point, New York to the British. His plans failed, and he defected and then fought for the enemy. As a result of these actions, Benedict Arnold, like Judas, is the by-word for betrayal and the antithesis of favor.

I. GOD DECIDED TO DESTROY ALL LIVING THINGS

The life and inspiration of the man Noah is the epitome of the understanding of divine favor in the worst of times. "And the LORD said, I will destroy man whom I have created from the face of the earth; both man, and beast and creeping thing, and the fowls of the air; for it repenteth me that I have made them" (Genesis 6:7). The sorrow and regret of man's actions are the basis of reference to God's repentance or *nakham* (Hebrew). The Lord's omniscient (all-knowing) foreknowledge did not preclude His sorrowful rejection of man's behavior and the judgment of all of creation. Noah, literally the best and loftiest of men with respect to grace-worthy behavior, represented the converse of what God's very nature deemed judgment-worthy in ancient times.

Genesis explains that the entire world was "corrupt" and "filled with violence" (Genesis 6:11–12). The first of these expressions, *corrupt*, means it was in moral and spiritual decay and thus destroyed from within. The second, *violence*, refers to the *actions of injustice* which permeated the population resulting in irreversible decadence.

» *Why do you think a world of people created by God turned its back on the Creator and turned instead to the very evil which assured the loss of God's favor and certain judgment?*

A. Wickedness on the Earth

The ultimate question of the age remains: *Why do people do good and why do people do evil?* The Bible explains the disfavor of Noah's generation by the Lord in two ways: "the wickedness of man was great in the earth" and "every imagination of the thoughts of his heart was only evil continually" (Genesis 6:5). Whatever good may have existed, it was continually subordinated to their evil natures and negated in their lives. Everything they conceived of in their minds resulted in evil purposes. It was a recipe for judgment.

Genesis attributes the *great* wickedness in the earth to the downward inclinations of the sins of the *flesh*, that is, the unbridled sinful nature: "My spirit shall not always strive with man, for that he also is flesh" (Genesis 6:3). The limited, though important, role of human conscience within the people failed miserably due to the condition of their hearts and minds. How far they had wandered from God's design and intention for humanity!

» *Do you think there is a point of no return with respect to the judgment of God? Explain.*

B. But Noah Found God's Favor

The demonstration of the mercy of the Lord is highlighted in the salvation of Noah. Neither worldwide judgment, nor its severity, can negate the goodness and love of the eternal Judge of all the earth. The divine disfavor and worldwide judgment which resulted from human sin were most certainly not divine reactions of a calloused, distant, or unconcerned bystander. Genesis is very careful to tell us not only of God's own sorrow amidst the loss, but to also emphasize how deeply "it grieved him at his heart" (Genesis 6:6). This expression in the Hebrew includes the variation in nuance of being *cut* and of being *hurt*. Some even suggest it means God's heart was broken. One thing is certain, God was not detached from them, but rather loved that wayward generation, which unfortunately valued evil and devalued the favor of the living God.

Noah stood in stark contrast to the fleshly failures of the wickedness of man before the flood. "But Noah found grace in the eyes of the Lord" (Genesis 6:8). In this verse, *grace* is from the word *khen*, translated interchangeably as *favor*. It is translated *favor* in Genesis 18:3, regarding Yahweh's appearance in the door of Abraham's tent. Abraham had just yielded to God's call by obeying the all-important command of circumcision. The faith of both Noah and Abraham was apparent in the living of their lives and, thus, demonstrable to the world. They lived in such a way as to show their faith.

II. GOD CALLED NOAH TO BUILD AN ARK

In Genesis we find that God commanded Noah to build "an ark of gopher wood" to the precise detail of divine specifications and that he was obedient (Genesis 6:14, 22). The writer of the Book of Hebrews emphasizes the *faith* aspect of this triumphant event in that Noah's entire response was that of believing God regarding "things not seen as yet" (Hebrews 11:7). The idea that catastrophe was imminent seemed like foolishness to the faithless, and the masses ignored the call of God in their generation, much as they do in modern times.

Jesus clearly links the generation of Noah and the last days. Matthew 24:37–39 says, "But as the days of Noah were, so shall also the coming of the Son of man be. For as in the days that were before the flood they were eating and drinking, marrying and giving in marriage, until the day that Noe entered into the ark, and knew not until the flood came, and took them all away; so shall also the coming of the Son of man be."

» *Imagine what it must have been like for Noah to experience a divine revelation of things that were as foreign to him as the rest of humanity. Would this have been easy to believe? Explain.*

A. He Was Ridiculed by Others

In II Peter the apostle also parallels Noah's generation with that of the last days: "Whereby the world that then was, being overflowed with water, perished" (II Peter 3:6). Though not explicit, it is not an unreasonable inference that end time mocking was being linked by Peter with an assumption of the ridiculing of Noah in Genesis. It is like an implicit echo from Noah's day revealing the heart of the end time generation: "Knowing this first, that there shall come in the last days *scoffers* walking after their own lusts" (II Peter 3:3).

Imagine how it must have been received by a people who saw a massive boat under construction on dry land and heard the preaching of Noah day after day warning of a coming judgment. Remember it was Jesus who lamented their attitude as the judgment approached. They demonstrated a sad, yet startling lack of concern. They were not bothered. They did not even have the ability of comprehending, as Jesus noted, that divine disfavor would result in their condemnation.

"And knew not until the flood came" (Matthew 24:39). Their annoyance and ridicule continued to the very moment of judgment. But then, of course, it was too late. The warning signs of judgment were meaningless to them, for their hearts were so impacted by the worst of sin that they were blind to their own need to entreat the grace of the God who designed them, the God who knew them best. (See Romans 1:20–32.)

» *What is the best way to get through to people who reject the Word of God and ridicule God's revelation regarding judgment and eternity?*

B. Noah Built the Ark by Faith

Imagine the burden carried by Noah and his family, not only being custodians of the truth of coming devastating judgment, but also having the responsibility of building the boat that would be their life-saving escape! Hebrews says Noah "moved with fear, prepared an ark to the saving of his house" and that he accomplished this amazing feat "by faith" (Hebrews 11:7). How else do four men build an ark approximately 450 feet long! They had more questions than answers. But they built it anyway. Faith is powerful.

Setting aside any discussion of the interpretation of the earth's advent of rain (Genesis 2:5–6), the world certainly had never seen anything approaching the magnitude of the judgment God revealed to Noah. Yet Noah believed God! He built the ark "to the saving of his house; by the which he condemned the world, and became heir of the righteousness which is by faith" (Hebrew 11:7). As sorrow gripped the very soul of the man of God, Noah, nonetheless, believed the Lord. He revered the revelation that the Flood—including the saving of his own family—served God's moral purposes.

III. GOD PLACED HIS FAVOR ON NOAH WHEN HE LIVED OUT HIS FAITH

Noah's righteous life engendered the favor of God which saved his entire family. The favor of the Lord, therefore, brought divine blessings. He lived out his faith—an obedient life before the Lord. First there was faith, then there was favor.

A. Noah and His Family Were Saved

The fateful, yet distinct, decree of the Lord in Genesis is repeated over and over. Judgment is the final verdict: "every thing that is in the earth shall die" (Genesis 6:17). With equal clarity God declared the righteous exception of Noah and his family. Noah found grace in the eyes of the Lord and became the spiritual exemplar of God's amazing grace.

Jesus accentuated the contrast when he said, "and the flood came, and destroyed them all" (Luke 17:27). Except for Noah's family, the entire world was lost to the judgment of the Flood. Peter twice referenced this exceptionalism of Noah in absolute terms. First, a "disobedient" world was destroyed and only a "few, that is, eight souls were saved" (I Peter 3:20). Then, Peter highlighted the extraordinary favor Noah obtained; salvation was limited to his family alone. "And [God] spared not the old world, but saved Noah the eighth person, a preacher of righteousness, bringing in the flood upon the world of the ungodly" (II Peter 2:5).

B. God Made a Covenant with Noah

All humanity was destroyed by the Flood, therefore, all mankind is included in the covenant promise of the rainbow: "neither will I again smite any more every thing living, as I have done, ... neither shall there any more be a flood to destroy the earth" (Genesis 8:21; 9:11). Therefore, with the destruction of the human family all mankind afterward necessarily descended from Noah and his family.

» *Why do you think the Lord gave the rainbow as the sign of the covenant He made?*

IV. GOD PLACES HIS FAVOR ON US WHEN WE LIVE OUT OUR FAITH

A. We Must Do What Is Good and Right

Genesis 6:9 tells us the favor bestowed upon Noah was specifically due to his relationship with God in the living out of his faith. "Noah was a just man and perfect in his generations, and Noah walked with God." His "generations" refers to Noah's peers, meaning he lived it out loud for all to see. The details of his walk with God included the essential elements of holiness and righteousness perfected in the heart by years of serving God.

The Hebrew word translated *perfect* includes being upright and holy, but also emphasizes the process. Noah had been perfected. The same word is used referring to God Himself in Deuteronomy 32:4: "He is the Rock, his work is perfect: for all his ways are judgment: a God of truth and without iniquity, just and right is he." Because he walked with God, Noah became like the Lord he loved and served!

Noah was also a just man, as all must be if they are to incur the favor of God. The word used here is *tzaddekk*, meaning righteous. (See Genesis 7:1.) The Psalmist used it in precisely the context of Genesis: "But let all those that put their trust in thee rejoice: let them ever shout for joy, because thou defendest them: let them also that love thy name be joyful in thee. For thou, Lord, wilt bless the righteous; with favor wilt thou compass him as with a shield" (Psalm 5:11–12).

B. God Is Pleased with Those Who Do What He Has Asked

Like the sacrificial actions of Nathan Hale in the early history of our nation, the biblical figure Noah in ancient times, and all the heroes of faith of Hebrews 11, blessings and favor follow when we do well and live well before God and others. God is pleased and the world around us is impacted by a life lived according to God's precepts.

The same word used of Noah's favor in Genesis is translated "grace" in Psalm 84:11. Its application remains as relevant today as in either Noah's or the Psalmist's generation. "For the Lord God is a sun and shield: the Lord will give grace and glory: no good thing will he withhold from them that walk uprightly."

⟩⟩⟩ INTERNALIZING THE MESSAGE

The favor of God is a much-desired longing in the hearts of those who know him. Heroes have impacted lives and earned the favored regard of generations, such as Nathan Hale's inspiring sacrifice. They were, nonetheless, ordinary people accomplishing extraordinary things. The heroics of a Noah, an Abraham, or an Esther do not presuppose some superhuman spiritual prowess. These men and women simply walked with God. They lived for him and pleased him. The powerful outcomes of their faith speak to us today of the enormous possibilities of faith in our own lives.

Reflecting Holiness

FOCUS THOUGHT

Because God makes us holy, we must live a life that reflects His holiness.

 FOCUS VERSES

I Peter 1:15–16

But as he which hath called you is holy, so be ye holy in all manner of conversation; Because it is written, Be ye holy; for I am holy.

 LESSON TEXT

I Peter 1:13–16

13 Wherefore gird up the loins of your mind, be sober, and hope to the end for the grace that is to be brought unto you at the revelation of Jesus Christ;

14 As obedient children, not fashioning yourselves according to the former lusts in your ignorance:

15 But as he which hath called you is holy, so be ye holy in all manner of conversation;

16 Because it is written, Be ye holy; for I am holy.

Numbers 14:1–9

1 And all the congregation lifted up their voice, and cried; and the people wept that night.

2 And all the children of Israel murmured against Moses and against Aaron: and the whole congregation said unto them, Would God that we had died in the land of Egypt! or would God we had died in this wilderness!

3 And wherefore hath the Lord brought us unto this land, to fall by the sword, that our wives and our children should be a prey? were it not better for us to return into Egypt?

4 And they said one to another, Let us make a captain, and let us return into Egypt.

5 Then Moses and Aaron fell on their faces before all the assembly of the congregation of the children of Israel.

6 And Joshua the son of Nun, and Caleb the son of Jephunneh, which were of them that searched the land, rent their clothes:

7 And they spake unto all the company of the children of Israel, saying, The land, which we passed through to search it, is an exceeding good land.

8 If the Lord delight in us, then he will bring us into this land, and give it us; a land which floweth with milk and honey.

9 Only rebel not ye against the Lord, neither fear ye the people of the land; for they are bread for us: their defence is departed from them, and the Lord is with us: fear them not.

⟫⟫ CULTURE CONNECTION

HACKED OR HOLY?

Don't know who to blame for technological frustrations these days? Blame the Russian hackers. While hackers from the Eastern hemisphere might be a standing joke, the reality of Russian interference in creating fake websites and hacking into various elements of information technology in various countries has been no laughing matter. Governments do what they please if it is in their own best interests it seems—perhaps spies from other countries also use similar methods.

Being a victim of hacking leaves one with an unsettled feeling. We want to be able to trust others better—to feel secure and untampered with. On a different level and in a different way, this is why rape and molestation are so abhorrent to humans. Our own body is our personal space—no one should invade that. Thus, everyone has a natural instinct for holiness. While government hackers tap away at keyboards, another concern is more present in citizens' minds: home invasion.

The body of the believer is devoted to the Lord. The enemy should not be allowed to hack into the files (mind and heart) or vandalize the house (use it for his liking). Apostolics should be more defensive of their bodies and minds than Americans are of their government's elections and websites. Only God should be authorized to inhabit and make changes in His temple.

⟫⟫ OUTLINE

I. GOD DELIVERED ISRAEL OUT OF EGYPT

II. JESUS SAVED US FROM OUR SIN

III. THE LORD CALLS US TO BE HOLY IN EVERY AREA OF OUR LIVES

⟫⟫ CONTEMPLATING THE TOPIC

After over four-hundred years of slavery, they were free. Pharaoh gave the order to let them go and let them be. Perhaps on the march out of Egypt, one of the Israelites thought back to a bedtime story his grandfather told him about a very distant grandfather named Abraham who had lived hundreds of years earlier. God promised Abraham, "Lift your eyes now and look from the place where you are—northward, southward, eastward, and westward; for all the land which you see I give to you and your descendants forever. And I will make your descendants as the dust of the earth; so that if a man could number the dust of the earth, then your descendants also could be numbered. Arise, walk in the land through its length and its width, for I give it to you" (Genesis 13:14–17, NKJV).

For those who still held out hope while baking bricks under Egypt's blazing sun, they knew they would not be slaves forever. God had prepared a land He had promised Abraham and his descendants, and God performed on that very promise the night Israel walked free out of Egypt. And as Moses and the nation soon realized, the greatest threat to return to Egypt was not from without: it was from within.

I. GOD DELIVERED ISRAEL OUT OF EGYPT

The Book of Exodus is written like a highlight reel. Some of God's most memorable miracles are recorded in Exodus. He plagued Egypt with ten plagues, parted the Red Sea for His people to pass, drowned the Egyptian army in the Red Sea, and inscribed ten commandments on tables of stone with His own finger. God clearly fought for Israel and against nations who fought against them because He wanted to bring Israel safely to the Promised Land.

Their journey from the Red Sea to the Jordan River was filled with victories great and small, leading them to a great land that flowed with milk and honey. Once they made it to the bank of the Jordan River, they could see the land in the distance. But they could not see the land well enough to know if it was safe to cross.

Moses sent twelve spies on a reconnaissance mission. The children of Israel waited anxiously to learn what the twelve spies discovered about their new home. After forty days all twelve spies returned. Israel waited with bated breath to hear their report. Ten who came back were shaken. Their faces were as white as a sheet; their knees were knocking. Numbers 13 reads they brought back an "evil" (slanderous) report. They talked only about giants guarding walled cities.

The other two spies were different. They were upbeat and optimistic. They excitedly showed the people grapes so large it took two men just to carry one cluster. Joshua and Caleb were ready to cross the Jordan and start life in the Promised Land. But when Israel took their vote, they voted to believe the report of the ten and refuse the report of the two. Even after all the miracles they had witnessed with their own eyes, and after waiting forty days for the report to come back, Israel decided to stay right where they were already camped.

» *If you had been Joshua or Caleb, how would you have tried to persuade Israel of victory? Why?*

Numbers 14 tells a tearful tale of a fearful people:

And all the congregation lifted up their voice, and cried; and the people wept that night. And all the children of Israel murmured against Moses and against Aaron: and the whole congregation said unto them, Would God that we had died in the land of Egypt! or would God we had died in this wilderness! And wherefore hath the Lord brought us unto this land, to fall by the sword, that our wives and our children should be a prey? were it not better for us to return into Egypt? And they said one to another, Let us make a captain, and let us return into Egypt. Then Moses and Aaron fell on their faces before all the assembly of the congregation of the children of Israel. And Joshua the son of Nun, and Caleb the son of Jephunneh, which were of them that searched the land, rent their clothes: and they spake unto all the company of the children of Israel, saying, The land, which we passed through to search it, is an exceeding good land. If the Lord delight in us, then he will bring us into this land, and give it us; a land which floweth with milk and honey. Only rebel not ye against the Lord, neither fear ye the people of the land; for they are bread for us: their defence is departed from them, and the Lord is with us: fear them not. (Numbers 14:1–9)

They were enslaved in fear between the land from which God delivered them and the land where God was taking them. They decided they would rather live in the wilderness on bread and water than move into the Promised Land and have to trust God to fight battles they could not win without Him. Worse yet, some even tried to turn the nation against their leaders and choose another leader who would lead them right back to bondage; right back to Egypt.

Because we live over three thousand years after Moses, we have the luxury of sitting in the film room and commenting on Israel's performance on the field. We saw what they saw, but they did not see what we see, at least not yet. They did not know how God was going to fell the giants and the walled cities. We often malign Israel for their lack of faith—and perhaps it is warranted—but many of us have done the same thing in our journey out of sin.

» **How would you describe your journey of faith and spiritual growth? What are some obstacles you have faced?**

II. JESUS SAVED US FROM OUR SIN

Jesus has saved all of us from sin. Even if you grew up in an Apostolic church and your first word was "revival," Jesus saved you from sin. If you grew up on the streets and spent most of your life in the bars and behind bars, Jesus saved you from sin. Jesus did not just save us from low self-esteem or a subpar lifestyle; He saved us from sin. And He did not just save us so we would have a more comfortable life; He saved us so we would have eternal life.

Salvation may be free to us, but it cost Jesus His life. He wrote the rules. He could have written the rules of redemption cheaply. To redeem us, He could have given thirty pieces of silver. That would have been fair since that is the price Judas valued Jesus. Judas sold Jesus to the men who wanted Jesus dead. But that price would not cost Jesus anything. God could mine silver from every silver mine and redeem every man, woman, boy, and girl if He wanted. But it would not cost Him anything.

Rather, the apostle Peter knew how expensive salvation was to Jesus when he wrote:

Knowing that you were not redeemed with corruptible things, like silver or gold, from your aimless conduct received by tradition from your fathers, but with the precious blood of Christ, as of a lamb without blemish and without spot. (I Peter 1:18–19, NKJV)

Jesus valued our soul higher than His own life. He died for us so we could live free from the prison of sin. Yet, like the nation of Israel—with their toes touching the cool river water of the Jordan—we have been known to think about going back to the very sin from which He saved us. Salvation is certainly free, but Jesus calls us to take up our cross daily and follow Him if we want to be His disciple (Matthew 16:24).

» **What does it mean to daily take up your cross?**

For years, Jen tried to keep it together, but her drug addiction was tearing her family apart. She had been born again as a young girl, but she was losing her faith to addiction. Some Sundays she showed signs of promise. She was worshiping, praying, even responding to the preached Word. Clearly the Spirit was winning this war. But the next week she was in trouble again, stealing from people she loved and people she did not even know, just to feed her addiction.

The judge in her city showed her mercy time and time again, but he could show no more mercy. Jen went to prison for years. She missed birthday parties and Christmas mornings and even one of her children's graduation. But during those years, God was reaching for her and she reached for God. She repented and gave her life back to God in prison. Ironically, she was more free in prison than when she had been out of prison.

The inmates and correctional officers saw a change in her and so did her family. When she was released, she was a different woman than when she had been sentenced. She was better. She was free. The church was happy to have her back. Her husband and children were happy to have her back. All of Heaven was happy to have her back. She was in the prayer room before service. Her worship was ablaze. She was transformed.

Jen was as faithful to church as the sun is to shine, but she missed one Sunday. Maybe she was working or sick or out of town. There was no cause to press the panic button because she missed one Sunday. Then she missed another and another and another. Soon she was leaving home at odd hours and coming home different. She had all the signs of addiction, but no one wanted to believe she had fallen back into that same trap.

Time told the tale. After being set free more than once from drugs and even from prison, Jen fell back into addiction. That addiction cost her another graduation and eventually, custody of her own children. No one around her understood how she could return to a lifestyle that had robbed so much from her, but we can say the same for Israel after leaving Egypt. How could anyone suggest they return to Egypt after they were slaves for hundreds of years? It is possible to forget the sorrow sin brings after we have been set free. We tend to romanticize the "good ole days." Do not fall for that trap. The enemy of our soul was never kind, is not kind, and will never be kind to us. He steals, kills, and destroys, but our God came to our world to give us life more abundantly.

Jesus taught us we cannot serve two masters. We will hate one and love the other (Matthew 6:24). Israel was given the choice to serve a Pharaoh bent on destroying them and their children or trusting God enough to serve Him to deliver them and their children. We too will serve a master determined to destroy us and our children or God who desires to deliver us and our children. We will not serve two masters, neither will we serve no master. Everyone will serve someone.

» *What can we as a church do for people who are enslaved to sin?*

III. THE LORD CALLS US TO BE HOLY IN EVERY AREA OF OUR LIVES

Moses and Aaron could not believe their eyes or ears. They knew the miracles God had just worked in plain sight for them. As they looked around at the people they loved, they saw despair on each face. God had defeated the most feared army in the then known world without Israel swinging one sword, but His own people did not trust Him to defeat the smaller armies of smaller cities.

Some of the would-be leaders were inciting panic. That is when Moses and Aaron fell on their faces before the entire nation of Israel. They were broken before the people. Israel was still wobbling as a newborn nation. Although they had celebrated hundreds of years as a nation, over four-hundred years of slavery stunted their growth. They were as unsteady as a toddler taking her first steps.

Joshua and Caleb ripped their clothes in despair. These men had spent over a month on the other side of the river. They had seen the walled cities and giants. They had something to say that Israel needed to hear:

The land, which we passed through to search it, is an exceeding good land. If the Lord delight in us, then he will bring us into this land, and give it us; a land which floweth with milk and honey. Only rebel not ye against the Lord, neither fear ye the people of the land; for they are bread for us: their defence is departed from them, and the Lord is with us: fear them not. (Numbers 14:7–9)

But their rally cry fell on deaf ears. The people starting clamoring to stone them. They wanted to kill the leaders, elect another leader, and return to Egypt. God had enough. Suddenly the glory of the Lord appeared in the tent of meeting in the sight of all the children of Israel. That was enough to stop all conversations about stoning and returning. God spoke with Moses and promised all the rebels who failed to trust God would wander in the wilderness until they all died. But not Joshua and Caleb. God rewarded them for their faith when the rest of the people were filled with doubt.

Our fight is not with a neighboring nation or a superpower wanting to enslave us. Our fight is with a more sinister foe: our fight is with sin. Since our fight is with sin, our goal is holiness. Our goal is to be like the one who fights for us. We are to be holy as He is holy. Holiness flows into every area of our lives. Holiness calls us to honesty when we would rather be dishonest. Holiness calls us to integrity when our resolve is weak and we think nobody will ever find out. Holiness calls us to humility when we would rather boast and brag about who we are rather than whose we are. Holiness calls us to speak in a way that glorifies God and edifies others. Any other speech that brings a reproach on God or brings others down has no place in the conversation of a Christian.

Holiness calls us to be careful of what we listen to and what we watch. Holiness determines our entertainment choices, and if our entertainment choices push us farther from God, they do not need to be our entertainment choices. Holiness calls us to respect our bodies as the temple of God's own Spirit, keeping our body clear of drugs or alcohol that could do irreversible harm to our body, our family, and our testimony.

Holiness calls us to dress modestly in a way that draws attention to God and not to ourselves. Even if the world around us does not value modesty and the purity it preserves, modesty is still beautiful in the eyes of God. Modesty helps us to be good stewards of our bodies and of our finances. Modesty is not concerned with the latest fashion or societal craze.

» *How can we best instill values of modesty and purity in the younger generation?*

⟫⟫ INTERNALIZING THE MESSAGE

We are not like God because we talk right, listen to the right music, wear the right clothes, and avoid drugs and alcohol. We have those disciplines and convictions because we want to be more like Jesus and heed the scriptural call to be holy as He is holy (I Peter 1:16). Jesus died for us to deliver us from sin, the very least we should do is live for Him. And by the grace and power of God, we must choose to live free from sin.

If you are struggling with wanting to return to sin because you are disappointed or disillusioned with God, take a lesson from a people who learned the hard way. Israel forgot the horrors of being enslaved to Egypt after they had been set free. It is possible for us to forget the horrors of being enslaved to sin after we have been set free. But what will keep us grateful for our freedom and wanting to be more like our God will be the time we spend with Him. We will see Him as He is and we will see sin as it is. Then we will see clearly to choose to live for Him, to love Him—to be like Him.

A Chosen Generation

FOCUS THOUGHT

As a chosen generation, we must share our testimony with the world.

 FOCUS VERSE

I Peter 2:9

But ye are a chosen generation, a royal priesthood, an holy nation, a peculiar people; that ye should shew forth the praises of him who hath called you out of darkness into his marvellous light.

 LESSON TEXT

I Peter 2:9–10

9 But ye are a chosen generation, a royal priesthood, an holy nation, a peculiar people; that ye should shew forth the praises of him who hath called you out of darkness into his marvellous light;

10 Which in time past were not a people, but are now the people of God: which had not obtained mercy, but now have obtained mercy.

Acts 13:44–49

44 And the next sabbath day came almost the whole city together to hear the word of God.

45 But when the Jews saw the multitudes, they were filled with envy, and spake against those things which were spoken by Paul, contradicting and blaspheming.

46 Then Paul and Barnabas waxed bold, and said, It was necessary that the word of God should first have been spoken to you: but seeing ye put it from you, and judge yourselves unworthy of everlasting life, lo, we turn to the Gentiles.

47 For so hath the Lord commanded us, saying, I have set thee to be a light of the Gentiles, that thou shouldest be for salvation unto the ends of the earth.

48 And when the Gentiles heard this, they were glad, and glorified the word of the Lord: and as many as were ordained to eternal life believed.

49 And the word of the Lord was published throughout all the region.

CULTURE CONNECTION

CHOSEN FOR WHAT?

"The millennial generation is all about being part of a greater purpose," writes Ahmad Raza in his article "Why a Purpose-Driven Mission is Key to Motivating Millennials" (December 12, 2016 at entrepreneur.com). According to recent research, 84% of young workers say it is more important to make a difference than to achieve professional recognition. Nine out of ten believe something more than profits should measure the value of a business.

The young adult generation has no problem with the biblical idea of being a "chosen generation." However, the millennial generation (those born after 1984) "dislikes bureaucracy and distrusts traditional hierarchies," says Raza. Young believers need to see more than institutions and traditions to remain a part of the church. This in-born sense of purpose and focus is answered best in the kingdom of God, if those leading can see clearly enough to help the younger ones see.

Karl Moore writes, "Millennials need direction and meaning, an interesting mixture of altruism and self-interest." They want to work at places that have a greater purpose than just making money. Their employers score big points if they fund an orphanage, make clean water in Africa, or rehome abandoned dogs ("Purpose, Not Paycheck" October 2, 2014 at forbes.com). They hate the dichotomy of such things as making a good income but never being available for one's own family or donating to a church that has a high-paid staff but makes no effort to help the local community.

A chosen generation knows their God-given meaning in life.

OUTLINE

I. SAUL WAS CHOSEN
   A. The New Birth
   B. As Newborn Babes We Are to Grow Up in Him

II. WE HAVE BEEN CHOSEN

III. WE HAVE BEEN TRANSFORMED TO BE A TESTIMONY TO OTHERS

CONTEMPLATING THE TOPIC

With every breath and heartbeat, Saul made it his mission to put an end to the Christians and the gospel they loved.

Saul tried to force many to recant Christ. He cost many Christians their lives. As he pulled them out of the safety of their homes into the dangers of the streets, mobs would often gather, take up stones, take the law into their own hands, and take the lives of Christians. Most of the time, Saul carted the Christians off to jail to be tried, and if they were found guilty of being a follower of Jesus, they were killed. Saul's hands were stained with the blood of just men and just women who were just following Jesus. But he was not finished. He gathered some intel that many of the Christians had fled for their lives one hundred miles away in Damascus. Murderous Saul had fire in his eyes and arrest warrants in his pocket, ready to bring Christians all the way back to Jerusalem to be tried and executed.

I. SAUL WAS CHOSEN

But on his murderous ride, God had enough of this zealot's misdirected zeal. God shone a light from Heaven so bright it knocked Saul from his horse to his knees. When he blinked and rubbed his eyes, he realized he was blind. Then he heard a voice from Heaven that asked, "Saul, Saul, why are you persecuting Me?" Saul was stunned. "Who are You, Lord?" And the Lord replied, "I am Jesus, whom you are persecuting."

When Saul realized he was fighting against the very One he should have been fighting for, he was frightened. Saul was Saul; Jesus was God. Fighting against God was like trying to shoo off a tornado with a baseball bat. He could not fight because he could not see. As far as he knew, he was as good as dead. But God was not thinking judgment; He was thinking mercy. Saul was not about to hear a lecture; he was about to hear the gospel.

From that road, his friends led a blinded, humbled terrorist into Damascus. Nobody in town knew God had been reaching for Saul, they just knew Saul was in town and they were in danger. But God was in control and He gave a Christian man named Ananias a vision to go to Saul and pray for him. When Ananias the hunted saw Saul the hunter, he called him "Brother Saul." And for the first time in his life, Saul felt grace because Saul heard the gospel: the gospel that the blood of Jesus was strong enough to forgive his past and the Spirit of God was able to fill his soul. Saul received his sight and the gift of the Holy Ghost.

Ananias then baptized him in the name of the very one Saul used to persecute: the name of Jesus Christ. God then used Saul to preach the very gospel he used to persecute because the gospel had the power to change even him. Saul was born with a zeal for Judaism, but he was born again with a zeal for Jesus Christ.

» *How can our lives be a testimony and an inspiration to others who do not know Jesus Christ?*

A. The New Birth

That is the power of the new birth. It is the power to change us from enemies of Jesus Christ to followers of Jesus Christ. Jesus clearly defined the new birth in John 3:3–5:

> *Jesus answered and said unto him, Verily, verily, I say unto thee, Except a man be born again, he cannot see the kingdom of God. Nicodemus saith unto him, How can a man be born when he is old? can he enter the second time into his mother's womb, and be born? Jesus answered, Verily, verily, I say unto thee, Except a man be born of water and of the Spirit, he cannot enter into the kingdom of God. (John 3:3–5)*

As we see throughout the New Testament, new birth brings water and Spirit baptism together into one conversion experience. Once we have repented of our sins, we are water baptized in the name of Jesus Christ for the remission of our sins. Then we receive the gift of His Holy Spirit. We find this pattern all throughout the book of Acts as men and women from all ages, backgrounds, races, and religions were born again. Their new birth changed them from the inside out.

While we may celebrate a child's birth by bringing balloons and sending cards to the brand-new parents, we all understand birth is only the beginning. That baby boy or girl is only beginning the growth process of becoming a man or woman respectively. The same is true with our new birth. We celebrate when someone is baptized in water in Jesus' name and baptized in the Spirit, and we rightly should. There is rejoicing in the presence of all the angels over one sinner who repents (Luke 15:10), but that brand-new baby boy or girl in God is just beginning to grow up into a mature man or woman in God. We are to grow up in Jesus once we have been born again.

» *What are some signs of spiritual growth in an individual's life?*

B. As Newborn Babes We Are to Grow Up in Him

Peter wrote in I Peter 2:2, "As newborn babes, desire the sincere milk of the word, that ye may grow thereby." We grow spiritually much like we grow physically—we eat. At first, we eat the milk of the Word. We hear and read the basics of the Bible. We learn some of the basic Bible stories like Noah and his ark, David and Goliath, and Daniel in the den of lions. The writer of Hebrews gave us a list of some Bible basics in Hebrews 6: faith, repentance from sin, water baptism, Spirit baptism, the resurrection, and judgment. Those are some of the Bible basics we learn when we are first born again.

But just as babies graduate from milk to meat as they grow older, so do we. We long for more to satisfy our soul and we learn about justification, redemption, propitiation, and sanctification. We feast on some Old Testament fare such as the Tabernacle, the priesthood, and the history of the nations of Israel and Judah. We seek and we see the deeper principles of God and we feed our souls. We seek a close relationship with God by building a prayer life outside our Sunday services. We grow up in Jesus by learning to walk with Jesus.

If you walk out the door each day without taking time to walk with God, you are not growing as you should. Each of us should have a place at home where we spend time with God in prayer. Turn the phone to airplane mode and spend uninterrupted time with God each day. He invites us to walk with Him and grow in Him. We ought to desire to accept His gracious invitation and spend time with Him. We need to feed ourselves on the Word of God throughout the week, not just on the weekend. Open up the Bible in a version you understand and your pastor recommends so you can learn more about God and His Word on your own. Before long, you will begin to take steps spiritually you were not taking earlier.

II. WE HAVE BEEN CHOSEN

All of us have room to grow in God. Even if you were raised in church and your first word was "revival," you have room to grow in God. But we do not grow in God just so we can tower over others spiritually. We grow in God so we can be a spiritual blessing to others. I Peter 2:9 reads, "But ye are a chosen generation, a royal priesthood, an holy nation, a peculiar people; that ye should shew forth the praises of him who hath called you out of darkness into his marvellous light."

We could pass a microphone around the room and hear testimonies of transformation from every one of us. God has called us out of darkness into His marvelous light for a purpose: that we should show forth His praises. When God saved Saul, He already knew what Saul would be and what he would do. God did not save Saul just for Saul; He saved him for others. Those others knew Saul's story. They witnessed him serve arrest warrants and death sentences to Christians of all ages. But when he began to preach the gospel he had once used to persecute, people paid attention.

Many who heard Saul's preaching were skeptical at first. The Bible tells us many doubted Saul was truly transformed. But there were also many who believed because they too had been transformed by the power of God. We may not have the same history as Saul, but we come from a life of sin just like he did, and God has transformed us. The others on the factory floor remember what you used to be and used to do, but they have seen a change in you. The other students in your dorm remember how you grew up and the parties you used to attend, but now they see you with a Bible and a smile and wonder what happened to you.

That is what happened to John and Ray. These two young men lived five minutes apart, but they were worlds apart. They grew up together, went to the same elementary, junior high, and senior high school together. During high school, John came to church at Ray's invitation, was baptized in Jesus' name, and filled with the Holy Ghost. Ray was thrilled but curious. He wanted to know what caused John to want to know about God. The two could not have been more different. John was into dirt bikes and Megadeth; Ray was into Steven Curtis Chapman and MarioKart.

For a few years, John worked as a screener for TSA and in his spare time, earned his blackbelt in one of the martial arts. Ray was the waterboy for the high school football team one season. He asked John what had attracted him to God since they were so different. John told him, "I pretty much did whatever I wanted. I listened to what I wanted. I hung out with anyone I wanted. I lived however I wanted. But no matter how much I had and how much I did, I was miserable. I woke up and hated everything I saw. I remember a time right after my grandfather died that I was in the dumps. But I saw you one day in school. Ray, you did not seem like anything ever got you down. You were different from all the others because your life offered me hope. Basically, I walked in darkness. I tried to navigate life in darkness. I stumbled in darkness. But in the middle of the darkness, I saw light. A ray of hope. You had something I did not have but wanted. I had more money and more muscles than you, but you had hope and I didn't."

» *Are you serving God because someone shared their testimony with you? Explain.*

III. WE HAVE BEEN TRANSFORMED TO BE A TESTIMONY TO OTHERS

We have been chosen by God, not just for us, but for others. We have been chosen by God to show forth His praises and share our testimony with the rest of the world. Our testimony is the same as Saul's: God called us out of darkness into His marvelous light. This week share your testimony with someone. Let them know what God has done for you and from where He has brought you. God has blessed us too richly to keep the blessing to ourselves.

Paul understood this because God gave him strict instructions to be a light to the Gentiles. This was foreign to his Orthodox Jewish mind. He did not want to associate with the Gentiles because they were not God's chosen people. They were not from the seed of Abraham. They could not trace their lineage back to one of the original twelve tribes of Israel, yet God still loved them and chose Paul to preach the gospel to them.

Paul's modus operandi was to preach to the Jews in the synagogue first, then preach to the Gentiles. However, the Jews were not happy with Paul preaching the same life-changing gospel message to the Gentiles he had just preached to them. They were upset and began arguing with Paul and Barnabas. Acts 13 does not tell us they disbelieved what Paul was preaching, but that because they were jealous of the Gentiles, they argued with Paul and Barnabas. Their jealousy grew quickly and wildly, causing Paul and Barnabas to leave for Iconium to preach the gospel there.

The Jews forgot the promise God made to Abram in Genesis 12, "I will make you a great nation; I will bless you and make your name great; and you shall be a blessing. I will bless those who bless you, and I will curse him who curses you; and in you all the families of the earth shall be blessed" (NKJV). God chose Abram, blessed Abram, and changed Abram to Abraham so he would be the father of the Jews and a blessing to the Gentiles. The Jews in Paul's day wanted to keep the message to themselves, but it is for them, their children, and all that are afar off, even as many as the Lord our God shall call (Acts 2:39).

» *What are some reasons we should not keep the message of truth to ourselves?*

▶▶▶ INTERNALIZING THE MESSAGE

We must remember God has changed us, chosen us, and called us out of darkness so we can be a light to the world around us. We must not be jealous when we have to park farther back in the parking lot because more people are coming to hear the gospel. We must not be envious when we walk into the sanctuary to find a family has already taken our seat. And we must not be upset when our pastor spends more time with new families to teach them Bible studies and is not able to spend as much time with us.

We must remember what it was like when we were first being born again. We must rejoice with those who are being born again and be there to help them in their discipleship journey just like our brothers and sisters were there to help us. We must remember we are changed, chosen, and called to be a light to people who walk in darkness so one day those who used to walk in darkness will also be a light to others.

Subject to One Another

FOCUS THOUGHT

Because Jesus served others, we are called to serve one another.

 FOCUS VERSE

I Peter 5:5

Likewise, ye younger, submit yourselves unto the elder. Yea, all of you be subject one to another, and be clothed with humility: for God resisteth the proud, and giveth grace to the humble.

 LESSON TEXT

I Peter 5:1–6

1 The elders which are among you I exhort, who am also an elder, and a witness of the sufferings of Christ, and also a partaker of the glory that shall be revealed:

2 Feed the flock of God which is among you, taking the oversight thereof, not by constraint, but willingly; not for filthy lucre, but of a ready mind;

3 Neither as being lords over God's heritage, but being examples to the flock.

4 And when the chief Shepherd shall appear, ye shall receive a crown of glory that fadeth not away.

5 Likewise, ye younger, submit yourselves unto the elder. Yea, all of you be subject one to another, and be clothed with humility: for God resisteth the proud, and giveth grace to the humble.

6 Humble yourselves therefore under the mighty hand of God, that he may exalt you in due time.

John 13:12–17

12 So after he had washed their feet, and had taken his garments, and was set down again, he said unto them, Know ye what I have done to you?

13 Ye call me Master and Lord: and ye say well; for so I am.

14 If I then, your Lord and Master, have washed your feet; ye also ought to wash one another's feet.

15 For I have given you an example, that ye should do as I have done to you.

16 Verily, verily, I say unto you, The servant is not greater than his lord; neither he that is sent greater than he that sent him.

17 If ye know these things, happy are ye if ye do them.

CULTURE CONNECTION

CLEANSING A DIFFERENT KIND OF DIRTY

Almost five children die every day from abuse. Americans filed over 7.4 million reports of child abuse in 2016 (*Child Maltreatment 2016* acf.hhs.gov). The dirt clinging to people today is even harder to wash than the filth on the feet of the disciples. Through us, Jesus Christ wants to wash the sin, shame, and hurts that a murky world creates.

Many deaths of neglected and abused children can be prevented. In most counties there are not enough family service workers to address the needs of so many children growing up in homes filled with addiction, sexual exploitation, mental illness, or selfish parents. Studies have shown that many deaths and abuse cases could be prevented only by volunteers. There is not enough funding to hire the staff needed to intervene in so many broken homes. However, there are enough neighbors who can be involved with children and families a few hours each week.

Who would be better to send into a hurting home than a believer who knows Jesus and is filled with His love and heart of service?

- The three-year-old whose single-mother needs someone to watch her daughter while she catches up on lost sleep between work and college.
- The foster child who is trying to find his way and adjust to life away from those who harmed him.
- The teenager who just is not lovable, but needs love so desperately from someone who has no ulterior motive.

Servanthood will change a dirty world.

▶▶▶ OUTLINE

I. JESUS TOOK ON THE ROLE OF A SERVANT
   A. Washed His Disciples' Feet
   B. Modeled Humility and Love
   C. We Are to Follow His Example

II. GOD WANTS US TO BE HUMBLE AND LOVE ONE ANOTHER
   A. Submit to One Another
   B. When We Humble Ourselves, He Will Lift Us Up

▶▶▶ CONTEMPLATING THE TOPIC

The New Testament calls believers to a life of service. Jesus explained that, in His Kingdom, the highest position one could possibly attain would be that of a servant (Matthew 20:27). He then became the ultimate model of servanthood, laying down His life to secure eternal salvation for all humanity. The apostle Paul later referred to himself and Timothy as "servants of Jesus Christ" (Philippians 1:1). Even a demon-possessed girl recognized that Christians were "servants of the most high God" (Acts 16:17).

Spirit-filled believers imitate Jesus' example by serving others. That service is not always appreciated by those they serve. Like our Lord, sometimes service involves suffering. (See Isaiah 52–53). But Paul assures us, "If we suffer, we shall also reign with him" (II Timothy 2:12).

The dinner bell truly reveals our appreciation for service. According to the Bureau for Labor Statistics, the average American household spent $3,008 eating out in 2015. (It's doubtful that number has decreased in the intervening years.) Blogger John Schmoll of FrugalRules.com shared the story of one family who spent a staggering $30,000 at restaurants over the course of a year.

Why are people willing to drop so much hard-earned money at their favorite dining establishments? Because someone else prepares the food, brings it to the table, refills the drinks, and then cleans up the mess when they leave. They are not buying a meal; they are paying for service.

I. JESUS TOOK ON THE ROLE OF A SERVANT

As in so many areas of life, Jesus calls His followers to walk a different path. (There is nothing wrong with visiting a restaurant after church, of course.) He outlined His life's mission by stating, "The Son of Man did not come to be served, but to serve" (Matthew 20:28, NKJV). And He certainly did. From the opening of His ministry until He ascended into Heaven, Jesus spent His days serving others.

Even His miracles were acts of service. When newlyweds ran out of wine at their wedding feast, Jesus came through with a special delivery (John 2:1–11). Whether He was healing the sick, calling the dead back to life, calming a storm, or providing a meal for a multitude, Jesus' miracles all were done in service to others.

The Lord saved one of His greatest illustrations of servanthood for the final week of His life. He assembled His disciples for one last meal together, and, when supper was finished, proceeded to teach them a lesson they never would forget.

A. Washed His Disciples' Feet

Any discussion of what happened next must begin with consideration of Jesus' identity. Before He was born, an angel appeared to Mary, His mother-to-be, and told her she would give birth to a boy who would "be great, and shall be called the Son of the Highest: and the Lord God shall give unto him the throne of his father David" (Luke 1:32). Her child would be a king—the King of Kings Who would sit on an eternal throne.

This makes Jesus' actions on this night even more astounding: the "Son of the Highest" prepared to wash the feet of the assembled guests, a task usually required of the lowest slave. The *IVP New Testament Commentary* cites a Jewish text which observes that washing feet was "something a Gentile slave could be required to do, but not a Jewish slave." While there may have been instances where one Jew might perform this task for a superior, Jesus clearly was the highest-ranking member of the group. He was their Rabbi, their Master. For Him to wash the disciples' feet was culturally unthinkable.

But John made it clear that Jesus was not having an identity crisis. He understood that "the Father had given all things into his hands, and that he was come from God, and went to God" (John 13:3). Because He understood His identity and purpose, He was comfortable fulfilling the role of the lowest servant. He knew that stooping to wash dusty feet did not diminish His eternal authority. He had nothing to prove.

Quoting the early church father Augustine, the *IVP New Testament Commentary* states, "The one into whose hands the Father had given all now takes his disciples' feet into his hands to wash them." The God Who created man from the dust of the earth began washing the dust from His disciple's feet.

» ***Why is the idea of washing someone's feet not something people like to consider?***

B. Modeled Humility and Love

In washing His disciple's feet, Jesus was demonstrating that they served a God who was willing to descend to the lowest levels to meet their most basic needs. God was not a distant deity who did not care about their daily challenges. He could calm the wind and the waves when necessary, but He also cared about more mundane matters. In Jesus Christ, God was willing to wrap Himself in a towel and wipe road grime from a traveler's feet.

Jesus revealed this even more clearly in succeeding chapters as He endured the shame and humility of the Cross. Washing feet was merely the introduction to a lesson that unfolded over the following days. At the Cross, God washed the sins of the world from the souls of men with His own blood.

Jesus' followers were stunned by their Master's actions. They did not fully comprehend His identity and mission, but they did grasp this was an unacceptable reversal of roles. Simon Peter even raised his voice in protest.

C. We Are to Follow His Example

Perhaps the reason Peter and his fellow disciples were so horrified by Jesus' actions is that it raised a very uncomfortable question: if washing feet was an acceptable task for the Master, what did that mean for His followers?

The disciples always had been preoccupied with position. They became embroiled in a dispute after the mother of James and John lobbied to have her sons elevated to a place of status in Jesus' Kingdom. The other disciples were angry because they secretly hoped to secure the same positions themselves. This prompted Jesus to explain that His Kingdom did not operate like worldly dominions (Matthew 20:20–28). On another occasion, Jesus warned His followers not to seek out the prominent seats at banquets, adding, "whosoever exalteth himself shall be abased; and he that humbleth himself shall be exalted" (Luke 14:11). Jesus wouldn't have offered this kind of advice if His audience had not needed it.

The disciples always seemed to have something to prove. Sometimes they were outwardly boastful—particularly Peter—while inwardly they appear to have wrestled with insecurity. They constantly jockeyed for position. Stooping to serve was out of the question. Their feet were coated with dust, but their spirit was contaminated with pride.

It is easy for present-day believers to fall into the same trap. We compare ourselves against others, trying desperately to stay a step ahead. We even may entertain the thought that certain tasks or roles are beneath us. We become frustrated when others secure positions of prominence, especially if we feel saddled with less glamorous responsibilities. We ask, "Why were they chosen instead of me? Why did they get that opportunity, while I was passed over?"

» *Why do you think insecurity makes it difficult to serve others?*

Paul addressed these attitudes in his letter to the Philippians, urging "Let nothing be done through strife or vainglory (selfish ambition or vain conceit, NIV); but in lowliness of mind let each esteem other better than themselves" (Philippians 2:3). In contrast, he challenged us to adopt the mindset of Jesus (Philippians 2:7–8).

True service is only possible when we possess genuine humility, and humility is only possible if we have a proper view of who we are in relationship to God. When we are secure in the knowledge that we are a child of the King, we will not feel threatened when we are called on to serve Him in humble circumstances. We know our seemingly humble role or task does not mean God loves us less than someone else who may, for the moment, serve in a place of greater prominence.

» *How does a proper understanding of our relationship to God empower us to serve others?*

II. GOD WANTS US TO BE HUMBLE AND LOVE ONE ANOTHER

Jesus knew the lesson He was sharing with His disciples that night would take time to digest. He even told Peter, "What I am doing you do not understand now, but you will know after this" (John 13:7, NKJV). Peter apparently spent time pondering Jesus' lessons on humility and servanthood, because he later shared them with the readers of his first epistle. (Do not be discouraged if it takes a while to learn some lessons!) He exhorted them to "be clothed with humility" (I Peter 5:5).

Some commentators suggest Peter was referring back to the night when Jesus "laid aside his garments; and took a towel, and girded himself" (John 13:4) for the purpose of washing the disciples' feet. (See Robertson's *Word Pictures of the New Testament*, for example.) Jesus was not merely putting on the garments of a servant; He was clothing Himself with a servant's attitude, which included humility. Peter was urging his fellow believers to adopt this same spirit of humility.

Peter also was implying that true humility will motivate us to voluntary submission. Submission may be an even less popular topic for modern readers than humility and servanthood, but it is a critical concept for Christians to grasp.

A. Submit to One Another

Peter began by urging the "younger" to "submit yourselves unto the elder." He then added, "Yea, all of you be subject one to another" (I Peter 5:5).

The English word *subject* is a translation of a Greek word which means, "a voluntary attitude of giving in, cooperating, assuming responsibility, and carrying a burden" (*Thayer and Smith Greek Lexicon*). Peter was telling his readers that submission is putting the needs and desires of others—especially the needs and desires of the church, the body of Christ—ahead of their own. It means choosing to cooperate with the team, even when the team's decision inconveniences us or contradicts personal desires.

True biblical submission is not the weak cowering before the powerful and mighty. Submission is not one person browbeating or manipulating another into conforming to their demands. Biblical submission occurs when one person voluntarily surrenders their rights, power, and privilege to serve another—even another who does not possess the same level of power or authority.

Jesus was the picture of perfect submission. He voluntarily chose to go to the Cross. He did not want to suffer and die, but He prayed, "Nevertheless not my will, but thine, be done" (Luke 22:42). On the night of His arrest, He observed that "twelve legions of angels" were at His disposal if He wished to order them into action (Matthew 26:53). But the angels stayed silent as Jesus submitted to the will of the Father. He was not dragged, kicking and screaming, to His death. He voluntarily surrendered His life for the sake of others.

Jesus demonstrated that the root of true biblical submission is not fear or manipulation: it is love. Jesus girded Himself in a towel and washed His disciples' feet because He loved them. "Having loved his own who were in the world," John wrote, "he loved them to the end" (13:1, NKJV). Because He loved them, He wanted to serve them.

When a believer is motivated by love, submission and service to others no longer feels burdensome. In fact, it can even become a delight.

» **How does love motivate true biblical submission?**

B. When We Humble Ourselves, He Will Lift Us Up

When Peter stressed the importance of humility (I Peter 5:5), he used the same Greek word, *tapeinophrosune*, that Paul used in Philippians 2:3 when he urged believers to, "in lowliness of mind...esteem other better than themselves." These two apostles wanted us to understand that humility causes us to rank the needs of others ahead of our own needs.

The only power than can cause this sort of mental shift is love. Nothing inspires humility like love. Paul said love "seeketh not her own" (I Corinthians 13:5). True love causes us to put others first.

A mother does not have to be prompted to spend hours caring for a sick child. She willingly stays at their bedside throughout the night, with little or no complaint. Why? Because she loves her child. No sacrifice is too great for love.

81

The husband or father rises early and voluntarily heads off to work each day because he loves his family. He may not enjoy his job, or find it particularly fulfilling, but that does not matter: he has submitted his own desires to the good of the people he loves. He humbles himself, serving them in love.

Jesus stressed the importance of our love for each other, telling His disciples, "A new command I give you: Love one another. As I have loved you, so you must love one another. By this everyone will know that you are my disciples, if you love one another" (John 13:34–35, NIV). The only way everyone will know believers love one another is if their humble acts of service demonstrate this love.

When Christians operate in love, they do not need to be begged, browbeat, or manipulated before they will serve others or God's Kingdom. They humbly and willingly put the needs of the Kingdom and the needs of others ahead of their own. Instead of loving to be served, they serve in love. They are not desperately trying to promote themselves or secure a position of honor. They know they are in the "mighty hand of God," and that, if they humbly wait on and serve Him, He will "exalt (them) in due time" (I Peter 5:6).

» *How can you serve someone this week?*

▶▶▶ INTERNALIZING THE MESSAGE

Remember object lessons? An object lesson involved someone using an ordinary object to share a Biblical lesson. Object lessons have fallen out of fashion in recent years, but they once were a popular part of many youth services. Jesus used a servant's towel to give His disciples an object lesson in service, humility, love, and submission.

But just witnessing Jesus' demonstration of these ideas was not enough. Jesus concluded His lesson by adding, "If ye know these things, happy are ye if ye do them" (John 13:17).

It is impossible to understand the power and joy of servanthood merely by hearing someone talk about the concept. Frankly, topics like "submission" and "humility" are not appealing. Most people do not get excited about sermons on these subjects. They would rather hear preaching and teaching about faith, healing, or deliverance.

It is difficult to grasp the power of servanthood until it is put it into action. Talking about it does not make a difference. It takes more than head knowledge. But when a person humbles themselves, submits to Jesus Christ and His Body, and serves others, they unlock power that cannot be found anywhere else. It uncorks a fountain of joy—the joy that comes from serving.

For I have given you an example, that ye should do as I have done to you. (John 13:15)

Faithful to God

FOCUS THOUGHT

As the world becomes more wicked, we must stand strong in our faith.

 FOCUS VERSE

Jude 1:3

Beloved, when I gave all diligence to write unto you of the common salvation, it was needful for me to write unto you, and exhort you that ye should earnestly contend for the faith which was once delivered unto the saints.

 LESSON TEXT

Genesis 5:21–24

21 And Enoch lived sixty and five years, and begat Methuselah:

22 And Enoch walked with God after he begat Methuselah three hundred years, and begat sons and daughters:

23 And all the days of Enoch were three hundred sixty and five years:

24 And Enoch walked with God: and he was not; for God took him.

Hebrews 11:5

5 By faith Enoch was translated that he should not see death; and was not found, because God had translated him: for before his translation he had this testimony, that he pleased God.

Jude 1:3–4, 14–15

3 Beloved, when I gave all diligence to write unto you of the common salvation, it was needful for me to write unto you, and exhort you that ye should earnestly contend for the faith which was once delivered unto the saints.

4 For there are certain men crept in unawares, who were before of old ordained to this condemnation, ungodly men, turning the grace of our God into lasciviousness, and denying the only Lord God, and our Lord Jesus Christ.

. . . . .

14 And Enoch also, the seventh from Adam, prophesied of these, saying, Behold, the Lord cometh with ten thousands of his saints,

15 To execute judgment upon all, and to convince all that are ungodly among them of all their ungodly deeds which they have ungodly committed, and of all their hard speeches which ungodly sinners have spoken against him.

CULTURE CONNECTION

THE AUTHOR OF OUR FAITH

William Sydney Porter was born in Greensboro, North Carolina, on September 11, 1862. In the early 1890's, Porter was employed as a teller and bookkeeper at the First National Bank in Austin, Texas. Regrettably, funds were unaccounted for during that time, and Porter was charged, convicted of embezzlement, and sentenced to five years in prison.

Though he had begun writing previously, he honed his skill greatly during his incarceration. Thinking that his current status might limit his publishing options somewhat, he selected a pen name of O. Henry. Under that pseudonym he became one of America's most prolific authors of the short story, at one point producing one a week for over a year.

His particular style incorporated one unique literary device. He was the master of the "twist" ending. Just when the readers thought they could anticipate where the plot line would proceed and how the characters would act, O. Henry would jar them with a totally unforeseen and unexpected development. The joy of reading his works was found largely in the last few lines when his mastery would be demonstrated.

In similar fashion, God has demonstrated His mastery over all in the final pages and lines of His written Word as well. There we can find the unfolded plan that He had in mind from the beginning. Unlike a work of O. Henry where reading the end first can spoil the pleasure, reading the end of God's book only enhances our joy on the journey! Small wonder that Jesus is called the Author of our faith!

OUTLINE

I. ENOCH WAS FATHFUL TO GOD

    A. He Prophesied to the Unfaithful

    B. He Contended for the Faith

    C. He Was Translated and Did Not
       Experience Death

**II. GOD WANTS US TO STAND STRONG IN
    OUR FAITH**

    A. We Must Contend for the Faith

    B. We Must Seek to Please God

CONTEMPLATING THE TOPIC

President Theodore Roosevelt lauded the virtues of faithfulness and perseverance during a May 7, 1903 address in San Bernardino, California. His comments apply to the Christian life as well.

Roosevelt reminded his audience of their pioneer heritage and the grit their predecessors displayed. "Remember that the chance to do the great heroic work may or may not come," he said. "If it does not come, then all that there can be to our credit is the faithful performance of every-day duty."

"If the time for the showing of heroism does come," he added, "you may guarantee that those who show it are most likely to be the people who have done their duty in average times as the occasion for doing the duty arose."

Our world emphasizes flashiness. Western culture celebrates talent, usually with little or no regard for character. God, on the other hand, rewards faithfulness. Flashiness may catch the attention of the masses and generate fifteen minutes of fame, but faithfulness catches God's eye. And while the world's favor quickly fades, the benefits of faithfulness are eternal.

I. ENOCH WAS FATHFUL TO GOD

Enoch is first introduced to us in "the book of the generations of Adam." (See Genesis 5:1.) Moses, the author of Genesis, offered minimal detail about Enoch's life. Enoch's story spans a mere seven verses (Genesis 5:18–24) and takes up just 97 words in the King James Version. More information is provided about Enoch's ancestors and offspring than his activities.

Interestingly, Genesis also does not record any words Enoch spoke. (We must wait until we reach the Book of Jude before learning what Enoch said.) But Genesis does offer insight into the sort of man Enoch was. Twice in seven verses, Moses observed that "Enoch walked with God" (Genesis 5:22, 24).

When all is said and done, our walk says far more than our words ever can express.

Enoch's walk with God was more than a casual stroll. He "walked with God after he begat Methuselah three hundred years, and begat sons and daughters" (Genesis 5:22). If Enoch had any inclination to abandon the path of righteousness, there undoubtedly were plenty of opportunities to do so. But Enoch was faithful through three centuries of the joys, sorrows, trials, travails, and triumphs that every life and family encounters.

Through it all, there was one constant: Enoch walked with God.

A. He Prophesied to the Unfaithful

The New Testament does offer a few details about Enoch's life that are not mentioned in the Old Testament account. When Jude warned the readers of his epistle about the dangers presented by false teachers, he hearkened back to Enoch for an example of how to confront ungodliness.

Jude cited a prophesy recorded in the Book of Enoch, an apocryphal work whose authorship is traditionally attributed to its namesake. Jude recorded Enoch as declaring, "Behold, the Lord cometh with ten thousands of his saints, to execute judgment upon all" (Jude 14–15).

Enoch's message had two elements: "the Lord cometh" (verse 14); and He will "execute judgment upon all" (verse 15). These words of warning echo throughout the Scriptures, including the New Testament.

Jesus Himself described the time of His return in similar language when He told the parable of the sheep and the goats (Matthew 25:31–46). He spoke of a day "when the Son of man shall come in his glory, and all the holy angels with him" (verse 31). Jesus explained He would sit on a throne of judgement, proclaiming rewards to those who had been faithful and pronouncing eternal punishment on those who had not.

Enoch lived may years before Jesus walked the earth, but this Old Testament patriarch clearly was attuned to the tenor of the end times. Like Paul, he understood the preaching of Christ's return is welcome news to those who believe and faithfully walk with God. (See I Thessalonians 4:18.)

But, as Enoch alluded, these are frightening words for unbelievers. For them, Christ's return will mark the beginning of their ultimate judgment. It will be a time of such terror that the wicked will beg the rocks to fall and crush them so they do not have to face "the wrath of the Lamb" (Revelation 6:16).

Nearly two thousand years have passed since Jude wrote his epistle, and much more time has elapsed since Enoch prophesied, but the contemporary church's mission remains identical to theirs. We also are called to preach the soon return of Christ and His impending judgment on an unbelieving world.

> *How should the knowledge of Christ's return and coming judgment affect our daily lives?*

B. He Contended for the Faith

Jude's urged his readers, both ancient and modern, to "earnestly contend for the faith which was once delivered to the saints" (Jude 3). Simon J. Kistemaker, author of the *New Testament Commentary* on this epistle, explains that, "The New Testament concept to *contend* is familiar to (Jude's) readers. In brief, it means to exert oneself without distraction to attain a goal." Kistemaker adds that, for Jude, the goal was to spread the true gospel and defeat heresy.

Jude introduced Enoch to his readers as someone who had successfully faced similar challenges. Enoch had not been afraid to verbally confront deception with truth. But while Enoch defended the faith with his words, he also promoted truth in another, equally important manner: his walk of faith served as a witness against his unbelieving contemporaries.

Enoch lived at a time when the world was descending into darkness. It would not be long before God would express His sorrow over humanity's sins and vow to start over through Noah's family. But while the world was hurtling towards judgment, "Enoch walked with God" (Genesis 5:22, 24). He did not allow himself to be dragged down by a degenerating culture. He remained faithful.

While it is important that we defend truth with our words, it is even more important to model it with our walk. Truth can never truly be defeated as long as someone, somewhere is faithfully living it out. The "Battle Hymn of the Republic," a popular nineteenth century patriotic song written by Julia Ward Howe, declares in verse that, "His truth is marching on." Truth does indeed march on, wearing the boots of faithful men and women who proclaim it in their everyday actions.

> *Who do you know of who successfully "contended for the faith" in a previous generation and has influenced you to do so in the present?*

C. He Was Translated and Did Not Experience Death

Genesis concludes its brief account of Enoch's life by describing his unusual exit from the earth: "And Enoch walked with God: and he was not; for God took him" (Genesis 5:24).

Moses offered scant detail about the nature of Enoch's departure, but the writer of Hebrews shed a bit of light on the subject. "By faith Enoch was translated that he should not see death," Hebrews 11:5 says, adding, "God had translated him." The theme of Hebrews 11 is, of course, faith, and the writer noted that Enoch's faith in God is what caused him to be "translated that he should not see death."

While we do not know exactly what happened, or how, we do know Enoch did not die a natural death. Hebrews uses the word *translated* (from the Greek *metatithemi*), which means "to transfer" or "to change." This word also carries the meaning of "to go or pass over."

In all of Scripture, only the prophet Elijah experienced a similar exit. (Jesus died before He rose again and ascended into Heaven.) But Paul promised that, at a future point in time, all believers who are alive on the earth will experience a similar transformation (I Corinthians 15:51–52).

» *How does being a Christian change your perception of death?*

II. GOD WANTS US TO STAND STRONG IN OUR FAITH

Our faith in God gives us hope that our end will be like Enoch's. But in the meantime, present-day Christians have something else in common with this ancient patriarch. We live in a fallen world that seems to slip a little farther every day. Jesus compared the world of Enoch's time ("the days before the flood") with the way things would be when He returned. (See Matthew 24:36–44.) Like Enoch, we are surrounded by wickedness. God's people feel His impending judgment looming over the horizon.

The believers in Corinth also lived in a wicked culture, so the apostle Paul encouraged them to, "Watch, stand fast in the faith, be brave, be strong" (I Corinthians 16:13, NKJV). Enoch did not have the benefit of Paul's encouragement, but he did "stand fast in the faith," and so can we. Enoch's life offers a roadmap that can help guide us to a successful end on our journey of faith.

A. We Must Contend for the Faith

As previously mentioned, Enoch contended for the faith during his lifetime. We also recognize that Jude's exhortation to "earnestly contend for the faith which was once delivered unto the saints" (Jude 3) applies to us, too.

But how do we imitate Enoch and fulfill Jude's command?

First, we can defend the faith with our words. If truth is going to be heard, it is up to us to speak it. This was the agenda of the early church. "They went forth, and preached every where" (Mark 16:20). Even their enemies confessed, "ye have filled Jerusalem with your doctrine" (Acts 5:28).

Peter urged us to, "be ready always to give an answer to every man that asketh you a reason of the hope that is in you with meekness and fear" (I Peter 3:15). If we are prepared, God will give us opportunities to share the message of truth with hungry hearts.

Sometimes it may feel that truth is at a disadvantage, especially when we consider the resources available to those who spread falsehood. But we must remember God is backing us up. We have the power of the Holy Ghost (Acts 1:8), the Gifts of the Spirit (I Corinthians 12, 14), and miraculous signs and wonders at our disposal (Mark 16:15–20). Truth always has prevailed, and it always will. Even when its preachers have been imprisoned and executed, the message of truth has slipped past the bars (II Timothy 2:9) and continued changing lives.

Preaching the truth is important, but nothing speaks louder than our lives. The most convincing argument for the veracity of the gospel is the transformed lives of believers. Peter told his readers that, in addition to being ready to defend their faith with words, they should make sure their conduct is "honorable among the Gentiles, that when they speak against you as evildoers, they may, by your good works which they observe, glorify God in the day of visitation." (I Peter 2:12, NKJV).

There is some debate as to what Peter meant by, "the day he visits us." "Some say that the phrase *the day he visits us* refers to the last day of this age when God judges everyone" (Simon J. Kistemaker, *New Testament Commentary*, *I Peter*). This interpretation is reflected in the New Living Translation's rendering of these words as, "they will give honor to God when he judges the world."

Two things are clear: our walk of faith serves as a witness to unbelievers in the present, and it will stand as a witness against them in judgment. Our hope and prayer are that our words and the witness of our faithful lives will convince them to obey the gospel before it is too late.

God has left us in this world to contend for the faith. With His help (and God certainly is helping us), we can remain faithful to our calling, just as Enoch was faithful to his.

» *What does it mean to "contend for the faith"?*

B. We Must Seek to Please God

Hebrews 11:5 offers perhaps the greatest commendation of Enoch's life. In explaining why Enoch was translated, the author of Hebrews said, "he had this testimony, that he pleased God."

As previously mentioned, the Bible does not give us many details regarding Enoch's life. There is no indication that he gave an astronomical offering, preached prestigious conferences, or founded an educational institution. There is no record that he built hospitals or orphanages or dug wells in rural villages on another continent. All that is said of him is that he "walked with God" (Genesis 5:22, 24).

Nothing pleases God more than people who faithfully walk with Him. We may never accomplish anything that impresses the world, but that will be alright, provided that our faithfulness pleases God.

Enoch was faithful when others were not. Enoch was faithful as the world around him grew increasingly wicked. Enoch faithfully walked with God, even when judgment waited in the wings.

If Enoch could walk with God under these circumstances, we can walk with God in our present age. And if we walk with God, we will have the same testimony he had: we "pleased God."

» *Why do you think faithfulness pleases God more than talent or accomplishments?*

▶▶▶ INTERNALIZING THE MESSAGE

Ask any leader which quality they appreciate most in a follower, and faithfulness probably will be near the top of their list. Talented people who are inconsistent and unreliable usually end up being replaced by someone who understands the importance of faithfulness.

Author Ryan Holiday highlights how faithfulness in small matters contributed to the ascendency of U.S. President James Garfield. In *The Obstacle Is the Way*, Holiday writes that Garfield "paid his way through college in 1851 by persuading his school, the Western Reserve Eclectic Institute, to let him be the janitor in exchange for tuition. He did the job every day smiling and without a hint of shame. Each morning, he'd ring the university's bell tower to start the classes—his day already having long begun— and stomp to class with cheer and eagerness." It was not long before Garfield had been promoted to professor, and, by age 26, he was the dean of the school.

Eventually, Garfield would be elected to lead the nation. Faithful adherence to daily duties helped take him from sweeping floors to living in the White House.

As Christians, our goal is not to live in a President's Mansion or a King's Palace, but we are striving for a heavenly home, where we will live eternally with Enoch and the rest of the faithful saints. The good news is the goal is within reach of anyone who is willing to be faithful.

Our faithfulness on this earth sends a message to the world around us. Our daily walk of faith is an important element of our witness. Every day that we faithfully walk with God, we are successfully contending for the faith in a wicked world.

As Theodore Roosevelt said, "all that there can be to our credit is the faithful performance of every-day duty." So stand strong, even when others are not. Be faithful. It matters more than we will ever understand in this life.

A Call to Persevere

FOCUS THOUGHT

When we feel pressure from the world to let go of our faith, we must instead choose to persevere to the end.

 FOCUS VERSES

Jude 1:20–21

But ye, beloved, building up yourselves on your most holy faith, praying in the Holy Ghost, Keep yourselves in the love of God, looking for the mercy of our Lord Jesus Christ unto eternal life.

 LESSON TEXT

Jude 1:17–24

17 But, beloved, remember ye the words which were spoken before of the apostles of our Lord Jesus Christ;

18 How that they told you there should be mockers in the last time, who should walk after their own ungodly lusts.

19 These be they who separate themselves, sensual, having not the Spirit.

20 But ye, beloved, building up yourselves on your most holy faith, praying in the Holy Ghost,

21 Keep yourselves in the love of God, looking for the mercy of our Lord Jesus Christ unto eternal life.

22 And of some have compassion, making a difference:

23 And others save with fear, pulling them out of the fire; hating even the garment spotted by the flesh.

24 Now unto him that is able to keep you from falling, and to present you faultless before the presence of his glory with exceeding joy.

⟩⟩⟩ CULTURE CONNECTION

LIQUIDITY IN THE WORLD MARKET

The Great Britain Pound faced ups and downs as talks about such things as Brexit hit the ears of world investors. A nation's money depends on its economy and other factors around the world. If the Pound is in trouble, investors might convert their money to Euros. If the Aussie Dollar hits a tailspin, the value of the Japanese Yen might rise in response. These ebb-and-flow changes in a country's coinage might be why we call it "currency" and describe financial markets with words such as "liquidity."

Some assets are more fluid than others. A person who owns a durable good such as grain, brick, wool, ore, or logs does not have a "liquid" asset. One must first find someone to buy those goods with money or trade for another good the supplier is in need of. Cash is a very liquid asset. At times, however, cash itself has been of no value when a government or economy fell apart. In such times, investors run to a timeless asset: gold. This yellow metal has maintained value throughout earth's history and can still be trusted to be liquid enough for a buyer to exchange it for cash, goods, or services as needed.

In the Kingdom, our "liquid asset" is the Spirit. Spirit-filled people access faith, love, joy, patience, self-control, humility, mercy, and many more "goods and services" in the Kingdom. Those without the Spirit are living bankrupt lives. Children of the King find that this "eternal gold" spends well anywhere.

⟩⟩⟩ OUTLINE

I. REMEMBER WHAT YOU HAVE BEEN TAUGHT

II. BUILD YOURSELF UP IN THE HOLY GHOST

III. KEEP YOURSELF IN THE LOVE OF GOD

IV. PERSEVERE TO THE END

⟩⟩⟩ CONTEMPLATING THE TOPIC

Persevere is a verb meaning, "to persist in anything undertaken; maintain a purpose in spite of difficulty, obstacles, or discouragement; continue steadfastly." Simply put, when we persevere, we refuse to give up.

Letting go and giving up is the temptation everyone faces when reaching the difficult stage of any project or endeavor. For this reason many give up when they get tired and the going gets tough.

Every music teacher can tell you many students give up after a short time especially if they are attempting to learn to play the piano. Learning to play the piano requires a lot more time and practice than most students realize. Practicing a musical instrument is not only strenuous, it is monotonous and unexciting. Playing the same piece over and over until it is mastered is nerve wracking.

Perseverance is required, not only to become a proficient musician, it is required to be proficient in any other area. Perseverance is the key to living a victorious life in Christ. "He that shall endure unto the end, the same shall be saved" (Matthew 24:13).

I. REMEMBER WHAT YOU HAVE BEEN TAUGHT

As believers, we have been taught the Christian principles that were designed to sustain us spiritually. Remembering these during duress will bolster our courage and help us to continue. Previous biblical lessons act as constant reminders of our direction and destiny. Long after our teachers are silent and the books are closed, lessons they taught live on in our memory. Often we hear their words echoing off the walls of the past.

As previous flight instruction has helped many beleaguered pilots to know what to do, previous Christian training and instruction have guided many believers through the turbulent pockets of wind when the foggy runway was nowhere in sight.

"Train up a child in the way he should go: and when he is old, he will not depart from it" (Proverbs 22:6). Training is the laying down of a track. Proper training provides, not only a way to proceed, but the right direction in which to proceed. A child may get off track momentarily, but as long as the track is there, he has something to return to. He may depart from the track, but the track will never depart from him. It is always there.

We all have problems with retaining what we read and study. But with practice we can improve our retention skill. Review and repetition are companions to retention. Going over past lessons can help anchor their truths in our minds. Meditation is also a great help for remembering. Whether we review past lessons literally or mentally, we keep them from gradually escaping our memory.

According to specialists in the area of the brain and memory, the brain retains everything it has ever received. Why then do we not remember everything? The problem is recall. Remembering has everything to do with recall. If we cannot remember something, it is because we cannot recall it. The information is there, but we cannot extract it from the memory bank. Evidence of this phenomenon often occurs when some incident, aroma, sound, or word causes us to remember something we thought we had forgotten. Sometimes even a song provides a backdrop for an experience long forgotten. It seems each note paints a vivid picture of a faded scene we thought was lost.

Remembrance and perseverance have a unique relationship with the three divisions of time; past, present, and future. What we have learned is obviously in the past. To remember is to call to the present something learned in the past. By remembering in the present the lessons of the past, we are encouraged to face the future.

What we as believers have been taught acts as a foundation upon which we build as we live this Christian life. The proper foundation provides stability to everything built thereon. If we have been taught right, our chances of surviving spiritually are much greater, especially if we will remember what we have been taught. A faulty foundation creates a condition of instability in everything built thereon and eventually will be the cause of the building failing.

We may not know the weakness of our structure until the storm comes. In the *Parable of the Two Foundations* in Matthew 7, both houses, the one built on the rock and the one built on the sand, remained intact until the rain descended, the floods came, and the winds blew. It was then that the house on the rock stood firm and the house on the sand fell (Matthew 7:24–27). Paul added, "If any man's work abide which he hath built thereupon, he shall receive a reward" (I Corinthians 3:14). This reward and the prize Paul referred to in I Corinthians 9:24 are the same. They represent what Jesus said in Revelation 2:10, "Be thou faithful unto death, and I will give thee a crown of life."

» *How can memory help a person persevere?*

II. BUILD YOURSELF UP IN THE HOLY GHOST

As body builders frequent the gym regularly to develop their physical bodies, soul builders frequent the church, the altar, and the Word regularly to develop their spiritual bodies. As a kid, this writer ordered a Charles Atlas course. He could identify with the scrawny picture of the young man in the advertisement. But he was enticed by the muscular form of the man who allegedly had benefited from such a course, for in the magazine advertisement they showed the before and after of the man. If you could see the writer today, you would probably say he wasted his time and money on the course. But he did learn something about dynamic tension, and it did help his self-esteem.

How do we build up ourselves in the Holy Ghost? This question can be answered by considering how physical things are built up. Recently there was a catastrophic flood in the writer's area. After much devastation, many low-lying properties had to be built up. One such area lies close to this writer's way to church. He has watched as acres have been gradually built up by truck after truck load of dirt being deposited in the low areas. One load dumped in a small area represents little improvement. But after hundreds and perhaps thousands of loads the area is noticeably higher.

This is the way believers build up themselves in the Holy Ghost. It is little by little. After one meal we cannot tell our child has grown. But after many meals, we notice a remarkable difference. Perhaps there is no noticeable growth after one church service, but after many services others can notice a difference in our growth.

Although there are illegal chemicals that can enhance a body builder's physique, the legal and healthy way to fitness is a regular regimen of exercise and strength training. May we as believers learn something from this. To build up ourselves in the Holy Ghost we must submit to a regular routine of spiritual things that are designed to bring us to maturity and full development as a Christian.

We are all conscious of how we look. Hours annually are spent in front of the mirror. Billions are spent annually on materials to apply to the skin to enhance beauty. But what would be people's response if they could look into God's mirror and see themselves as they really are? If they could, more time and money would be spent in the effort to improve their spiritual image.

The challenge to build ourselves up in the Holy Ghost reveals that when we receive the Holy Ghost, we are not at the point of completion but at the point of beginning. When a young teenage boy receives a body-building course in the mail, it does not mean he has the physique now that he may have after the course's application.

The Holy Ghost is the Comforter; one called alongside to help. We understand scripturally that this helper is Jesus. When He comes into our lives, we have something that will develop us spiritually, if we will let it. For example, we have the potential of the fruit of the Spirit in our lives at the inception of the Holy Ghost. But there must be a development of this fruit. We have love, for the Scripture says, "The fruit of the Spirit is love" (Galatians 5:22), but that fruit is in its embryonic stage. It is a seed that must develop into a tree. The more we love the more developed and strong our love becomes.

» *How can we develop our spiritual bodies like we develop our physical bodies?*

III. KEEP YOURSELF IN THE LOVE OF GOD

These seven words—Keep Yourself in the Love of God—especially the preposition "in," seem to establish the love of God as a place. If it is a place, it is an area we enter and reside in. It can also be thought of as a relationship entered through the portal of the Holy Ghost. For Paul said, "The love of God is shed abroad in our hearts by the Holy Ghost" (Romans 5:5). As a believer, once we arrive at the place and in the relationship, we must do everything we can to remain there; to make that our domicile.

Note that this seven-word injection is in the form of an imperative sentence. The "you" is implied. Simply, the word is commanding: you keep yourself. No one else is going to keep you there. "Work out your own salvation with fear and trembling" (Philippians 2:12). We are all answerable to God for our actions. No one else can be blamed for our lack of proper response to this injunction.

The love of God is a dimension that is higher than any relationship established by doctrine. Response to doctrine is cerebral. Response to the love of God is visceral. Simply, our mind sorts through the confusion of ideas and settles on an understanding of doctrine. Our heart responds to that doctrine and establishes a relationship with the God of that doctrine as we obey Him.

» *Discuss the difference between the mind and the heart.*

Although the Word says, "Take heed unto thyself, and unto the doctrine; continue in them: for in doing this thou shalt both save thyself, and them that hear thee" (I Timothy 4:16), Jesus said, "By this shall all men know that ye are my disciples, if ye have love one to another" (John 13:35). I Peter 4:8 says, "And above all things have fervent charity among yourselves."

Calvinism teaches that once we are in the love of God, it is not possible to ever lose that relationship. This doctrine teaches that once a person is saved, they cannot be unsaved or lost. If this were true, there would be no need to persevere. Once saved, a believer could relax and never again be concerned about being lost. Simply, once on the track that leads to Heaven, there could never be a chance of derailment. This doctrine nullifies the validity of verses like, "If ye do these things, ye shall never fall" (II Peter 1:10), and "Now unto him who is able to keep you from falling" (Jude 1:24). The term keep would have never been used if there was no need to keep. Our spiritual security is in Christ, but it is conditional. If eternal security were personally unconditional, it would be impossible to backslide or even blaspheme the Holy Ghost.

> *In what ways can we keep ourselves in the love of God?*

IV. PERSEVERE TO THE END

The highway is a better metaphor than a railroad track to explain our journey with the Lord. The verse, "From which some having swerved have turned aside unto vain jangling" (I Timothy 1:6), would not make sense if we could not leave the track. Jesus said, "I am the way" (John 14:6). The Greek term translated way means road. When we begin our journey with the Lord, we join the traffic on the road, not the trains on the track.

Although salvation begins in its embryonic stage when a person comes to the Lord, it is a process. It is not complete until the end of the process. For this reason the Word says, "He that shall endure unto that end, the same shall be saved" (Matthew 24:13). "Receiving the end of your faith, even the salvation of your souls" (I Peter 1:9). And, "We are not of them who draw back unto perdition, but of them that believe to the saving of the soul" (Hebrews 10:39). Simply, we are not saved until we persevere to the end. Salvation is a journey that must be completed to enjoy its ultimate reward.

If a person is eastbound on Interstate 70 in St. Louis, Missouri, headed for Columbus, Ohio, he is still in Missouri even though he may turn around and head westbound toward Denver, Colorado. Because he is headed toward Columbus does not mean he is in Columbus. Repentance is a turning around on the road of life. "There is a way that seemeth right unto man, but the end thereof are the ways of death" (Proverbs 14:12). A person on the road to hell who turns around and heads toward Heaven in the opposite direction has repented. Because he is on the road to Heaven does not mean that he is in Heaven. He who is in St. Louis, Missouri, headed for Columbus, Ohio, and turns around and heads toward Colorado is still in St. Louis. But he that shall keep traveling westward on Interstate 70 toward Colorado shall be in Colorado if he does not change directions.

John Stephen Akwari, a Tanzanian, who represented Tanzania in the marathon at the 1968 Summer Olympics, dislocated his right knee and injured his shoulder when he was involved in a pile-up with other athletes nearing the halfway point of the race. Although he was advised to drop out of the race, he pressed on. Most everyone had left the stadium when he finally limped over the finish line. When Akwari was asked why he persevered, he said, "My country did not send me 5,000 miles to start the race. They sent me to finish the race."

Enduring to the end is the believers' goal. Paul said, "Know ye not that they which run in a race run all, but one receiveth the prize? So run, that ye may obtain" (I Corinthians 9:24). It is the prize at the end of the race that we seek. Eternal life will be worth all the struggle.

» *What does it mean to persevere in living for the Lord?*

▶▶▶ INTERNALIZING THE MESSAGE

Many years ago a common laborer in a distant state received a letter from his father-in-law telling of a rich ore strike in his area. The laborer excitedly made his way to his father-in-law's domicile and began to make serious plans to dig. The ore was so shallow that it was possible to dig with a shovel to mine it. He and his friend dug and dug, but found no ore. After days of disappointment he decided to give up and return home. A few days after he returned home he received a letter from his father-in-law stating that another man began to dig in the same hole and made a rich strike within a few inches.

How often do we give up when we are so close to our answer? Is it possible to give up when we are as close as one praise from the promise? Israel gave up at Kadesh-barnea which was on the border of the land promised to them by the Lord. As a result, they wandered for 40 years before coming that close again. It was not until all the older people had died that God led the young people into their promised land.

Legend has it that when Christopher Columbus was asked by his mariners, "What are you going to do when you are not sure where you are and whether you have enough supplies to continue?" Columbus allegedly is said to have replied, "Sail on and on and on." Let us say with Columbus, as well as with Paul, "We are not of them who draw back . . . but of them that believe to the saving of the soul" (Hebrews 10:39).

SPRING 2020

The Living Word
SERIES

Sharing His Mission

LESSON
MANUAL

Lesson Manual

© 2019 Pentecostal Publishing House • 36 Research Park Court • Weldon Spring, MO 63304
www.pentecostalpublishing.com • All rights reserved.
Manufactured in USA, March 2020, 1932011

EDITORIAL STAFF
Editor in Chief: Robin Johnston
Associate Editor, Curriculum: Lee Ann Alexander
Word Aflame Adult Editor: Jonathan McClintock

WRITERS
James Littles
Ron Wofford
Daniel Koren
Gayla Baughman

Jarrid Younkin
John Moore
Dorsey Burk
L J Harry

CONTENTS

SHARING HIS MISSION

by Jonathan McClintock

The role *mission* plays in an organization is crucial to that organization's success. William Craig, writing for Forbes.com, suggested that "high-performance organizations are linked to being mission-driven companies" ("The Importance of Having a Mission-Driven Company"). In fact, he found that a worker who actually buys into and is driven to do his work based on the company's mission, more than a paycheck, is more likely to invest in the company for the long haul and is 30 percent more likely to grow into a "high performer." In other words, the most successful workers are those who find themselves motivated more by the mission than they are by the money.

In the church this concept also holds true. Individuals who are motivated by the mission rather than the benefits of living for Jesus Christ are more satisfied in their walk with God, live with more joy, and rarely waffle on their level of commitment.

The mission of Jesus Christ was summed up in one verse, Luke 19:10: "For the Son of man is come to seek and to save that which was lost." Everything Jesus did revolved around this one purpose. God came and manifested Himself in flesh for the sole purpose of reconciling the world back into relationship with Him. And this was the mission for which He trained His disciples during His three years of ministry.

While standing on the mount, Jesus declared to His followers, "Go ye into all the world, and preach the gospel to every creature" (Mark 16:15). Jesus told them the message of the gospel was what would save the lost and build the church. And for His followers to build His church, they would have to buy in to the mission.

As disciples of Jesus Christ, our motivation must be found in the mission, not the many benefits promised in His Word. Yes, blessings will come and His promises are sure, but commitment to the mission is the most important call every believer has received.

LESSON MANUAL

This Lesson Manual has been developed with the goal of providing teachers numerous options to assist in preparation and delivery of each lesson.

In each lesson you will find a Focus Thought, Focus Verse, and Lesson Text that lay a foundation and give direction for the material that is to be presented. Questions are dispersed throughout the body of each lesson to provoke thought and spark discussion. We urge teachers to use these questions as a means of helping students apply each portion of the lesson.

> » *How does God being "all knowing" bring you comfort?*

STUDENT WORKBOOK

The Student Workbook has been organized in such a way that students are given the tools to not only follow the major points of each lesson but will also have a tool to further their personal discipleship and devotion throughout the week.

1. The Focus Thought, Focus Verse, and Culture Connection have been included in the Student Workbook.
2. The Lesson Outline has also been included to give the student a template to follow as the lesson is being taught. In addition, certain parts of the outline correspond with the daily discipleship prompts in the Approach section. This is designed to show what part of the lesson corresponds to the particular day's lesson text and application questions.
3. The Approach section is designed to give the student daily discipleship prompts by including portions of the lesson and application questions. The flexibility of this section allows for the student to follow along and interact during class, to become familiar with the lesson content before class, or to spend time in review during the week following class.
4. The Ask and Apply questions are presented for the purpose of helping the student contemplate the truths of Scripture and the content of the lesson. The first of the questions in each set is taken directly from the Lesson Manual, while the second question in each set is an additional prompt designed to help the student apply what is being taught.

POWERPOINTS

To access your FREE PowerPoints visit: Pentecostalpublishing.com/wappt

God with Us

FOCUS THOUGHT

God manifested Himself in flesh to be with us.

 FOCUS VERSE

Matthew 1:23

Behold, a virgin shall be with child, and shall bring forth a son, and they shall call his name Emmanuel, which being interpreted is, God with us.

 LESSON TEXT

Matthew 1:18–23

18 Now the birth of Jesus Christ was on this wise: When as his mother Mary was espoused to Joseph, before they came together, she was found with child of the Holy Ghost.

19 Then Joseph her husband, being a just man, and not willing to make her a publick example, was minded to put her away privily.

20 But while he thought on these things, behold, the angel of the Lord appeared unto him in a dream, saying, Joseph, thou son of David, fear not to take unto thee Mary thy wife: for that which is conceived in her is of the Holy Ghost.

21 And she shall bring forth a son, and thou shalt call his name JESUS: for he shall save his people from their sins.

22 Now all this was done, that it might be fulfilled which was spoken of the Lord by the prophet, saying,

23 Behold, a virgin shall be with child, and shall bring forth a son, and they shall call his name Emmanuel, which being interpreted is, God with us.

Isaiah 7:14

14 Therefore the Lord himself shall give you a sign; Behold, a virgin shall conceive, and bear a son, and shall call his name Immanuel.

ON FRONTIER'S FRONT LINES

In 2010, three major airline companies were in the middle of merging, so the chief executive officer (CEO) of Frontier Airlines made a bold move before the merger. He disguised himself as a Frontier employee to see what it felt like to be a Frontier employee. Bryan Bedford left the comfort and security of his executive office and worked on the front lines of Frontier Airlines. One of his first jobs was emptying the lavatory after a flight. Bedford got his hands dirty—quite literally.

Everyone thought he was just a fledgling flight attendant. They did not know the CEO of their company had come to work alongside them. When he finally explained who he was and why he was there, they were amazed that their CEO would step down from his lofty office to be with them. We applaud executives who want to better their employees by becoming a rank-and-file employee themselves, but how amazing that we worship a God who wanted to save us by becoming one of us.

God did not just leave the safety of a corner office and personal parking space; He left the safety of Heaven and the angelic chorus of "holy, holy, holy" for the dangers of Earth and a murderous mob's cry of "crucify." He came because He wanted to be near us, with us, even within us. Of all the names whereby we know God, one of the sweetest is Emmanuel, for He is God with us.

>>> OUTLINE

I. GOD HAS ALWAYS DESIRED TO BE NEAR US

  A. Near the Brokenhearted

  B. Near Those Who Call on Him

II. GOD SENT OTHERS TO REPRESENT HIM TO HIS PEOPLE

  A. The Priests Ministered to God for the People

  B. The Prophets Spoke to the People for God

III. GOD CHOSE TO MANIFEST HIMSELF IN FLESH TO BE WITH US

  A. Emmanuel: "God with Us"

  B. He Will Never Leave Us nor Forsake Us

>>> CONTEMPLATING THE TOPIC

Companies develop gimmicks to get their target audience's attention. In the same way, as individuals, we do whatever we can to get our message across. It requires some strategy to wrestle attention away from preoccupations in favor of the issue at hand, whether it is cleaning a room or buying a new cell phone. We all look for the perfect way to get and hold another person's attention.

Scripture illustrates God's challenge in getting and holding humanity's attention. Adam and Eve successfully blocked out the Creator's daily conversations long enough to pursue the option of determining what was right and wrong for themselves. This initial attention deficit disorder resulted in removal from their home. God still sought their attention, provided them with clothing, explained the consequences of their actions, and promised a day in the future when the serpent's head would be bruised. God's ultimate effort to gain human attention came when He manifested Himself in the flesh.

From the very beginning, God created men and women to be in relationship with Him. However, God gave Adam and Eve the free will to either choose or reject that relationship. Trees, plains, and oceans have no option but to wave as affirmation of God's glorious creative and sustaining acts. Birds, beasts, and sea creatures must worship as well. Adam and Eve's choice to reject God's preferences for their lives brought separation from the Creator.

I. GOD HAS ALWAYS DESIRED TO BE NEAR US

That first bite of forbidden fruit elicited a strange response from God. He sought relationship restoration rather than executing judgment. The Bible records the many efforts God has made to restore full relationship with humanity. While one lesson cannot uncover all of God's relationship efforts, the brokenhearted and those who call on Him provide examples of God's initiatives.

A. Near the Brokenhearted

The LORD is nigh unto them that are of a broken heart; and saveth such as be of a contrite spirit. (Psalm 34:18)

David penned this psalm while living outside of Israel. To avoid Saul's wrath, the future king sought political asylum in Abimelech's territory. The peace ended when David feigned mental illness and suffered expulsion from the king's court. Refusing to fight against his own people left David relying completely on the Lord for his safety. He began by blessing the Lord and remembering God's responsiveness to his cry (Psalm 34:1–4).

Suffering provides an opportunity to experience God's missionary nature. The human condition guarantees people will have this opportunity at many points across their lifespan. Sadly, society around us provides many examples of people who try to care for their own brokenheartedness. The same was the case in David's day. When God's people suffer, they encounter the Lord's deliverance.

God will always be near those in need; the only question is whether we will experience His nearness as an awareness of His mercy or if we will encounter the bitterness that follows unresolved suffering. Suffering provides a gracious gift to experience God's nearness that self-sufficiency can never provide.

» *What strategies can people use to focus on God's nearness during suffering rather than giving most of their attention to reducing the pain or sorrow?*

B. Near Those Who Call on Him

Psalm 145 includes many wonderful ways to praise this God who seeks relationship. Egypt thought the gods created humans to do the work of the gods. On the other hand, Israel took the opportunity for generations to share the ways God had worked on their behalf (Psalm 145:4). They spoke of Yahweh's wonderful works, great goodness, and righteousness (Psalm 145:5–7). The psalmist gave the reader many reasons to praise God because of all He had already done (Psalm 145:8–13). David went so far as to say the Lord opened His hand "and satisfiest the desire of every living thing" (Psalm 145:16).

The ability to see God's majestic care for all creation set up God's people to be a residing place for God's Spirit. They knew no box, building, or mountain could contain the Creator who sought relationship with them. The Lord gave Moses directions for making a holy space where this covenant God could dwell among His chosen people. While they could do nothing to earn God's favor, they would need to learn how to appropriately call on His name and maintain purity before Him.

Sadly, Israel's example also showed rejection would come when they did not abide in this relationship. Isaiah's first prophecy spoke of a wrong relationship with God, who sought to be tabernacled among them. Their lack of faithfulness caused God to reject their offerings. Their refusal to call on God in truth (Psalm 145:18) caused their God to call them a harlot and to bring His judgment on them.

> » **Why did Israel struggle with being faithful to God? In what ways do we mirror their struggles?**

II. GOD SENT OTHERS TO REPRESENT HIM TO HIS PEOPLE

God chose one family to be the pipeline to bless all nations. Abram left Ur to search for a city made without human hands. Although he never got there, he dedicated his life to the journey. God formed a covenant with Abraham and his family. Yahweh would be their God if they would obey and follow Him alone.

When Israel grew to the strength of a nation in Egypt, God heard the cry of His covenant people and delivered them. As He had appeared to Abraham and Jacob, He would now appear to all the people. God settled on the mountain, and the people recognized the risk of being so close to God. The Old Testament provides a record of God's effort to purify and bless His people so all the world would follow them. He sent priests and prophets to represent His desire to abide with them.

A. The Priests Ministered to God for the People

All of Israel's neighbors had priests to help them appease their gods and give them victory over their enemies. Israel's priests, however, proclaimed the startling message that only one God existed, and that one God wanted to be in a special tabernacled relationship with them. While God called Israel to be a kingdom of priests on behalf of the world (Exodus 19:6), Aaron and his family would need to show them how to stand in the risky territory between their holy God and all the sinful people of the world (Exodus 28–29).

Much of the priests' work centered on the Tabernacle—the place where God chose to be present in a special way. All Israelite life revolved around the Tabernacle. In the journey to the Promised Land, they placed their tents around the Tabernacle when they camped, and they followed it when they moved. The pillar of fire and pillar of cloud visibly reminded all the people that God was with them. Eventually, with the construction of Solomon's Temple, Jerusalem became the place where Yahweh placed His name.

Priests protected the holiness of the Tabernacle and of the people. They taught the Law in a way that key principles of clean and unclean as well as holy and unholy could be understood by all the people. They diligently worked to maintain their own purity, so they could live between their holy God and people who sought to keep the covenant.

Human failure to keep the covenant required the priests to perform their mediatorial role. Sacrificial offerings restored both the person bringing the offering and the Tabernacle where God chose to dwell. Representing people to a holy God carried a very heavy responsibility.

> **God uses His people as a royal priesthood to take the world's needs to Him in prayer. How should you pray for needs in your community and nation at this time?**

B. The Prophets Spoke to the People for God

Priests did not serve alone in the gap between a sinful people and a holy God. Prophets functioned as God's messengers to the people. Jesus would later weep over Jerusalem for its tendency to honor the graves of the prophets. They liked the idea of God's voice being with them, but they rejected the words these men and women spoke on God's behalf.

Prophets lived precarious lives. One does not need much imagination to feel the tension when Nathan challenged all-powerful and all-sinful King David with "thou art the man" (II Samuel 12:7). The king's misuse of power for sexual favors and murder threatened God's plan to use Israel as a light to the nations. Nathan highlighted the failure. The king repented. God forgave.

Elijah lived under a cloud of danger even while he experienced God's sustaining miracles of being fed by a raven's beak and a widow's hand. Ahab and Jezebel wanted the nation to serve both Yahweh and Baal. The test at Mount Carmel set the stage for Baal to fail while Yahweh answered by fire. Elijah experienced emotional and spiritual crises while running from the monarchs. The episode illustrates the reality that prophets were not perfect men, even as they carried a perfect God's words. Elijah saw sins in kings, but he could not see his own self-centeredness when he accused God of having no other followers. God's desire to speak to the people brought fallible men and women into the dangerous gap between God's holiness and human failures. Prophets could speak true words, but they could not fix the people nor themselves.

The prophets saw both nations fall and God's absolute commitment to preserving a remnant to fulfill His promises. Isaiah witnessed the king's refusal to engage in a conversation with God to save Jerusalem (Isaiah 7:10–16). He also saw the promised child who would carry the government on His shoulder and would be "called Wonderful, Counsellor, The mighty God, The everlasting Father, The Prince of Peace" (Isaiah 9:6).

III. GOD CHOSE TO MANIFEST HIMSELF IN FLESH TO BE WITH US

Perhaps we have all heard someone say, "That cannot end well." The observer might be watching boys compete with bottle rockets or national leaders debate over a Supreme Court appointment; in either case fireworks will ignite destruction.

The ultimate concern for a sure explosive outcome results from observing God's persistent efforts to bridge the gap between His holiness and a fallen creation. God has pledged not to take the ultimate action to destroy all creation as He considered with Noah. The rainbow serves as God's promise not to solve the problem that way.

The Gospel writers did not see Jesus' birth as a second or third attempt that followed previous failed efforts to bridge the gap. Instead the New Testament writers saw the Old Testament law, with its priests and prophets attempting to bridge the gap, as a schoolmaster to bring us to Christ (Galatians 3:24). Priestly and prophetic ministry helped all to see how radical the breach actually was between God and humanity. Rules, animal sacrifices, and prophetic utterances could never make humanity holy enough for God to be with people.

» *Why do we need God in order to be holy?*

A. Emmanuel: "God with Us"

While God demonstrated grace through Moses, the Law only provided mediated grace. Grace and truth came personally into human existence by Jesus Christ. Anything less than the Incarnation would fail to achieve God's desire to reconcile the world unto Himself (II Corinthians 5:19). The gap required truth that named sin and rebellion against God. The gap also required a grace mechanism to make God's desire to be among people possible. Jesus became that grace tool.

> *Therefore the Lord himself shall give you a sign; Behold, a virgin shall conceive, and bear a son, and shall call his name Immanuel. (Isaiah 7:14)*

The original prophecy of the virgin's child named Emmanuel was to a hard-hearted king who was too busy solving his own problems to engage in a conversation with God's prophet. Ahaz refused to acknowledge Yahweh's presence in time of national crisis. Fortunately, as wearying to God as it might be (Isaiah 7:13), human stubbornness cannot stop God's plan.

The second giving of the prophecy seemed to be a far less critical juncture. Joseph faced ridicule and shame from others rather than the armies that had confronted his ancestor. The pregnant, unwed teen carried no less than the conception of the Holy Spirit. The shame to be confronted was the shame and sin of all humanity. The dream brought comfort and provided direction for an engaged Hebrew man, but the child to be born brought hope to all humanity. Joseph still had to address the shame of going through with the marriage to an unwed mother, but now he knew why.

Angels carried messages to a number of people in the Old Testament, but none compared to this message. God planned to do the impossible. As great as the virgin birth was, the source of the seed in Mary's womb was not the main miracle Joseph heard. God not only wanted to be with sinful humanity, but He would bridge the gap by coming Himself.

God was present with Israel in theophanies, such as the burning bush, but He had never been present as a member of humanity. The very idea was scandalous. Emmanuel's presence would be complete rather than just in appearances. He had to be seen and handled (I John 1:1). He had to grow and mature (Luke 2:52). He had to pray to overcome His own desire to solve the holiness-sin gap through a less painful means (Luke 22:42–44).

B. He Will Never Leave Us nor Forsake Us

Many parents have had to retrace their steps on a long journey to find their toddler's lost blanket or stuffed animal. They cannot face the hours of turmoil as the child tries to go to bed without the comfort item. Psychologists call this a transitional object. The child uses the constant companion when facing stress or when alone. Being without the item brings stress. Most children will grow out of the need for their one-eyed stuffed rabbit. The object is put in a memory box for later or just forgotten as something else becomes more interesting.

Emmanuel did not come to be a transition object. Humans will never become so holy they no longer need the Savior's grace. Separation from God, other people, and creation as a whole will not just go away because the population has gotten smarter, more economically advantaged, or has found a way to distribute resources in a way that is fair to everyone. Humans will always need "God with us." The Creator made us this way.

》》》 INTERNALIZING THE MESSAGE

When the early disciples heard Jesus was leaving and they could not follow, they became afraid. They had grown used to Jesus being near. Even if a storm blew up on the lake, Jesus would come walking on the water. The Savior told them they did not yet have a complete understanding of God's intent to be with them.

The disciples thought they were losing something when Jesus went away. Instead Emmanuel took on a whole new dimension. He was with them, but soon He would be in them (John 14:17–18). He would live, and so would they. With the Holy Spirit, people can confidently know without a doubt that Emmanuel is still God with us.

Complete Submission

FOCUS THOUGHT

Since Jesus modeled submission to both earthly and heavenly authority, we must also be in submission to the authority in our lives.

 FOCUS VERSES

Luke 2:51–52

And he went down with them, and came to Nazareth, and was subject unto them: but his mother kept all these sayings in her heart. And Jesus increased in wisdom and stature, and in favour with God and man.

 LESSON TEXT

Luke 2:41–52

41 Now his parents went to Jerusalem every year at the feast of the passover.

42 And when he was twelve years old, they went up to Jerusalem after the custom of the feast.

43 And when they had fulfilled the days, as they returned, the child Jesus tarried behind in Jerusalem; and Joseph and his mother knew not of it.

44 But they, supposing him to have been in the company, went a day's journey; and they sought him among their kinsfolk and acquaintance.

45 And when they found him not, they turned back again to Jerusalem, seeking him.

46 And it came to pass, that after three days they found him in the temple, sitting in the midst of the doctors, both hearing them, and asking them questions.

47 And all that heard him were astonished at his understanding and answers.

48 And when they saw him, they were amazed: and his mother said unto him, Son, why hast thou thus dealt with us? behold, thy father and I have sought thee sorrowing.

49 And he said unto them, How is it that ye sought me? wist ye not that I must be about my Father's business?

50 And they understood not the saying which he spake unto them.

51 And he went down with them, and came to Nazareth, and was subject unto them: but his mother kept all these sayings in her heart.

52 And Jesus increased in wisdom and stature, and in favour with God and man.

AMBER ALERTS

If Mary and Joseph could have, they would have used an Amber Alert, but they lived long before smartphones. When they were in the middle of their long walk home, they realized Jesus was not with them. When they asked family and friends caravanning with them, they all looked around and then looked at each other. No one knew where Jesus was.

If you have been in a crowd of people during an Amber Alert, you have probably observed the scene of phones ringing and vibrating all at the same time. After looking at their phones, everyone's face shows signs of stress and worry. The Amber Alert imparts the sinking knowledge that a child has gone missing. But for two deputy sheriffs, one particular Amber Alert would prove to save two scared children.

While on patrol, the two deputies spotted an RV on the side of the road. They stopped to help the three stranded people but could not repair it, so they called for a tow truck. After the truck towed the RV, the officers received the Amber Alert and realized three-year-old Leah and four-year-old Jordan must have been inside the RV. They called the tow truck driver who told them where the individuals were staying. The deputies contacted the local police, who arrested the three adults and safely returned the two missing children.

Mary and Joseph trekked back to Jerusalem. After three days they found twelve-year-old Jesus in the Temple. He was safe, and wonder of wonders, this preteen was teaching the teachers.

>>> **OUTLINE**

I. FESTIVAL OF PASSOVER

  A. The Custom of Joseph and Mary Was to Attend in Jerusalem

  B. Jesus Was Twelve Years Old

II. JESUS WAS LEFT BEHIND

  A. His Family Accidentally Left Him

  B. Unaware He Was Not with Them

III. HIS FAMILY SEARCHED FOR HIM

  A. Jesus Was in the Temple

  B. Listening and Asking Questions

  C. The People Were Amazed at His Understanding

IV. MARY QUESTIONED JESUS

  A. "I Must Be about My Father's Business"

  B. Jesus Submitted to His Parents

  C. We Should Submit to Both Earthly and Heavenly Authority

>>> **CONTEMPLATING THE TOPIC**

Driving through different parts of North America reveals that not all drivers are created equal. It is also evident the different road signs mean different things to different people.

Perhaps the most challenging of all is the yield sign. The word alone should make it obvious what needs to happen—to give up your right of way to someone else. But in all honesty, it does not happen all the time.

Maybe it is partially because within our own human nature, yielding is not an easy thing to do. We like to be in control. We do not like yielding to anyone or anything. Submission is not something we enjoy or always do willingly.

Jesus became the ultimate example of willing submission. The way He entered this world, lived His life, and then left this world is a pattern for each of us to exemplify. In so doing we will find that the greatest blessings in this life are tied to a submissive spirit.

I. FESTIVAL OF PASSOVER

Passover is a special time in the lives of the Jewish people. It is a time of remembering and celebrating their deliverance from Egyptian bondage. It occurs in the spring and is connected to the barley harvest. During this time there is an offering of the firstfruits of the barley harvest.

A. The Custom of Joseph and Mary Was to Attend in Jerusalem

In our Scripture setting, we are told the custom of Joseph and Mary was to journey to Jerusalem and be there for Passover. In ancient times, such a trip would be quite an undertaking. The journey for this family from Nazareth to Jerusalem would be approximately eighty miles and take nearly three days. The women were not required to be in Jerusalem for Passover, but the presence of Mary shows us she was devout in her beliefs. It also lets us know she was submitted to her husband and to God in her worship.

This is significant in helping us understand that Jesus would have grown up making this annual trip. As He grew He would become familiar with the events surrounding Passover. It is estimated there were at least 2 million people in Jerusalem during Passover in the days Jesus lived, so He became somewhat comfortable moving among the press of the crowd.

B. Jesus Was Twelve Years Old

The Book of Luke tells the story of Jesus' birth and His being presented to Simeon at the Temple in Jerusalem. It skips over the early childhood years of Jesus and picks the story back up with Jesus coming to the Temple during the annual pilgrimage to celebrate Passover. This Passover was significant in the life of Jesus because of His age at the time.

Although the Jewish practice of bar mitzvah (a ceremony in which a thirteen-year-old Jewish boy is proclaimed ready to take his place in public worship) had not been instituted yet, at age twelve the religious instruction for Jesus would have become intense and focused. He would have been taught that He was soon to be considered a man and, therefore, would have obligations concerning life and worship.

» *Would you trust a twelve-year-old today to make adult decisions? Why or why not?*

II. JESUS WAS LEFT BEHIND

We may wonder, how could Mary and Joseph have lost Jesus? How could they have let the Son of God out of their sight for even a few moments? Yet, somehow, as they were returning to Nazareth, they realized Jesus was nowhere to be found. He had seemingly disappeared. No doubt it would have been a confusing and hectic time as families gathered their belongings and started the long journey back home. Being mentally and physically exhausted, it would be easy for them to overlook a few details. But still we wonder, how could they leave their son behind?

A. His Family Accidentally Left Him

To be fair to Mary and Joseph, we cannot totally blame them. It is within the realm of possibility for them to assume Jesus was somewhere in the crowd following along. Keep in mind, He was twelve years old and was expected to start acting like an adult. Also, immediate families would travel with their larger extended families. For that reason alone, the parents could have assumed Jesus was simply with other family members.

Leaving Him behind was not an intentional act on their part. It was not an indication they were not concerned for Him or did not love Him. Quite simply, it just happened. They had raised Him right and perhaps assumed He had been to enough Passover celebrations to know when it was time to head home.

B. Unaware He Was Not with Them

On the first evening of their journey, Mary and Joseph realized Jesus was not with them. Perhaps while making camp for the night and beginning to prepare dinner, they began to wonder where He was. After all, a twelve-year-old boy is going to eat.

They began to move among their family members and traveling companions asking about Jesus. Time and again they were told He had not been seen. At some point maybe they began trying to recall the last time they had seen Him. It had to have been while He was in the city since He had not been seen on the journey.

> » *What emotions do you think Mary must have felt when she realized Jesus was not with them?*

III. HIS FAMILY SEARCHED FOR HIM

Like any mother or father would, Mary and Joseph began the search for Jesus.

A frantic search among the travelers was soon underway. From one group to the next, they went looking for their son. Time and again they were told He had not been seen since they left. All they knew to do was return to Jerusalem and see if something had happened to Him there.

A. Jesus Was in the Temple

From one place to another they went. Undoubtedly they went to the places they thought a twelve-year-old boy might go: the marketplace where food was sold, the areas where other children would be playing, perhaps even by the well where others would congregate.

It may have been a little while before they considered looking in the Temple. After all, how many twelve-year-olds want to hang out there? Can you imagine their surprise when they found Him in the Temple expounding the Word of God to the elders gathered there? Luke 2:46–47 states, "And it came to pass, that after three days they found him in the temple, sitting in the midst of the doctors, both hearing them, and asking them questions. And all that heard him were astonished at his understanding and answers."

> » *How willing would you be to listen to a twelve-year-old teach you a Bible study?*

B. Listening and Asking Questions

His parents must have stood there in amazement at what was happening before their eyes. Their son was in deep discussion with these much older men. By the looks on the men's faces, they were in awe of the knowledge and wisdom of this young lad. Take notice though, the Word says Jesus was "hearing them, and asking them questions." He was in no way trying to be a know-it-all. He was willing to humbly listen to the words they were saying and then ask His questions. He understood the power of submitting Himself before trying to share what He had to say.

C. The People Were Amazed at His Understanding

In the process the people were amazed that such a young man could have the wisdom and insight He did. With every question and every response, they simply sat in awe. It would have been obvious to Mary and Joseph that their son was something special.

They understood a little of who He was. They knew a little concerning why He had come into the world. But on this day, something changed in their view of Him. Even though they were still His parents, they began to realize He was not just their little boy anymore. He was becoming the man the angels had told them about all those years before.

IV. MARY QUESTIONED JESUS

Even at that, Mary was still a momma. She was still upset and wanted some answers. "Where in the world have you been?" "Do you have any idea what you have put us through?" "We were not sure if you were dead or alive." "Who do you think you are to just go off and do your own thing without telling me or your dad where you were going?" "You just wait until we get home and we'll see about this."

It is indeed an interesting time of life when young people begin to test the limits of their freedom. Parents can have a difficult time letting them stretch too far. Sometimes we forget Jesus was a normal young man, and Joseph and Mary were normal parents. The tension of such a situation would have been real.

» *Do you think Mary was slightly angry or just concerned? Explain.*

A. "I Must Be about My Father's Business"

All eyes would have turned to Mary and Joseph as they approached Jesus. People would have heard the conversation between the parents and their child. They anxiously waited to see how Jesus would respond. Would He be the typical young person and get a surly attitude, replying with some smart comment? Would He be embarrassed and simply try to walk away?

His response was compelling. In no way was it disrespectful. He looked at His mother and simply said, "Wist ye not that I must be about my Father's business?" (Luke 2:49). He was torn between the two worlds of childhood and adulthood, recognizing this was an adult moment for Him, and He wanted them to realize that.

They did not fully understand what He was saying. In their minds it was not yet time. The day would come, but it would not be today. Even though they recognized

16

His wisdom and knowledge, they did not fully understand what He was saying. Luke 2:50 tells us, "And they understood not the saying which he spake unto them."

B. Jesus Submitted to His Parents

Amazingly, we read in verse 51, "And he went down with them, and came to Nazareth, and was subject unto them: but his mother kept all these sayings in her heart." He willingly left those gathered in the Temple and went home with His parents. He was submissive to the parental authority God had placed Him under while on earth.

What an incredible example! While He had the power to do as He willed, He chose to submit. He could have risen up and demanded they go on their way and let Him stay and do His Father's work. Instead, He simply did what Mom and Dad asked Him to do. He returned home with them.

» *What is it about Jesus' spirit and attitude here that stands out?*

C. We Should Submit to Both Earthly and Heavenly Authority

Philippians 2:5–8 speaks to us about true submission: "Let this mind be in you, which was also in Christ Jesus: who, being in the form of God, thought it not robbery to be equal with God: but made himself of no reputation, and took upon him the form of a servant, and was made in the likeness of men: and being found in fashion as a man, he humbled himself, and became obedient unto death, even the death of the cross."

The life of Jesus is a perfect pattern of one who submitted to earthly and spiritual authority. Jesus willingly gave up personal desires to submit to the plan of God. That plan required submitting to man and God. Refusing to submit to either one is not total submission.

⟫⟫ INTERNALIZING THE MESSAGE

Paul wrote, "Wherefore God also hath highly exalted him, and given him a name which is above every name" (Philippians 2:9). In other words, when we submit, we release God to elevate and promote us to places where we can be the most effective for Him.

Our prayer today should be, "Lord, let the mind that was in Christ Jesus be in me today. Let me submit myself to the authority You have placed over me in this life and most of all help me to submit myself to Your spiritual authority. And then Lord, use me for Your glory."

Be Baptized

FOCUS THOUGHT

To be participants in the New Covenant, we must be baptized in the covenant name of Jesus.

 FOCUS VERSES

Matthew 3:14–15

But John forbad him, saying, I have need to be baptized of thee, and comest thou to me? And Jesus answering said unto him, Suffer it to be so now: for thus it becometh us to fulfil all righteousness. Then he suffered him.

 LESSON TEXT

Matthew 3:13–17

13 Then cometh Jesus from Galilee to Jordan unto John, to be baptized of him.

14 But John forbad him, saying, I have need to be baptized of thee, and comest thou to me?

15 And Jesus answering said unto him, Suffer it to be so now: for thus it becometh us to fulfil all righteousness. Then he suffered him.

16 And Jesus, when he was baptized, went up straightway out of the water: and, lo, the heavens were opened unto him, and he saw the Spirit of God descending like a dove, and lighting upon him:

17 And lo a voice from heaven, saying, This is my beloved Son, in whom I am well pleased.

Acts 2:38

38 Then Peter said unto them, Repent, and be baptized every one of you in the name of Jesus Christ for the remission of sins, and ye shall receive the gift of the Holy Ghost.

Colossians 2:11–12

11 In whom also ye are circumcised with the circumcision made without hands, in putting off the body of the sins of the flesh by the circumcision of Christ:

12 Buried with him in baptism, wherein also ye are risen with him through the faith of the operation of God, who hath raised him from the dead.

I Peter 3:21

21 The like figure whereunto even baptism doth also now save us (not the putting away of the filth of the flesh, but the answer of a good conscience toward God,) by the resurrection of Jesus Christ.

⟫⟫ CULTURE CONNECTION

BAPTIZING THE BAPTIZER

Imagine an elementary school art teacher showing Picasso how to paint. Or a high school basketball coach teaching LeBron James how to shoot. Or a weekend worship leader teaching Chris Tomlin how to lead. Now imagine you are the art teacher, the coach, or the worship leader. Now you know how John the Baptist felt. If we measured inadequacy in gallons, John the Baptist felt a Mediterranean Sea full of inadequate.

Yet Jesus came to him one day to be baptized by him. Little did John the Baptist know the reality of his words that Jesus would baptize us with the Holy Spirit and fire. He wanted to hand the divine Picasso the brush, but Jesus put the brush back in John's hand and assured him they were in the right places. Although Jesus had never sinned and never would, He needed to be baptized in order to fulfill all righteousness.

Perhaps God has asked you to do something you feel inadequate to complete. Maybe your mind is having a difficult time reconciling everything your faith is telling you. But you must remember, God's ways are perfect. If He asked you to do something beyond your ability, He will give you the ability to do what He has asked of you. We must simply trust Him and obey His direction.

⟫⟫ OUTLINE

I. JOHN THE BAPTIST
A. Preached to the People
B. "He That Cometh after Me"

II. JESUS CAME TO JOHN TO BE BAPTIZED
A. John Refused at First
B. To Fulfill All Righteousness

III. REASONS FOR OUR BAPTISM
A. New Covenant Entrance through the Covenant Name of Jesus
B. Identifies Us with Jesus
C. A Clear Conscience
D. A Command
E. For the Forgiveness or Remission of Sins

⟫⟫ CONTEMPLATING THE TOPIC

A minister was trying to convince his audience that one did not have to be submerged in water to be baptized. Going to the story of the baptism of Jesus, the minister pointed out that John was baptizing *in* the Jordan River, but this did not necessarily mean they were going *into* the water. The minister stated that the original word for *in* could mean "in close proximity to, around, or nearby." He said the Ethiopian in the desert did not really go *into* the water but just needed to be nearby it so Philip could put some on him.

Afterward a listener walked up to the minister and congratulated him, "Reverend, that message cleared things up for me. You know the story of the disciples being in a bad storm on the Sea of Galilee? Now I know they were close to that storm but not really in it. And it warms my heart to know Paul was only around that old jail but not actually in it. And you know that part about people being cast in Hell? Well, it is nice they will only be nearby the lake of fire but not actually in it. By the way, next Sunday I plan to be in church, meaning I shall be in close proximity to it," he said, pointing to the golf course next door.

19

I. JOHN THE BAPTIST

A. Preached to the People

Beyond being the emcee for Jesus, John had a message that prepared people for this main event on earth's stage. John called the people to turn in a new direction. If they could not realize they had been doing life wrong, they would not accept the new life Jesus was bringing in. For John, repentance was not an emotion or a moment of prayer, but a changed life accompanied with confession of sins (Matthew 3:6). There are clear marks of such a conversion. John said fruit must appear in people's lives. If not, they would be destroyed in the fire (Matthew 3:8–10).

» *How did your conversion involve both a change of thinking and acknowledging your sins?*

Typical of a rabbi at the time, John baptized his followers. John's baptism signified these followers were stepping out from the mundane religious tradition around them and becoming heartfelt and personal in pursuing God and showing kindness to their fellow man (Luke 3:10–14). John, however, preached baptism for remission or removal of sin. This new message prepared listeners for the complete form of baptism that would come in the name of Jesus with the power of His shed blood to wash away their sins. After Jesus completed His work with the Resurrection and Ascension, John's baptism had to be replaced with baptism in Jesus' name (John 1:29, 36; Acts 4:12; 19:1–6).

B. "He That Cometh after Me"

John knew he had come to prepare the way of God, and God would appear as a man whom John would baptize. In other words, John knew Jesus was "God with us." John announced the one coming after him was greater than he was because He existed before John. Jesus was born six months after John. But John knew Jesus was more than just a man who had been born.

John was a Holy Ghost preacher. Though John came to introduce water baptism, he also declared that Jesus came to introduce Spirit baptism. Many people today believe Jesus simply came to forgive our sins; however, John had already been preaching about a cleansing of sin. He made it clear that the purpose of Jesus coming was to bring us the Spirit infilling (Matthew 3:11). What John was doing with water, Jesus would introduce with the Spirit—total saturation. Those who reject the message of the gift of the Holy Ghost have rejected the very reason Jesus came; they have denied Christ.

» *What are some passages that show Jesus spoke about the Spirit baptism throughout His ministry?*

John, who did no miracles, had huge crowds coming to hear his clear and challenging message about turning from sin. John was a holiness preacher. It was not enough for people to confess their sins; they must turn from their sinful actions and pursue righteousness instead. Those pursuing holiness do not live for personal gain, strife, greed, pride, or other fleshly motives. John lived a separated life in a very extreme sense and did not suffer from being "culturally irrelevant" or "judgmental and narrow minded." John knew difficulty and persecution had a way of separating the uncommitted from the resolute.

John preached about Heaven and Hell. This should not be surprising, but many Jews had come to deny the existence of an afterlife. John warned that those who did not repent and were not baptized would be eternally lost, and he preached a very narrow message that believers should also receive the Spirit that He who was coming after him was bringing.

II. JESUS CAME TO JOHN TO BE BAPTIZED

A. John Refused at First

John refused to baptize people who were not doing it unto repentance. If their hearts were filled with pride and hatred, he instead showed them the error of their ways through his preaching. For truly, baptism will not save those who choose to continue to harbor hatefulness and pride in their hearts, refusing to repent of their sins.

At first John refused to baptize Jesus when he said, "I need to be baptized by You" (Matthew 3:14, NKJV). With Jesus, John refused not because of a "sin disqualifier" but because of a "sinlessness disqualifier." This Man Christ Jesus did not need washing or cleansing of sin. John knew he was impure in his own eyes once he looked into the eyes of Jesus.

B. To Fulfill All Righteousness

When John resisted baptizing the Lord, Jesus responded by saying this was to fulfill all righteousness. Righteousness should be the motivation behind all we do. It is right for all of us, as Jesus pointed out to His relative John (Matthew 3:15). When a person starts asking, "Do I have to do this to be saved?" that person is demonstrating a glaring lack of a foundational desire to fulfill all that is right in God's eyes.

Jesus came to take on the sins of the world and usher true believers into a Spirit-filled life. In baptism Jesus identified with sinful humanity. On the cross He took on the sins of the whole world.

John had been told he would see the Spirit descending on the one who would baptize with the Spirit (John 1:33). While water baptism into Jesus Christ effectively removes sins and responds to a person's faith, it also parallels the Spirit immersion which totally consumes the believer's life. Spirit baptism and water baptism go together. Biblically, when one occurred, the other followed closely along with it (Acts 2:38, 41; 8:16–17; 10:47; 19:5–6; Romans 6:3–5; Titus 3:5).

» *Which came first for you, water or Spirit baptism? Explain.*

III. REASONS FOR OUR BAPTISM

The word *baptism* was a new word created around the time of the early English Bible translations. Catering to those who believed baptism to include sprinkling or pouring, the translators transliterated the Greek *baptizo* as "baptize" rather than create a theological war by actually translating the word. The true translation of that word could be "immersion." John immersed or submerged the people in the Jordan River.

A. New Covenant Entrance through the Covenant Name of Jesus

A covenant is a binding contract between two individuals. Abraham entered into covenant with the Lord. In that covenant the Lord called His name over the believer (Genesis 22:16; Psalm 105:9; Hebrews 6:13). He called His name over Jacob in covenant as well (Genesis 28:13–15). He called His covenant name over the descendants of Israel (Exodus 6:4–8; Deuteronomy 5:2–3). He promised to bring others into His covenant, a covenant for those who would return and others who would come to Him (Isaiah 59:21; Jeremiah 31:31–34; Hebrews 8:4–13; 12:18–24; 13:20).

The prophets declared that a believer was to "call on the name of the Lord." This did not mean only to vocalize the name, but to enter into covenant with the one whom that name represented. The new believer Saul—who would become better known by his Greek name Paul—was told by the servant of the Lord to rise up and invoke the name of the Lord to wash away his sins (Acts 22:16). Each recorded baptism in Scripture was done by the minister calling the name of the Lord Jesus Christ over the new inductee (I Corinthians 1:12–13).

B. Identifies Us with Jesus

In baptism, we take on Christ. Those who have been immersed into the Lord Jesus have put on Christ—the old self has been buried and is over with, by faith (Galatians 3:27). In the unseen realm, we are like Jesus. While others might not see a physical change after baptism, the enemy sees the new creature. The believer's past identity has been hidden (Colossians 3:3). As children of God, we must see ourselves through this new lens. By reckoning ourselves dead to sin and alive to God, we overcome the old patterns of sin (Romans 6:3–14).

> » *How do you see yourself when you try to look at yourself through God's eyes?*

C. A Clear Conscience

Baptism washes away the sins of the past. While some make a theological argument that water cannot wash away sins, they have overlooked the act of faith in the finished work of Christ. This is not about the power of water and its ability to rinse away dirt from the body. Baptism is an act of faith in the power of Christ to wash away sin. Water immersion is simply an act of faith that God acknowledges. Baptism brings one to the end of self and gives a fresh start with a clear conscience. Just as water preserved Noah and his family in the ark, water immersion into Jesus protects the believer from the coming destruction (I Peter 3:21).

D. A Command

When we have a heart after the Lord, there is no need to twist our arms to make us obey the Lord. A converted heart wants to fulfill all righteousness. Simply because the Scriptures command us to be baptized is reason enough to do it. We do not have to fully understand all the significance and meaning of the act to do it. It is essential that we come with a humble heart, confess and turn from the past life of rebellion against God, and be immersed in water in the name of Jesus.

E. For the Forgiveness or Remission of Sins

Some have tried to say baptism *for* the remission of sins means *because of* our sins having already been washed away. However, baptism was first understood as initiation into a covenant. No one was baptized *because* they had made a covenant but *in order* to make the covenant. The Greek word behind the English word *for* never carries the meaning "because of" in Scripture. It always carries the sense of "into" or "toward" as in the sense of "in order to obtain" something. The end goal of water baptism in Jesus' name is the cleansing from sin.

The key passage to show this case strongly is Matthew 26:28 where Jesus tells us His blood is for the remission of sins. Jesus did not shed His blood because sins were already washed away. One must be baptized in Jesus' name for sins to be removed and for the work of the blood to complete its work in their lives.

» *How does it change the importance and meaning of baptism when one realizes it is necessary for washing away sins?*

▶▶▶ INTERNALIZING THE MESSAGE

Researchers say the human mind develops highways, or well-used paths, in certain patterns of thinking. For example, once you have built the "how to ride a bicycle" path between the left and right hemispheres of the brain, you will always be able to ride a bike. Certain paths may never be built, such as doing algebra, which will make such mental tasks harder to learn later in life. The old life of sin can build superhighways that will be abandoned when we begin to travel the highway of holiness.

This is where new believers actively disassociate themselves from their old identities. Believers must count themselves as truly dead to sin and those old pathways of behavior (Romans 6:11). That four-lane highway of greed or pride gets abandoned when we learn a new direction: generosity and humility. The fist that once tightened and drew back to strike those with whom we disagreed must now reach out a hand to help those who struggle (Romans 6:13). Living the life of holiness and separation from sin is how we act on what the Lord has declared about us. We overcome the sinful ways by the power of His Spirit (Romans 8:13).

It Is Written

FOCUS THOUGHT

Jesus showed us how to resist Satan and overcome temptation by the power of God's Word.

 FOCUS VERSE

Luke 4:4

And Jesus answered him, saying, It is written, That man shall not live by bread alone, but by every word of God.

 LESSON TEXT

Matthew 4:4, 7, 10

4 But he answered and said, It is written, Man shall not live by bread alone, but by every word that proceedeth out of the mouth of God.

. . . . .

7 Jesus said unto him, It is written again, Thou shalt not tempt the Lord thy God.

. . . . .

10 Then saith Jesus unto him, Get thee hence, Satan: for it is written, Thou shalt worship the Lord thy God, and him only shalt thou serve.

Luke 4:1–4

1 And Jesus being full of the Holy Ghost returned from Jordan, and was led by the Spirit into the wilderness,

2 Being forty days tempted of the devil. And in those days he did eat nothing: and when they were ended, he afterward hungered.

3 And the devil said unto him, If thou be the Son of God, command this stone that it be made bread.

4 And Jesus answered him, saying, It is written, That man shall not live by bread alone, but by every word of God.

⟫⟫ CULTURE CONNECTION

FOMO

One of life's greatest temptations is represented by four letters: FOMO. Known as the fear of missing out, it is one of the highest-octane fuels for temptation. Frans de Waal, a primatologist at Emory University, conducted an experiment on two capuchin monkeys to evaluate the power of FOMO.

In the experiment, de Waal rewarded the monkeys when they completed a simple task. All they had to do was hand a rock to the researcher. When they handed him the rock, he handed them a cucumber. When he gave the same reward to both monkeys for completing the same task, they were content.

But when he gave one monkey a grape while giving the other a cucumber, he saw markedly different results. The monkey who was perfectly content only seconds earlier with earning a cucumber began shrieking, baring his teeth, thrashing in his cage, and pounding on the table to show his anger. He was enraged because he wanted what he did not have.

The enemy of our soul is no kinder. He fills up his five-gallon jar of temptation in hopes of filling us with discontentment, envy, jealousy, covetousness, and resentment—a deadly cocktail of emotions.

In our day FOMO is still a formidable foe. It still lures us to the bar and urges us to open wide and drink up this deadly cocktail. But we are not missing out on anything in this life when we are living the abundant life Jesus gave His life to give us. So fill up on the precious Word of God, and when the tempter tempts you to drink his cocktail, be ready to say, "It is written."

⟫⟫ OUTLINE

I. JESUS WAS LED BY THE SPIRIT INTO THE WILDERNESS
    A. Fasted for Forty Days
    B. Tempted by the Devil

II. TURN THESE STONES TO BREAD
    A. Satisfy Your Physical Hunger
    B. It Is Written

III. JUMP FROM THE PINNACLE OF THE TEMPLE
    A. Test God
    B. It Is Written

IV. BOW BEFORE ME
    A. Offer Worship to the God of This World
    B. It Is Written

V. OVERCOMERS BY THE WORD OF GOD

⟫⟫ CONTEMPLATING THE TOPIC

Temptation goes with the territory. It is inevitable—a part of life none of us can avoid. As long as we are living in the flesh, temptation will come our way. We will never outgrow it or mature beyond it.

I. JESUS WAS LED BY THE SPIRIT INTO THE WILDERNESS

In the Book of Matthew, we receive insight into two of the most significant events in the life of Jesus. These occurred at the beginning of His public ministry. First, Jesus was baptized by John. Then Matthew shared the account of Jesus' temptation in the wilderness.

Over the course of a lifetime, we learn there are times when temptation follows closely on the heels of great spiritual experiences. After a great worship service where God has blessed us, even temptations we have long forgotten can resurface. The key is to stay as led of the Spirit on Monday as we were on Sunday.

Interestingly, the Bible tells us Jesus was led of the Spirit into the wilderness for the very purpose of being tempted by the devil. The Spirit directed Him to a place of aloneness and separation. In some ways this can be difficult to understand. Why would God lead someone to a place where He knows the person will be tempted? Would it not be better to keep the person in a spiritual environment where temptation would have little to no power or influence?

No doubt God can do that. But there are times when He will lead us to places in our lives where our spirituality can be tested, proven, and strengthened, so we must stay close to Him and His Word. Many people fall into temptation because they do not practice the necessary spiritual disciplines of prayer, fasting, and reading the Word.

» *Why is it important to spend time on spiritual disciplines?*

A. Fasted for Forty Days

The very word *fasting* may cause some to cringe. We do not like the idea of not eating or drinking anything for any period of time. Our flesh craves to be satisfied with natural things and rebels against being denied. For some, the thought of giving up even one meal for spiritual reasons is a formidable undertaking. Imagine doing what Jesus did and fasting for forty days.

For almost six full weeks He denied His physical appetite. He refused to give in and take nourishment into His body.

It was a time of spiritual warfare. Such a season demanded the spirit be strong and ready for battle. The only way to accomplish this was to deny the flesh and feed the spirit. Prayer and fasting were critical to Jesus overcoming the temptations He would face throughout His ministry. Without preparing the spiritual man, surely He would fall in a weak moment. In His humanity, He may not have known all He was about to encounter. Yet, in His spirit, He was well able (just as we are) to recognize when a spiritual struggle was taking place.

B. Tempted by the Devil

And sure enough, the devil showed up. He did not show up at the Lord's baptism. He waited until Jesus was in the wilderness, denying Himself of the food He would need for strength in His body. The devil likes to show up in our weak moments. He does not always arrive when things are going well and we are full of the Holy Spirit. No, he tries to choose his moments of temptation carefully. After all, if he knows we are in a strong spiritual season, why would he bother showing up at all? But on the other hand, if he can catch us when we are weak, he thinks he has half the battle already won.

II. TURN THESE STONES TO BREAD

Temptation offers an answer for a need or desire. It presents something that will satisfy the appetites of the flesh. The first thing the devil suggested that Jesus do was to turn the stones in the wilderness into bread that could be eaten.

The challenge was prefaced with the words, "If thou be the Son of God." This challenged Jesus' identity. It was an attempt to appeal to the Lord's pride in order to get Him to prove His identity. The devil knew if he could successfully stir up the ego of Jesus, he might get Jesus to yield to temptation. And Satan did so by not only appealing to Jesus' ego but also to His hunger. It was kind of a "come on Jesus, You can prove You are the Son of God and also take care of Your hunger at the same time."

» *What areas of pride in our lives often fall prey to temptation?*

A. Satisfy Your Physical Hunger

We understand that as we fast, the spiritual man is made more sensitive and is strengthened. However, anytime we fast we are going to feel hungry. If we fast long enough, we may feel really hungry. After a certain period of time with no food, a person may start to feel weakness as well. In a natural sense, we can avoid that by satisfying our physical hunger. Eat something. Break the fast.

We could easily assume the devil realized those physical tendencies our bodies experience during a fast. The devil knew Jesus was physically hungry and would naturally want to satisfy that physical hunger. He was planting a thought of satisfying the hunger when he said, "Turn these stones into bread."

» *Can you discipline your physical hungers to the point where they do not control you? Explain.*

B. It Is Written

The temptation is not what destroys us. Not responding correctly to the temptation is what destroys us. The power of choice belongs to us, just as it did to Jesus. We can look at what Jesus did to find what we need to do.

First, Jesus did not give in, nor did He simply ignore the temptation. Instead, He confronted it head-on. He did not confront it with His own ideas or thoughts. He leaned on the Word of God. He knew the Word was forever settled in Heaven and Earth, and it would not fail Him, especially in times of temptation.

27

Jesus boldly looked at the devil and said, "It is written, Man shall not live by bread alone, but by every word that proceedeth out of the mouth of God" (Matthew 4:4). By appealing to the Word of God, Jesus was appealing to the highest authority known to humanity. When we use the Word to counter the attacks of the devil in our lives, we literally place God on the battlefield and not just our own flesh. When we do that, we cannot be defeated.

III. JUMP FROM THE PINNACLE OF THE TEMPLE

During times of temptation, the flesh can do some strange things. It can either embrace what God is doing or challenge what God is doing. In the wilderness the devil was tempting Jesus to challenge God.

A. Test God

In our wilderness moments of temptation, it can be easy to question God. We may wonder if God really cares at all. Our minds may run rampant with thoughts that we may not survive this or that God will not save us if we start to fall.

To prove the point, the devil took Jesus to a pinnacle of the Temple and told Him to jump. The devil also whispered in Jesus' ear that it would be okay; God would send angels to catch Him. During times of temptation, we may become disillusioned and subject to deception. When that occurs, we might do things that sound good at the moment, but we would never have done otherwise. Jesus refused to allow that to happen to Him.

B. It Is Written

Once again Jesus appealed to the Word of God. From the pinnacle He declared to the devil, "Thou shalt not tempt the Lord thy God" (Matthew 4:7). In other words, He was not going to put God to the test just because He was being tested. He was going to have faith in God and hold to the promises of the Word of God.

It would be easy during times of temptation to try and put God on the spot—to challenge Him to prove He really is God. We must remember that the process of facing temptation strengthens our faith and our walk with God. Foolishly challenging Him will serve no good purpose. Rather, appealing to the Word and standing firm will deliver us in due season.

» *Why is knowing God's Word and putting it to memory crucial to gaining victory over temptation?*

IV. BOW BEFORE ME

Beyond fleshly temptations are spiritual temptations. Jesus was not immune to this simply because He was God manifested in the flesh. He still had to submit Himself to the Spirit of God when He was tempted by the devil.

A. Offer Worship to the God of This World

The devil was well acquainted with true worship. He knew what it was like to be in the presence of God and offer worship to Him. The reason the devil was removed from his place in Heaven was partly due to his desire to be worshiped like God was worshiped.

That desire has never left him. When confronting Jesus in the wilderness, the last area of temptation the devil brought was for Jesus to worship him. He mistakenly thought that being in the wilderness would make Jesus feel as if He has been forgotten and forsaken. Since we all have an inherent need to express worship, the devil thought Jesus was prime for a redirection of His worship.

Once again the devil missed it by a million miles. He allowed his desire for worship to overshadow just how committed Jesus was. If Jesus did not succumb to turning stones to bread and jumping off of a pinnacle of the Temple, there was no chance He was going to cease His worship. Jesus knew that if our worship falls to temptation, so will everything else.

B. It Is Written

This time Jesus was much bolder and more straightforward. We get the sense there was fire in His eyes as He got as close to the devil as He could and said, "Get thee hence, Satan: for It Is written, Thou shalt worship the Lord thy God, and him only shalt thou serve" (Matthew 4:10).

Amazingly, after this the devil left Jesus, and God sent angels to minister to Jesus. Once the devil realized Jesus' worship could not be shaken, he knew any further temptation would be futile.

» **Do you make a sincere effort to hide God's Word in your heart? Explain.**

V. OVERCOMERS BY THE WORD OF GOD

We must never underestimate the value of the Word of God in our lives. God's Word is our wellspring of hope and encouragement. During times of temptation, His Word is a source of supernatural strength in fighting off the enemy. II Corinthians 10:4 lets us know, "For the weapons of our warfare are not carnal, but mighty through God to the pulling down of strong holds."

David knew this lesson well. He realized that hiding the Word in his heart would help him not to sin against God (Psalm 119:11). He also knew the Word was a lamp to his feet and a light to his pathway (Psalm 119:105). On the battlefield with Goliath, David boldly declared the power of the name and the Word of the Lord (I Samuel 17). Because he did so, God gave him a great victory.

▶▶▶ INTERNALIZING THE MESSAGE

When we commit ourselves to regularly studying and applying the Word of God in our lives, we are fortifying ourselves for our wilderness experiences. We can overcome the temptations of the flesh and spirit by standing and declaring the Word of God to the enemy we face. Whether it be our physical appetites, our spiritual struggles, or being challenged in our worship, the Word of God remains our best defense.

Follow Me

FOCUS THOUGHT

Jesus calls all of those who wish to be His disciples to follow Him.

 FOCUS VERSE

Matthew 4:19

And he saith unto them, Follow me, and I will make you fishers of men.

 LESSON TEXT

Matthew 4:18–22

18 And Jesus, walking by the sea of Galilee, saw two brethren, Simon called Peter, and Andrew his brother, casting a net into the sea: for they were fishers.

19 And he saith unto them, Follow me, and I will make you fishers of men.

20 And they straightway left their nets, and followed him.

21 And going on from thence, he saw other two brethren, James the son of Zebedee, and John his brother, in a ship with Zebedee their father, mending their nets; and he called them.

22 And they immediately left the ship and their father, and followed him.

Mark 2:13–14

13 And he went forth again by the sea side; and all the multitude resorted unto him, and he taught them.

14 And as he passed by, he saw Levi the son of Alphæus sitting at the receipt of custom, and said unto him, Follow me. And he arose and followed him.

Luke 9:23

23 And he said to them all, If any man will come after me, let him deny himself, and take up his cross daily, and follow me.

CULTURE CONNECTION

1,046,593

One of the most well-known athletes in our time is Tom Brady. Since 2000 he has played quarterback for the New England Patriots. Before New England drafted him to join their team, 198 other players were chosen ahead of him in the NFL draft. Every one of those teams and their owners are wondering how many Super Bowl wins they would have if they had drafted Tom Brady.

But people are divided on him. Some people love him; some do not even like him. Some love him enough to want to know where he is at all times. They want to be close to him, maybe to get his autograph or to take a selfie with him. One such fan designed a website that can tell you exactly how many yards you are from Tom Brady at any given time—howfaramifromtombrady.com. Right now, according to the website, I am 1,046,593 yards away from him.

I do not know how accurate the website is. I doubt Tom Brady wears a GPS tracker, but if someone wanted to find him, doubtless this website could be used as a starting place. Some people are not content just to follow him on social media; they want to actually follow him around. But for a fan, that is standard operating procedure. If a fan of something as trivial as sports can become so intent on tracking a mortal man, how much more should followers of Jesus be intent on seeking Him? Jesus is calling all of us to follow Him, but following Him is more than just checking in on Sunday and giving online on Wednesday. Followers want to know where He is. They want to see Him. Look like Him. Talk like Him. Act like Him. Be like Him. Followers want to be near Him, so they can be with Him.

Tom Brady may be 1,046,593 yards away, but Jesus is just one prayer away.

 OUTLINE

I. JESUS CALLED HIS DISCIPLES
A. Follow Me
B. I Will Make You Fishers of Men

II. ALL WHO WISH TO BE DISCIPLES MUST FOLLOW HIM
A. Follow the Same Path
B. Mirror His Actions

III. TO FOLLOW IS TO OBEY
A. Leave Behind
B. Take Up the Cross

IV. TO FOLLOW IS TO SERVE
A. Serve God
B. Serve Others

CONTEMPLATING THE TOPIC

Most couples will say "I do" to that momentous question asked by the pastor before God and gathered witnesses. Young men and women spend months agonizing over invitation patterns and reception venues. Eventually they will find the limit to their wedding funds and begin to make choices on what to keep and what to abandon.

The couple will sign one piece of paper and say the simple three letter pledge. Life changes as they know it. The loving couple has no idea what the future holds, but they make the commitment of a lifetime. Faithful couples will adjust and grow together through the birth of children, career changes, unemployment, and care for each other during the aging process. Two little words served as the pledge to love until "death do us part."

Disciples experience even greater long-term consequences when they accept Jesus' call to follow Him. With joy we accept the offer of remission of sins and the infilling of the Holy Spirit. We discover spiritual giftings and the wonder of new life in Christ. Disciples learn the journey is much more than that initial decision to repent. We learn of the many dimensions of spiritual maturity that await us.

I. JESUS CALLED HIS DISCIPLES

Jesus' first sermon called all humanity to repentance and announced the dawning of a new age (Matthew 4:17). The rest of Jesus' life served to expand, support, and illustrate this foundational thesis statement. That simple sermon will eventually condemn all who chose to find their own way and reject the restoration opportunity provided by the Creator who entered His creation to restore all things to Himself (II Corinthians 5:19).

This new Rabbi possessed greater authority than any other speaker. John the Baptist, the strangely dressed prophet who baptized followers in the Jordan River, proclaimed Jesus to be the Lamb of God (John 1:36).

A. Follow Me

Peter and Andrew knew of Jesus from their time following John the Baptist. (See John 1.) Perhaps they had seen Jesus' baptism, heard the thundering voice, and experienced the wonder of a dove settling on Jesus' shoulder. They could feel the electric current of change in the air. They had no idea how much impact the young Rabbi's simple command, "Follow me," would make on their lives (Matthew 4:19).

Jesus called the brothers to follow Him. He did not a call them to a school of philosophy or a body of authoritative texts. Jesus called them to an ever-deepening relationship with Him. They could not know the path obedience would take. They could not know the unmeasurable awe of witnessing a person brought back to life or the avalanche of pain resulting from denying their teacher in just a few years.

Students can master texts by memorizing, debating, and teaching. But a relationship with the Savior can never be mastered. Paul pointed to this reality with the heart cry, "That I may know him" (Philippians 3:10). That knowledge could only come through pursuing Jesus' power and suffering. Rather than simply reading a text, the siblings followed the Incarnate Word.

» *What is the difference between being invited to have a relationship with Christ and being called to know the Bible?*

B. I Will Make You Fishers of Men

Jesus found Peter and Andrew while they were casting their nets. Jesus chose these active men. The men did not choose Him, as other students chose their teachers. Following Jesus was too uncomfortable and uncertain for some who self-selected to become disciples (Matthew 8:19–20). Jesus did not follow conventions of putting family first (Matthew 8:21–22; 12:46–50). The other brothers, James and John, also left their father and family in the boat as they followed Jesus.

Jesus always chose people from where they were and transitioned them toward full living. He promised only one reward to the brothers; they would become fishers of men. They understood fishing. They knew men. Now they would learn the wisdom, heart, and actions needed to collect people for the Kingdom. Jesus would change the metaphor for farming folks. Rather than fish for men, they could respond to the Master's commission to go into the harvest. Both farmers and fishermen would draw freely from their places of labor and let the Master do the sorting later (Matthew 13:24–30, 46–50). They could love and care for the field in such a powerful way because they were free from separating good from bad—they made all welcome.

II. ALL WHO WISH TO BE DISCIPLES MUST FOLLOW HIM

Some people find peace by knowing their steps are ordered by the Lord. They trust the Lord will stoop down and move their shoe in the right direction if they start to make the wrong step. This pre-Christ perspective celebrates the gifts of following God's laws. For those who follow Jesus, the principle goes much deeper. Rather than trusting the given law, disciples rely on walking with the Lord.

A. Follow the Same Path

By definition, disciples follow Jesus. They cannot do otherwise. Disciples trust the one who allocates talents and responsibilities (Matthew 25:14–30). They trust the one who distributes spiritual gifts to the body in accordance with His divine will (I Corinthians 12:11–12).

Following Jesus sets the direction. Nothing describes this daily choice better than the call to repentance. New converts make a 180-degree turn from following their own will to surrendering to Christ. This decision will set the course for subsequent repentance moments. As we die daily, our repentances will become course corrections. Disciples repent of all thoughts, actions, and emotions that are out of sync with the Teacher. Living as a disciple helps identify those areas of misalignment, confess them to fellow travelers, and receive the impact of fervent prayer (James 5:16–20).

Following Jesus sets the pace. The Master calls for constant, daily walking. The race requires patient runners rather than sprinters (Hebrews 12:1). Keeping pace with the Master enables disciples to engage in highly demanding moments of spiritual work as well as seasons of rest. Trusting Him to be the pacesetter helps us to ask the right questions (Acts 1:6–8), pray the right prayers, and use our spiritual gifts at the right time. We do not rush to the finish line; we let Jesus set the pace.

Finally, following Jesus sets the purpose. The early disciples had to learn why they were called. They thought they were in on the ground floor of a new kingdom and should be rewarded as such (Mark 10:35–40). That thinking came from the world around them rather than from following Jesus. They learned their purpose was to make disciples wherever the Lord led them. The purpose was clear. All the disciples had to do was follow.

» *Why do we sometimes need correction in our direction, pace, or purpose?*

B. Mirror His Actions

Mirroring Jesus' actions represents a daunting task for disciples. Nothing should inspire disciples more than Jesus' declaration of those who believe on Him, "Greater works than these shall he do" (John 14:12). Jesus' ministry caused disciples to marvel and understand Jesus had come from the Father (John 5:36). These greater works would come through prayer, following Jesus' commandments, responding to the Spirit, and living by Jesus' love principle (John 14:13–21).

Mirroring Jesus' actions begins with accepting a new identity in Jesus. Like Nathaniel, we may ask, "What good comes from our people?" Nathaniel had no evil or guile in his spirit, but he could not see the capacity of being spiritually productive (John 1:45–51). His city had not produced a great prophet or leader. Why would that change now? Following Jesus reveals the potential He places in us (John 15:16).

Following Jesus develops new thought and action patterns. For example, accomplished musicians will study a new piece of music, learn how the masters have played it, and practice. Practice will begin with a much slower tempo than will be performed in the concert halls. The actions must become engrained in the mind and fingers.

Some disciples struggle with inactivity while others struggle with hyperactivity. Disciples correct their behavior by following the Teacher.

» *What is something specific the Spirit is calling you to do to bring you closer in line with His actions?*

III. TO FOLLOW IS TO OBEY

King Saul is not the only one who thought sacrifice would make up for a lack of obedience. Paul had to inform the Roman church, as well as the church today, that willful disobedience to God's will was incompatible with the life of grace. (See Romans 6.) Grace has broken sin's control and provided forgiveness for occasional sin. But disciples do not follow the Teacher just to experience forgiveness. Grace also empowers us to live as agents of reconciliation in the world. Such a call requires obedience.

"And he said to them all, If any man will come after me, let him deny himself, and take up his cross daily, and follow me" (Luke 9:23).

A. Leave Behind

Obedience begins with self-denial. This foundational work of grace sets the trajectory for following Jesus like nothing else. The disciples' call required them to leave their nets, boats, parents, and tax table. Jesus taught His followers that they could not have dual citizenship. They must choose which master they will serve (Matthew 6:24).

Leaving is not always easy. Some who considered following Jesus left the journey before they even got started. They were not willing to leave family, property, or dreams that had just come true. Leaving our old lifestyles forces us to continually reject the common sense or collective wisdom of our culture. Even good rules must be put aside for the lifestyle Jesus desires (Matthew 5:38–48). We must indeed put away the works of the flesh (Galatians 5:16–21) and even our childish understandings of faith (I Corinthians 13:11; Hebrews 5:12–14).

Fortunately, grace does not give up. Jesus went out of His way to invite Peter for a reconciliation conversation (Mark 16:7). He also called Peter to dinner—a place where the disciple could truly discover that his love for Jesus was deep enough to let go of some things, so he could feed Jesus' sheep (John 21:12–17).

B. Take Up the Cross

Following and obeying Jesus requires taking up a cross. This startling image came on the heels of great revelation. The cross call did not come with the invitation to drop the nets. Personal crosses had to be connected to a deeper revelation of Jesus' identity. He is both the Christ and the suffering one. He would gracefully lay down His own life. He would inform His followers that they must do the same.

Jesus handled His cross by seeing what was ahead and despising the cross's shame. Obedience requires disciples to take similar steps. We must "press toward the mark" as a people who have not yet attained our goal. Counting all things as loss enables disciples to look forward without shame or fear (Philippians 3:13–15).

Jesus trusted the Father's will. He knew the Spirit would quicken Him from the grave after three days. Since He knew He would live again, momentary death held no shameful loss or lasting stench of decay.

IV. TO FOLLOW IS TO SERVE

To follow Jesus is to serve like Jesus. God's redemptive plan unfolded by sending a suffering servant rather than a messianic warrior. By serving, Jesus fulfilled the human mandate to tend to God's creation. Jesus served those around Him, whether it was a child in need or disciples with dirty feet. Following Jesus always requires the posture of a servant to God and to others.

A. Serve God

God created people with needs for secure living, belonging, and purpose. The Garden of Eden provided the perfect place for humanity to flourish. Then sin broke everything. No longer could people joyfully live in service of the Creator without fear. Following Jesus opened the door to freely serve and flourish again. Going through the door of serving God and others requires faith and ongoing spiritual maturity.

Salvation represents so much more than a ticket to eternal life. Jesus told His followers that new power would come with the Holy Spirit. Followers receive spiritual giftings as individual members of the body and as the body as a whole. (See I Corinthians 12; Romans 12.) Serving God starts by recognizing spiritual giftings.

Stewards freely serve by holding their master's goods in trust. They seek to live worthy of the master's trust. Stewards have only one evaluation standard: faithfulness (I Corinthians 4:2). Living in the shadow of the Cross removes competition and the pressure to succeed or prove self-worth. Stewards know they are lavishly loved by God and seek His pleasure alone. Other goals fall short of a follower's potential.

Loving and serving God becomes visible as we live out the second of the great commandments—loving others as we love ourselves.

» *How can we live out the second of the great commandments?*

B. Serve Others

Scripture boldly recounts the lives of men and women of faith. Hebrews 11 reveals the catalog of faithful people as well as chief failures. All manner of vices spring from biographical sketches of those listed. The New Testament tells a similar story. Paul called himself chief among sinners. Peter denied his Master and could have easily lost the Kingdom keys. By being restored to God through Christ, disciples reorient their lives from self-centeredness to living on behalf of others.

Peter's life provides wonderful snapshots to grasp the magnitude of disciple transformation. Peter went fishing in self-pity. When the Lord did not live up to Peter's expectations, Peter shamefully denied his friend. Yet Jesus called Peter again. This recall centered on loving Jesus by serving the Shepherd's sheep. Peter did not get sheep of his own; he would only find purpose and value by using his gifts to bless other people.

Peter wanted to know if John would have to pay the same stewardship price (John 21:21). He had not yet learned the pleasure that comes from giving up personal prerogatives to follow Christ (I Peter 2:16–25). By the end of Peter's life, he had a more mature perspective. He encouraged fellow elders to fulfill their stewardship responsibilities for the right reasons. If they would reject all forms of pride and serve others with the humble mind of Christ, they would gain the opportunity to cast all anxiety on their Lord (I Peter 5:1–7).

» *How does serving others impact our anxiety?*

▶▶▶ INTERNALIZING THE MESSAGE

Disciples serve in many ways. Jesus included caring for children, visiting the sick and those in prison, giving water to the thirsty, and casting out demons. James called the church to go beyond well wishes of "be warmed and filled" and actually do something about the need. James and Paul both believed the servant role included hearing each other's confession and praying (James 5:16–18) as part of bearing one another's burdens (Galatians 6:1–2). Tabitha shared the love of God by making garments (Acts 9:35–36).

All followers have gifts to share. They love the one who called them so much that they follow His example. Following Jesus prepares disciples to serve others.

The Disciples' Prayer

FOCUS THOUGHT

It is important for us to pray after the manner Jesus taught His disciples to pray.

 FOCUS VERSE

Matthew 6:9

After this manner therefore pray ye: Our Father which art in heaven, Hallowed be thy name.

 LESSON TEXT

Matthew 6:5–15

5 And when thou prayest, thou shalt not be as the hypocrites are: for they love to pray standing in the synagogues and in the corners of the streets, that they may be seen of men. Verily I say unto you, They have their reward.

6 But thou, when thou prayest, enter into thy closet, and when thou hast shut thy door, pray to thy Father which is in secret; and thy Father which seeth in secret shall reward thee openly.

7 But when ye pray, use not vain repetitions, as the heathen do: for they think that they shall be heard for their much speaking.

8 Be not ye therefore like unto them: for your Father knoweth what things ye have need of, before ye ask him.

9 After this manner therefore pray ye: Our Father which art in heaven, Hallowed be thy name.

10 Thy kingdom come. Thy will be done in earth, as it is in heaven.

11 Give us this day our daily bread.

12 And forgive us our debts, as we forgive our debtors.

13 And lead us not into temptation, but deliver us from evil: For thine is the kingdom, and the power, and the glory, for ever. Amen.

14 For if ye forgive men their trespasses, your heavenly Father will also forgive you:

15 But if ye forgive not men their trespasses, neither will your Father forgive your trespasses.

Luke 18:1

1 And he spake a parable unto them to this end, that men ought always to pray, and not to faint.

ECHO

Jesus taught us to pray. Paul admonished us to pray. Our pastors remind us to pray. But some days we are busy, forgetful, lazy, or carnal. Some days we just do not pray. We want to pray, we know we need to pray, but we do not always pray. But when someone tells us their woes, we remember the power of prayer. "I'll pray for you." We say it, we mean it, but we do not always do it. Why? Most of the time, it is because we forget.

Enter *Echo Prayer*, an app for iPhone and Android designed to help people keep track of those who need prayer. It is designed to keep our prayer list for us and even remind us to pray. You can set a reminder to pray at a certain time of the day or for a certain prayer request. And when God answers your prayer, click "answered," dance a dance of joy, and keep praying for the rest of the people on your list.

Given the sincerity of prayer, let us hope we can mature beyond needing a phone alarm to call us to prayer, but in some way we must discipline ourselves to keep our promise to pray for people who ask for our prayers. And God will keep His promise when He tells us He is listening to us. Our prayers plus God's power will produce answered prayers.

 OUTLINE

I. WHEN YOU PRAY

   A. Not as the Hypocrites

   B. Pray in Secret

   C. Not Vain Repetition

II. AFTER THIS MANNER

   A. Praise

   B. Pronounce

   C. Petition

   D. Penitence

   E. Proclaim

III. ALWAYS TO PRAY AND NOT TO FAINT

CONTEMPLATING THE TOPIC

When the doctor diagnosed her with leukemia, Nona Freeman soon learned this would be the end of her work on the mission field. She fumed about having only been there three years and already being too ill to do anything more. She was too embarrassed to ask friends to pray. However, her husband got word to one prayer warrior without Nona knowing.

For two weeks Nona struggled in such pain and weakness that she could not pray for herself. One night she had given up hope of living, but the Lord gave her a dream. She saw a man kneeling to pray, drew nearer to hear him, and recognized her praying friend. In her dream she heard him rebuke that disease, and instantly she felt something like an electric shock shoot through her body. Immediately she was awake with clarity and comfort—no more pain. She could not help but tell many of what the Lord did for her. She said, "I now know how Hezekiah the king must have felt when the sentence of death was given him by the prophet, followed by God's graciously adding years to his life when he prayed" (Nona Freeman, *Bug and Nona on the Go*).

I. WHEN YOU PRAY

Jesus taught His disciples the new way of life in the Kingdom. He did not see prayer as an option or an addition to a disciple's life, but a norm. Jesus declared, "When you pray," as a clear marker that this activity is to be typical of a disciple, not exceptional. There is no such thing as a praying disciple—those who do not pray are not disciples.

Since this exercise would be core to a believer's identity, Jesus cleared up the confusion caused by religious behaviors and defined what prayer should be. To institutionalized religion, prayer is a routine, an obligation, and an empty ritual intended to make good things happen. For Jesus, prayer was much more.

» *Do you view prayer as an event or lifestyle? Why?*

A. Not as the Hypocrites

For some, prayer was a mask or an act—hence Jesus called them "hypocrites," meaning "actors." They put on a front they wanted others to see. Even today people know they look good to other Christians if they pray. Perhaps their prayer over their meal is sometimes for self-glory rather than to give God thanks. Even in a Pentecostal church, people can affect the right posture in prayer, they can weep, or they can lift their hands and shout "hallelujah!" with the intent of looking good to others. One must be careful not to slip into "a vague devotional mood" as C. S. Lewis described. Prayer must be much more than duty or display.

B. Pray in Secret

Rather than prayer being a presentation or a public demonstration, prayer is to be a private strategy. Jesus tells us to be like a city on a hill that all can see, but we are not to do our spiritual works in public. What the world sees of us in public will be fueled by the prayer we do in private. Those who show off with fancy prayers and projected religious behavior are hollow on the inside and powerless in private. Those who connect to their source of power in the unseen areas will have evidence of that in public.

C. Not Vain Repetition

Sadly, too many people get into a rut of prayer that does nothing. The religious institution values such rituals and memorized prayer because it is measurable. However, prayer is a conversation. Conversations have no perfect formula or measurable data like a lecture or recitation. Conversations are as fluid and flexible as the persons involved. Repeating words over and over does not make a conversation. A quality conversation connects hearts. When one or both speakers are moved, that is effective conversation.

In keeping with what the Lord Jesus taught about prayer, His earthly brother helped us understand more when he wrote, "The effectual fervent prayer of a righteous man availeth much" (James 5:16). Effective prayer does something. Prayer is not a destination, but a journey.

» **What great things have you seen occur from your prayers?**

II. AFTER THIS MANNER

Jesus intended His disciples to pray with certain parameters. This "pattern prayer" for disciples was not to be repeated word-for-word with empty, rote memorization. That would go against what Jesus taught. This prayer structure shows a disciple what aspects are included in a healthy conversation with Jesus.

The most overlooked word in the prayer is the first: "Our." Prayer should be for others and not just self. It should bring unity and not division. Even though a disciple prays in a private place, prayer pulls the body together through one Spirit.

A. Praise

Too often a prayer begins with a problem as its focus rather than the source of our answers. Effective prayer begins with uplifting the Lord Himself and recognizing the greatness of the one to whom we pray. By saying "Father"—which Jesus would have spoken in the Aramaic, *Abba*, essentially meaning "Daddy"—Jesus shows us how personally and confidently we can approach the Lord in prayer.

Approaching the Lord respectfully makes us pause and temper our approach to Him. It is too easy to not be interested in Him and just be interested in getting something for self. Witchcraft and paganism are about what the powers do for the person. Other religions are about serving "me." The faith of Jesus is first about what we do to serve the Master of the universe.

» **Does your prayer time tend to begin with problem or praise?**

B. Pronounce

Next, before we ask for what we want in prayer, there is another important stopping point of prayer. Non-disciplined prayers often include people asserting their will on God: "Lord, I need You to do this. Father, make this happen for me. God, I want this and this and this." By beginning with His will, our requests will come in the right spirit. By getting the right perspective in prayer, we may find we do not need to ask for some things at all.

C. Petition

As our priority, we pray the kingdom of God into existence. All around us exist the kingdoms of the flesh (self-rule), the human system, and Satanic forces. These kingdoms operate on three levels for those without Christ. First, the flesh is a kingdom of one—a person inside his or her own skin, ruled by personal desires, making choices against God's plan. Second, the forces of this world intimidate and pressure even good people to do those things that are against God's desire for humanity. Often the personal drive of a human finds a place for expression in this network of selfishness, which encourages sin and rebellion against God. Third, the devil's kingdom works behind the scenes, literally, taking advantage of people who are living in sin. Satan and his forces drive people to do things they cannot explain and forever regret.

A child of God is strategically placed to expand the kingdom of light. By prayer we fight the forces of Hell and drive back the dark plot on earth's inhabitants. In the home, street, neighborhood, city, region, and country, the disciple prays God's kingdom into existence until it becomes the mountain that fills the whole earth. Human strength cannot build this empire—only the King and His forces can expand God's kingdom. Believers know the strengths of the kingdom of darkness in their area: abuse, alcoholism, doctrines of demons, and so on. Pray specifically to oust those evil elements of this present world and pray the solution that the kingdom of God will bring: gentleness, clear minds, apostles' doctrine, and so on.

» *What features of the kingdoms of this world should you pray against in your area?*

As humble servants we show up in the presence of the King and get our orders. This means a disciple consistently lays down personal desires and puts the Father's will in that place. Knowing what God's will is makes it easier for us to pray. Pray for others that the will of God be done in their lives: healing, financial supply, joy, and much more.

The Lord wants to hear our requests. We come to Him not to make demands of our wants and wishes, but to ask for the things we need. The promise of provision is now, the promise of prosperity and abundance is in the life to come. While the Lord often blesses His people with much more than necessary, we can stand in strong faith knowing He will give us everything we need—for this we can ask confidently.

This is not a weekly prayer. Jesus expects His followers to come in prayer daily. This relationship and conversation should grow day by day and not become a dead ritual.

Jesus is the Bread of Life. We must feast on Him to stay alive spiritually. This occurs in prayer and digging into Scripture. By prayer, we feast on Him each day.

D. Penitence

As disciples we cannot stay in harmony with the Lord and be in disharmony with others. We cannot expect God to do for us what we will not do for others. Unforgiveness is an open door for the devil and a closed door for Jesus. In case the disciples missed the importance of this element of the prayer, Jesus quickly taught on this principle after He finished the prayer.

The Lord does not lead anyone into temptation. By praying this we remind ourselves that temptation is never God's idea. By praying this daily, we are reminded that we will be tempted and might fall if we are not watchful. This prayer helps us stay alert to the strength we have in the one from above who holds us up from total devastation.

We should never think our victory is our own.

Disciples know their own weaknesses and the temptations that are a struggle. Therefore, we pray this prayer for ourselves as well as for others. We know our "no" zones, which trigger other things in our lives. As we pray for others ("lead us not"), we pray for each person's different areas of struggle. This is not a blanket prayer or a magic bullet. It is a pattern for us to pray specific prayers. Jesus exemplified this aspect of the prayer when He prayed for Simon that though Satan would try to sift Simon out of the Kingdom, Simon would be converted and help strengthen the others.

Disciples take action in prayer against the enemy of their children, friends, and families. We stand up boldly in prayer for new believers who are growing in their faith. No Bible study or worship song packs the power of what an hour in prayer can do to push back the onslaught of the enemy against vulnerable new believers. We call out the strongman by name and tell him the edict from Heaven: he has no place in these lives and must let them go.

E. Proclaim

While our prayer time may glance toward what the devil and his kingdom are doing, we never finish focused on what is wrong. We focus on the King and His kingdom of righteousness. We exalt the Lord and exult in His presence: "Lord, it is Your kingdom. You are the King of my life. Your kingdom grows until it fills all the earth."

A child of God stands on the winning side. We acknowledge that as we step away from our season of focused prayer. Recognizing that none of these things are done by one's own power, we acknowledge the Giver of all good things: "It is Your power, Lord. You have done all these things. You have answered my prayer for healing. You have delivered my son-in-law from his addiction. You have done all things well."

Finally, we must make sure to do prayer the same as we do every other aspect of life: do it for the glory of God. Every prayer God answers and every time He intervenes in human affairs, His brightness and His glory are increased.

III. ALWAYS TO PRAY AND NOT TO FAINT

Prayer is not an activity for weak or weary people. It takes guts and determination to pray. However, we need not be physically powerful. Jesus explained that even a little elderly woman could get what she wanted by petitioning continually. Her prayers were not in hope that the judge loved her or cared about her situation; her petitions persisted because she knew the law was in her favor. We come to the Lord as those who have nothing of any value to offer Him, but we can come boldly because we know He cares about us.

At times it becomes easy to complain more than we pray. We talk troubles rather than declare triumph. Effective prayer persists because of what the Lord has promised. Some promises and prophecies are not received because someone did not endure in prayer until the answer came.

One of the best illustrations of persistent prayer is Jesus on the eve of His death. His flesh cringed at the thought of dying. Though He had prepared for this moment long before and confidently announced it to His disciples, He went to the garden to pray in private. Jesus began by acknowledging His right to ask based on relationship: "Father." Never stepping out of His servant role, Jesus prayed as a man to God, much as we do, surrendering His human will or desire for survival to the great will or divine design. He patterned for us how to petition in our times of need.

The purpose of His prayer and that of His disciples around Him in the garden was not to enter into temptation. They slept while He persisted in prayer. Jesus prayed for an hour and then woke His disciples to get them praying with Him and for their own sakes. So consumed by the dire situation, Jesus returned to a lonely place of prayer. The pressure was too much for His flesh to handle, and His pores broke out in bloody sweat as tiny vessels ruptured beneath the skin. He returned to wake the men and urge them to pray again. He returned to prayer once more, praying the same thing. He persisted until He conquered the temptation.

Finally, the answer came. Jesus got what He requested: a submitted will. His fears were gone. He awoke the disciples after His three-hour prayer vigil. The enemy was upon Him. The temptation to run was before Him, but He did not flinch. He had steeled Himself against the fear so much that when Simon Peter tried to fight back, our Lord turned to Him and spoke as if He had never had a struggle with the idea of this tortuous death before Him: "Shall I not drink the cup which My Father has given Me?" (John 18:11, NKJV).

» *What does it mean to "always pray and not faint"?*

⟫⟫ INTERNALIZING THE MESSAGE

This model prayer of Jesus is not our only New Testament example of how to pray. Prayers of Paul in his letters show the same elements (Ephesians 1:15–23; 3:14–21; Philippians 1:3–11; Colossians 1:3–22). Like the Lord's "Our Father which art in heaven," Paul began his prayers with thanks to the Father, acknowledging His role in their lives. The apostle prayed that the eyes of their understanding would be opened to God's plan. The most remarkable aspect of each of these prayers is how praying for others would lead the beloved apostle to end by elevating Jesus in such a fashion that much of our formative doctrine is based on his prayer endings.

Hosanna!

FOCUS THOUGHT

Because Jesus is our King, we should honor Him with worship and praise.

 FOCUS VERSE

Mark 11:9

And they that went before, and they that followed, cried, saying, Hosanna; Blessed is he that cometh in the name of the Lord.

 LESSON TEXT

Zechariah 9:9

9 Rejoice greatly, O daughter of Zion; shout, O daughter of Jerusalem: behold, thy King cometh unto thee: he is just, and having salvation; lowly, and riding upon an ass, and upon a colt the foal of an ass.

Mark 11:1–11

1 And when they came nigh to Jerusalem, unto Bethphage and Bethany, at the mount of Olives, he sendeth forth two of his disciples,

2 And saith unto them, Go your way into the village over against you: and as soon as ye be entered into it, ye shall find a colt tied, whereon never man sat; loose him, and bring him.

3 And if any man say unto you, Why do ye this? say ye that the Lord hath need of him; and straightway he will send him hither.

4 And they went their way, and found the colt tied by the door without in a place where two ways met; and they loose him.

5 And certain of them that stood there said unto them, What do ye, loosing the colt?

6 And they said unto them even as Jesus had commanded: and they let them go.

7 And they brought the colt to Jesus, and cast their garments on him; and he sat upon him.

8 And many spread their garments in the way: and others cut down branches off the trees, and strawed them in the way.

9 And they that went before, and they that followed, cried, saying, Hosanna; Blessed is he that cometh in the name of the Lord:

10 Blessed be the kingdom of our father David, that cometh in the name of the Lord: Hosanna in the highest.

11 And Jesus entered into Jerusalem, and into the temple: and when he had looked round about upon all things, and now the eventide was come, he went out unto Bethany with the twelve.

Luke 19:39–40

39 And some of the Pharisees from among the multitude said unto him, Master, rebuke thy disciples.

40 And he answered and said unto them, I tell you that, if these should hold their peace, the stones would immediately cry out.

CULTURE CONNECTION

FLASH MOB

Imagine you are seated at Chick-fil-A with your classic chicken sandwich and mountain of waffle fries laid out in front of you. You only have thirty-five minutes left on your lunch break before you need to head back to the office to finish up the day. Just as you are about to pray over your lunch, sixty people around you stand up, nod to each other, and begin to sing.

Should you run and hide or stand and sing? You did not plan for a choir concert, but you are in the middle of one, in the middle of a flash mob. A flash mob is a phenomenon where a group of people coordinate a time and place to sing together. A group of sixty Christians from several churches planned a flash mob on July 7, 2018, at a Chick-fil-A in Nashville, Tennessee. One of the beauties of worship is we can worship Jesus anywhere, at any time.

We do not have to clock out on worship when the pastor dismisses church on Sunday. We can worship Jesus anywhere, at any time. It does not have to be in a flash mob, but if it is, I hope your waffle fries do not get cold.

OUTLINE

I. JESUS WAS PROPHESIED TO BE THE COMING KING
A. Just
B. Having Salvation
C. Humble

II. TRIUMPHAL ENTRY
A. Riding on a Colt
B. Coats and Palm Branches
C. The Meaning of Hosanna

III. REBUKE BY NON-WORSHIPERS
A. Quiet the Crowd
B. If These Hold Their Peace

IV. JESUS IS OUR KING
A. Hosanna! He Has Saved Us!
B. Worship and Praise

CONTEMPLATING THE TOPIC

When we read the story of Creation, especially about the forming of human beings, we realize we were created to be worshipers of God. He uniquely designed us with a desire to know Him and to worship Him. With all the ability God gave to humankind, nothing is greater than our ability to lift our hearts, our voices, and our hands in praise to our Creator.

However, God also designed us to be able to exercise the power of choice. Just because we were all created to worship does not mean everyone will worship. It is a personal decision each individual must make. For many, this is one of the hardest decisions. There is a battle raging within concerning who will sit on the throne of our lives.

For those who know Him as both Savior and King, worship is no struggle at all. Worship is the expression of a heart of gratitude from those who have been redeemed. It is how we recognize who He really is to us. Worship is the connecting force in our relationship with God.

I. JESUS WAS PROPHESIED TO BE THE COMING KING

To a people who had been oppressed and enslaved, the promise of a King who would redeem them would have been reason to rejoice. The prophet Zechariah told the Israelites to rejoice greatly and to shout. In other words, emotional worship was the order of the day. Their Deliverer was coming, and they would leave bondage forever.

A. Just

The first thing the prophet Zechariah pointed out about the Messiah was "He is just," meaning He is perfect and morally righteous (Zechariah 9:9). There would be no sin found in Him. Further, He would fulfill the law of God completely.

To be perfect He would have to be in right relationship with God and man. We know He was in a right relationship with God because He submitted to the will of the Father. We know He was in right relationship with man because He was compassionate, generous, and merciful.

B. Having Salvation

The people did not need the blessing of material things. They were not looking for better homes or better jobs. This was not about getting an education or saving for retirement. While none of those things are bad in and of themselves, those were not the things for which Israel was looking. No doubt the days spent in oppression had made them long for such things, but there was something deep in their hearts they wanted even more. They were looking for salvation.

However, their idea of salvation and God's idea of salvation were different. They longed for salvation from their enemies, while the ultimate plan of God would be the salvation of their souls. That is exactly what Zechariah told them their King would bring to them. He would indeed bless them materially, but even more so, He would bless them spiritually. As they sought Him, He would reward them.

Jesus said in Matthew 6:33, "But seek ye first the kingdom of God, and his righteousness; and all these things shall be added unto you." When we truly express our worship to God for bringing us salvation, and we seek His kingdom above anything else, He blesses us beyond measure.

» *What is there in your life that may be coming between you and seeking first the kingdom of God?*

C. Humble

Most people would expect a king to arrive, well, like a king. He would come in pomp and circumstance. His bearing would be regal, he would be dressed in the finest of clothing, and he would wear the most expensive crown. People would shower him with applause and kind words. There would be important meetings and special accommodations made for a king.

But not this King. No, He would not be attended by servants and have all the finery of other kings. He would not walk with a strut and a demeanor that demanded attention. His transportation would not be a fine stallion that would be the envy of any horseman. Not at all. Rather, this King would arrive and live humbly. In fact, Zechariah said He would be lowly. Think about that for a moment. What if you were in Israel and heard that? I mean, what kind of a king arrives lowly? How could one who has such a humble demeanor ever be a victorious King? Yet the prophet declared that their King would be lowly.

» *What other passages of Scripture speak to you about the humility of Jesus?*

II. TRIUMPHAL ENTRY

A. Riding on a Colt

True to the prophecy, Mark 11:1–7 tells how a young colt came to be the transportation for the King. Jesus commanded His disciples to go to a nearby village where they would find a young, unbroken colt. They were to untie the colt and bring it back to Jesus. If anyone stopped them and asked what they were doing, they were to simply tell them the Lord needed the colt. This had to be a God thing because if someone did that today, that person would be charged with being a horse thief.

The disciples had to be wondering why Jesus would want to ride into Jerusalem on a colt. It may have made little sense to them. But the colt symbolized peace, and Jesus was bringing peace. The word peace in the Greek means "to set at one again." It meant to take that which was broken and put it back together. Jesus was coming as a King in order to put man and God back together.

The disciples brought the young colt to where Jesus was. As they saw Him preparing to ride the colt, they put their garments on the back of the colt where Jesus would sit. They were doing their best to make Him comfortable.

» *Do you see the colt symbolizing anything else in this passage? Explain.*

B. Coats and Palm Branches

At that time approximately two million people had gathered in the city for the Feast of the Passover. A great multitude of these people lined the streets where Jesus was making His triumphal entry. There would have been citizens of Jerusalem and others from nearby places like Bethany and Bethphage. Their purpose was to be there for Passover, but that quickly changed when they heard Jesus was entering the city.

Their actions on that day showed how they viewed Him. The people began to take off their outer coats and spread them in front of Him. They also cut off tree branches and laid them down before Him. This was a common practice performed for kings of that day.

47

C. The Meaning of Hosanna

Mark 11:9–10 gives us some great insight when it says, "And they that went before, and they that followed, cried, saying, Hosanna; Blessed is he that cometh in the name of the Lord: Blessed be the kingdom of our father David, that cometh in the name of the Lord: Hosanna in the highest."

By their proclaiming of "Hosanna in the highest," they were elevating Him far above any earthly king. The word *hosanna* actually has a two-fold meaning. The first meaning is "save us."

What words could have been more fitting on that day? How significant that this was during Passover, the celebration of God saving the firstborn of Israel prior to their exodus from Egypt. For centuries the Jewish people had been looking for their Messiah. Their hearts' longing was for salvation. By using the word *hosanna*, they were saying He was not only their King—He was also their Messiah.

The secondary meaning of *hosanna* is as an expression of joy and celebration. What better reason to feel joy and to celebrate than to know the King of kings has arrived. He may have arrived lowly, but He held all power in His hands. He may have ridden on a colt that day, but there will come a day, according to Revelation 19:11, when He will ride on a white horse of victory.

» *What are some contrasts between how those crying "Hosanna" were worshiping and how some worship today?*

III. REBUKE BY NON-WORSHIPERS

A. Quiet the Crowd

It is interesting that the ones who were asking Jesus to silence the worship of His followers were the religious elite of the day. They had all the traditions and practices of religion down to perfection. They just simply did not like nor accept heartfelt, emotional worship.

Since they did not enjoy it, they did not want anyone else to enjoy it either. They quickly instructed Jesus to rebuke His disciples—to be quiet, zip their lips, put a stopper in it, calm down, quit getting excited. To the Pharisees, worship should be dignified and proper. They did not see the need for exuberance and emotion in the name of worship.

B. If These Hold Their Peace

Instead of silencing the worshipers, Jesus warned the Pharisees about the dangers of trying to stop heartfelt worship. He also wanted them to understand how much God valued worship. By doing this, Jesus was actually condemning their half-hearted, practiced-to- perfection, weak form of worship.

His words to them stopped them in their tracks. They had never heard such a thing before. Jesus boldly declared, "If these should hold their peace, the stones would immediately cry out" (Luke 19:40).

God will be praised. And if men hold their peace, then nature will cry out in worship.

IV. JESUS IS OUR KING

Revelation 17:14 says, "These shall make war with the Lamb, and the Lamb shall overcome them: for he is Lord of lords, and King of kings: and they that are with him are called, and chosen, and faithful." This passage beautifully shows us who our King is. He is victorious over death, Hell, and the grave. He will conquer Satan at the end of time and bind him forever.

A. Hosanna! He Has Saved Us!

If ever the world needed a Savior, it is today. While we may be born again and preparing to go to Heaven, our cry ought to be, "Hosanna! Come and save us!" Our hearts should be homesick for Heaven, causing us to continually pray, "Even so, come Lord Jesus."

For thousands of years of human history, people have looked for a Savior. Since the Day of Pentecost, the church has longed for their Savior to take them out of this world. We know He has saved us; now we are waiting for that day when He will call His bride home forever.

B. Worship and Praise

While we wait with anticipation for that day, we must maintain until He comes (Luke 19:13). During the time of waiting, our worship must be continual. We need to keep fresh fire on the altar of our lives through our praise to Him.

We each have a choice. God will not make anyone worship Him. He will not pressure us to do what we were created to do. The decision is totally in our hands. But we must never forget that if we hold our peace, all of creation still sings their song to Him. All of nature lifts itself in worship to Almighty God.

God responds to our worship. As we lift our hands and our voices to Him, He takes note. We are never more at one with God than when we are fulfilling our God-given purpose by being true worshipers.

⟫⟫ INTERNALIZING THE MESSAGE

Having a sense of purpose is one of the greatest needs any person has. Fulfilling that purpose is one of the greatest accomplishments any person can achieve. We tend to pursue what we are passionate about and call it "fulfilling our purpose." But what would happen if we began pursuing what God is passionate about? What would happen if we began to fulfill our two-fold God-given purpose of 1) being a worshiper and 2) leading others to be worshipers? Perhaps God would begin to bless our lives in ways we cannot even imagine. "But seek ye first the kingdom of God" (Matthew 6:33).

The House on the Rock

FOCUS THOUGHT

Just like the wise man, we must build our lives upon the Rock.

 FOCUS VERSE

Matthew 7:24

Therefore whosoever heareth these sayings of mine, and doeth them, I will liken him unto a wise man, which built his house upon a rock.

 LESSON TEXT

Matthew 7:24–27

24 Therefore whosoever heareth these sayings of mine, and doeth them, I will liken him unto a wise man, which built his house upon a rock:

25 And the rain descended, and the floods came, and the winds blew, and beat upon that house; and it fell not: for it was founded upon a rock.

26 And every one that heareth these sayings of mine, and doeth them not, shall be likened unto a foolish man, which built his house upon the sand:

27 And the rain descended, and the floods came, and the winds blew, and beat upon that house; and it fell: and great was the fall of it.

Ephesians 2:19–22

19 Now therefore ye are no more strangers and foreigners, but fellowcitizens with the saints, and of the household of God;

20 And are built upon the foundation of the apostles and prophets, Jesus Christ himself being the chief corner stone;

21 In whom all the building fitly framed together groweth unto an holy temple in the Lord:

22 In whom ye also are builded together for an habitation of God through the Spirit.

Colossians 1:23

23 If ye continue in the faith grounded and settled, and be not moved away from the hope of the gospel, which ye have heard, and which was preached to every creature which is under heaven; whereof I Paul am made a minister.

⟫⟫ CULTURE CONNECTION

OCEANFRONT VIEW

One drive to the beach is all you need to see houses worth millions of dollars because of their million-dollar-views. Some houses are beautiful. Some need a little work. But they are the envy of most inland homeowners because of where they are built. Beachfront homeowners can wake up in the morning, draw back the drapes, and watch dolphins playing in the waves. Or they can watch the sun as it makes its climb into the eastern sky over the sea signaling a new dawn.

Their backyard is the ocean. Those houses are perfect for calm days with just enough sunshine to stay warm and just enough breeze to stay cool. But nobody wants to be near them when a hurricane is swirling. In 2004, four hurricanes came to visit the state of Florida: Hurricanes Charley, Frances, Ivan, and Jeanne. Those houses with such enviable views of the Atlantic or the Gulf of Mexico were reduced to rubble by the time the four storms left town. They were built, not on solid, stable rock, but on shifting, unstable sand.

The view from the solid, stable rock may not be as breathtaking as the oceanfront view, but when the wind howls and the rains pound, you will be grateful you built your house on a firm foundation. Storms do not care whose last name is on the mailbox or how many zeros are on your paycheck. Heed the wisdom of Jesus. While the sun is shining, build your house for the days when it is not. Build your house on a rock.

⟫⟫ OUTLINE

I. BUILDING A HOUSE
  A. Blueprints
  B. Strong Foundation

II. FOOLISH MAN
  A. Foundation of Sand
  B. Storm Destroyed His House

III. WISE MAN
  A. Foundation on Rock
  B. House Survived the Storm

IV. SURE FOUNDATION
  A. Gospel of Jesus Christ
  B. God's Word

⟫⟫ CONTEMPLATING THE TOPIC

Jesus likened us, in our relationship with Him, to one who builds a house. A wise builder builds on a firm foundation. If we choose to base our foundational belief system on the Word of God, our faith will be able to withstand the rains, floods, and winds that batter against us.

I. BUILDING A HOUSE

The prospects of moving into a home where everything is new is exhilarating. However, a lot of work goes into building a new construction "from the ground up." This adage is ever so true when building a house. It starts with the ground. Proverbs 24:27 gives wise advice to the builder concerning the first work: "Prepare thy work without, and make it fit for thyself in the field; and afterwards build thine house." In other words, make sure things are done in order. Start with the ground. Make sure the earth beneath the foundation is solid.

» **What do you think Proverbs 24:27 means by "make it fit for thyself in the field"?**

A. Blueprints

When building a house, the first things set into motion are designing the plans and drawing the blueprints. The blueprints reveal every aspect of the completed construction—what the house is going to look like down to the finest detail. Blueprints are meant to guide the contractors so there is no question where everything is to be located. Blueprints are the detailed plan of the finished product.

God has given us blueprints for our spiritual houses. His Word is the blueprint and has all we need to make sure everything is included in our houses. Not only does His Word guide us with the plan for salvation, but it gives directions on how to live a victorious life, resist sin, and overcome temptation.

A successful journey through life begins with God's plan. We must build our spiritual houses on Jesus Christ and the truth of His Word. Jesus pointed to Himself as the source when He said, "I am the way, the truth, and the life: no man cometh unto the Father, but by me" (John 14:6).

Our relationship with God begins when we believe in Jesus and surrender our lives to Him. Surrender leads to obedience as we follow His plan. The basic plan starts with repentance. Repentance is turning from the old path, making an about-face, and walking in God's way. Matthew wrote, "Jesus began to preach, and to say, Repent: for the kingdom of heaven is at hand" (Matthew 4:17). The disciples understood and followed the example of Jesus: "They went out, and preached that men should repent" (Mark 6:12).

The apostles followed the blueprint set forth by Jesus, even after His ascension. "Repent ye therefore, and be converted, that your sins may be blotted out" (Acts 3:19). (See also Matthew 9:13; Luke 15:10; 24:47; II Corinthians 7:10; II Peter 3:9.)

After repenting of our sins, we begin to desire more of His presence in our lives. Through obedience to His Word, we are then baptized in Jesus' name, just as the blueprint specified. Baptism was instructed by Jesus, "He that believeth and is baptized shall be saved; but he that believeth not shall be damned" (Mark 16:16). As the church was established in Acts, Peter shared the plan of salvation with the crowd that gathered after the outpouring of the Holy Spirit in the upper room.

Feeling the conviction of sins, they asked what they should do. "Then Peter said unto them, Repent, and be baptized every one of you in the name of Jesus Christ for the remission of sins, and ye shall receive the gift of the Holy Ghost" (Acts 2:38). The new believers were all baptized in water in the name of Jesus. The proper response to the message of Jesus was always the same, "When they heard this, they were baptized in the name of the Lord Jesus" (Acts 19:5). Baptism was essential for all those who believed. (See also Acts 8:12, 14–16; 10:47–48; Romans 6:3–4; Ephesians 4:5.)

When we follow the blueprint precisely and take on the name of Jesus in baptism, we are promised the gift of the Holy Ghost. The gift of the Spirit comes through our faith in Christ Jesus and obedience to His Word. There are times when this precious gift is given before baptism. (See Acts 10:47–48.) Repentance and baptism are not works to earn the Holy Spirit. We cannot earn this gift. These are simply responses of obedience and expressions of our faith in the death, burial, and resurrection of Jesus Christ.

Jesus paid the price by giving His life on the cross, shedding His blood as the atonement for all our sins (I John 2:2). All we have to do is surrender ourselves to God and allow His Spirit to move into our hearts. As this happens, we will begin speaking in other tongues as the Spirit gives us utterance. (See Acts 2:38.) In the New Testament church, everyone who received the Holy Ghost spoke with tongues. (See Acts 2:3–4; 10:44–46; 19:6.) The blueprint included that very important aspect of the Holy Ghost, so we would have no question what it looks and sounds like to receive the gift of the Holy Spirit.

B. Strong Foundation

As we read the Word of God, we discover what He desires for our lives. Our obedience to the Word of God provides a solid foundation upon which to build our faith. Jesus said, "If ye love me, keep my commandments" (John 14:15). Not only are we wise to obey Christ's commandments, but we show our love for Him when we do so. Just as the wise man built his house upon the rock, building our faith on the Word of God is the only secure foundation. This strong rock gives us confidence that no matter what comes our way, we will be safe because our foundation is strong, grounded, and secure in truth.

II. FOOLISH MAN

Jesus referred to the man who built his house on sand as being the foolish man. It is common knowledge that sand does not provide a stable foundation for construction. For anyone to attempt to build a foundation on sand certainly marks such a person as lacking in wisdom.

» *What do you think the Bible is referring to when it calls a foundation "sand"?*

A. Foundation of Sand

Sand is an unstable platform for a foundation. It is porous and shifts when saturated by water. A storm could easily compromise the strength of a sand-supported foundation. We can liken this to those who may know what the Bible teaches and yet disregard parts of it as unnecessary for their salvation. Or it could be those who choose what verses to believe and obey over other verses that, in their opinion, are not Heaven or Hell issues. When we dissect the Word and begin to value one part above another, we are in danger of weakening the foundation and threatening the structure.

B. Storm Destroyed His House

The foolish man lost everything because he chose the wrong foundation. When the storm began to pour rain on his house, the foundation began to erode. When the winds began to blow, the house had no stable structure to keep it together and began to weaken and fall apart.

The Bible talks about how other doctrines not founded in truth will toss us "to and fro." These are called winds of doctrine. Paul admonished believers, "That we henceforth be no more children, tossed to and fro, and carried about with every wind of doctrine, by the sleight of men, and cunning craftiness, whereby they lie in wait to deceive" (Ephesians 4:14). If we have the truth firmly established in our hearts, these other doctrines will have no impact on our lives. The teaching set forth by Jesus Christ and established by the apostles in the New Testament is the only true doctrine. Paul admonished Timothy to make sure others did not teach another doctrine: "That thou mightest charge some that they teach no other doctrine" (I Timothy 1:3). False doctrine denigrates the purity of God's Word. It adds things that were not intended and leaves out important commandments that were intentionally placed there. It appears the foolish man built his house on false doctrine, which did not withstand the onslaught of opposition.

III. WISE MAN

The man who built his house on the rock is acclaimed for his wisdom. He anticipated the worst that could happen, and then he planned accordingly. When we begin this spiritual journey with the Lord, we should look down the road and prepare for the worst that could happen. Then we should do all we can to build into our relationship that which will help us survive. If we anticipate sickness and prepare our faith to lean on God and His providence, the disease will not destroy our faith. Even if we experience sickness unto death, our faith can remain if we are securely grounded in God. He knows the beginning from the end and has our destiny in His hands.

A. Foundation on Rock

The Scripture calls the man who built his house on rock wise. Perhaps many opportunities arose to deviate from the foundation on rock. At times in our lives it may seem easier because the materials that are most accessible are not the ones that are the sturdiest. When building our relationship with Jesus Christ, we cannot compromise when it comes to laying down the foundation, no matter how inconvenient it may seem. The very base of our faith is at risk if we choose anything else but rock.

The Book of Isaiah informs us our foundation should be the Lord God: "Behold, I lay in Zion for a foundation a stone, a tried stone, a precious corner stone, a sure foundation: he that believeth shall not make haste" (Isaiah 28:16). The Rock of our foundation is that "precious corner stone," Jesus Christ. Paul also referred to Jesus Christ being the "chief corner stone" in his letter to Ephesus: "And are built upon the foundation of the apostles and prophets, Jesus Christ himself being the chief corner stone" (Ephesians 2:20). There is no other option. The Rock, Jesus Christ, is the only safe foundation we should build upon.

B. House Survived the Storm

Building on rock physically gives such a firm foundation that the house is never compromised, even in the greatest storm. There are people who go through horrendous experiences and seem to come out with their faith even stronger.

We cannot know what storms will come our way. Not all storms are from the enemy. Sometimes life brings troubles that come from being in this broken world. Sickness, loss, broken relationships, and other calamities can be the result of simply living in this world. We can be assured that whatever the source of our pain and suffering, if our foundation is solid, we have a better chance of surviving, even if we are a little battered in the process.

» *How can you develop a firm foundation to carry you through trying situations?*

IV. SURE FOUNDATION

Watching people renovate old, dilapidated homes has become extremely popular. People buy old homes and upgrade them to like-new condition. They renovate them to look more modern and then sell them to satisfied customers. It is fascinating to see the progress and enjoy the drama of renovation. The most challenging setbacks come when contractors discover problems with the foundation. If there is something wrong with the foundation, everything else must stop until it can be corrected.

Our spiritual foundation is even more critical than a natural foundation. We should inspect our foundation often to make sure it has not been compromised. If we see an area that is in question or God reveals something to us that is lacking, we should give it our full attention right away. Whatever it takes to bring the foundation back up to code is worth the sacrifice. We want to make sure our basis of belief is established on a sure foundation of truth.

» *Name some habits and lifestyles that could be a detriment to our spiritual foundation.*

A. Gospel of Jesus Christ

The gospel of Jesus Christ is central to our doctrinal foundation. When Jesus walked on this earth, He had a mission statement. It was outlined as He read from the scroll of Isaiah in the synagogue in Nazareth: "The Spirit of the Lord is upon me, because he hath anointed me to preach the gospel to the poor; he hath sent me to heal the brokenhearted, to preach deliverance to the captives, and recovering of sight to the blind, to set at liberty them that are bruised" (Luke 4:18). The mission of Jesus Christ was the foundation and focus of His ministry on earth. Networked in His mission was His example to us. As we watch His life unfold and His ministry come to fruition, we can align our own lives with His perfect example. He was a perfect blueprint for us to follow.

B. God's Word

Today we may not have Jesus walking beside us in a physical form as He did when He was on earth. However, we do have His Word to guide us and help us build a firm foundation. God's Word is relevant for every era and every person, no matter the age, race, or geographical location.

The writer of Hebrews declared, "For the word of God is quick, and powerful, and sharper than any twoedged sword" (Hebrews 4:12). The New King James Version translated it, "For the word of God is living and powerful."

The word *quick* in the King James Version is taken from the word *quicken*, which comes from the root word meaning "to make alive." Just as God quickened Adam by breathing His breath into him, God breathes life into us through His Word. This tells us that God's Word is alive and powerful. It is living. It is the breath of God speaking to us.

God's Word is a solid foundation because it was established before time and lives on forever. "For ever, O LORD, thy word is settled in heaven" (Psalm 119:89). God's Word is eternal. It is an absolute truth we can put our trust in because it has been in existence from the beginning of time. "In the beginning was the Word, and the Word was with God, and the Word was God" (John 1:1). Knowing God's Word is not separate from Him but is His very essence makes His Word stand above all other texts ever written. His Word breathes life into us as we read it.

» *How can we utilize God's Word more in our daily lives?*

⟫⟫ INTERNALIZING THE MESSAGE

Building on the Rock gives us hope that the foundation will not change. God's truth will always be the same because God does not change. His Word was established outside the restricted box of time. It is not subject to the past, present, or future. It is forever "settled in heaven" (Psalm 119:89). The Bible also says Jesus Christ is the same yesterday, today, and forever. (See Hebrews 13:8.) We must continue believing this unchanging truth, so our foundation stands firm until the end.

Since truth does not change, we can be assured it is genuine and unadulterated. The doctrinal truths in God's Word will not waiver. If we continue to stand on the firm foundation of Jesus Christ, the Chief Cornerstone, we will have the firm foundation of truth that will withstand any storm.

Good Soil

FOCUS THOUGHT

Like the good soil, we must hear and receive the Word, allowing it to produce fruit in our lives.

>>> FOCUS VERSES

Mark 4:8, 20

And other fell on good ground, and did yield fruit that sprang up and increased; and brought forth, some thirty, and some sixty, and some an hundred. . . . And these are they which are sown on good ground; such as hear the word, and receive it, and bring forth fruit, some thirtyfold, some sixty, and some an hundred.

>>> LESSON TEXT

Mark 4:3–10; 13–20

3 Hearken; Behold, there went out a sower to sow:

4 And it came to pass, as he sowed, some fell by the way side, and the fowls of the air came and devoured it up.

5 And some fell on stony ground, where it had not much earth; and immediately it sprang up, because it had no depth of earth:

6 But when the sun was up, it was scorched; and because it had no root, it withered away.

7 And some fell among thorns, and the thorns grew up, and choked it, and it yielded no fruit.

8 And other fell on good ground, and did yield fruit that sprang up and increased; and brought forth, some thirty, and some sixty, and some an hundred.

9 And he said unto them, He that hath ears to hear, let him hear.

10 And when he was alone, they that were about him with the twelve asked of him the parable.

. . . . .

13 And he said unto them, Know ye not this parable? and how then will ye know all parables?

14 The sower soweth the word.

15 And these are they by the way side, where the word is sown; but when they have heard, Satan cometh immediately, and taketh away the word that was sown in their hearts.

16 And these are they likewise which are sown on stony ground; who, when they have heard the word, immediately receive it with gladness;

17 And have no root in themselves, and so endure but for a time: afterward, when affliction or persecution ariseth for the word's sake, immediately they are offended.

18 And these are they which are sown among thorns; such as hear the word,

19 And the cares of this world, and the deceitfulness of riches, and the lusts of other things entering in, choke the word, and it becometh unfruitful.

20 And these are they which are sown on good ground; such as hear the word, and receive it, and bring forth fruit, some thirtyfold, some sixty, and some an hundred.

⫸ CULTURE CONNECTION

BROADCASTING

Broadcasting is a modern marvel. It is possible to sit in a radio station in one city and broadcast a signal of songs to another. One Oklahoma station employee from KOMA recalls getting requests from listeners in South Australia. That is not even on the same continent. Now that we have internet access and online streaming, people who have never been to our church can be a part of our services. But as broadcasters understand, those who broadcast give up control of who receives the signal.

That is the same method Jesus referred to in the Parable of the Sower. But Jesus was not referring to radio stations; He was referring to seed. When the sower sowed his seed for a harvest, he broadcast the seed all over the field. There was no way to control where the seed fell, which is why some fell on wayside ground, some on stony ground, some on thorny ground, and thankfully, some fell on good ground. It would be safer and more economical to drop each seed carefully into the plowed soil. Less seed would be lost, but the sower would also reap less harvest.

We are not called to inspect the soil; we are called to sow the seed. It is up to God and the hearers where the seed falls and how it grows.

 OUTLINE

I. THE SOWER AND THE SEED
- A. The Wayside
- B. Stony Ground
- C. Thorny Ground
- D. Good Ground

II. THE PARABLE EXPLAINED
- A. The Sower
- B. The Seed
- C. The Wayside
- D. Stony Ground
- E. Thorny Ground

III. THE GOOD SOIL
- A. Hear the Word
- B. Receive the Word
- C. Bring Forth Fruit

⫸ **CONTEMPLATING THE TOPIC**

Have you ever wondered what it takes to be an effective gardener? How many of us have set out to grow something, whether a full garden or simply a small houseplant? We quickly learn that cultivating a plant is not simple work. One source describes part of the challenge of effective growing by saying, "Some people might think that weeds are the most troublesome element to deal with in a garden. It is probably more accurate to say this: the number one thing that will disappoint and dishearten a gardener is working with soil that is difficult to manage or just plain unproductive" (http://www.garden-counselor-lawn-care.com/why-is-soil-so-important.html).

Soil quality and condition are vital to successful growing, whether it is a potted plant or one's spiritual life. Jesus revealed the importance of soil in the Parable of the Sower and the Seed. As disciples of Jesus, our great desire is to produce spiritual fruit.

I. THE SOWER AND THE SEED

The Parable of the Sower marked a turning point in the ministry of Jesus and introduced a larger section of parables, while serving as an interpretive guide for those who followed. This parable is one of only two included in each of the synoptic Gospels.

The setting of this parable is the Sea of Galilee, with Jesus sitting inside a boat facing the shore while teaching the crowd on the shore. One author noted, "Most of the Roman Empire's inhabitants were rural peasant farmers or herders . . . often ignored . . . but Jesus ministered frequently among this class" (Craig S. Keener, *The IVP Bible Background Commentary: New Testament*). Jesus was at home in both the major metropolitan centers and the rural areas of His day.

The context of this parable would have grabbed the attention of the crowd. Most likely the people hearing the words of Jesus that day either grew their own fruits and vegetables, herded their own meat, or did both. In North America we are several steps removed from field to table, but not so in Jesus' time. Therefore, a story about a farmer sowing seed, while a very common experience to them, would also stir their interest. Many in the crowd must have wondered, *How is this great Teacher going to draw significance from our daily existence?*

In this lesson the Master Teacher emphasized many things. He highlighted the sower, the seed, the soil, and the Kingdom, telling the listener truths about each.

A. The Wayside

Jesus began the parable by telling the audience of a sower, or farmer, who went out to sow. Some of the seed "fell by the way side, and the fowls of the air came and devoured it up" (Mark 4:4). Luke added that the wayside-fallen seed "was trodden down, and the fowls of the air devoured it" (Luke 8:5). The wayside refers to "a path traversing the unenclosed fields. The unproductiveness is due of course to the hardness of the trodden soil. Jesus adds that the birds devoured the seed, and this is due to its lying on the surface without penetrating it" (*International Critical Commentary: New Testament*). Other authors suggest a common practice of the era was to sow before the ground was plowed. This seed then simply got no traction because the ground was too hard for it. The seed at the wayside not eaten by birds was trampled on by people as they walked to and fro. The wayside, as Jesus' audience would certainly know, was not a place where effective growth happened.

B. Stony Ground

Next Jesus said some of the seed fell on stony ground. This is not to be understood as seed falling directly on rock, but the seed fell on a thin layer of soil that had rocks just below the surface. If the sower had not plowed first, he would be unaware of the rocks just beneath the surface. The seed sprouted rather quickly, but its lack of roots was its demise. The stony ground permitted no roots to form.

C. Thorny Ground

Then Jesus said some of the seed fell on thorny ground. This seed landed where other seed was. That does not seem like a bad position to be in—with other seed. However, the other seed was not the same. It was seeds of thorns or briers. The seed that fell on thorny ground was not alone, but it was not with seed that would foster its growth. Jesus said the seeds of briers and thorns choked the grain, causing it to be unfruitful. Often the thistles were unseen. "They may have just been cut or burned, leaving roots from which thistles could grow with the seed to choke it out" (Keener). Even though this portion of the soil may have looked fine on the surface, lurking below were dangerous elements that would hold back and destroy fruit-bearing growth.

D. Good Ground

Lastly, Jesus mentioned the seed that fell on good ground and produced a crop that "sprang up and increased; and brought forth, some thirty, and some sixty, and some an hundred" (Mark 4:8). "All the figures Jesus reports here are very good yields" (Keener). The seed mixed with good ground produced a crop. The seed was the same in each instance; the determining factor was the soil. The soil on which the seed falls is a significant part of this parable.

II. THE PARABLE EXPLAINED

Jesus moved on to explain the parable to His disciples after helping them see why He was now speaking to them in parables. In Mark 4:9 Jesus declared, "He that hath ears to hear, let him hear." He encouraged the disciples to hear and listen to what He said, but it seems they were having trouble understanding. Verse 10 reports that when they were alone, they asked Jesus about the parable. Their question served as the backdrop for Jesus' explanation of the parable and also His rationale for using parables.

A. The Sower

Jesus reported in Mark 4:14, "The sower soweth the word." Jesus is the first sower, just as He is the firstfruits of the Resurrection and the author and finisher of our faith. He has an active role in the sowing; He did then and He does now. In this parable and during His earthly ministry, He sowed to those in the crowd. The further extension is that those who sow what Jesus sowed are also sowers. Sowing is a straightforward task, but it is not an easy task. The sower must be fully convinced the sowing will bear fruit. If not, over time the sower will become discouraged, frustrated, or bored. But when the sower believes the sowing will bear fruit, the sower continues sowing. The truth from the known realm of agriculture is that a sower scatters something of value in order to reap something of value. So too in the Kingdom, a sower spreads something of value with the hope of reaping.

B. The Seed

"The sower soweth the word" (Mark 4:14). The seed of the sower is the Word of God. When we speak the Word of God, we are sowing the words of eternal life. Is it any wonder the Bible has had such an impact on human history?

If one is sowing something other than the Word, the value is limited. How easy it is when witnessing, teaching, or preaching to get off track and ramble on about other things. All who have ever attempted sowing the Word have been guilty of doing something else while making the effort to sow the Word. It requires intentional focus from the sower to keep the discussion, Bible-study session, sermon, or lesson centered on the Word of God. That is the duty of the sower. One who does not expound the Word is not sowing anything of eternal value.

A grave danger for sowers who do not focus exclusively on the Word is they could become distracted with popular fallacies of the day. Sowers must sow the Word regardless of how it differs with popular notions of the age. Courageous sowers diligently and rightly divide the word of truth, ensuring the seed they sow is the Word of God. Sowing the false ideas of pop-culture or even other well-meaning people can lead to false doctrine. Sow the Word.

» *What are some practical ways we can "sow the Word"?*

C. The Wayside

Earlier we described the wayside, but in this passage, Jesus explained the spiritual implications of the wayside. The hardness of the soil prohibited growth. This happens in churches and in individual hearts. The seed is sown and some falls in a place where it has no chance to grow. What may seem to be a purely natural phenomenon was suddenly understood by the hearers as a deeply spiritual circumstance. "When they have heard, Satan cometh immediately, and taketh away the word that was sown in their hearts" (Mark 4:15). Satan promotes the hardening of hearts through bitterness, anger, envy, and disappointment, but ultimately the condition of the heart is determined by the hearer.

Unfortunately, having a hard heart means God's Word has not impacted the person, creating a prime opportunity for the adversary to swoop in and steal away any lingering seed. What a disturbing description! An enemy comes in and snatches away the seed that was sown. This enemy will do everything he can to see that the seed is snatched away from someone's heart.

Here we see another important truth about the sower, the seed, and the field. Jesus reported the seed was stolen from the heart of the hearer by the adversary. So the heart was the receptor of the Word. *Heart* is the most often used scriptural word, in both Old and New Testaments, to describe "the integrating center of man as a rational, emotional, volitional being" (*Dictionary of Paul and His Letters*). Another way to say or think of it is the heart "is the seat of human will and desire" (*Dictionary of the Later New Testament and Its Developments*). When the Bible speaks of the heart, it means the essence of humanity. The seed of the Word of God connects to the essence of humanity, yet people are responsible to cultivate the soil of their hearts so the Word will bear fruit in their lives.

» *Have you ever worked to lead someone to the Lord only to learn, as time went on, the soil of that person's heart was hard? Explain.*

D. Stony Ground

Earlier we learned that the stony ground was not necessarily a gravel field; it was ground with just a thin layer of soil covering the rocks underneath. The sun caused the seed to sprout up quickly, but the hardness of the rocks meant no roots could form, so depth of growth was destroyed.

Since the common practice of the era was to not plow until after sowing, the sower would be unaware of the conditions just below the surface. This is a true analogy of any who sow seed even today. Often we do not know what is below the surface—our task is to sow as effectively as we can. Time will tell whether the soil beneath the surface is good for growing. Additionally, as hearers of the Word, our task is to stir up the fallow ground, or as God said through His prophet Jeremiah, "Break up your fallow ground" (Jeremiah 4:3). Stony ground can destroy growth, but it can be plowed up for better results.

» *When working with those whose hearts seem to be "stony ground," what have you found to be effective?*

E. Thorny Ground

The thorny ground is where thorns and thistles were trimmed or even burned down, but the roots remained. As mentioned previously, here the seed fell where other seed was. Unfortunately, the other seed would not facilitate the new seed's growth and production of fruit.

How many people in churches are in this category? Probably all have known those who did not want to continue following God's Word but wanted to have a semblance of God, so they aligned themselves with thorns and thistles. Thorns and thistles are around the church, but they do not produce fruit.

Jesus said the cares of this life and the deceitfulness of riches choke out the seed and block it from being fruitful. Disciples must carefully guard their hearts to discern whether any thistles are trying to grow. Some helpful questions are: Am I continuing to give to God's kingdom? Am I serving in the church? Is my life bearing fruit? Am I focused on the things of the world? Do my thoughts about life, spiritual freedom, and consecration focus on God's Word or the carnal notions of popular culture?

We must not let the thistles choke us out.

III. THE GOOD SOIL

Thankfully not all soil was challenged. Some seed fell on good soil; when that happened fruit followed. Productivity depends on receptivity: "The contrast between the unproductive and the productive soils . . . illustrates the contrast between those in Israel who were rejecting the message of the kingdom and the disciples who received the message of the kingdom" (Mark L. Bailey, "The Parable of the Sower and the Soils"). In the life and ministry of Jesus, we find a profound dichotomy between those who believe (people from every nation, tribe, and tongue) and those who do not believe (the leaders of the Jewish people, those God called to be His own and blessed with the revelation of the first covenant). The truth of the good soil is the revelation that anyone, anywhere can receive the message of the Kingdom, mix it with faith and obedience, and live a life that is productive spiritually.

» **What does "good soil" look like?**

A. Hear the Word

Those who bore fruit heard the Word. They were in position to hear what God was saying. Their hearts were not so filled with other things that the Word could not get through. Hearing is significant because we know faith comes by hearing (Romans 10:17).

B. Receive the Word

Hearing is a prelude to receiving the Word. But we can hear the Word and discard it. The thin soiled places of every human heart would like to do that every time a word comes that challenges. The call from God is to hear the Word, understand it, and then apply it to our hearts. Receiving the Word into our spirits is how to be the good soil described in the parable. This is why prayer before and after church services is so important. Sometimes it is very clear to us that God is working on our hearts through His Word, yet at other times we are not so sure. But when we pray, we allow God's Spirit to illuminate His Word to us and help us receive it.

» **What are some ways we receive the Word?**

C. Bring Forth Fruit

Paul lists fruit of the Spirit in Galatians 5:22–23. Spiritual fruit is the sign of a healthy Christian life. When we do our part to ensure the ground of our hearts is receptive and the seed is sown in our hearts, spiritual fruit is the natural result. We do not cause the growth; only God can make things grow. But God, by giving humans free will, has given people the ability to prohibit spiritual growth in their lives. The illustration of the farmer is especially relevant. The farmer sows seed and cultivates and fertilizes the field. But the farmer does not bring rain or cause the sun to shine. Only God can do that. Therefore, as we work with God, He will bring the increase into our lives. The seed of His Word is powerful, producing an abundant harvest.

⟫⟫ INTERNALIZING THE MESSAGE

We must prepare our hearts to be good soil, so we are able to receive the Word. The Bereans "received the word with all readiness of mind, and searched the scriptures daily" (Acts 17:11). It is important to receive the Word with a heart that is ready to obey. This means we are prepared, with an open heart and a committed spirit, and we accept God's instructions without hardness.

In Remembrance of Me

FOCUS THOUGHT

We must keep in our remembrance the sacrifice Jesus made for us.

 FOCUS VERSE

Mark 14:22

And as they did eat, Jesus took bread, and blessed, and brake it, and gave to them, and said, Take, eat: this is my body.

 LESSON TEXT

Mark 14:17–26

17 And in the evening he cometh with the twelve.

18 And as they sat and did eat, Jesus said, Verily I say unto you, One of you which eateth with me shall betray me.

19 And they began to be sorrowful, and to say unto him one by one, Is it I? and another said, Is it I?

20 And he answered and said unto them, It is one of the twelve, that dippeth with me in the dish.

21 The Son of man indeed goeth, as it is written of him: but woe to that man by whom the Son of man is betrayed! good were it for that man if he had never been born.

22 And as they did eat, Jesus took bread, and blessed, and brake it, and gave to them, and said, Take, eat: this is my body.

23 And he took the cup, and when he had given thanks, he gave it to them: and they all drank of it.

24 And he said unto them, This is my blood of the new testament, which is shed for many.

25 Verily I say unto you, I will drink no more of the fruit of the vine, until that day that I drink it new in the kingdom of God.

26 And when they had sung an hymn, they went out into the mount of Olives.

I Corinthians 11:23–26

23 For I have received of the Lord that which also I delivered unto you, That the Lord Jesus the same night in which he was betrayed took bread:

24 And when he had given thanks, he brake it, and said, Take, eat: this is my body, which is broken for you: this do in remembrance of me.

25 After the same manner also he took the cup, when he had supped, saying, This cup is the new testament in my blood: this do ye, as oft as ye drink it, in remembrance of me.

26 For as often as ye eat this bread, and drink this cup, ye do shew the Lord's death till he come.

CULTURE CONNECTION

LEST WE FORGET

September 11 is one of those days that most people remember where they were when they heard the news. Even the busiest business people stopped what they were doing to watch as passenger planes rocketed into the World Trade Center, the Pentagon, and a remote field in rural Pennsylvania. No one could believe the sheer terror brought on by the terrorists who overpowered the pilots and weaponized the planes. And everyone was amazed at the selfless heroism of the first responders and passengers to sacrifice themselves for people they did not even know.

Each year, on the anniversary of that unthinkably dark day, we pause in the morning to remember the sacrifice of the first responders, passengers, and workers. And we say their names, so we do not forget them or their sacrifice. Jesus knows we are prone to forget, so He instituted a way for us to remember His sacrifice. We call it communion, the Lord's Supper, the Last Supper, or Eucharist. It is a sober celebration for the blood He shed for us and for His body that was broken for us.

He was not the victim of a terrorist plot; He was the protagonist in the greatest story ever told. The Romans and the Jews did not take His life; He willingly laid it down. Jesus died so we can live. The next time our church celebrates communion together, remember Him. Remember His sacrifice. And remember that the same one who came to die for us is coming back for us.

OUTLINE

I. PREPARATION FOR THE PASSOVER
    A. A Man with a Water Pitcher
    B. Upper Room

II. JESUS WITH THE TWELVE
    A. A Betrayer
    B. Is It I?

III. LORD'S SUPPER INSTITUTED
    A. The Bread
    B. The Cup

IV. THIS DO IN REMEMBRANCE OF ME
    A. Practice of Communion
    B. Remember on Purpose

CONTEMPLATING THE TOPIC

Parents often fear potential dangers that might come to their children. Therefore, moms and dads focus their parenting to reduce as many risks as possible. When the little one becomes mobile, parents childproof their home. Electrical sockets get covered, and dangerous objects are removed from surfaces the child might reach.

When the child starts moving into public spaces, many parents start introducing phrases like "stranger danger" into the child's vocabulary. Parents want to protect their child from kidnapping and abuse at the hand of a stranger. Parents believe children must learn this phrase because little ones do not have an innate distrust of others. Children need to remember not to get into cars with strangers, because not remembering could be catastrophic. However, as adults we may continue to distrust those who are different from us.

Fear of strangers resides deep in the human spirit. Violence has threatened people in all periods of human history. The ministry of Christ, however, witnessed to a new way of living. Jesus called His followers to love their enemies rather than fear them. The only way for these new disciple behaviors to become a reality is to form new memories of how to respond to other people. Jesus willingly died at the hand of those who did not like Him. He offered His own experience as a new tool to create new memory possibilities in His followers.

I. PREPARATION FOR THE PASSOVER

Jesus and His followers had deep memories of freedom from abusive people. Passover played a significant role in both their memories of liberation and their identity as a people. Passover recreated the liberation from Egypt and pointed forward to a time when God would free them from Roman rule. Every neighborhood in Jerusalem would have engaged in house cleaning, preparation for the special meal, and welcoming extended family to the celebration.

A. A Man with a Water Pitcher

The disciples initiated the Last Supper preparations. In the past they had not attended to the daily needs of Jesus or of His followers. Those moments provided the context for multiplying the bread and fish so all could be fed. On this occasion they asked Jesus where He would like to have His Passover dinner, rather than just assuming everything would happen in an orderly fashion.

Jesus' directions to find a man carrying water sounded more foreign to His original audience than it would for us today. Carrying water in Jerusalem at that time would have been a woman's work. The unusual occurrence of a man carrying water would have certainly gotten the attention of the two men.

B. Upper Room

The disciples followed the servant all the way to his master's house. There they asked the house owner for the room prepared for their Master. Following Jesus frequently meant sleeping and eating outdoors. They had heard more teaching during walks through fields, on a hillside, in a boat, or on the Temple grounds than they had heard inside of buildings. This night they would eat inside in accordance with the Law and to provide memory guides for the future.

» *Do you think these disciples sensed something was about to happen that evening? Why or why not?*

II. JESUS WITH THE TWELVE

The twelve apostles represented the twelve tribes of Israel. Jesus chose them to follow Him, learn His identity, accept their new mission, and continue His work to the whole earth.

A. A Betrayer

Deliverance always incudes dying. Without dying, too much of the old bondage comes into the new phase of life. The Passover meal included a sauce made of dried fruits, spices, and wine or vinegar to help reflect on the first Passover when Israel triumphantly left Egypt's death. Worshipers would dip their unleavened bread and bitter herbs into the sauce to remember where they had been and reflect on the hope before them.

Jesus chose the bitter herb dip to reveal how the coming deliverance would include death by betrayal. Contemporary Gospel readers see the threads of the betrayer woven throughout the story. The original diners did not have the insight of reading the completed story. They did not realize how isolated Judas was from the other eleven. They assumed following Jesus predestined all of them to reigning with the Messiah in His new kingdom.

B. Is It I?

Jesus revealed His pending death after the confession in Caesarea Philippi. This new revelation that one of them would betray Jesus brought sorrow on all of them. What started as a remembrance of God's deliverance quickly degenerated into self-questioning. One of them would end all their hopes.

Each disciple asked the Master, "Is it I?" Remembering the Lord's Supper calls disciples today to ask the same question. Like Judas, contemporary betrayers would be better off to have never known life than to turn back on Jesus' mission.

» *How does unrepented betrayals hinder you from celebrating the Supper?*

III. LORD'S SUPPER INSTITUTED

Jesus looked forward to that special Passover. The day had come for Him to fulfill His purpose. As captain of our salvation, He lived to suffer so He could offer cleansing to all. (See Hebrews 2:9–11.) Jesus chose a new meal for new covenant people—a meal of bread and cup.

A. The Bread

> And as they did eat, Jesus took bread, and blessed, and brake it, and gave to them, and said, Take, eat: this is my body. (Mark 14:22)

Jesus fed the multitudes in the wilderness as a sign of His delivering power. All participants linked the bread to Moses' manna, but Jesus wanted them to eat of the new bread that gave life. John 6 records Jesus' teaching on eating the bread of His body. This new bread would bring eternal life. The Lord's Supper included four acts which still guide us today.

Act 1: Jesus Received the Bread

Jesus received the bread on the table just as He had received the five loaves from the boy when thousands needed to be fed. He chose the most common staple of daily living to create the symbol of grace. In death He took the common nutrients of daily living and transformed them into a means of grace.

The common things of life become something else when placed in Jesus' hands. Disciples freely give their master everything they have. They do not hide their shame or keep honor for themselves. Instead they place all in Jesus' hands. He removes all shame and empowers the smallest gifts to become holy, Kingdom resources for the mission ahead.

Act 2: Jesus Blessed the Bread

As our true High Priest, Jesus took His blessing role quite seriously. His words brought life to all He blessed, even children, lepers, tax collectors, common fishermen, and prostitutes. All who place what they have in Jesus' hands receive the favor of God.

Those who follow Jesus do so to fulfill His missionary purposes. All good and perfect blessings come from above, from the one who will never turn from His commitment to bless those begotten by the word of truth. These blessings serve as a sign for many more to come (James 1:17–18). These blessings provide the resources to love our neighbors as ourselves. In the Lord's Supper, disciples actively receive and count those blessings.

» *How do these first two acts challenge you?*

Act 3: Jesus Broke the Bread

Following Jesus contains several paradoxes. If you want to gain your life, you must first lose it. If you want to live, you must first die. Jesus' broken body reminds us that we too have the privilege of being broken with purpose.

More frequent celebrations of the Lord's Supper would help the contemporary church recognize the value of suffering in Kingdom living. Sadly, many disciples follow the old way of pain avoidance rather than the new way of life in the Spirit. Rejecting suffering is to dip in the bitter bowl rather than partaking of the blessed bread. Learning to value brokenness will require Gethsemane-like prayer. Believers should take solace in the fact that seasons of brokenness always happen in the Lord's hands. Jesus never lets us suffer alone.

Act 4: Jesus Shared the Bread

When all of life is placed in God's hands, nothing gets wasted. All things work for His glory. Jesus shared His life with whoever was willing to follow for more than just the loaves and the fishes.

Brokenness produces blessings for others, even as the kernel of wheat's death brings life for those who get to eat its bread. Disciples never represent the end users of the Lord's Supper. They receive so they have something to give. Worship transforms disciples from wanting to get something from the Lord to wanting to share their blessings with others. Sharing our blessings with others further increases our capacity to receive gracious gifts.

» *How do these final two acts challenge you?*

B. The Cup

And he took the cup, and when he had given thanks, he gave it to them: and they all drank of it. And he said unto them, This is my blood of the new testament, which is shed for many. (Mark 14:23–24)

The cup represented the greatest shift that would take place during that passion week. The Old Testament conveys the wonder of God's desire to be among humanity and restore all things back to Himself. The call of Abram in Genesis 12 included potential blessings for all nations.

The Passover meal provided the context of the covenant shift. New Covenant blood would be spilled for many. No longer would Old Covenant bulls, rams, and goats provide the Band-Aid of holiness needed to keep the people clean enough for God to dwell with them.

The New Covenant could take effect once the testator died. Jesus willingly poured out His blood, so all could be reconciled to God. The first enactment of that grace-dispensing meal had everyone drinking from one cup. While sharing a cup upsets contemporary readers, the power of the shared cup belongs firmly in the Lord's Supper. All members of the table either drink of the New Covenant cup together or they do not drink at all. As Paul would later state, we also eat of one bread because we are of one body.

That first enactment emptied the cup. In the twenty-first century, many people want a spiritual buffet where they can pick and choose the parts they enjoy. The offered cup must be drained, just as Jesus completely emptied His life. When believers willingly drink deeply and completely, they experience the overwhelming work of grace.

IV. THIS DO IN REMEMBRANCE OF ME

And when he had given thanks, he brake it, and said, Take, eat: this is my body, which is broken for you: this do in remembrance of me. (I Corinthians 11:24)

Modern neuroscience helps us understand that memories do not rest in a set of filing cabinets in the brain. Human memory does not work like saving computer files on a hard drive or in the cloud. Memories draw from different parts of the brain. Some memories store facts and events, while other memories relate to skills, habits, or classical conditioning where one stimulus gets linked to another. Recalling a past memory includes smells, emotions, and sights, in addition to the facts.

Recalling a memory actually remaps the human brain. The brain develops new connectors and branches for information to be transmitted. God's creative genius in making the human nervous system still holds wonderful new discoveries. These new discoveries make some interesting connections to the biblical text. For example, Paul expressed the ability to have a renewed mind by thinking on good things. Modern science has confirmed the possibility of creating new pathways in the brain by practicing such new thought patterns. Rather than processing information through fear patterns, believers develop a new mind where hope rules. Rather than living to serve themselves, they obtain the mind of Christ where they live on behalf of others.

A. Practice of Communion

Communion feeds the body of Christ rather than individuals in the body. The one loaf and one cup element of the Lord's Supper reminds us to celebrate the sacrament as a group of believers rather than for personal edification. The early church included breaking of bread in its core functions following the second upper room experience. Communion belongs in the context of the apostles' doctrine, fellowship, and prayer

(Acts 2:42). The rest of the Book of Acts demonstrates the consequence of a people who lived in these four practices.

The New Testament does not give specific guidelines for worship like Moses' sacrificial system. Perhaps this flexibility exists as a way to take the whole gospel to the whole world. Drums and colorful dance in African worship will look and sound different from zither music in India or guitars in Latin America. While our music styles differ, the Lord's Supper serves to unify the whole body of believers. By Acts 20 the church had developed a rhythm of celebrating communion on the first day of the week. Paul's first Corinthian letter shows us the Supper had long existed in the life of the church. The Corinthian church failed to celebrate the Supper as one body, thus they ate unworthily.

B. Remember on Purpose

The Lord's Supper serves as a wonderful memory device. Memories triggered by feeling the bread's texture, tasting wine or grape juice, hearing the Lord's words, and sharing the time with disciples of all ages guide the church in celebrating the Supper. A biblical understanding of memory fits well with contemporary neuroscience discoveries.

- Memories recount events from the past. Each time we remember Jesus' sacrifice, it takes on new layers of meaning. New disciples freshly experience deliverance. Elder saints remember the power of Christ's body and blood through decades of faithful service. Each remembering moment changes the memory to include the present realities.
- Remembering Christ transforms current identity. When believers make room for the body and blood of Christ to be experienced, they open themselves for transformation. Such New Covenant moments bring holiness, unity, spiritual gifting, and focus on missionary service.

> **How does a biblical understanding of remembering affect the way you approach the Lord's Supper? How does the Supper transform your outlook on tomorrow?**

▶▶▶ INTERNALIZING THE MESSAGE

Extended-family meals fill the table with people who care for each other and have a shared story. Such meals can be as simple as a pizza or as elaborate as a meal prepared by a trained chef. Memories make the meal a celebration. When disciples gather around the Lord's table, they hear of the torn body and poured blood, but the meal must be a celebration rather than a wake. Remembering the Lord makes the difference. He paid the price for everlasting joy. He opened the door for faithfully living in the Spirit.

Disciples have the choice of dipping in the bitter bowl or sharing the bread and cup. All shame and sorrow disappear when we share Jesus' offering rather than betraying His mission. Remembering the wonder of the meal creates new possibilities as brothers and sisters take fresh steps to be salt and light in a hurting world. Feasting at the table provides the sustaining nourishment to do so. We leave the table in the power of the Spirit.

Watch and Pray

FOCUS THOUGHT

As disciples of Jesus Christ, we must watch and pray so we do not enter into temptation.

 FOCUS VERSE

Matthew 26:41

Watch and pray, that ye enter not into temptation: the spirit indeed is willing, but the flesh is weak.

 LESSON TEXT

Matthew 26:36–46

36 Then cometh Jesus with them unto a place called Gethsemane, and saith unto the disciples, Sit ye here, while I go and pray yonder.

37 And he took with him Peter and the two sons of Zebedee, and began to be sorrowful and very heavy.

38 Then saith he unto them, My soul is exceeding sorrowful, even unto death: tarry ye here, and watch with me.

39 And he went a little farther, and fell on his face, and prayed, saying, O my Father, if it be possible, let this cup pass from me: nevertheless not as I will, but as thou wilt.

40 And he cometh unto the disciples, and findeth them asleep, and saith unto Peter, What, could ye not watch with me one hour?

41 Watch and pray, that ye enter not into temptation: the spirit indeed is willing, but the flesh is weak.

42 He went away again the second time, and prayed, saying, O my Father, if this cup may not pass away from me, except I drink it, thy will be done.

43 And he came and found them asleep again: for their eyes were heavy.

44 And he left them, and went away again, and prayed the third time, saying the same words.

45 Then cometh he to his disciples, and saith unto them, Sleep on now, and take your rest: behold, the hour is at hand, and the Son of man is betrayed into the hands of sinners.

46 Rise, let us be going: behold, he is at hand that doth betray me.

⟫⟫ CULTURE CONNECTION

SEALS

They say it only lasts for six months, but it has been referred to as the longest six months some people will ever endure. It is known as BUD/S: Basic Underwater Demolition/SEAL training in Coronado, California. For six months instructors push young, aspiring Navy SEAL candidates to their limits. The first phase is the toughest. It is even referred to as "Hell Week." On average, two of every three young military men or women dreaming to be a Navy SEAL call it quits during the first phase. But a slim remnant press further, even though their bodies are screaming to quit. Self-will presses them past the pain until they hear the instructors say, "Hell Week is secured."

Their instructors are not their enemies, for without the training, SEALs may not survive in the arena of war. If captured, the enemy will push them even further than their instructors pushed them. So they train . . . and train . . . and train. So do we. We do not train with push-ups and underwater missions, but we train our bodies and our spirits to talk to God and to hear His voice. And we train our bodies to glorify Him, not just to satisfy us.

If we are weak, our enemy will pounce on us to destroy us every chance he sees, but thankfully, Jesus gave us the weapon of prayer. Through prayer we can stay close to God and far from temptation. And when we pray, we know God hears us and will help us because He loves us.

⟫⟫ OUTLINE

I. JESUS PRAYED AT GETHSEMANE
   A. Sorrowful and Troubled
   B. Let This Cup Pass from Me

II. DISCIPLES WERE SLEEPING
   A. Spirit Is Willing
   B. Flesh Is Weak

III. JESUS SURRENDERED HIS WILL
   A. Thy Will Be Done
   B. Betrayed by a Friend

IV. WATCH AND PRAY
   A. Surrender to the Will of God
   B. Strength When Tempted

⟫⟫ CONTEMPLATING THE TOPIC

With each passing year, our world seems to be moving further away from God. However, in times of peril, it is interesting how many people who never pray publicly turn to God when tragedy strikes. The United States Homeland Security Digital Library holds a copy of Concurrent Resolution 223 that allowed the use of the Capitol rotunda for a private prayer vigil after the tragedy of the airplanes that crashed into the twin towers of the World Trade Center in 2001. It states, "Permitting the use of the rotunda of the Capitol for a prayer vigil in memory of those who lost their lives in the events of September 11, 2001" (www.hsdl.org).

As members from both houses of Congress gathered in the rotunda that day, Christian Americans rejoiced at the representation of faith among the leaders. They hoped things would change for the country and prayer would become a higher priority from the governmental offices right down to the homes of the citizens. But, disappointingly, after the tragic event fell further into the past, the memories were less horrendous, and people reverted back to their old habits, leaving God out of their lives.

I. JESUS PRAYED AT GETHSEMANE

A. Sorrowful and Troubled

It is hard to imagine what was running through our Savior's mind while He agonized in the garden. Being God manifested in the flesh, He knew the future. He knew His purpose was to give His life for the sins of humanity, but He also knew what would transpire before that victory was achieved. The pain and suffering must have been heavy on His mind. Being God did not diminish what the flesh would have to go through. His purpose was to suffer excruciating pain on behalf of generations of those bound by sin. In His journey from the garden, He would have to ascend into the depths of Hell before the work was complete.

The pain and suffering were not the only things on Jesus' mind as He agonized In the Garden of Gethsemane. He bore the sins of the world on His shoulders. I John 2:2 says, "And he is the propitiation for our sins: and not for ours only, but also for the sins of the whole world." It is hard to imagine the magnitude of heaviness, sorrow, and emotional pain this caused Him. Sin is a heavy burden that pulls its victims down, even to the point of death. "Then when lust hath conceived, it bringeth forth sin: and sin, when it is finished, bringeth forth death" (James 1:15). The emotional trauma of sin's finished product multiplied millions of times must have been excruciating. On the cross, Jesus bore all our sins. It was imperative for Jesus to carry our sins to provide atonement for them.

» *What are the emotions you feel when you think about the Crucifixion? Why?*

B. Let This Cup Pass from Me

Jesus cried out as the time was nearing for Him to accomplish His mission through suffering. He experienced every sensation we experience in the flesh. "There hath no temptation taken you but such as is common to man" (I Corinthians 10:13). By the foreknowledge of God, Jesus knew what was going to transpire in the last few hours of His life on earth. However, the thought of the suffering involved affected Him as it would any of us. With this great responsibility on His shoulders, His flesh struggled with His spirit. This cup of suffering seemed too much for Him to endure. He ultimately surrendered, but not without evidence of struggle. "And being in an agony he prayed more earnestly: and his sweat was as it were great drops of blood falling down to the ground" (Luke 22:44).

» *What is the significance of Jesus sweating "great drops of blood" in this passage?*

II. DISCIPLES WERE SLEEPING

Nothing is more miserable than trying to keep awake when we are weary. This must have been how the disciples felt that night. The evening was late; it was past the time to be in bed. When Jesus chided them, they probably felt a twinge of guilt, but they were still unable to keep their eyes open.

A. Spirit Is Willing

When God wakes us up in the middle of the night to pray, our spirit is compelled to obey. We are stirred when the Lord wakes us up and guides us to our place of prayer.

Those are the moments we may feel as David felt standing before Goliath with a sling and a few stones. He knew God was going to fight this battle. His spirit was willing and strong. He served a God who had fought for him in the past. God delivered him from the lion and the bear; this was not too hard for the Lord. (See I Samuel 17.) David's courage came from the confidence he had gained in past battles he had won with God at his side.

When God tells us to do something and we know beyond a shadow of a doubt it is His voice, no devil in Hell can stop us. When God shakes us and wakes us up in the middle of the night, our desire is to do His bidding. At that bidding we rebuke the enemy, we challenge legions of demons, and we speak the Word of faith, expecting healing. The very last words Jesus spoke to His disciples were an example of a spirit that is willing. He said, "And these signs shall follow them that believe; In my name shall they cast out devils; they shall speak with new tongues; they shall take up serpents; and if they drink any deadly thing, it shall not hurt them; they shall lay hands on the sick, and they shall recover" (Mark 16:17–18). This courage was evoked by confidence in what Jesus said.

B. Flesh Is Weak

There are times when the spirit is willing, but the flesh is weak. We may be kneeling in obedience to God's call and realize an hour later that we have fallen asleep. Jesus offered an out for His disciples. He understood they were mere mortals and the flesh was not as strong as the spirit. It seems He gave them a generous dose of grace. God knows when we are tired and weary. He extends an extra measure of mercy on us when we at least show the effort. The time is not lost. Nothing is lost with God. "And we know that all things work together for good to them that love God, to them who are the called according to his purpose" (Romans 8:28).

If we are tired and feel we have failed the Lord, we should take a moment and let Him turn it into something good. Even if we did not get in the hour we hoped for, a few moments of obedience goes a long way with the Lord. (See I Samuel 15:22.)

» *Why is our flesh so weak?*

III. JESUS SURRENDERED HIS WILL

A. Thy Will Be Done

Jesus was honest and transparent when He prayed, "O my Father, if this cup may not pass away from me, except I drink it, thy will be done" (Matthew 26:42). Jesus surrendered His will to the will of the Father. His purpose for coming to earth would be fulfilled in His obedience.

B. Betrayed by a Friend

The best place to be when crisis comes is on our knees in prayer. Jesus desired His disciples to join Him, but when they did not, He persevered on His knees. The will of the Father would move forward, even to the extent that someone Jesus loved very much would betray Him. However disappointing, this was all part of the plan for the rest of God's purpose to be accomplished.

Whatever Judas felt when he kissed Jesus to identify Him for the soldiers, afterward he was filled with regret. Using an endearing gesture was all part of the deception. Jesus knew what the kiss really meant. Rather than being an endearing traditional greeting between friends, this time it was a signal used to destroy Jesus. Yet Jesus responded in a loving, gentle way, "Friend, wherefore art thou come?" (Matthew 26:50).

Jesus' response to Judas is truly the mark of a Savior. In the midst of betrayal with a most hideous, grossly tragic ending, Jesus, knowing the outcome of that kiss, still called Judas His friend. At the conclusion of His betrayal, Jesus was still reaching for the precious soul of one He loved.

Is it possible for us to love souls so much that in the midst of betrayal, abuse, or the most despicable treatment, we could still be compassionate toward those people to the point of calling them friends? As our example, Jesus would be pleased if we could portray this type of unconditional love toward others. Jesus declared this kind of love when He was preaching the Sermon on the Mount. He admonished His listeners, "Ye have heard that it hath been said, Thou shalt love thy neighbour, and hate thine enemy. But I say unto you, Love your enemies, bless them that curse you, do good to them that hate you, and pray for them which despitefully use you, and persecute you" (Matthew 5:43–44).

IV. WATCH AND PRAY

Matthew 26:41 reveals the benefit of watching and praying. "Watch and pray, that ye enter not into temptation." Watching and praying is a mighty duo. Praying is an extraordinary tool in itself, but keeping a watchful spirit, not only for the tactics of the enemy but also for the deliverance of the Lord, injects our prayer with faith. We pray with expectation, watching and waiting for God to show Himself mighty. If we could remove the cataracts from our spiritual eyes, we would see how anxious God is to answer our prayers and come to our rescue when we are into trouble. The following verse of Scripture gives us a glimpse of the emotional desire the Lord has for meeting the needs of His children: "For the eyes of the LORD run to and fro throughout the whole earth, to shew himself strong in the behalf of them whose heart is perfect toward him" (II Chronicles 16:9). When we pray with expectation, we literally watch for the salvation of the Lord.

» *How can we pray with expectation?*

A. Surrender to the Will of God

According to the dictionary, *surrender* means "to yield to the power, control, or possession of another upon compulsion or demand; to give up completely or agree to forgo especially in favor of another" (www.merrian-webster.com). When we think of surrender, we may visualize someone looking down the barrel of a gun, hands raised in surrender. At that moment nothing is more important to that person than surrendering his will to the person holding the gun (except in the event he has been commanded to recant his faith).

When people are seeking God, the gesture of raising their hands up is a sign of yielding their will to the will of God. "Know ye not, that to whom ye yield yourselves servants to obey, his servants ye are to whom ye obey; whether of sin unto death, or of obedience unto righteousness?" (Romans 6:16). The reality is, we serve whom we obey. We cannot divide our loyalty between two choices. "No man can serve two masters: for either he will hate the one, and love the other; or else he will hold to the one, and despise the other. Ye cannot serve God and mammon" (Matthew 6:24).

When we completely surrender, God can move in and work with the fallow ground of our submitted spirits. Surrendering to the will of God is essential for God to work in us.

B. Strength When Tempted

Jesus was our greatest example of how to fight temptation. When He went into the wilderness to fast and pray, He was grossly accosted by the devil. However, Jesus used the Word of God to combat the enemy. (See Matthew 4:4, 7, 10.) Through this example Jesus taught us how powerful a tool the Word of God is. Satan was defeated and finally gave up.

The Scripture outlines the power and ability of the Word. "For the word of God is quick, and powerful, and sharper than any twoedged sword, piercing even to the dividing asunder of soul and spirit, and of the joints and marrow, and is a discerner of the thoughts and intents of the heart" (Hebrews 4:12).

> » *Discuss the verses of Scripture Jesus used to defeat the devil in the wilderness. Can we use those same verses today to win our battles? Explain.*

〉〉〉 INTERNALIZING THE MESSAGE

Prayer is important for us to consider. There is much that could be said about the effects of prayer, the power of prayer, and the testimonies of miracles performed through prayer.

As we move through our daily routines, we must take time to reflect on God's will, not only for the future, but for the present. "God, what do You want me to do right now about this situation?" Stopping and taking a moment to pray about a decision could change the course of our lives.

God wants to be involved in every decision we make. If we are in tune with His daily preferences in our decisions, when that life-altering decision comes our way, we will be able to turn to God, hear His voice, and make the right decision.

Made Free

FOCUS THOUGHT

Jesus died for us so we could live free from the penalty of sin.

 FOCUS VERSE

John 19:30

When Jesus therefore had received the vinegar, he said, It is finished: and he bowed his head, and gave up the ghost.

 LESSON TEXT

John 19:28–30

28 After this, Jesus knowing that all things were now accomplished, that the scripture might be fulfilled, saith, I thirst.

29 Now there was set a vessel full of vinegar: and they filled a spunge with vinegar, and put it upon hyssop, and put it to his mouth.

30 When Jesus therefore had received the vinegar, he said, It is finished: and he bowed his head, and gave up the ghost.

Romans 6:17–23

17 But God be thanked, that ye were the servants of sin, but ye have obeyed from the heart that form of doctrine which was delivered you.

18 Being then made free from sin, ye became the servants of righteousness.

19 I speak after the manner of men because of the infirmity of your flesh: for as ye have yielded your members servants to uncleanness and to iniquity unto iniquity; even so now yield your members servants to righteousness unto holiness.

20 For when ye were the servants of sin, ye were free from righteousness.

21 What fruit had ye then in those things whereof ye are now ashamed? for the end of those things is death.

22 But now being made free from sin, and become servants to God, ye have your fruit unto holiness, and the end everlasting life.

23 For the wages of sin is death; but the gift of God is eternal life through Jesus Christ our Lord.

⟫⟫ CULTURE CONNECTION

MAD GAB

Mad Gab is a fun word game. Short phrases are printed on little cards, and the phrases are broken down into little words. The player's job is to figure out the phrase by piecing the words together and sounding them out. It sounds simple, but it is not. For example, the player may read "pea sank white" on the card, but that translates into "peace and quiet."

The fun of Mad Gab is listening to players say the right answer—often with what sounds like an accent—but most of the time, they have no idea what they are saying. Mad Gab came out in the twentieth century, but I found a game of Mad Gab unwittingly played in the Book of Matthew in the first century. But this was not a game because the stakes were life and death.

Jesus had struggled up Calvary, carrying our cross. Roman soldiers slammed Him down on the rugged timber and nailed His healing hands to the cross. Some passersby came walking up to Jesus, filled with rage, though most did not even know why. (See Matthew 27:39–40.) Then the religious leaders chimed in. They pointed to the cross and screamed to the crowd, "He saved others; himself he cannot save" (Matthew 27:41–42). When Jesus heard their rant, the corners of His parched mouth began to crack and smile, because He heard truth amidst the madness.

When Jesus was given the choice between saving our lives and saving His own, He chose to save our lives rather than His own. The Romans did not take His life; He willingly died so we could live. Perhaps if they had listened to their own words, they would have understood what He was doing. As Christian author Max Lucado wrote, "He would rather die for us than live without us." That, my friend, is amazing grace.

⟫⟫ OUTLINE

I. JESUS WAS CONDEMNED TO DIE
   A. Innocent and without Sin
   B. Led Away to Be Crucified

II. GOLGOTHA
   A. King of the Jews
   B. What I Have Written I Have Written

III. SOLDIERS TOOK HIS GARMENTS
   A. A Seamless Coat Like a Priest's Garment
   B. Let Us Not Rend It

IV. IT IS FINISHED
   A. Gave Up the Ghost
   B. Salvation's Plan Was Accomplished

V. MADE FREE THROUGH HIS DEATH
   A. Free from Sin
   B. Servants of Righteousness
   C. God's Gift of Eternal Life

⟫⟫ CONTEMPLATING THE TOPIC

In the United States, fallen veterans are honored for making the ultimate sacrifice to defend the lives of others. Until the events of September 11, 2001, this ideal had become routine, simply a day off from work. Only after the events of that horrible day have the people of the United States again realized the value of life. People were paralyzed as they watched the events unfold, as rescue workers ran into buildings people were desperately trying to escape. Almost twenty years have elapsed since that fateful day, and Americans still feel the impact of that day and the idea of a life sacrificed to save others.

I. JESUS WAS CONDEMNED TO DIE

A. Innocent and without Sin

Pontius Pilate was the Roman prefect for Jerusalem during the time of Jesus. As prefect his primary role was to maintain law and order within the boundaries of his jurisdiction. Jerusalem was notorious for uprisings and civil disobedience in defiance of Roman rule. The Bible names Pontius Pilate as the one who ultimately condemned Jesus to death on the cross. Yet the Bible also tells us Pilate was conflicted. He stated before the mob, "What evil hath he done? I have found no cause of death in him" (Luke 23:22). At this point Pilate was ready to release Jesus, yet the crowd became hostile and demanded Jesus be crucified. Pilate, under pressure to maintain order by oath, chose to send an innocent man to His death.

B. Led Away to Be Crucified

The Gospel of Matthew tells us that after Pilate condemned Him, Jesus was led away to a common hall where a group of soldiers stripped Him, placing a scarlet robe on Him and a crown of thorns on His head. They spat on Him, beat Him, and mocked Him. They then replaced the scarlet robe with His original garment and took Him away to be nailed to the cross. Luke 23:26 states, "And as they led him away, they laid hold upon one Simon, a Cyrenian, coming out of the country, and on him they laid the cross, that he might bear it after Jesus." The Bible goes on to tell of the crowd that followed Jesus and the women who bewailed and lamented Him. The Creator of all things, manifest in the Man Christ Jesus, was subjected to great pain and humiliation at the hands of those He created.

» *Have you ever stood by and watched as someone was subjected to cruel harassment by a large group of people? Explain.*

II. GOLGOTHA

We read in John 19:17, "And he bearing his cross went forth into a place called the place of a skull, which is called in the Hebrew Golgotha." Just the name alone provides a dismal picture of a place that had become synonymous with death. Even today, items containing toxic elements have a skull displayed on the package to warn that the contents can cause death if ingested. Death on Golgotha was not pleasant. It was the final place of execution for those condemned to die by crucifixion.

A. King of the Jews

Jesus was referred to as King twice in His lifetime. The first was at His birth when shepherds and kings sought Him. They hailed Him as King and bowed before Him, bearing gifts. All this honor was given despite the fact this royal Baby was born and housed in a manger. The idea of a king being born, especially one that would cause men to travel a far distance, put fear into King Herod. He sought to destroy Jesus in order to protect his throne.

The second time Jesus was referred to as King was before His death at the hands of the Jewish leaders. When Jesus was crucified, Pilate had a placard put above Him on the cross; it read: King of the Jews.

B. What I Have Written I Have Written

A famous line from Shakespeare's play *Macbeth* says, "What's done, is done." This phrase is often heard in modern society to denote something that cannot or will not be changed. When the Jewish leaders saw the sign hung above the head of Jesus, stating "KING OF THE JEWS," they protested to Pilate, who had written the phrase on the sign (John 19:19). They stated it should say, "He said, I am King of the Jews" (John 19:21). But Pilate, who was disgusted by this whole proceeding, simply proclaimed, "What I have written I have written" (John 19:22). The Bible tells us Pilate had physically washed his hands before the crowd, proclaiming he was washing his hands of the situation. It is obvious from his actions that Pilate's last action in the affair of Jesus' crucifixion was to make the sign. So disappointed with himself for giving in to the pressure of the mob and condemning an innocent man to death, he was finished with the matter and nothing so trivial as a sign was going to be changed.

» *Have you ever faced a situation that left you feeling so conflicted you just decided you were done with it? Explain.*

III. SOLDIERS TOOK HIS GARMENTS

John 19:23 states, "Then the soldiers, when they had crucified Jesus, took his garments, and made four parts, to every soldier a part; and also his coat."

A. A Seamless Coat Like a Priest's Garment

The detail of the coat having no seam held special meaning to the Jewish people of that era. Exodus 28:32 states, "And there shall be an hole in the top of it, in the midst thereof: it shall have a binding of woven work round about the hole of it, as it were the hole of an habergeon, that it be not rent." These are the instructions by God given to Moses of the garment to be worn by the high priest, the only authorized person to enter the Holy of Holies and offer atonement for the sins of the Israelites. The garment was to have no seam.

B. Let Us Not Rend It

The significance of the seamless coat does not end with the relevance to the garment worn by the high priest. Leviticus 21:10 states, "And he that is the high priest among his brethren, upon whose head the anointing oil was poured, and that is consecrated to put on the garments, shall not uncover his head, nor rend his clothes." While Jesus was in no position to rend his own clothes, the soldiers could have easily divided the garment into equal parts as souvenirs. While some may not see this text as being relevant to the events at the Crucifixion, the fact the soldiers opted not to rend the garment maintained the integrity of Jesus as the ultimate High Priest.

IV. IT IS FINISHED

John recorded the last words of Jesus, "It is finished" (John 19:30). Matthew and Mark state Jesus cried with a loud voice, but John records Jesus' final utterance. All the prophecies about His crucifixion were complete. The pain, agony, and humiliation faded with the sunlight. What lay ahead for the followers of Jesus was uncertain; what was certain was that His death to atone for the sin of all humanity was finished.

A. Gave Up the Ghost

Though the Gospel of Luke does not record Jesus giving up the ghost, there does not appear to be any specific reason for this omission. The other Gospels record this event of Jesus as if it were within His control to release His spirit. There is no doubt it was within His control. He had walked on water, healed the sick, made the blind to see, and brought the dead to life again. Jesus was God manifest in the flesh. There was nothing at any time that was not within His control. John 1:3 states, "All things were made by him; and without him was not any thing made that was made." All these events were foretold by God through the prophets of old. It was a plan of His design in order to reconcile sinful man to Himself.

B. Salvation's Plan Was Accomplished

When Peter preached after the Holy Ghost had come, he said, "Therefore let all the house of Israel know assuredly, that God hath made the same Jesus, whom ye have crucified, both Lord and Christ" (Acts 2:36). Messiah had come and Peter told the Jews gathered in Jerusalem that not only had they missed Him, but they had killed Him. God had walked among men and had been put to death by the very people He created. The apostle Paul would go on to write, "For when we were yet without strength, in due time Christ died for the ungodly. For scarcely for a righteous man will one die: yet peradventure for a good man some would even dare to die. But God commendeth his love toward us, in that, while we were yet sinners, Christ died for us" (Romans 5:6–8). The penalty for sin is death, a debt that was paid by the death of Jesus.

» *Why should we often reflect on the price that was paid for our salvation?*

V. MADE FREE THROUGH HIS DEATH

The writer of Hebrews stated, "But we see Jesus, who was made a little lower than the angels for the suffering of death, crowned with glory and honour; that he by the grace of God should taste death for every man. For it became him, for whom are all things, and by whom are all things, in bringing many sons unto glory, to make the captain of their salvation perfect through sufferings" (Hebrews 2:9–10). Only because He was willing to die are we free.

A. Free from Sin

Time and again in the New Testament it is written that Jesus died to free us from our sins. John 8:36 states, "If the Son therefore shall make you free, ye shall be free indeed." Paul wrote in Galatians 5:1, "Stand fast therefore in the liberty wherewith Christ hath made us free, and be not entangled again with the yoke of bondage." These are but a couple of examples telling us of the freedom His death has given humanity over sin. We understand that we must have faith in Him, repent of our sins, be buried with Him in baptism, and be born again through the infilling of His Holy Spirit. Then we are commanded to live a life of submission to His will and fulfill our purpose in His kingdom.

» *If complacency kills, can we lose out on freedom by being stagnant through complacency?*

B. Servants of Righteousness

Paul wrote to the church at Rome about servitude, to both the flesh and the spirit. He explained that after conversion, we are no longer servants to our flesh, but we are servants to God unto righteousness. Righteousness is defined as "acting in accord with divine or moral law" (Merriam-Webster). God promised in Jeremiah 31:33, "I will put my law in their inward parts, and write it in their hearts." The Spirit of God desires to show us how to live a life of righteousness. Our choices still matter; there is no autopilot when it comes to living for God.

C. God's Gift of Eternal Life

God has given many gifts to humanity. His greatest gift was giving His Son as a sacrifice for our sins. After Jesus' resurrection, He gave us the gift of the Holy Ghost— His Spirit living inside of us. These gifts culminate in the ultimate gift as stated in Romans 6:23: "For the wages of sin is death; but the gift of God is eternal life through Jesus Christ our Lord." This life is temporary, or finite, but we are promised eternal life through Jesus Christ.

» *Can you fathom what it means to live forever? Explain.*

⟩⟩⟩ INTERNALIZING THE MESSAGE

Former US President John F. Kennedy once said, "The cost of freedom is always high, but Americans have always paid it. And one path we shall never choose, and that is the path of surrender, or submission." As Christians we should have an even greater understanding of the price of freedom. Ours is the kind of freedom that transcends international borders, even transcending the limitations of this life. Jesus made the ultimate sacrifice to secure our salvation from sin. It is imperative we live for Him, and through strengthening our relationship with Him, we should desire to live a life of righteousness.

Power of the Resurrection

FOCUS THOUGHT
We can have new life because Jesus rose from the dead.

 FOCUS VERSES

Luke 24:6–7

He is not here, but is risen: remember how he spake unto you when he was yet in Galilee, saying, The Son of man must be delivered into the hands of sinful men, and be crucified, and the third day rise again.

 LESSON TEXT

Luke 24:1–12

1 Now upon the first day of the week, very early in the morning, they came unto the sepulchre, bringing the spices which they had prepared, and certain others with them.

2 And they found the stone rolled away from the sepulchre.

3 And they entered in, and found not the body of the Lord Jesus.

4 And it came to pass, as they were much perplexed thereabout, behold, two men stood by them in shining garments:

5 And as they were afraid, and bowed down their faces to the earth, they said unto them, Why seek ye the living among the dead?

6 He is not here, but is risen: remember how he spake unto you when he was yet in Galilee,

7 Saying, The Son of man must be delivered into the hands of sinful men, and be crucified, and the third day rise again.

8 And they remembered his words,

9 And returned from the sepulchre, and told all these things unto the eleven, and to all the rest.

10 It was Mary Magdalene and Joanna, and Mary the mother of James, and other women that were with them, which told these things unto the apostles.

11 And their words seemed to them as idle tales, and they believed them not.

12 Then arose Peter, and ran unto the sepulchre; and stooping down, he beheld the linen clothes laid by themselves, and departed, wondering in himself at that which was come to pass.

I Peter 1:3–5

3 Blessed be the God and Father of our Lord Jesus Christ, which according to his abundant mercy hath begotten us again unto a lively hope by the resurrection of Jesus Christ from the dead,

4 To an inheritance incorruptible, and undefiled, and that fadeth not away, reserved in heaven for you,

5 Who are kept by the power of God through faith unto salvation ready to be revealed in the last time.

EMPTY TOMBS SPEAK LOUDER THAN WORDS

Skeptics who do not believe Jesus rose from the grave suggest reasons why His tomb is empty. One theory suggests Jesus only swooned on the cross; He did not die. Then when He was placed in the tomb, the cool, damp air in the tomb revived Him, and He walked out under His own power. But having just been beaten, crucified, pierced, and tightly wrapped in graveclothes, it seems highly unlikely Jesus would have healed in just three short days.

Others have suggested the women who reported His resurrection just had the wrong address—they went to the wrong tomb. Even if they were so bleary-eyed that they could not see straight, the Romans only had to march the women to the right tomb and show them the lifeless body of their Lord, and Christianity would have been squashed before it began. But they could not because His body was not in the tomb.

The last popular theory is the same theory the Romans propagated in their day: the disciples stole Jesus' body. But these are the same disciples who huddled behind locked doors, fearing for their lives. They did not want to die, yet they were all willing to die preaching the truth of the Resurrection. If they stole Jesus' body, surely one of the disciples would have caved under the threat of death and led the authorities to His body.

Those are three of the primary alternate theories skeptics have suggested for the empty tomb, but they all point to the same indisputable evidence. Whether they want to admit it or not, the tomb is empty.

>>> **OUTLINE**

I. FIRST DAY OF THE WEEK
  A. Stone Was Rolled Away
  B. Two Angels Appeared
  C. He Is Risen

II. REMEMBER HIS WORDS
  A. Delivered into the Hands of Sinners
  B. Crucified
  C. Rose Again the Third Day

III. THE WOMEN TESTIFIED
  A. Unbelief
  B. Peter Ran to the Tomb

IV. THE POWER OF THE RESURRECTION
  A. New Birth
  B. Living Hope
  C. An Inheritance That Can Never Perish

>>> **CONTEMPLATING THE TOPIC**

The last week had been a struggle for Mary Magdalene, Joanna, Mary, the mother of James, and other women who had been with them. Jesus, their friend and teacher—the one they hoped was the promised Messiah—had been crucified. Even though they were standing a distance from the three crosses, they saw the Roman soldier's sword pierce His side. They watched the water and blood gush from the wound. Every conceivable emotion rolled around in their hearts: the emptiness of losing a loved one; the disappointment of dashed dreams; the anger at the Roman soldiers who killed Him; the confusion of misunderstanding His teaching; the hopelessness of dying faith; and the bitterness of wasted time, money, and energy.

Although emotionally weary and physically exhausted, the women rose before dawn on the first day of the week and, carrying spices, went to the tomb of Jesus. They went to anoint the body of Jesus, to finish preparing Him for His burial. This was the last act of love they could perform for Jesus. Their concern was the sealed stone blocking the grave. How could they get the grave open?

I. FIRST DAY OF THE WEEK

A. Stone Was Rolled Away

The nagging question bothering the two Marys, Joanna, and the other women as they climbed the rocky trail to the tomb was, *How can we get the stone rolled away?*

The tomb belonged to Joseph of Arimathea, a wealthy member of the Sanhedrin, who secretly followed Jesus. It was a new, unused tomb, cut into the limestone, and had a stone that sealed it. The stone may have been circular like a wheel, but it was probably square (cork-shaped) as they were "much, much more common than round (disk-shaped) ones" (www.biblicalarchaeology.org).

» *Why do you think Joseph of Arimathea asked for the body of Jesus since he was a secret disciple? How would that affect his standing in the Jewish community?*

Because of the concerns of the Jewish religious leaders, Pilate ordered the tomb be sealed. That process involved stretching a string across the stone covering and sealing the tomb after authorities inspected it to ensuring the body was secure.

Scripture explains that guards were commanded to stand at attention by the tomb.

> *The Roman guard was a sixteen-man unit that was governed by very strict rules. Each member was responsible for six square feet of space. The guard members could not sit down or lean against anything while they were on duty. If a guard member fell asleep, he was beaten and burned with his own clothes. But he was not the only one executed, the entire sixteen-man guard unit was executed if only one of the members fell asleep while on duty. (www.blueletterbible.org)*

Consequently, the women faced three major obstacles in opening the tomb:
1. A large, heavy stone blocked the entrance to the tomb. Who would roll it away?
2. The seal of the Roman governor authenticated the tomb. Anyone breaking the seal would face death.
3. Roman soldiers guarded the tomb. Their failure would result in death.

» *How do you think the women expected to overcome these obstacles?*

Imagine the women's total amazement as they rounded the bend to the tomb and found the Roman soldiers had fled the scene. The governor's seal had been broken, for the stoned had been rolled away. The tomb was open.

B. Two Angels Appeared

> *And, behold, there was a great earthquake: for the angel of the Lord descended from heaven, and came and rolled back the stone from the door,*

and sat upon it. His countenance was like lightning, and his raiment white as snow. (Matthew 28:2–3)

The women were astonished to see the angel sitting on the large grave stone. Terrified by the heavenly being, the women bowed their faces to the earth. The angels said: "Why seek ye the living among the dead? He is not here, but is risen" (Luke 24:5–6).

C. He Is Risen

The women did not expect the Resurrection. They carried spices to anoint the body to help mask the stench of decay. They had not understood the words of the Lord. The angelic announcement took them totally by surprise. Slowly they digested the message of the empty tomb. Jesus was not there, for He had conquered death, Hell, and the grave. He was alive.

» **Why did the women—and the disciples—fail to understand the prophecies of the Resurrection? Have you failed to understand some promises of God? Explain.**

The women looked around them. Jesus' borrowed tomb had been new, never used. It was hewn out of the limestone hill, without a back entrance. As the tomb was unused, Jesus' body could not be confused with any others. The Roman seal verified that His body had been in the tomb. The stone blocking the entrance to the tomb and the band of Roman soldiers testified that no one could have secretly entered the grave and stolen the body. All these facts supported the words of the angels.

II. REMEMBER HIS WORDS

A. Delivered into the Hands of Sinners

Hope and joy replaced disappointment and despair as the women absorbed the words of the angels: "Remember how he spake unto you when he was yet in Galilee, saying, The Son of man must be delivered into the hands of sinful men, and be crucified, and the third day rise again" (Luke 24:6–7).

The women were aware of the facts of the previous week. They knew Judas had betrayed Jesus with a kiss in the Garden of Gethsemane. They knew Jesus had been dragged illegally before the Sanhedrin and before Pilate. They knew He had been beaten and sentenced to death. Yes, Jesus had been "delivered into the hands of sinful men" (Luke 24:7).

B. Crucified

The women had stood off in the distance as the Roman soldiers nailed Jesus to the cross and planted Him between two thieves. Crucifixion was the cruelest form of death employed by the Romans.

Roman crucifixions were designed to cause maximum pain for a prolonged period—victims' feet and wrists were usually nailed to a wooden cross, which would hold them upright while they suffered a slow and agonizing death, often taking several days . . . .

As such, it was usually carried out only for the execution of slaves in Roman society . . . ; the bodies were often left on the cross to rot or to be eaten by animals, but in some cases, they were removed and buried. (www.livescience.com)

As the angels had reminded the women, Jesus had foretold His death by crucifixion. Perhaps they had failed to grasp the significance of His words because of the horror of crucifixion. Surely God would not allow His Son to suffer such inhuman brutality. Yet they saw the pounding of the nails, the mocking soldiers, and the blood and water. They witnessed the Crucifixion.

C. Rose Again the Third Day

The angels proclaimed, "He is not here, but is risen" (Luke 24:6). On the first day of the week, three days after the Crucifixion, the women stood at an empty tomb. The inconceivable truth overwhelmed them. Joyfully they ran to tell the glorious news to the disciples, who had possibly gathered in Bethany.

John's account of Jesus appearing to Mary Magdalene seems to conflict with the chronology of Matthew, Mark, and Luke. Tim Chaffey harmonizes the accounts in his article "Christ's Resurrection—Four Accounts, One Reality" in *Answers* magazine. He suggests that after seeing the open tomb, Mary Magdalene ran to Jerusalem to tell Peter and John, leaving the other women—at least four more—at the tomb to hear the words of the angels. He further suggests that Mary returned with Peter and John and then lingered nearby, where Jesus appeared to her. This is a logical deduction based on Mary's statement to the presumed gardener. Had she heard the words of the angel, she would have known Jesus was alive and would not have been weeping in despair.

III. THE WOMEN TESTIFIED

A. Unbelief

Just like Mary would have been had she waited, the other women were astounded at the declaration of the angels. The scent of the spices they had carried to anoint the body of Jesus testified to their unbelief. They had fully expected to see the broken body of Jesus in Joseph of Arimathea's tomb. The empty tomb mystified them. The words of the angel stupefied them.

» *Have you ever seen an angel? If so, describe it.*

As comprehension dawned on the women, their despair turned to unspeakable joy. Leaving the spices behind—the costly spices suddenly became meaningless—the women raced to tell the disciples that Jesus was alive. He had risen from the dead, just as He had promised.

B. Peter Ran to the Tomb

Even though Peter saw the empty tomb and the graveclothes lying there, he did not totally grasp the significance. Undoubtedly the other disciples did not understand either. Perhaps that is the reason Jesus, prior to His ascension, opened the disciples' "understanding, that they might understand the scriptures, and said unto them, Thus it is written, and thus it behoved Christ to suffer, and to rise from the dead the third day: and that repentance and remission of sins should be preached in his name among all nations, beginning at Jerusalem" (Luke 24:45–47).

IV. THE POWER OF THE RESURRECTION

A. New Birth

What is the significance of the Resurrection? What truth did Peter fail to grasp as he looked at the empty tomb and the graveclothes?

The Resurrection gives meaning to the death and burial of Jesus Christ. If Jesus had not risen from the dead, then He would have simply been another zealous religious leader who was martyred or died a natural death (e.g., Buddha). By being resurrected, He conquered death, Hell, and the grave (I Corinthians 15:12–15).

When we experience the new birth, we die to our sins in repentance, we are buried with Christ in baptism, and we arise to walk in the fullness of the Holy Ghost. This echoes the death, burial, and resurrection of Christ. Because He arose from the dead in power and victory, we too can live in victory over sin and in the power of the Holy Ghost. Christianity is the only religion that has a risen Savior.

B. Living Hope

Bill and Gloria Gaither's classic song says, "Because He lives, I can face tomorrow." The reality of a living Christ gives us hope. The resurrected Christ proves no power on earth can stand against our Savior. He won the battle and triumphed over evil. When the despair and cares of the world oppress us, we can shout, "My Saviour lives. Because He lives, my sins are forgiven and His Spirit lives inside me."

Peter said it well: "Blessed be the God and Father of our Lord Jesus Christ, which according to his abundant mercy hath begotten us again unto a lively hope by the resurrection of Jesus Christ from the dead, to an inheritance incorruptible, and undefiled, and that fadeth not away, reserved in heaven for you" (I Peter 1:3–4).

C. An Inheritance That Can Never Perish

Not only do we have a living hope while on earth, we are promised an inheritance that can never perish. Peter described it as being incorruptible, undefiled, eternal, and reserved for us in Heaven.

Someday our mortal bodies will put on immortality, and then we will be with the Lord forever (I Thessalonians 4:14–18).

John's description of the New Jerusalem boggles our minds, for we cannot fathom the beauty and splendor of the eternal city. As Paul wrote, "But as it is written, Eye hath not seen, nor ear heard, neither have entered into the heart of man, the things which God hath prepared for them that love him" (I Corinthians 2:9). Our finite minds are incapable of imagining the grandeur and glory of Heaven.

However, we are not anxious to see streets of gold and gates of pearl. Sure, the walls of jasper and the rainbow of colors in the foundation of New Jerusalem will be breathtaking. But what we long for is to be in the presence of Jesus. Dwelling eternally in His presence is the greatest inheritance we could ever receive.

» **What excites you most about Heaven?**

⟫⟫ INTERNALIZING THE MESSAGE

The message of the Resurrection is the capstone of the gospel. Many religions teach basic moral ethics, such as the Nobel Eightfold Path of Buddhism. The founders of some religions have been martyred. But Christianity is the only religion that has a risen Savior. The story of the death and burial of Jesus Christ would be incomplete without His rising from the dead. His resurrection gives meaning to His sacrificial death. It proves that the power of evil has been defeated. And because He lives, we can live in victory.

The message of the Resurrection should motivate us to "live soberly, righteously, and godly, in this present world; looking for that blessed hope, and the glorious appearing of the great God and our Saviour Jesus Christ; who gave himself for us, that he might redeem us from all iniquity, and purify unto himself a peculiar people, zealous of good works" (Titus 2:12–14).

The message of the Resurrection reminds us that as Christ lives eternally, so shall we. Just as Jesus kept His promise about rising the third day, He will also keep His promise about returning for His saints. We do not know when it will be, but the signs of His returning are all around us. As the Resurrection proved Christ's victory over death, His returning will bring eternal life to those who believe in Him. The Resurrection proves He is alive forevermore.

Sharing His Mission

FOCUS THOUGHT

As disciples of Jesus Christ, we are commanded to share the gospel message with everyone.

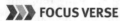 **FOCUS VERSE**

Mark 16:15

And he said unto them, Go ye into all the world, and preach the gospel to every creature.

LESSON TEXT

Matthew 28:16–20

16 Then the eleven disciples went away into Galilee, into a mountain where Jesus had appointed them.

17 And when they saw him, they worshipped him: but some doubted.

18 And Jesus came and spake unto them, saying, All power is given unto me in heaven and in earth.

19 Go ye therefore, and teach all nations, baptizing them in the name of the Father, and of the Son, and of the Holy Ghost:

20 Teaching them to observe all things whatsoever I have commanded you: and, lo, I am with you alway, even unto the end of the world. Amen.

Mark 16:15–16

15 And he said unto them, Go ye into all the world, and preach the gospel to every creature.

16 He that believeth and is baptized shall be saved; but he that believeth not shall be damned.

Luke 24:46–47

46 And said unto them, Thus it is written, and thus it behoved Christ to suffer, and to rise from the dead the third day:

47 And that repentance and remission of sins should be preached in his name among all nations, beginning at Jerusalem.

Acts 1:8

8 But ye shall receive power, after that the Holy Ghost is come upon you: and ye shall be witnesses unto me both in Jerusalem, and in all Judæa, and in Samaria, and unto the uttermost part of the earth.

CULTURE CONNECTION

MISSION STATEMENTS

Not all mission statements are created equal. Corporate bigwigs hire other bigwigs to brainstorm around a conference room table and devise the perfect, pithy mission statement for their company. It will be the marching orders whereby the company does business. Some are excellent; some could use a little work.

Avon's mission statement weighs in at 249 words and includes six core aspirations. That is about 229 words too long. Albertson's exists "to create a shopping experience that pleases our customers; a workplace that creates opportunities and a great working environment for our associates; and a business that achieves financial success." Their word count is a little better, but those twenty-nine words do not tell us if Albertson's sells tires or makes drinking straws. In case you are curious, Albertson's is a grocery store chain.

Jesus would have made the corporate bigwigs proud. His mission statement is specific, short, and easy to remember. "Go into all the world and preach the gospel to every creature." Jesus' mission statement tells us to go everywhere and tell everyone. Jesus has called us to go into all the world and make disciples.

The next time you wonder what God created you to do, remember these short verses at the end of the Gospels: go and make disciples. Jesus gave His life to give His church this mission.

OUTLINE

I. HIS MISSION

    A. The Spirit of the Lord Is upon Me

    B. Seek and Save the Lost

II. SHARING HIS MISSION

    A. Go

    B. Preach the Gospel

    C. Baptize

    D. Teach and Make Disciples

CONTEMPLATING THE TOPIC

Jesus came "to seek and to save that which was lost" (Luke 19:10). Jesus came to bring reconciliation to God and man (II Corinthians 5:14–21). This mission of Jesus motivated everything He did; it was His Father's business. The Bible is clear that the lost were never far from the mind of Jesus Christ. He did not come for notoriety, to establish an earthly kingdom, or to live in luxury. He came to save the lost.

I. HIS MISSION

We see clearly from Scripture that Jesus came with one mission in mind—to seek and save the lost. Who were the lost Jesus came to save? Everyone, for "all have sinned, and come short of the glory of God" (Romans 3:23). How, then, was Jesus going to save everyone? By accepting their repentance and then baptizing them with the Holy Spirit (David S. Norris, *Big Ideas*). This message of baptism in the Holy Spirit was so important that we see Jesus proclaim to the disciples that He will baptize them with the Holy Spirit (Acts 1:5). And later in Acts 11:16 when Peter retold what happened at the home of Cornelius he said, "Then remembered I the word of the Lord, how that he said, John indeed baptized with water; but ye shall be baptized with the Holy Ghost." The context of this account in Acts 11 is Peter explaining to those in Jerusalem what happened in Caesarea. He explained that while he was still speaking to the gathered group of Gentiles, the Holy Spirit fell on them and they began to speak with tongues.

We may envision Peter somewhat bewildered that God had poured out the Holy Spirit on Gentiles just as He had on Jews, yet while Peter considered it, the words of Jesus illuminated his mind, "You shall be baptized with the Holy Spirit" (Acts 11:16, NKJV). Jesus was not limiting His seeking and saving to only Jews. By Cornelius and his household being filled, the disciples learned the mission of Jesus was to reach everyone.

Jesus came to seek and save the lost, and He achieved His mission through the Cross and by baptizing with the Holy Spirit.

» *Do you see how the mission of Jesus is fulfilled when someone obeys the gospel through repentance, baptism in Jesus' name, and receiving the gift of the Holy Spirit? Explain.*

A. The Spirit of the Lord Is upon Me

Luke 4:16–22 records a day when Jesus went to a synagogue in Nazareth on the Sabbath. Bible scholars are unsure of when the synagogue became prominent in Judaism, but it is clear that by the time of Jesus, it was an accepted form of covenant continuity and worship (Leon Morris, Tyndale *New Testament Commentaries: Luke*). As the Jewish people became vassals of other nations and were not able to practice worship as freely at the Temple, synagogues became important. Some scholars believe the synagogue Jesus attended in Luke 4 was the very synagogue He attended as a child (J. Dwight Pentecost, *The Words and Works of Jesus Christ*).

It is possible local synagogue leaders invited Jesus to read and to preach or that Jesus indicated His desire to read that day by standing up to read (Morris). (See Luke 4:16.) Whether invited to speak or taking the initiative Himself, one thing is clear: when the Law or Prophets were read, the reader would stand, and then after reading, it was customary for the speaker to sit down while teaching or preaching. This is what Jesus did.

"When He had opened the book, He found the place where it was written" (Luke 4:17, NKJV). Some suggest the synagogue was ordered according to a lectionary calendar, and this particular reading was the reading assigned for the day when Jesus arrived. The plain wording of the text indicates that is not the case. Luke says Jesus found the place where it was written. He knew exactly what He wanted to say that day, and He knew the particular passage. He was a prepared preacher. He stood up and read from Isaiah 61:1–2, where the prophet prophesied about the coming Messiah and His anointing. Jesus referred here to His anointing that occurred at His baptism (Norris, *I Am*).

In His ministry Jesus was an anointed man of God. It seems clear that Jesus understood His anointing by God as power for His ministry. Jesus is unique because all the fullness of the Godhead dwelt in Him bodily (Colossians 2:9), yet as a man, He needed the anointing of God to accomplish His ministry. From a human perspective, this might seem unnecessary; after all, Jesus is fully God. Why then would He need anointing from God to perform His ministry? Could He not simply do it as the mighty God in Christ? He could have done it that way, but that would not have been congruent with the Incarnation. God created Jesus as both fully human and fully divine. One example is the way Jesus helped John the Baptist understand the importance of Jesus being baptized. He was baptized, not because of sin, but "to fulfil all righteousness" (Matthew 3:15). In a similar way, Jesus, as a man, was anointed by God to perform His ministry. This serves as an example to believers, and that is the point.

> **When you witness to others, have you experienced the anointing of God helping you? What was it like?**

B. Seek and Save the Lost

As mentioned in the beginning of the lesson, the mission of Jesus was seeking and saving. Let us look further at the specifics of this mission. First, Jesus sought the lost. One effective way to understand this is by the contrast Jesus illustrates of Himself versus the Pharisees. Pharisees in the time of Jesus layered the law of Moses with many additional human traditions, putting burdens on people they were not capable of fulfilling (Matthew 23:4, 13). By neglecting the "weightier matters of the law," the Pharisees had further corrupted themselves (Matthew 23:23). Jesus affirmed they should have kept the Law. But it was their additions to it that prohibited them and others from doing so. Worse, their oral traditions allowed them to dissociate themselves from any who did not measure up to their false views. So they had little regard for the lost. People like Zacchaeus, the woman at the well, or the woman who washed Jesus' feet with her tears would be excluded and avoided according to the false notions of the Pharisees. The Kingdom was not open to them; they were lost.

But Jesus sought them out. Examples fill the Gospels, proving that Jesus sought the lost. Perhaps the greatest scriptural illustration of this is Luke 15, where the stories of the lost coin, the lost sheep, and the lost son are told. In each story something of value is lost and someone searches for it. The searchers in the stories are the woman, the shepherd, and the father. Each one looks diligently and longingly for the lost. At the end of each of those stories, Jesus says those who found the missing items rejoiced and celebrated. Verses 7 and 10 tell us there is joy in Heaven when one repents.

Jesus not only seeks, but He has the power to save. Looking at the story of the lost son from Luke 15, consider that the lost son is different from the other two lost items that precede his story in the chapter. Aggressive searches take place for the lost sheep and the lost coin, but little is told about the coin and the sheep. But when the narrative shifts to the story of the lost son, much is told of him. His rejection of the father, his running away from the father's house, and his realization that he was wrong are all key elements of the story. The lost son has volition; he has to make a choice to return to the father's house. But once his choice is made—once he realizes he is no longer fit to be a son but only a servant—the focus of the narrative shifts from him to the father. It is then the father runs to him, restores him, and rejoices with him. The father had the power to save. The father represents God, and Jesus was telling His hearers that God has the power to save even lost sons. We know God performed His saving power in the Man Christ Jesus. His atoning death on the cross and subsequent outpouring of the Holy Spirit on those who repent tell the tale. He runs to, restores, and rejoices with all who repent, are baptized in His name, and receive the gift of the Holy Spirit. Jesus seeks and saves the lost.

II. SHARING HIS MISSION

Jesus came to seek and save the lost. Our mission is the same. In our lesson text, Jesus explained the components of our mission and the tasks we need to perform to do it effectively. Before looking deeply at those passages, let us look at missions and mission statements.

Business management experts have cautioned that not having mission statement clarity can sidetrack an enterprise. While the church is certainly more important than any business enterprise, it is still beneficial for churches to have a mission statement that derives from Jesus' mission of seeking and saving the lost. One writer described a mission as follows: "a broad, brief, biblical statement of what the organization is supposed to be doing" (Aubrey Malphurs, *Ministry Nuts and Bolts*). A mission is not a vision and it is not a purpose statement; mission describes what the church is doing. A mission statement should be concise enough to fit on a T-shirt (Malphurs).

» *If you had one, what would be your ministry mission statement?*

A. Go

Jesus commanded the disciples to go—a seemingly simple command, yet one even they were challenged to fulfill. Many have noted it was the persecution of the church in the Book of Acts that propelled it beyond the walls of Jerusalem. Going can be challenging. One writer said it this way, "The start stops most." How true that is. But the command is to go.

The disciples faced obstacles to going. Initially the Romans regarded them as a sect of Judaism and treated them in similar ways, but the disciples faced persecutions from the Jews very early on (Acts 3–4; 6–7). Eventually the Romans persecuted the church as well. The threat of persecution was a significant obstacle. But the leaders of the church were not deterred. They received the mission from Jesus and moved forward in faith.

We too have obstacles. The church will always be opposed by the world, the flesh, and the devil. But the command to us is the same as it was to them: go. When disciples focus on the challenges, they lose faith. But when they focus on God's Word, they are invigorated.

» **Where is God directing you to go? What is holding you back?**

B. Preach the Gospel

Going is essential, but what is done as one goes is just as important. The disciples left Jerusalem and proclaimed the gospel. They had no beautiful church buildings in which to gather and proclaim the Word of God. They simply told people Jesus died, was buried, and rose again the third day (I Corinthians 15:1–4). The first church met in homes for worship and preaching, but their preaching of the gospel also took place in many other locations (Acts 16:13; 17:22). The disciples lived in a world with many religions. Their world was pluralistic, where various religions were celebrated but none claimed preeminence. Theirs was a deeply immoral society with little or no sense of decency. Immorality was publicly displayed and practiced as worship of idols. But still the disciples preached the gospel. They told the good news of Jesus, and God confirmed His Word.

For those whose temperaments are introverted, preaching the gospel can be challenging. Some suggest practicing telling what the Lord has done for you. It is also helpful to recognize that preaching the gospel happens not only behind a pulpit but also over a dinner table, on a break at work, and in a myriad of other places. Many excuse themselves from this task because they are not preachers. But God calls all His people to tell His gospel. Some decline the offer of telling the good news out of a sense of political correctness; after all, some say, politics and religion are the two things people in a polite society are not supposed to discuss.

Certainly there are significant challenges for those who work in secular employment. One helpful principle is understanding that the gospel of Jesus is the gospel of peace. In Ephesians 6:15 Paul taught the Ephesian church that part of the whole armor of God was the shoes of the "gospel of peace." The gospel does not bring conflict to people. Conflict comes from the sinfulness of the human heart and the evil of the adversary. The gospel brings peace. Realizing we offer peace through the gospel can greatly encourage us to tell God's good news. Through the gospel, disciples offer peace with God. To someone stuck in the turmoil of sin, nothing can be greater.

C. Baptize

Jesus commanded the disciples to baptize in His name. In Mark 16:16 Jesus declared, "He that believeth and is baptized shall be saved." Baptism is an essential part of salvation. "Repentance and water baptism together complete the full work of forgiveness" (David K. Bernard, *The New Birth*). Baptism has many scriptural purposes though there is no scriptural record of baptism for the purpose of public confession (Bernard). We are "buried with him by baptism into death: that like as Christ was raised up from the dead by the glory of the Father, even so we also should walk in newness of life" (Romans 6:4). Baptism also served as a spiritual circumcision of the heart (Colossians 2:11–12). Jesus commanded His disciples to baptize, and they did as He commanded.

Disciples of Jesus today will baptize those who desire to be saved. Churches fulfilling the mission of Jesus are baptizing people on a regular basis.

D. Teach and Make Disciples

Lastly, Jesus told the disciples to begin teaching and making disciples. Through His earthly ministry, Jesus gave the pattern; now the disciples too were responsible to spread His love and grow His kingdom. In Matthew 28:18–20 Jesus told the disciples that all authority in Heaven and on Earth had been given to Him, further proof that He would enable them to fulfill the task and no obstacle could stop them. When commissioning them to go, Jesus told them to go and teach because all authority belonged to Him. The disciples were not going forth to teach and make disciples in their own authority; they went forth on the wave of Jesus' authority. They were commanded to teach, make disciples, and baptize, because all authority belonged to Jesus.

One of the overlooked portions of this passage is the final clause in Matthew 28:20. Jesus said, "I am with you alway, even unto the end of the world." Most Christians want the presence of God and even claim it as a promise from the Bible. It is important to note the context of Scripture when the promise of God's presence is given. For example, God promised Moses He would be with him in Exodus 3; however, that promise of presence was contingent on Moses doing what God was calling him to do. This passage is very similar. God conveys His abiding presence to those who abide in Him and do His will. Those claiming to follow Him but not abiding in Him or doing His will cannot expect God to be with them in the same way.

▶▶▶ INTERNALIZING THE MESSAGE

Churches do many things and many of those things are very important. But the church must never lose sight of the truth that their reason for existence is to glorify God and make disciples. Let us not become sidetracked or distracted with the cares of this life and lose our commitment to our true purpose and mission.

SUMMER 2020

The Living Word

SERIES

God Is Faithful

LESSON
MANUAL

Lesson Manual

© 2019 Pentecostal Publishing House • 36 Research Park Court • Weldon Spring, MO 63304
www.pentecostalpublishing.com • All rights reserved.
Manufactured in USA, June 2020, 1942011

EDITORIAL STAFF
Editor in Chief: Robin Johnston
Associate Editor, Curriculum: Lee Ann Alexander
Word Aflame Adult Editor: Jonathan McClintock

WRITERS
John Moore
Jared Runck
Ron Wofford
Tim Bollmann

Michael Sparks
Micah Johnson
Brian Roberts
John Hanson

CONTENTS

GOD IS FAITHFUL

by Jonathan McClintock

Some people cannot be counted on. Perhaps that is why it is refreshing to find people who do what they say they will do. But if we are honest with ourselves, no matter how many times we do come through on our word, there will be moments in time when our promise to do a particular thing will end in disappointment. Why? Because we are humans, with limitations, and we are unable to control every circumstance and situation we face. No matter how faithful we want to be, our humanity will fail us at times.

On the eve of Jesus' arrest in the Garden of Gethsemane, Jesus looked at Peter and told him that before the rooster crowed in the morning, Peter would deny Jesus three times. Upon hearing this, the bold apostle looked back at Jesus and declared, "I will never deny You." In fact, Peter's declaration did not stop there. He even insisted that not only would he not deny Jesus, but he would die for his Lord if it came to that.

But only a few short hours later, Peter found himself in a situation he had never anticipated. The pressure around him began to build. The heat was turned up as he stood by the fire and tried to deflect the probing questions of those gathered in the courtyard. And in a few moments of weakness, Peter denied he even knew who Jesus was. The third and final denial was punctuated with profanity, only seconds before the sound of the crowing rooster reverberated in his ears. In his moment of weakness, Peter's faithfulness faded.

However, when the Bible tells us God is faithful, we can be certain of that fact. When pressures squeezed Jesus, He remained faithful. When the heat was turned up on Jesus, He remained faithful. And when others were unfaithful to Him, even then He remained faithful to them. Nothing challenges the faithfulness of our God.

John the Revelator gave us a picture of the unending faithfulness of our God. While in the Spirit on the Lord's Day, John caught a glimpse of our triumphant Savior, proving that even at the end of time, He will still be faithful: "And I saw heaven opened, and behold a white horse; and he that sat upon him was called Faithful and True" (Revelation 19:11). His faithfulness will endure to the end.

LESSON MANUAL

This Lesson Manual has been developed with the goal of providing teachers numerous options to assist in preparation and delivery of each lesson.

In each lesson you will find a Focus Thought, Focus Verse, and Lesson Text that lay a foundation and give direction for the material that is to be presented. Questions are dispersed throughout the body of each lesson to provoke thought and spark discussion. We urge teachers to use these questions as a means of helping students apply each portion of the lesson.

> » *How does God being "all knowing" bring you comfort?*

STUDENT WORKBOOK

The Student Workbook has been organized in such a way that students are given the tools to not only follow the major points of each lesson but will also have a tool to further their personal discipleship and devotion throughout the week.

1. The Focus Thought, Focus Verse, and Culture Connection have been included in the Student Workbook.
2. The Lesson Outline has also been included to give the student a template to follow as the lesson is being taught. In addition, certain parts of the outline correspond with the daily discipleship prompts in the Approach section. This is designed to show what part of the lesson corresponds to the particular day's lesson text and application questions.
3. The Approach section is designed to give the student daily discipleship prompts by including portions of the lesson and application questions. The flexibility of this section allows for the student to follow along and interact during class, to become familiar with the lesson content before class, or to spend time in review during the week following class.
4. The Ask and Apply questions are presented for the purpose of helping the student contemplate the truths of Scripture and the content of the lesson. The first of the questions in each set is taken directly from the Lesson Manual, while the second question in each set is an additional prompt designed to help the student apply what is being taught.

POWERPOINTS

To access your FREE PowerPoints visit: Pentecostalpublishing.com/wappt

God Will Supply

FOCUS THOUGHT
God takes care of His people.

FOCUS VERSE

I Kings 17:16
And the barrel of meal wasted not, neither did the cruse of oil fail, according to the word of the LORD, which he spake by Elijah.

LESSON TEXT

I Kings 17:1–4; 8–16
1 And Elijah the Tishbite, who was of the inhabitants of Gilead, said unto Ahab, As the LORD God of Israel liveth, before whom I stand, there shall not be dew nor rain these years, but according to my word.

2 And the word of the LORD came unto him, saying,

3 Get thee hence, and turn thee eastward, and hide thyself by the brook Cherith, that is before Jordan.

4 And it shall be, that thou shalt drink of the brook; and I have commanded the ravens to feed thee there.

. . . . .

8 And the word of the LORD came unto him, saying,

9 Arise, get thee to Zarephath, which belongeth to Zidon, and dwell there: behold, I have commanded a widow woman there to sustain thee.

10 So he arose and went to Zarephath. And when he came to the gate of the city, behold, the widow woman was there gathering of sticks: and he called to her, and said, Fetch me, I pray thee, a little water in a vessel, that I may drink.

11 And as she was going to fetch it, he called to her, and said, Bring me, I pray thee, a morsel of bread in thine hand.

12 And she said, As the LORD thy God liveth, I have not a cake, but an handful of meal in a barrel, and a little oil in a cruse: and, behold, I am gathering two sticks, that I may go in and dress it for me and my son, that we may eat it, and die.

13 And Elijah said unto her, Fear not; go and do as thou hast said: but make me thereof a little cake first, and bring it unto me, and after make for thee and for thy son.

14 For thus saith the LORD God of Israel, The barrel of meal shall not waste, neither shall the cruse of oil fail, until the day that the LORD sendeth rain upon the earth.

15 And she went and did according to the saying of Elijah: and she, and he, and her house, did eat many days.

16 And the barrel of meal wasted not, neither did the cruse of oil fail, according to the word of the LORD, which he spake by Elijah.

5

CULTURE CONNECTION

GOD PROVIDES IN EVERY SITUATION

Marcus and Renee Brainos were on their first deputation as UPCI missionaries to France. They had planned to spend part of the winter in Canada and had outfitted their three children with warm outerwear. But Marcus only had an older coat, and Renee did not really have anything warm enough for the trip. The kids were taken care of, so Renee had decided to manage until she could find something without straining their budget.

One Sunday, after ministering at a church in Arkansas, the pastor's wife gave Renee a package from a lady in their church. That morning, as this lady was leaving for church, the Lord spoke to her about a very warm Italian leather coat she had in her closet. "That coat belongs to the wife of the missionary couple at church today. Take it to her."

When Renee was given the coat, she was shocked and then became a little nervous that it would not fit. But she immediately thought, *If God sent this to me, then why would it not fit?* Not only did it fit, but there were also very warm gloves in the pocket. The lady had started to remove them but felt instructed to leave them as well.

God knows our every need and is faithful to provide. Sometimes He asks us to go into situations that require things we do not have, but He knows those needs before we do and already has a plan.

 ## OUTLINE

I. ELIJAH PROPHESIED
A. No Dew or Rain
B. Sometimes God Gives an Unpopular Word

II. ELIJAH AT THE BROOK CHERITH
A. Ravens Fed Him
B. The Lord Takes Care of Those Who Trust Him

III. WIDOW OF ZAREPHATH
A. Gave Her Last Meal to the Prophet
B. Meal and Oil Never Ran Out
C. The Lord Takes Care of Those Who Put Him First

IV. GOD WILL SUPPLY
A. We Must Trust in the Lord
B. We Must Put God First

CONTEMPLATING THE TOPIC

On May 25, 1961, United States President John F. Kennedy told Congress of his intentions to send a man to the moon and return him safely to Earth by the end of the decade. The challenge to do such a thing was monumental since the technology to achieve such a task had not yet been invented. Ultimately, the National Aeronautics and Space Administration (NASA) would receive billions of dollars in funding to ensure they would have all they needed to achieve the goal of reaching the moon. Though there were tragedies and setbacks along the way, on July 20, 1969, Neil Armstrong stepped onto the surface of the moon, successfully completing the challenge that had been set forth.

After President Kennedy's challenge, the US government supplied the needs of NASA. As Christians we often trust God to provide for our needs. Yet some believers feel, at times, that God withholds or does not provide for our needs. Philippians 4:19 states, "But my God shall supply all your need according to his riches in glory by Christ Jesus." This promise is written and cannot change. Then why do we feel God is not providing for our needs at times? We often experience tragedies and setbacks on the road of life. But through it all, we can trust God will still provide what we need.

I. ELIJAH PROPHESIED

A. No Dew or Rain

The prophet Elijah boldly stood before King Ahab and delivered a message declaring the judgment of God was going to fall upon Israel. In modern society, standing before a world leader expressing your opinion without fear of retribution seems reasonable. In the days of Elijah, a strongly worded opinion to the ruler of the land could bring swift and brutal punishment, even death. Elijah had the task of telling King Ahab that his nation would suffer from drought, seeing no rain or dew for the foreseeable future. Knowing the king's heart, God gave Elijah personal directions to flee the area after giving the message to the king. Not only did God give Elijah an opportunity to avoid the wrath of Ahab, but God sent Elijah to a place where he would find protection and provision. This mission must have been difficult for Elijah, but his obedience to God gave him the courage to go forward and complete the difficult task he had been given.

B. Sometimes God Gives an Unpopular Word

Jonah received an unpopular word from God. God commanded Jonah to go to Nineveh and tell the people to repent or face His wrath. This word did not sit well with Jonah as there was a contentious history between Israel and Nineveh. Instead of going to Nineveh as directed, Jonah went to Joppa and boarded a ship sailing for Tarshish. A storm arose, which caused the ship and crew to be in peril. When Jonah confessed his responsibility, the crew tossed Jonah overboard into the sea. Jonah was swallowed by a great fish, where he spent the next three days and nights. Once Jonah was delivered from the fish, he went straight to Nineveh and completed the task God had originally given him.

Elijah was far more obedient than Jonah. However, this did not make his task any easier. There are times when we as individuals—or as the collective body of Christ— receive an unpopular word from God. Sometimes the Word of God that comes from the pulpit of our local assembly is not popular. In Jonah 4 we see the prophet proclaiming his discontent with the task God had given him. Eventually he submitted to the authority of God and obeyed, just as Elijah had obeyed God.

» *How do you handle an unpopular word from God, with compliance or disregard?*

II. ELIJAH AT THE BROOK CHERITH

The expression "God works in mysterious ways" is applicable to Elijah's situation. Why would the God of all things tell His prophet to go and hide by a small creek? Certainly God could destroy or vanquish anyone who stood against His chosen prophet. This situation demonstrates how God operates with divine understanding. The word Elijah received was to tell Ahab about the impending judgment and then hide at the Brook Cherith. Elijah did not question God. He simply complied with the directive he was given by the Creator.

A. Ravens Fed Him

The irony is thick when looking at the choice God made in the way he would feed Elijah. The raven has long been associated with darkness or evil doings. Many stories and poems have been written using the raven as a symbol of evil or darkness. Most famous in modern times is the poem "The Raven" by Edgar Allan Poe. It portrays a raven talking to a man distraught at the loss of his love and grappling for sanity. Even more ironic in the case of Elijah is that wild animals, or wild birds in this case, approached a human being to bring him food. Birds are always skittish around humans and other creatures that approach them, and rarely do they feel comfortable approaching humans.

The Bible does not give many details on what happened to Elijah during his stay at the Brook Cherith, only that he was fed by the ravens. Imagine if someone had come across the prophet during his stay at the brook. What would this person have witnessed? Elijah was healthy and vibrant during a time of drought and famine. Even more amazing were the ravens bringing him food. A person who saw ravens as evil creatures might be overcome with fear seeing them freely approaching and bringing food to the prophet. That vision alone could cause men to stay away for fear the prophet held some power over creatures associated with darkness. Yet God used ravens to feed His prophet. With this in mind, we can see some logic in why God would have used this method to care for the man He was protecting. In His own way, God provided both nourishment and protection for Elijah.

» *How has God provided for you or others in a manner you could only describe as miraculous?*

B. The Lord Takes Care of Those Who Trust Him

Elijah had good reason to trust in the Lord. Not only had the Lord given Elijah direction to hide, but He gave Elijah safe passage and supplied his needs. Further study of the prophet provides numerous examples of the awesome power of God. Elijah was no different than any other human being. He simply obeyed and trusted in the Lord. Only when we trust in God can we be witness to greater miracles. Our trust grows as our relationship with the Lord develops into something more than just the occasional prayer.

David is another good example of a man who trusted God. We see the divine hand of the Lord protecting and providing for David. Each miraculous event in the life of David was greater than the last. These demonstrated how God prepared David for greater challenges and how David was growing in his trust in God. Our trust in God must grow beyond all human reasoning. Our trust in God is not optional. For Him to operate in our lives, we must trust Him and submit to His will. Psalm 9:10 states, "And they that know thy name will put their trust in thee: for thou, LORD, hast not forsaken them that seek thee."

8

III. WIDOW OF ZAREPHATH

Elijah received a word from God commanding him to leave the brook and go to a place called Zarephath. There he would find a widow God had instructed to care for the prophet.

She was a God-fearing woman based on two facts from Scripture. First, God told Elijah He had commanded a widow to take care of him. Only those in relationship with God would likely heed His voice. Secondly, when Elijah asked her for bread, she told him she did not have enough. When the prophet told her the word of the Lord, she immediately left to make him bread. Her obedience demonstrated the depth of her faith.

A. Gave Her Last Meal to the Prophet

A closer look at the interaction between the widow and the prophet reveals how our human nature can give us pause when trusting God. The initial request by Elijah was simply for a vessel of water. The widow immediately set out to fulfil his request. As she was walking away, Elijah called out to her and asked that she bring him some bread. This request caused her to hesitate for a moment as she informed Elijah she only had enough meal to make bread for herself and her son. She further stated she had come to gather two sticks in order to prepare the bread "that we may eat it, and die" (I Kings 17:12). In other words, she had enough meal to make one small morsel of bread; then she and her son would resign themselves to die from starvation. Elijah commanded her to make him some bread first, assuring her God would make sure her barrel would never be empty. In obedience to the word of God, she made the bread.

Hesitation in the face of imminent danger or uncertainty is an instinctive human reaction. Firefighters train to run toward dangerous situations in order to overcome the instinctive fear to flee. Their training is long and arduous, so when the moment arises, they can perform their duties. The widow demonstrated the natural hesitation of her humanity, yet when the word of God came forth, she immediately relied on her spirituality to overcome her fear. We must work daily in prayer and study to grow our faith in God.

» *What are you doing to grow your faith in God?*

B. Meal and Oil Never Ran Out

Imagine a drought and famine so severe that it would cause a widow to proclaim the impending death of herself and her son for lack of food. Elijah asked her to trust in the Lord and first make a morsel of bread for him; then the Lord would provide an abundance of meal and oil. I Kings 17:15–16 states, "And she went and did according to the saying of Elijah: and she, and he, and her house, did eat many days. And the barrel of meal wasted not, neither did the cruse of oil fail, according to the word of the LORD, which he spake by Elijah." Because of her faith and obedience, God was able to perform the miracle proclaimed by His prophet.

Faith and obedience are inseparable. The Bible tells of a man named Naaman, a powerful man within Syria who also happened to be a leper. Naaman heard about the prophet Elisha and was told this man of God could heal his leprosy. He journeyed to the house of Elisha, only to be greeted by a messenger. II Kings 5:10 states, "And Elisha sent a messenger unto him, saying, Go and wash in Jordan seven times, and thy flesh shall come again to thee, and thou shalt be clean." Naaman was not pleased with this situation, but he was desperate. Verse 14 explains, "Then went he down, and dipped himself seven times in Jordan, according to the saying of the man of God: and his flesh came again like unto the flesh of a little child, and he was clean." If Naaman had refused to obey what God had told him to do via the prophet, he would not have been healed of leprosy.

C. The Lord Takes Care of Those Who Put Him First

Every character in the Bible who put God first has always enjoyed God's provisions. Even when the situation is less than desirable, God still provides for those who put Him first. Joseph was betrayed by his own brothers and sold into slavery. They had become jealous of Joseph being held up as the most blessed son of their father. Joseph ended up living many years as a slave, and his father thought he was dead. Joseph worked hard and was held in high regard by his master, Potiphar. One day Potiphar's wife tried to seduce Joseph, but he fled. She lied to her husband saying Joseph had attacked her. Joseph was sent to prison an innocent man and remained incarcerated for years. But because he was able to interpret dreams, Pharaoh called Joseph to his court to tell Pharaoh what his dreams meant. When Joseph gave the interpretation to Pharaoh, he elevated Joseph to the second most powerful man in Egypt. When Joseph's brothers came to Egypt looking for food, Joseph was in a position to help save his family and was eventually reunited with his father. Joseph was obedient to God throughout his ordeal. In Genesis 50:20 Joseph told his brothers, "But as for you, ye thought evil against me; but God meant it unto good, to bring to pass, as it is this day, to save much people alive."

» *Why is it difficult to put God first when it may feel like He has put you last?*

IV. GOD WILL SUPPLY

God will supply our needs if we trust in Him and put Him first. This sounds easy, yet we struggle with it daily. It is imperative to understand we must first trust God and then choose to put Him first in every aspect of our lives.

A. We Must Trust in the Lord

Trust in God is the first step of faith. We cannot be saved without putting our trust in the Lord. Even when we do not understand all that is happening, we must trust He has our best interests at heart. Too often we reason ourselves out of trusting God by interfering with His work. Moses told the Israelites to "stand still, and see the salvation of the LORD" (Exodus 14:13). As human beings we always try to control every aspect of our lives and circumstances. This is impossible. Trusting God enables us to rely less on ourselves and more on Him. Proverbs 3:5–6 states, "Trust in the LORD with all thine heart; and lean not unto thine own understanding. In all thy ways acknowledge him, and he shall direct thy paths."

B. We Must Put God First

The New Testament records Jesus saying, "But seek ye first the kingdom of God, and his righteousness; and all these things shall be added unto you" (Matthew 6:33). Today's society rejects the idea of putting anything or anyone before oneself. Yet God teaches us to put Him first and He will supply all our needs. We must be cautious and understand that what we need and what we want can be two very different things. Sometimes we overlook the thing we need and focus on the thing we want. Often we want material things, positions of power or prestige, or a particular romantic partner; these make us lose focus. We must remember, if we put God first, He will supply all we need.

» *What indicators demonstrate someone is putting God first?*

⟫⟫ INTERNALIZING THE MESSAGE

If you saw someone drowning and swam out to assist, could you save the person if the person fought your efforts? It is highly unlikely you would be able to pull that person to safety because in the struggle you would become fatigued and put your own self at risk of drowning. In the height of panic, people often neglect assistance because they do not trust those who are offering help. If the drowning person does not submit to your direction, allowing you to help, the person will simply drown.

This principle can also be applicable to us spiritually. If we do not trust God, He cannot help us. The world often criticizes God for not forcing help upon us. God has given us free will. His love will not force us to submit to anything we do not wish. Therefore, we must build our relationship with God to the point of trusting Him beyond reason. His Word promises in Deuteronomy 31:6, "Be strong and of a good courage, fear not, nor be afraid of them: for the LORD thy God, he it is that doth go with thee; he will not fail thee, nor forsake thee."

God Hears Elijah's Prayer

FOCUS THOUGHT

God honors His preachers' prayers.

 FOCUS VERSE

I Kings 17:24

And the woman said to Elijah, Now by this I know that thou art a man of God, and that the word of the LORD in thy mouth is truth.

 LESSON TEXT

I Kings 17:17–23

17 And it came to pass after these things, that the son of the woman, the mistress of the house, fell sick; and his sickness was so sore, that there was no breath left in him.

18 And she said unto Elijah, What have I to do with thee, O thou man of God? art thou come unto me to call my sin to remembrance, and to slay my son?

19 And he said unto her, Give me thy son. And he took him out of her bosom, and carried him up into a loft, where he abode, and laid him upon his own bed.

20 And he cried unto the LORD, and said, O LORD my God, hast thou also brought evil upon the widow with whom I sojourn, by slaying her son?

21 And he stretched himself upon the child three times, and cried unto the LORD, and said, O LORD my God, I pray thee, let this child's soul come into him again.

22 And the LORD heard the voice of Elijah; and the soul of the child came into him again, and he revived.

23 And Elijah took the child, and brought him down out of the chamber into the house, and delivered him unto his mother: and Elijah said, See, thy son liveth.

⟫⟫ CULTURE CONNECTION

BAYOU BARTHOLOMEW

In July of 1989, Jerry Self and his brother-in-law were faced with the reality that in three hours, five-hundred acres of sweet potatoes would be under water. Twelve inches of rainfall had pushed the Bayou Bartholomew out of its banks, and it had reached the edge of Jerry's farmland. In desperation he called his pastors, A. J. and Dwight Fulton, to come pray for a miracle.

Both pastors arrived quickly. The men sat on a log that had floated to the edge of the field out of the bayou, and they began to pray.

After the pastors left, Jerry continued to monitor the water and found it had stopped rising. Believing the water had crested, Jerry checked the water levels north and south of him, only to learn the water was still rising.

Jerry continually checked the gauges and spoke with other farmers, again to receive the same report: the water was still rising. He went back to his fields, wondering what he would find, but the water continually stayed back.

For thirty days the water threatened, but it never rose higher than where the four men had sat and prayed.

Just as God heard Elijah's prayer, He hears the prayers of those He calls to watch over His people.

⟫⟫ OUTLINE

⟫⟫ CONTEMPLATING THE TOPIC

It is no secret that, in every sector, United States society is experiencing a crisis of authority. From the childhood vaccination debates to the election of President Trump, skepticism of the "tried and true" and "the expert" has gripped the nation. In 2017, secular social scientist Tom Nichols published *The Death of Expertise: The Campaign against Established Knowledge and Why It Matters*, exploring the troubling aspects of this trend. For Nichols, this "death of expertise" is rooted in "a rejection not only of knowledge, but of the ways in which we gain knowledge and learn about things. Fundamentally, it's a rejection of science and rationality, which are the foundations of Western civilization itself" (thefederalist.com).

However, Nichols' analysis, though intriguing, seems to miss the real issue. The ultimate source of this growing skepticism is not a loss of faith in "expertise," as such, but a loss of faith in "experts." The crisis of authority is not a crisis of scientific rationality but a crisis of personal integrity.

I. CRISIS IN THE ERA OF THE KINGS

A. The Rise of King Ahab

After the death of the Northern Kingdom's first king, Jeroboam, the nation almost instantaneously plunged into a protracted civil war. Baasha, of the tribe of Issachar, overthrew Jeroboam's son Nadab after two years (I Kings 15:26–28), only to have his own son, Elah, assassinated after two years by his captain Zimri (I Kings 16:8–10). Zimri himself reigned a grand total of seven days before being overthrown by another military captain Omri, who was able to finally bring stability (I Kings 16:15, 23). What is missing entirely in the story of Omri's rise to power is any sort of "prophetic mandate" for his actions. Even the ill-fated Zimri had at least the credible authorization of the prophet Jehu ben Hanani for his attack on Elah. (See I Kings 16:1–4, 7).

Though little is said of Omri in the Bible, his greatest military accomplishment (conquering Moab) is mentioned in the famous Moabite Stone. In other words, Omri and the dynasty that followed him were among the first kings after Solomon to have an international reputation and pivotal role in the ancient Near Eastern geopolitical drama. A key part of the reason for Omri's power and prominence was his alliance with the king of Sidon, which made the Northern Kingdom a vital link in international trade, bringing Israel into a new era of wealth and political influence.

B. The Rise of Idol Worship

None of this is mentioned in the Bible narrative for a very specific reason. The way Omri sealed his covenant with the king of Sidon was to have his son, Ahab, marry the Sidonian princess Jezebel. The Sidonians were worshipers of the false Canaanite god Baal. For the writer of Kings, this spelled disaster for the nation, for it meant the reintroduction of a loathsome false god into Israel's national life.

That is why the writer of Kings included the following note in the narrative of Ahab's ascension to power (I Kings 16:34): "In his days did Hiel the Beth-elite build Jericho: he laid the foundation thereof in Abiram his firstborn, and set up the gates thereof in his youngest son Segub, according to the word of the LORD, which he spake by Joshua the son of Nun." Not only does this text demonstrate the prophetic stature of Joshua, but it also symbolizes "the striking reversal between Israel's triumph under Joshua and their tragedy under Ahab" (Bruce K. Waltke, *An Old Testament Theology*). Under Ahab, Baal worship was not simply tolerated—it was promoted as the official "state religion" of Israel. (See I Kings 16:31–33.)

God's explicit purpose for giving the Israelites the Promised Land was to punish the Canaanites for their false worship. (See Genesis 15:13–16; Joshua 3:10.) The marriage of Ahab and Jezebel represented the very "undoing" of Israel's conquest of the land under Joshua, even to the rebuilding of the evil city of Jericho.

C. The Demands of Obedience Never Change

There are two important lessons to draw from the story of Ahab's rise to power. First, God is not impressed or moved by worldly standards of success. Most historians agree that Omri and Ahab were two of the most powerful kings Israel had ever known. In fact, at the Battle of Qarqar, King Ahab was able to field an army of ten thousand infantry soldiers and two thousand chariots and was essentially the military leader of the coalition that confronted the Assyrian king Shalmaneser III (Victor P. Hamilton, *Handbook on the Historical Books*). However, despite the military and economic might of Omri and Ahab, they failed the one test of "good success" (Joshua 1:8)— they were not faithful to God or His covenant.

The second important lesson to draw from these stories is that God's demands for obedience never changed. Though centuries separate the time of Joshua from the time of Ahab, God still abhorred the gods of the Canaanites and all that their worship entailed. Not the "cultural shift," nor the "need for economic stability," nor the desire for "international recognition" were sufficient reasons for sacrificing Israel's strict loyalty to God. The actions of Omri and Ahab were sinful because they were rooted in a lack of trust in God to provide those things in His own way and time.

» *Why are worldly definitions of success both so attractive and so dangerous?*

II. THE PORTRAYAL OF ELIJAH

A. A Man of Purpose

Into this charged religious and political arena stepped the mysterious man Elijah. Perhaps what is most noticeable is how little we know about him. No one is quite sure of the whereabouts of Tishbi, Elijah's hometown. The writer of Kings does not provide us with the name of Elijah's father or even the tribe to which he belonged. The only thing we know about Elijah is the meaning of his name: "Yahweh is my God." And perhaps, in the end, that is all we need to know about him. Elijah's name was his mission: he was a prophet raised up by God to combat the state-sanctioned rise of false worship.

B. A Man of Prayer

The only other thing we know about Elijah is he was a man of prayer. A grand total of fourteen separate prayer sessions are recorded in I Kings 17–19. Three things are noteworthy about Elijah's prayers. First, his prayers are striking in their simplicity. The Bible is no stranger to lengthy prayers. (See, for example, I Kings 8:22–53.) However, Elijah's prayer in chapter 17 was almost breathtakingly brief. "O LORD my God, I pray thee, let this child's soul come into him again" (I Kings 17:21). Later, in Matthew's record of the Sermon on the Mount, Jesus extolled this kind of prayer: "But when ye pray, use not vain repetitions, as the heathen do: for they think that they shall be heard for their much speaking. Be not ye therefore like unto them: for your Father knoweth what things ye have need of, before ye ask him" (Matthew 6:7–8).

Second, Elijah's prayers are notable for their honesty. Especially in his encounter with God on Mount Horeb in I Kings 19, Elijah was very open with his own feelings of isolation and perhaps even despair. Like David and the other psalmists, Elijah demonstrated honesty to be the hallmark of fervent prayer. In his honesty Elijah became for the apostle James a "model" man of prayer (James 5:17).

Finally, Elijah's prayers were notable in their persistence. He prayed three times for the widow's son to be resurrected (I Kings 17:21); he prayed seven times for the rains to fall and end the three-year-long drought (I Kings 18:43). In Luke 18:1 we find Jesus' Parable of the Unjust Judge was intended to teach this very lesson, "that men ought always to pray, and not to faint."

» **Besides honesty and persistence, what are two or three other keys to effective prayer you have discovered in your own life?**

C. The Importance of Spiritual Authority

In the Old Testament, Elijah was an iconic example of spiritual authority. It is often forgotten that Baal's role in the Canaanite pantheon was as the god of storms (lightning and rain). When Elijah announced: "As the LORD God of Israel liveth, before whom I stand, there shall not be dew nor rain these years, but according to my word" (I Kings 17:1), he was directly challenging Baal's claims. According to the Canaanite Baal myth, drought signaled the "death" of the god; in effect, when Elijah stormed into Ahab's presence that day, Elijah, through Yahweh's power, "killed" Baal.

Elijah's spiritual authority may have been demonstrated in miraculous signs and wonders, but it was clearly rooted in Elijah's prayers. Charles H. Kraft was correct in saying, "Spiritual authority is in direct proportion to spiritual intimacy" (*The Evangelical's Guide to Spiritual Warfare*). As with all other forms of authority, spiritual authority comes with associated responsibilities. A pastor who has been granted spiritual oversight of a congregation has a spiritual obligation to uphold his congregants in intercessory prayer. At the end of his life, Samuel, the prophet and judge, said to the children of Israel: "Moreover as for me, God forbid that I should sin against the LORD in ceasing to pray for you" (I Samuel 12:23).

There is one final truth about the nature of spiritual authority revealed in the Elijah stories: spiritual authority must grow and develop. The stories recorded in I Kings 17 show a definite progression in terms of the prophet's own authority. As Richard D. Nelson puts it: "Elijah moves from passive to active readiness. In the first story he simply obeys and is fed. In the second, he reports what God will do. In the third, he takes an active role and the Lord listens to him" (*First and Second Kings*). If Elijah had not undergone these three tests of faith—each increasing the level of required trust exponentially—it is more than likely he would not have been adequately prepared for the showdown with the false prophets of Baal in I Kings 18. The raising of the widow's son convinced Elijah once and for all that God does hear and answer prayer, and He can do miracles that have never been seen before.

III. THE POWER OF A PRAYING PREACHER

A. The Widow First Trusted Elijah

The stories recorded in I Kings 17 form a kind of interlocked narrative, united by their focus on the problem of imminent death and the divine gift of life via miraculous means (Nelson). One cannot tell the story of the resurrection of the widow's son without including, in some way, the prior story of the miraculous provision of food for the prophet, the widow, and her son (for over two years). It must be noted that Zarephath was in Sidonian territory, the "heart" of Baal's country. Elijah had taken his fight against the false god to the god's own "homeland."

The text makes it clear this widow prepared the meal Elijah requested with the last bit of food she had been saving for her and her son. She had so much faith in the prophet's words that she was willing to risk starvation in her obedience. The text is also clear that the widow acted "according to the saying of Elijah" (I Kings 17:15). Prior to her encounter with the prophet Elijah, this woman had been a worshiper of Baal; she did not know nor worship Yahweh, the God of Elijah. She acted, at least at first, on her faith in the prophet. There was something about Elijah himself that inspired trust, hope, and courage in this woman.

» *Do you think you would be able to trust in and act upon a word from a man or woman of God like this widow did? Why or why not?*

B. The Widow Was Led to Trust in God

Because of her courageous act of obedience to God's word through the prophet Elijah, miraculous provision occurred. However, an even greater miracle is that this poor Sidonian widow came to be a believer in the God of Elijah. This can be seen in her grieved petition after the death of her son: "What have I to do with thee, O thou man of God?" (I Kings 17:18). The widow then recognized that Elijah's spiritual authority came from the one true God, not from himself or from any of the gods of the Sidonians who had proven unable to provide sustenance during the drought and famine.

What followed was the first recorded resurrection story in the Bible. Because of this Sidonian widow's faith and the prophet Elijah's persistent prayers, God performed a miracle He had never performed before—raising a person from the dead. It was this final miraculous sign that elicited the widow's full confession of faith: "Now by this I know that thou art a man of God, and that the word of the LORD in thy mouth is truth" (I Kings 17:24).

C. The Importance of Spiritual Integrity

It is important to notice that the woman believed in the prophet before she believed in the prophet's God. The trustworthy character of the prophet led the woman to trust in the character of the God whom the prophet proclaimed. If the widow had not trusted Elijah, she would have continued with her original plan, and that meager

17

meal would have been her last. But because she chose to trust the prophet, her life and her son's life were saved.

In addition, the widow's decision to trust required that Elijah present himself (and his God) as trustworthy. In other words, Elijah's character and demeanor in these stories are crucial to the widow's discovery of the true character of God. Elijah was not simply called to represent God by performing mighty signs and wonders in His name; more fundamentally, Elijah was called to represent God by exhibiting His characteristic faithfulness to His covenant promises.

A life of spiritual authority is rooted in a life of spiritual integrity. And a life of spiritual integrity can only be rooted in a quest to consistently model the character of God revealed fully in Jesus Christ. Without the integrity of Christ-like character, spiritual authority becomes a weapon that is wielded for one's own benefit rather than for the cause of Christ and His kingdom. Sadly, many have been driven away from God because those who claim to represent Him do not display spiritual integrity. We should thank God every day for the blessing of spiritual leaders who lead with integrity.

» *Name two or three ways spiritual integrity might be differentiated from integrity of character. Can one exist without the other? Why or why not?*

⟫⟫ INTERNALIZING THE MESSAGE

A baker in a little country town bought the butter he used from a nearby farmer. One day he suspected that the bricks of butter were not full pounds, and for several days he weighed them.

He was right. They were short of the advertised weight, and he had the farmer arrested. At the trial the judge said to the farmer, "I presume you have scales?"

"No, your honor."

"Then how do you manage to weigh the butter you sell?" inquired the judge.

The farmer replied, "That's easily explained, your honor. I have balances and for a weight I use a one-pound loaf I buy from the baker."

Warren Buffet, chairman and CEO of the investment company Berkshire Hathaway, once said: "In looking for people to hire, look for three qualities: integrity, intelligence, and energy. And if they don't have the first one, the other two will kill you." We live in a world that is hungry for leadership with integrity, especially spiritual leadership. We also live in a world where that kind of leadership is in increasingly short supply. Today the world of Christendom is being rocked by abuse scandals that make the televangelist scandals of the 1980s appear tame and almost trifling.

At its root this cultural "search for integrity" is the cry of a heart that longs for something to believe in that will not disappoint or fail. We know the only fulfilling end for such a quest is a relationship with God, the only one who is ultimately trustworthy and unchanging.

The Lord, He Is God

FOCUS THOUGHT
God is God alone and has all power.

 FOCUS VERSE

I Kings 18:39
And when all the people saw it, they fell on their faces: and they said, The Lord, he is the God; the Lord, he Is the God.

LESSON TEXT

I Kings 18:30–39
30 And Elijah said unto all the people, Come near unto me. And all the people came near unto him. And he repaired the altar of the Lord that was broken down.

31 And Elijah took twelve stones, according to the number of the tribes of the sons of Jacob, unto whom the word of the Lord came, saying, Israel shall be thy name:

32 And with the stones he built an altar in the name of the Lord: and he made a trench about the altar, as great as would contain two measures of seed.

33 And he put the wood in order, and cut the bullock in pieces, and laid him on the wood, and said, Fill four barrels with water, and pour it on the burnt sacrifice, and on the wood.

34 And he said, Do it the second time. And they did it the second time. And he said, Do it the third time. And they did it the third time.

35 And the water ran round about the altar; and he filled the trench also with water.

36 And it came to pass at the time of the offering of the evening sacrifice, that Elijah the prophet came near, and said, Lord God of Abraham, Isaac, and of Israel, let it be known this day that thou art God in Israel, and that I am thy servant, and that I have done all these things at thy word.

37 Hear me, O Lord, hear me, that this people may know that thou art the Lord God, and that thou hast turned their heart back again.

38 Then the fire of the Lord fell, and consumed the burnt sacrifice, and the wood, and the stones, and the dust, and licked up the water that was in the trench.

39 And when all the people saw it, they fell on their faces: and they said, The Lord, he is the God; the Lord, he is the God.

A GRANDPA'S PRAYER

On Friday, December 8, 2017, Rick Carter received a call that his four-month-old grandson was admitted to A. I. duPont Hospital for Children. He was having trouble breathing, his heart was racing, and he was running a fever. Twenty-four hours later the doctors still had no diagnosis and were struggling to stabilize him.

Two days later, on Sunday, December 10, Pastor Steven Beardsley preached a sermon entitled "The Test." What grabbed Rick's attention was his pastor's emphasis that to pray for miracles and healings, a pastor is not always needed because we serve the same God and have the same power within us.

By Monday evening the doctors had diagnosed Bryce with RSV, but he was not better and was looking at another week in the hospital. Rick told his daughter, "I'm coming to pray."

Rick stood alone in the room, holding Bryce. Rick laid his hand on the baby's chest and began to pray. "God, I am stepping out in faith and enacting what my pastor preached. I am Your servant and if You choose not to heal Bryce, You are still God. Please heal Bryce and let him be released tomorrow."

Instantly Rick felt the warm presence of God lay upon his hand and go into Bryce's chest. Bryce began to convulse in his arms and scream. He was shaking and moving so much, Rick thought he was going to drop him. At that moment, the alarms started going off, alerting the nurses' station that there was a problem.

As this was happening, Rick could hear nurses and doctors running to the room. When the first hand touched the doorknob, Bryce was at complete peace and smiling at Rick. The next day, Bryce was released from the hospital at 10:00 AM; all his vital signs were normal and stabilized.

>>> OUTLINE

I. SAMARIA HAD TURNED TO FOLLOW BAAL
  A. Ahab and Jezebel Led the People to Follow Baal
  B. Leaders Can Influence the Hearts of Their Followers

II. SHOWDOWN ON MOUNT CARMEL
  A. The God Who Answers by Fire
  B. We Can Be Confident That Our God Will Answer

III. PROPHETS OF BAAL BUILT AN ALTAR
  A. Offered Their Sacrifice
  B. Those Who Serve False Gods Have No Hope

IV. ELIJAH REBUILT AN ALTAR
  A. Prepared His Sacrifice and Prayed
  B. Those Who Serve the True God Have Hope

V. THE LORD, HE IS GOD
  A. We Serve the One True God
  B. We Have Hope Because God Has All Power

>>> CONTEMPLATING THE TOPIC

During the 1960s a family accepted a global missions assignment to a remote African village. Several Christian missionaries had tried unsuccessfully to establish a church in that particular area, but the village witch doctor held great power over the people of the village. They had seen him do mystical acts that brought them into submission under his power. He was successful in driving off the previous missionaries, and the people of the village were witnesses to these acts. Believing him to have special powers from numerous gods, they were understandably hesitant to embrace another religion.

The missionary family arrived and set up a small hut for church. They held services faithfully, worshiped, sang, prayed, and preached. They interacted daily with the villagers, who welcomed them. However, the villagers did not discuss religion or attend any functions the missionaries offered. The witch doctor told the missionaries that their God was weak and they would leave within ninety days. This family was not weak in faith and knew with all confidence they served the one true God. A full calendar year passed, and the missionaries continued faithfully in their duties, holding services each week. Desperate for a move of God, they sought an answer from God in prayer to confirm their calling to this place that seemed hopeless to receive God.

One Sunday the entire village showed up for service. While the missionaries were ecstatic, they were also puzzled by the sudden turnout. Every villager was baptized that day, even the witch doctor. After a few days, the missionaries were approached by the witch doctor. They asked him what had happened to bring about the sudden change of heart. The witch doctor told them that like their predecessors, he began to slowly poison their water supply the first day they arrived in the village. It usually took a few weeks before the missionaries would be so physically ill they had no option but to leave their work and the village to seek medical assistance. The witch doctor went on to say that not only had he poisoned their water, but he had continued to increase the poison each week for the past year.

The amount of poison he last put in the water was enough to kill a herd of elephants, yet this family never suffered one day of sickness throughout the entire year. When the villagers asked him what was happening, he told them, "Surely they serve a true God that He has protected them from certain death." So He led the entire village to their service to learn about their God.

▶▶▶ SEARCHING THE SCRIPTURES

I. SAMARIA HAD TURNED TO FOLLOW BAAL

I Kings records the plight of Israel as each leader took them further and further away from serving God. I Kings 16:30–31 tells us, "Now Ahab the son of Omri did evil in the sight of the LORD, more than all who were before him. And it came to pass, as though it had been a trivial thing for him to walk in the sins of Jeroboam the son of Nebat, that he took as wife Jezebel the daughter of Ethbaal, king of the Sidonians; and he went and served Baal and worshiped him" (NKJV).

A. Ahab and Jezebel Led the People to Follow Baal

Ahab inherited a kingdom that had been led astray for generations. The significance of his tenure was not because of his disobedience so much as it would be the time God would reveal His might and power to the people of His promise. Ahab's marriage to Jezebel brought the situation of Israel's sin to a greater depth. I Kings 16:32–33 states, "He set up an altar for Baal in the temple of Baal that he built in Samaria. Ahab also made an Asherah pole and did more to arouse the anger of the LORD, the God of Israel, than did all the kings of Israel before him" (NIV). The people of Israel followed along as if they had forgotten what God had done for them.

Much like in our society today, the gift of salvation purchased at Calvary seemed to have been lost on a generation seeking self-pleasure and personal fulfillment through the lust of the flesh. Much like in I Kings, humanity today suffers from short-term memory based on carnal desires passed from generation to generation.

» *What are some ways our world today reflects the days of King Ahab?*

B. Leaders Can Influence the Hearts of Their Followers

The Bible gives us numerous examples of leaders who influenced their subordinates—some for good, others for evil. Ahab and Jezebel must have given the people of Israel some false sense that Baal would offer them hope and peace like they had never known. Perhaps the idea of living and fulfilling any desire was appealing. Whatever the reason, the people received and followed the influence given by their leaders. Only a few of the prophets would stand strong for the law of God in the face of adversity. Many of us today are facing similar circumstances; our beliefs are questioned and mocked by those who proclaim faith, yet they serve a different master entirely.

» *How do our world leaders influence people today?*

II. SHOWDOWN ON MOUNT CARMEL

Every good story has a showdown between good and evil. The characters are developed through the story line, culminating in a climactic showdown at the anticipated moment of suspense. The Bible is unique in this literary technique in that the timing of the showdown is never when we anticipate. Lamentations 3:25–26 tells us, "The LORD is good unto them that wait for him, to the soul that seeketh him. It is good that a man should both hope and quietly wait for the salvation of the LORD."

It would be over four hundred years before God would deliver the children of Israel from the bondage of the Egyptians. Waiting on the Lord often brings out the worst in humanity. When Moses was on Mount Sinai, the children of Israel became impatient and made an idol to worship. This act was within a short time of the Red Sea crossing. As Ahab came into power, the Israelites had once again turned their backs on God. The prophet Elijah would stand as the representative of God.

In I Kings 18:19 Elijah told Ahab, "Now therefore send, and gather to me all Israel unto mount Carmel, and the prophets of Baal four hundred and fifty, and the prophets of the groves four hundred, which eat at Jezebel's table." The stage was set. Elijah would stand before all of Israel and declare that the Lord, He is God.

A. The God Who Answers by Fire

Fire is unlike any other natural element that destroys. It is a force of nature with unlimited destructive power. God has unlimited power. Just like Moses before him, Elijah knew God could demonstrate His power in any way He deemed fit for the occasion. He knew God would use fire to consume the offering He would present before the Lord. The situation concerning Israel's disobedience in worshiping Baal had come to a point where only a massive demonstration of the power of God would turn them back to worshiping Him. Only an all-consuming fire would vanquish the enemies of God.

The Bible tells us Hell will be a place of unquenchable fire, a place where all the enemies of the Lord will spend eternity. Yet the Bible also uses fire to demonstrate the all-consuming power of the Holy Ghost. Matthew 3:11 records the words of John the Baptist, "I indeed baptize you with water unto repentance: but he that cometh after me is mightier than I, whose shoes I am not worthy to bear: he shall baptize you with the Holy Ghost, and with fire." This fire consumes us and gives us authority and power to profess the Word of God and demonstrate His power through signs, wonders, and miracles.

B. We Can Be Confident That Our God Will Answer

The Bible promises God will never forsake us, even though it also gives examples of His people feeling forsaken by God. This is where our faith must come into play. Our relationship with God must be made strong through daily prayer, worship, and Bible study. Only then will our faith hold up when we feel forsaken. During those times we must rely on the words given to us by divine Scripture. Psalm 86:7 states, "In the day of my trouble I will call upon thee: for thou wilt answer me."

The examples of holy men in Scripture demonstrate that each had a relationship with God that was nurtured faithfully. When we see faithful men and women of God today doing miraculous things, we can infer they have a faithful relationship with God. Often they speak of hearing from God, giving testimony to what He has spoken into their lives and ministries. It is important to understand that any time God speaks to us, it will always comply with the Word He has given us through the Scriptures.

» *Have you known someone to claim to have received a word from God, but it went against Scripture? Explain.*

III. PROPHETS OF BAAL BUILT AN ALTAR

The Bible does not give a detailed description concerning the particular altar the prophets built for Baal; it only tells us an altar existed where they placed the bullock. We can assume that with four hundred and fifty prophets of Baal, it most likely was a sizable structure. The various means of worship and sacrifice to the false god would have been taken into consideration during construction. There is no mention of any particular material that was used or any particular manner of design. Simply stated, an altar existed for the Baal prophets to offer their sacrifice to their god.

Our modern society has many "altars"; some have a specific design, while others do not. Some people worship technology, while others simply worship the theories and discoveries offered by science. There are too many "altars" to name, yet we all know of the false gods we encounter every day.

A. Offered Their Sacrifice

The prophets of Baal must have been pleased at this opportunity to demonstrate the greatness of their god. They were great in number, so surely this proved their god was great also. The Bible records that after they prepared the bullock, they began to cry out to Baal. After some time had passed with no response, they began to climb on the altar and cry out even more. After more time had passed, Elijah began to mock them, saying their god must not be able to hear them. Perhaps he was on a long journey and was not available or perhaps he was sleeping so deeply they would need to cry louder to arouse him from his slumber. After several hours of no response, Baal's prophets began to cut themselves in desperation. At no time during this process does the Bible declare they ever gave up on Baal.

Too often in society, people will "go down with the ship." In other words, they will not relent from their position, even in the face of certain destruction or failure. Pride is the reason many people will not concede a position. Blinded by their arrogance, they often go to greater extremes to prove themselves superior or not in error. We have seen this behavior in the church when men and women have failed to humble themselves and repent. Proverbs 16:18 states, "Pride goeth before destruction, and an haughty spirit before a fall."

B. Those Who Serve False Gods Have No Hope

Jeremiah 10:2 states, "Thus saith the LORD, Learn not the way of the heathen, and be not dismayed at the signs of heaven; for the heathen are dismayed at them." There is no hope in anything outside the one true God. Those who serve Him are consistently blessed with goodness, while those who serve false gods and idols are consistently wrought with sin and the consequences that arise from it. God has declared that we should serve no other gods. Deuteronomy 12:30 tells us, "Take heed to thyself that thou be not snared by following them, after that they be destroyed from before thee; and that thou enquire not after their gods, saying, How did these nations serve their gods? even so will I do likewise." Israel had fallen into Baal worship, and God would stay true to His Word by destroying those who served Baal.

» *Can you list some things people worship that will not offer them hope?*

IV. ELIJAH REBUILT AN ALTAR

The first thing we should notice when Elijah proceeded to build his altar to the Lord is the deliberate actions he executed. The New Testament declares in I Corinthians 14:40, "Let all things be done decently and in order." God has a design in everything He does. The Scriptures give no detail on how the altar to Baal was constructed, yet when we read about Elijah's altar, we are given a list of details. I Kings 18:31–32 records, "And Elijah took twelve stones, according to the number of the tribes of the sons of Jacob, unto whom the word of the LORD came, saying, Israel shall be thy name: and with the stones he built an altar in the name of the LORD: and he made

24

a trench about the altar, as great as would contain two measures of seed." There is purpose in the details and the order in which things are presented before the Lord. Throughout all sixty-six books of the Bible, God demonstrates order and purpose.

It is noteworthy that Scripture states Elijah built the altar before the people of Israel. It implies that the altar of God was in a state of disrepair. Elijah worked to restore it to service. It is also important to note that it took some labor on the part of the prophet to restore the altar. When we fail God, often our prayer life goes into disrepair. We must work and repair what has been broken by our disobedience. Yet God will restore us time and again because of His love for us.

A. Prepared His Sacrifice and Prayed

Restoring the altar to God was only the beginning for Elijah. I Kings 18:33 states, "And he put the wood in order, and cut the bullock in pieces, and laid him on the wood, and said, Fill four barrels with water, and pour it on the burnt sacrifice, and on the wood." Once again Elijah performed his task of preparing the sacrifice according to the law of Moses. In painstaking detail the prophet went about his duties preparing the sacrifice and the elements of the altar to be presented to the Lord at a prescribed time. One detail was not part of the sacrificial ritual—Elijah had the altar and sacrifice doused in water three times. The altar, wood, and sacrifice were completely wet. This would make it impossible for any human to ignite the sacrifice with fire. When the time came, Elijah offered up his prayer to God. He prayed the Lord would turn the hearts of His people, so they would know He was God. The fire of the Lord fell and consumed the sacrifice, the word, the stones, the water, and even the dust. When the people of Israel saw it, they fell on their faces and declared, "The LORD, he is the God; the LORD, he is the God" (I Kings 18:39).

B. Those Who Serve the True God Have Hope

Romans 5:3–4 states, "And not only so, but we glory in tribulations also: knowing that tribulation worketh patience; and patience, experience; and experience, hope." Those who serve the Lord have always had hope, even during times of great tribulation. The children of Israel had the hope of a deliverer during the four hundred years they were held in bondage by Egypt. Jesus has come, and we now have the blessed hope of salvation and eternal life. No one can escape the consequences of sin, yet we can all overcome by the sacrifice of God through His Son, Jesus. The glorious hope we have is recorded by miraculous events in the Old and New Testaments. No other religion, philosophy, or even science gives the promise of eternal life. The hope found in serving God is beyond comprehension.

V. THE LORD, HE IS GOD

Psalm 100:3 states, "Know ye that the LORD he is God: it is he that hath made us, and not we ourselves; we are his people, and the sheep of his pasture." The idea of only one God has lived long beyond the multiple false gods of antiquity. There are some religions that still serve multiple gods, yet the significance that one God made Himself known to the world has caused many religions to embrace only one god. They may still serve a false god, yet the impact of the power of the one true God cannot be denied.

A. We Serve the One True God

Many claim to serve the one true God. Therefore, it stands to reason that the Lord would validate Himself to those who serve Him. God has always revealed Himself to His people in some fashion. Since the Day of Pentecost, He has revealed Himself to the individual believer through the infilling of the Holy Ghost. No other religious group outside of Christianity makes such a claim, to have the Spirit of God living within the believer. This unique characteristic not only sets us apart from others because it is different, but it sets us apart because of the power it gives us. Deuteronomy 4:35 states, "Unto thee it was shewed, that thou mightest know that the LORD he is God; there is none else beside him." Once we have received His Spirit, there is no doubt whom we serve.

» *Have you ever struggled with doubt? How did you overcome it?*

B. We Have Hope Because God Has All Power

Our hope comes from God. Romans 15:13 states, "Now the God of hope fill you with all joy and peace in believing, that ye may abound in hope, through the power of the Holy Ghost." God created all things in Heaven and in Earth. He spoke it all into existence, yet He has a love for humanity that surpasses all understanding. The Creator could have easily destroyed humanity after the Garden, yet He instead chose to redeem them. The power of love is greater than any power we know. It influences us to make choices that defy logic, that go beyond logical reasoning. I John 4:8 states, "He that loveth not knoweth not God; for God is love." You cannot know God if you do not love others as He does.

⟫⟫⟫ INTERNALIZING THE MESSAGE

The witch doctor from the village mentioned at the beginning of this lesson witnessed firsthand the power of the one true God. Neither he nor the other villagers could deny what they had witnessed. When God puts His Spirit within us, we cannot deny that something miraculous has occurred. Ezekiel 11:19–20 states, "And I will give them one heart, and I will put a new spirit within you; and I will take the stony heart out of their flesh, and will give them an heart of flesh: that they may walk in my statutes, and keep mine ordinances, and do them: and they shall be my people, and I will be their God." Elijah was faithful to God and led Israel to a place where they would see His awesome power in full demonstration. Just like the men and women of Israel from that era, we can know today that the Lord, He is God.

God Sees All

FOCUS THOUGHT

Because God sees all things, we should seek to please Him with our actions.

 FOCUS VERSE

I Kings 21:20

And Ahab said to Elijah, Hast thou found me, O mine enemy? And he answered, I have found thee: because thou hast sold thyself to work evil in the sight of the LORD.

 LESSON TEXT

I Kings 21:1–7, 17–20

1 And it came to pass after these things, that Naboth the Jezreelite had a vineyard, which was in Jezreel, hard by the palace of Ahab king of Samaria.

2 And Ahab spake unto Naboth, saying, Give me thy vineyard, that I may have it for a garden of herbs, because it is near unto my house: and I will give thee for it a better vineyard than it; or, if it seem good to thee, I will give thee the worth of it in money.

3 And Naboth said to Ahab, The LORD forbid it me, that I should give the inheritance of my fathers unto thee.

4 And Ahab came into his house heavy and displeased because of the word which Naboth the Jezreelite had spoken to him: for he had said, I will not give thee the inheritance of my fathers. And he laid him down upon his bed, and turned away his face, and would eat no bread.

5 But Jezebel his wife came to him, and said unto him, Why is thy spirit so sad, that thou eatest no bread?

6 And he said unto her, Because I spake unto Naboth the Jezreelite, and said unto him, Give me thy vineyard for money; or else, if it please thee, I will give thee another vineyard for it: and he answered, I will not give thee my vineyard.

7 And Jezebel his wife said unto him, Dost thou now govern the kingdom of Israel? arise, and eat bread, and let thine heart be merry: I will give thee the vineyard of Naboth the Jezreelite.

. . . . . .

17 And the word of the LORD came to Elijah the Tishbite, saying,

18 Arise, go down to meet Ahab king of Israel, which is in Samaria: behold, he is in the vineyard of Naboth, whither he is gone down to possess it.

19 And thou shalt speak unto him, saying, Thus saith the LORD, Hast thou killed, and also taken possession? And thou shalt speak unto him, saying, Thus saith the LORD, In the place where dogs licked the blood of Naboth shall dogs lick thy blood, even thine.

20 And Ahab said to Elijah, Hast thou found me, O mine enemy? And he answered, I have found thee: because thou hast sold thyself to work evil in the sight of the LORD.

A GOD OF DETAILS

Wendy's husband passed away unexpectedly while they were pastoring. After gaining the strength to move on with her life, she moved to New York. The move was a good change, and God provided her with a nursing job, at which she excelled.

Wendy's son Keith had been waiting for a heart transplant for almost four years, but he had no way of acquiring the level of care he would need after the surgery. While Wendy was in town visiting him, she asked, "Am I going to need to come here for you to get your transplant?" Keith was quite startled and in his gentle, kind way, he responded that he would never ask her to make that sacrifice.

As they were talking, the pastor walked over and joined the conversation. After hearing their conversation, the pastor told them of a recent meeting he had been in. That very week a group of church leaders had been trying to formulate a plan to get Keith the help he needed. They decided it would only work if they could somehow get Wendy to help, but she would need to quit her job and move back to the area.

Within two weeks of that conversation, Wendy was offered two jobs. Both made it possible for her to work from home and move back to help Keith through the transplant process. Within a few months, Wendy moved and Keith's transplant was a success.

God sees the needs of His people, and when we seek to please Him and care for one another, He works out all the details.

>>> OUTLINE

I. GOD IS OMNISCIENT
A. Knows All Things
B. His Knowledge Should Bring Us Comfort

II. NABOTH HAD A VINEYARD
A. An Inheritance from His Fathers
B. Ahab Wanted Naboth's Vineyard
C. God Knows the Enemy Wants to Take What We Have Been Given

III. JEZABEL DEVISED A PLAN
A. Naboth Was Falsely Accused and Stoned
B. Ahab Let the Injustice Happen
C. God Knows the Enemy Will Try to Steal, Kill, and Destroy

IV. GOD REVEALED THE TRUTH TO ELIJAH
A. Nothing Is Hidden from the Lord
B. We Must Seek to Please the Lord

>>> CONTEMPLATING THE TOPIC

The only survivor of a shipwreck was washed up on a small, uninhabited island. He prayed fervently for God to rescue him. Every day he scanned the horizon for help, but no hope was in sight. Exhausted from the effort, he finally resigned himself to living out his life on the island all alone.

Eventually he managed to build a little hut out of driftwood for protection from the elements and to store his few possessions. One day after scavenging for food, he arrived home to find his little hut in flames, the smoke rolling up to the sky. Just when he thought things could not possibly get any worse, they did. Suddenly everything he had was lost. He was stunned with grief and anger. "God, how could you do this to me?" he cried. He simply could not believe God would allow this to happen to him with all that had already gone wrong in his life.

Early the next day, however, he was awakened by the sound of a ship approaching the island. He could hear its foghorn blaring from beyond the coastline. Soon a small group of sailors arrived in a rowboat. They had come to rescue him. "How did you know I was here?" the weary man asked the sailors. "We saw your smoke signal," they replied.

It is easy for us to forget that God sees what we do not see. Our human eyesight is limited by barriers, walls, doors, and horizons. In our humanity we may forget God is not limited by what limits us. Regardless of how bad life gets at times, we need to remember that God sees it all and is working for our good beyond what we can see.

⟩⟩⟩ SEARCHING THE SCRIPTURES

I. GOD IS OMNISCIENT

It used to be that if we were assigned a research paper in school, we would go to the library and pull books off the shelf for research. We were limited only by the number of books available.

Today we simply search Google for a topic, and more resources are at our disposal than we could possibly ever read through. Computer technology and the internet have expanded our ability to acquire information and knowledge, almost beyond comprehension. Even at that, we are finite and are limited in what we actually know. The smartest among us still does not know everything there is to know.

But God is omniscient. There is nothing unknown to Him. He knows what Google knows and even more. Isaiah 40:13–14 states, "Who can fathom the Spirit of the LORD, or instruct the LORD as his counselor? Whom did the LORD consult to enlighten him, and who taught him the right way? Who was it that taught him knowledge, or showed him the path of understanding?" (NIV).

A. Knows All Things

Omniscience is defined as "the state of having total knowledge; the quality of knowing everything." For God to truly be sovereign over His creation, He has to be all knowing. The Bible tells us His knowledge is so vast, He even knows the minutest details, like the number of hairs on your head or every time a sparrow falls to the ground. No detail is so small that God does not know it. No knowledge or thought is so deep that it is beyond Him.

Psalm 139:15–16 declares to us just how omniscient God is when it comes to our person: "My frame was not hidden from you, when I was being made in secret, intricately woven in the depths of the earth. Your eyes saw my unformed substance; in your book were written, every one of them, the days that were formed for me, when as yet there was none of them" (ESV). Can you imagine that? Before you were even formed, God knew the design of the days that would be in your future. We make our plans and think we know what we are going to do or what is going to happen. But really, only God knows with certainty what tomorrow holds.

» *Does the fact that God knows everything bring you fear or bring you comfort? Explain.*

B. His Knowledge Should Bring Us Comfort

Realizing God knows everything should be the source of security and comfort for us. The foundation of our faith is based on the facts that God does not change and that God knows everything. The reason you can trust Him is because He knows everything. According to Hebrews 4:13, nothing is hidden from God: "Neither is there any creature that is not manifest in his sight: but all things are naked and opened unto the eyes of him with whom we have to do."

While for some this would be a reason to tremble in fear, to those who are born again and are faithfully serving Him, it is a comfort. Just to know God sees everything, no matter how hidden it is to the eyes of man, means God is aware at all times of what is happening to each of us. His knowledge of what we do not know means He has answers and solutions that we will never find on our own.

II. NABOTH HAD A VINEYARD

I Kings 21:1–13 tells of a man named Naboth who owned a vineyard. Owning land meant a certain amount of security for the person and the person's family. A vineyard in that day would have been of great value due to the demand for wine for both common people as well as the military. Great value would be placed on such a piece of land, not only for what it produced presently, but also for what it would provide in the future.

» *Is there something you own that gives you a certain sense of security because you own it?*

A. An Inheritance from His Fathers

In ancient times many people did not own land but would farm land and sell whatever was produced on the land. Considering that the majority of people were not wealthy and had limited means, if a man owned property, he would be considered much better off than the man who merely farmed the land of someone else.

In this case, Naboth had inherited the vineyard. This means he understood the worth and the price that had been paid for it by his forefathers. Not only was there value in the land itself, but it would also have had significant emotional value to him and his family. The vineyard was not something to treat casually or sell off just to make life easier.

» *What things have you inherited that have great value to you?*

B. Ahab Wanted Naboth's Vineyard

God is a merciful God. Ahab should have known this better than most. In I Kings 20 God extended mercy to Ahab during a time when it seemed Ahab would be defeated by Ben-hadad, king of Syria. The Lord told Ahab that victory would be his in spite of how much it looked like things would not go his way.

After God brought His word to pass, evidently something changed inside of Ahab. Instead of being thankful for what God had preserved, Ahab began to selfishly desire the vineyard of Naboth, which was located next to the palace. Ahab wanted to turn it into a vegetable garden instead of a vineyard.

He offered Naboth a certain price, which Naboth refused. Instead of simply accepting no as an answer, Ahab became despondent and depressed. He should have been content with what he already had, but his greed caused him to be consumed with what he did not have.

C. God Knows the Enemy Wants to Take What We Have Been Given

We need to remember that God sees all. He knows we have an adversary who is roaming about, seeking whom he may devour. Our enemy not only wants to devour us, but he wants to devour any good thing God brings into our lives.

The blessings of life that we have, our walk with God, and our families are all precious and valuable. Many of these blessings are a part of our spiritual inheritance. The devil would like nothing better than to bargain them away from us. And if we are not willing to make a bargain, he will do everything he can to destroy us. God sees everything and knows this about our enemy. Nothing is hidden from God, even the plans of our enemy.

III. JEZEBEL DEVISED A PLAN

When Ahab returned home, he was distraught, refused to eat, and spent most of his time in bed with his face turned toward the wall. Jezebel noticed this and asked him, "Why is thy spirit so sad, that thou eatest no bread?" (I Kings 21:5).

A. Naboth Was Falsely Accused and Stoned

Ahab was quick to tell her of Naboth's refusal to sell the vineyard. Being the evil person she was, Jezebel took it upon herself to devise a plan to kill Naboth and give the vineyard to Ahab. She instructed Ahab to get up and cheer up. She told him she would take care of everything.

Her plan involved writing devious letters and signing Ahab's name to them. The plot was carefully laid out to call an assembly and have Naboth accused of blasphemy. The tragic result was he was carried outside of the city and stoned to death.

» *Have you ever been unjustly accused of something? How did you feel?*

B. Ahab Let the Injustice Happen

Perhaps one of the most intriguing aspects of the story is that Ahab silently sat back and let a good man be put to death in order to fulfill his own selfish desires. No doubt Ahab knew that what was being done was wrong. He also knew God had blessed him by giving him victory over his enemies. Yet he overrode all of that and allowed an injustice to occur.

31

C. God Knows the Enemy Will Try to Steal, Kill, and Destroy

Jesus said in John 10:10, "The thief cometh not, but for to steal, and to kill, and to destroy." God is ever aware that the enemy of our souls will do anything he can to keep us from succeeding at living for God.

The enemy may approach us with kindness, offering to bargain with us for what is valuable. He may even offer a high premium for us to sell out. The Lord knows the struggle the flesh has with temptation. His response to the temptation of the devil in the wilderness is still the best approach we can take. Our response should be to appeal to the Word of God and say, "It is written."

II Corinthians 2:11 tells us we are not ignorant of the devices of the enemy. Through the leading of the Spirit, God makes us aware of the approach of the enemy in our lives. Naboth was a great example of standing his ground and not yielding to the devices of the enemy when tempted.

IV. GOD REVEALED THE TRUTH TO ELIJAH

Unknown to Naboth, God would reveal all of this to the prophet Elijah. Just because Naboth had lost his life did not mean God would turn a blind eye to what Ahab and Jezebel had done.

The Lord revealed to Elijah what Ahab had done and where Elijah could find Ahab— in Naboth's vineyard enjoying the spoils of his evil actions. A swift and terrible judgment was pronounced by the man of God to Ahab. Elijah told Ahab that because of the great evil he had done, he would lose his prosperity and dogs would lick up his blood in the same place where they licked the blood of Naboth after his stoning.

A. Nothing Is Hidden from the Lord

Ahab and Jezebel failed to realize that nothing is hidden from the Lord. I Corinthians 4:5 declares, "Therefore judge nothing before the time, until the Lord come, who both will bring to light the hidden things of darkness, and will make manifest the counsels of the hearts: and then shall every man have praise of God." In other words, God sees all; nothing is hidden from Him. He will bring out in the light those things that were formed against us in the darkness. Once they are exposed, He will execute judgment on them.

Regardless of what we have gone through, God has not turned a blind eye toward us. He sees everything. The pain and suffering we endure has not slipped by Him unnoticed. God is ever aware and will not let such things go unpunished.

> » *Can you think of a situation where you observed someone doing evil while acting as if God was not watching?*

B. We Must Seek to Please the Lord

Our desire must be to please the Lord. Naboth took no thought for the wealth that could have been gained by selling the vineyard. Rather, he was more concerned with what was pleasing to the Lord. God not only sees the evil acts of our enemy, He also sees the righteous acts of our own hearts. While the enemy will be judged for his evil, we will be blessed for our righteousness.

Proverbs 16:8 tells us, "Better is a little with righteousness than great revenues without right." Naboth was more content with a vineyard that produced what it did and having a righteous heart than he ever would have been by selling out just for money.

⟩⟩⟩ INTERNALIZING THE MESSAGE

In Psalm 139:7 the psalmist asked the questions, "Whither shall I go from thy spirit? or whither shall I flee from thy presence?" In many ways such questions are rhetorical. The psalmist knew there was nowhere he could go where God would not see him.

The same is true for us today. God sees all. Nothing is hidden from Him. To the sinner this could be a frightening proposition. But to the faithful it is one of the greatest comforts we can know in this life. The knowledge that God watches over everything that happens to us should bring us great confidence in Him.

There will be times when others will treat us unjustly. It will hurt and could cause us to turn aside from trusting God. However, the story of Naboth should be an encouragement to us that God will not allow evil to go unnoticed or unpunished. He is faithful to those who are faithful to Him.

Focus on Following

FOCUS THOUGHT

No matter the distractions, we must choose to focus on following the Lord.

 FOCUS VERSE

II Kings 2:2

And Elijah said unto Elisha, Tarry here, I pray thee; for the LORD hath sent me to Beth-el. And Elisha said unto him, As the LORD liveth, and as thy soul liveth, I will not leave thee. So they went down to Beth-el.

 LESSON TEXT

II Kings 2:1–4; 11–15

1 And it came to pass, when the LORD would take up Elijah into heaven by a whirlwind, that Elijah went with Elisha from Gilgal.

2 And Elijah said unto Elisha, Tarry here, I pray thee; for the LORD hath sent me to Beth-el. And Elisha said unto him, As the LORD liveth, and as thy soul liveth, I will not leave thee. So they went down to Beth-el.

3 And the sons of the prophets that were at Beth-el came forth to Elisha, and said unto him, Knowest thou that the LORD will take away thy master from thy head to day? And he said, Yea, I know it; hold ye your peace.

4 And Elijah said unto him, Elisha, tarry here, I pray thee; for the LORD hath sent me to Jericho. And he said, As the LORD liveth, and as thy soul liveth, I will not leave thee. So they came to Jericho.

. . . . .

11 And it came to pass, as they still went on, and talked, that, behold, there appeared a chariot of fire, and horses of fire, and parted them both asunder; and Elijah went up by a whirlwind into heaven.

12 And Elisha saw it, and he cried, My father, my father, the chariot of Israel, and the horsemen thereof. And he saw him no more: and he took hold of his own clothes, and rent them in two pieces.

13 He took up also the mantle of Elijah that fell from him, and went back, and stood by the bank of Jordan;

14 And he took the mantle of Elijah that fell from him, and smote the waters, and said, Where is the LORD God of Elijah? and when he also had smitten the waters, they parted hither and thither: and Elisha went over.

15 And when the sons of the prophets which were to view at Jericho saw him, they said, The spirit of Elijah doth rest on Elisha. And they came to meet him, and bowed themselves to the ground before him.

⟫⟫ CULTURE CONNECTION

BE THE AFTERSHOCK

The first rattling of an earthquake is referred to as the mainshock. However, once the initial shaking subsides, there are usually aftershocks. Aftershocks are caused by the readjusting of the plates that were shifted during the mainshock. The bigger the earthquake, the more aftershocks and the longer they can last. The earthquake of 1906 in San Francisco is reported to have had aftershocks that affected Southern California, Nevada, Oregon, and Arizona.

When an earthquake happens, there is no question of whether there will be aftershocks; they always follow. There are safety protocols and guidelines on how to prepare for earthquakes and their aftershocks, but scientists have not discovered any method to stop them. Once an earthquake begins, there is no stopping what will follow.

The earthquake makes its mark, and the aftershock follows in its path. Aftershocks are so consistent that scientists can determine a range in which they will occur. There is not a question of if, but when.

As disciples of Christ, what would happen if we were to become the true aftershock of Jesus? If we follow Him consistently, others will have no doubt of who Jesus is, and what He does will naturally flow through us. We can be His aftershock, following His lead and helping those He has touched to adjust to a new life in Him.

⟫⟫ OUTLINE

I. THE LORD SENT ELIJAH SEVERAL PLACES
   A. Elijah Told Elisha to Stop Following
   B. The Lord Wants to Know If We Will Continue to Follow Him

II. SONS OF THE PROPHETS BROUGHT DISTRACTION
   A. Elisha Told the Distractions to Be Quiet and He Kept Following
   B. We Must Choose to Focus, Despite the Distractions

III. ELIJAH PERMITTED ELISHA TO MAKE A LAST REQUEST
   A. A Double Portion
   B. God Honors the Prayers of Those Who Follow Him

IV. ELIJAH WAS TAKEN AWAY IN A FIERY CHARIOT
   A. Elisha Kept His Eyes on the Mantle
   B. Where Is the Lord God of Elijah?
   C. God's Power Follows Those Who Follow Him

V. NO MATTER THE DISTRACTIONS, WE MUST FOCUS ON FOLLOWING THE LORD

⟫⟫ CONTEMPLATING THE TOPIC

In 2015, reports show that 3,477 people were killed and an estimated additional 391,000 were injured in motor vehicle crashes involving distracted drivers; 10 percent of fatal crashes, 15 percent of injury crashes, and 14 percent of all police-reported traffic crashes were reported as being affected by distractions; 9 percent of all drivers fifteen to nineteen years old involved in fatal crashes were distracted at the time of the crashes (this age group has the largest proportion of distracted drivers at the time of fatal crashes); 551 non-occupants (pedestrians, bicyclists, and others) were killed in distraction-affected crashes (https://www.enddd.org). In each year following, these statistics have increased.

Distracted driving comes in three different forms: (1) Cognitive distraction or mental distraction is when a driver's mind is not focused on driving. Talking to another passenger or being preoccupied with personal, family, or work-related issues are some examples. Even listening to a favorite podcast or radio station can put a driver at risk; the audio can take the

35

focus away from driving and the overall surroundings. (2) Visual distraction occurs when a driver looks at anything other than the road ahead. Even checking a child's seat belt while driving is visually distracting. Electronic devices for the car, such as GPS devices and portable DVDs or digital entertainment systems, also distract drivers. (3) Manual distraction happens when a driver takes one or both hands off the wheel for any reason. Some common examples include eating and drinking in the car, adjusting the GPS, or trying to get something from a purse, wallet, or briefcase.

The highway of life is also filled with distractions that take our focus off following the Lord. It is easy to be turned aside by the little things of life and to lose focus on what really matters. We need to always remember that those momentary glances at things that detract from following God could prove to be spiritually fatal.

⟫⟫ SEARCHING THE SCRIPTURES

I. THE LORD SENT ELIJAH SEVERAL PLACES

The story of Elisha following Elijah provides us insight into what it means to remain focused on the journey. After choosing to follow Elijah, Elisha returned home and said some final goodbyes to life as he had known it. He would be leaving behind his mother and father and the security of a future already laid out for him.

Elisha had no way of knowing that the journey with Elijah would take many twists and turns. Perhaps Elisha thought the anointing would simply be his because he had accepted the mantle. He may not have realized there would be a long season of simply following, in order to receive all God had for him.

The two left Gilgal together. Soon after, Elijah turned to Elisha and told him the Lord was sending Elijah to Bethel. From Bethel he would be instructed to go on to Jericho. The stay in Jericho would be brief as the Lord further instructed Elijah to travel to Jordan. Elisha was finding out that following was much more involved and strenuous than he perhaps had first thought.

A. Elijah Told Elisha to Stop Following

At each point along the journey, Elijah turned to Elisha and told him to remain in the place he found himself presently. Elijah told Elisha to stay in Gilgal, then in Bethel, and then in Jericho. Each destination brought a straightforward instruction to "stay."

No doubt it would have been somewhat discouraging and disheartening to Elisha to be told to quit following, time and time again. After all, he had accepted the mantle and wanted to follow the prophet of God. He had left all he had ever known, and following after Elijah had become everything to him. And yet Elisha continued to follow.

» *Why do you thnk Elijah kept offering to let Elisa stay behind?*

B. The Lord Wants to Know If We Will Continue to Follow Him

In living for God, the journey is not always as easy as we expect. Many times we feel a major hurdle or stop sign has been thrown into our pathway. Other times life seems to be going along fine, and we anticipate great things happening. Then, suddenly, distractions appear that could easily take our focus off the Lord.

The Lord wants to know if we will continue to follow Him. He knows how easily we can be distracted from what really matters. Several times in Scripture the Lord tested people's commitment to see whether they would remain faithful followers. Moses had to lead Israel through the wilderness in search of the Promised Land. Abraham had to follow God to the top of Mount Moriah when it would have been easier not to go. Simon Peter had to follow Jesus by walking on a stormy sea. When many others had ceased following Jesus, He asked the disciples, "Will you also go away?"

God knows it is easy to follow Him when He is answering our prayers and saying "yes" to our requests. But there will be times when it seems as if everything in life has turned upside down, and the journey could come to a standstill. In those times God finds out just how committed we are to following Him.

> *Can you recall a time when it seemed as if it would be easier to just stop instead of continuing to follow the Lord? Explain.*

II. SONS OF THE PROPHETS BROUGHT DISTRACTION

Every day we are surrounded by noise—the noise of traffic and workplaces, the noise of family and homelife, and even the noise that comes with being at church. Among the noise are voices. Voices are constantly vying for our attention and seeking influence in our lives.

The challenge is to know which voices to listen to and which ones are merely distractions. Elisha was surrounded by the noises of his day as well as the voices of the sons of the prophets. It would seem they were well-intentioned voices. Each stop on the journey brought an audience of these men before Elisha.

Quite honestly, they were telling him the truth. But to Elisha they were just stating the obvious, telling him things he already knew would happen. In so doing they became a distraction that could have caused him to lose focus.

A. Elisha Told the Distractions to Be Quiet and He Kept Following

How would Elisha respond? What would he do with the distractions that kept showing up at every place he went following Elijah? Perhaps Elisha would give in to the voices and become discouraged after realizing the elder prophet would indeed be taken from him.

Better yet, maybe Elisha should stop and reason with the sons of the prophets and try to explain why he was doing what he was doing. Maybe he should just agree with them and convince himself that all this following was foolishness. After all, he had followed the prophet all over the world and back again.

Elisha chose the wisest response of all. He refused to allow the distractions to change his direction. Although the voices were speaking truth, Elisha knew if he gave

37

in to them, he would quickly lose his way. By speaking to the voices and silencing them, Elisha allowed his focus to remain steadfastly on Elijah.

B. We Must Choose to Focus, Despite the Distractions

Every distraction requires a decision. It is totally up to us what we will do when distractions come. We can yield to them and lose sight of where God is taking us, or we can refuse to allow them to turn us aside from the journey. These are decisions only we can make.

However, without a made-up mind willing to stay focused on God, it is nearly impossible to faithfully follow Him. At times we will have to take authority over the distractions in order to be successful. II Corinthians 10:5 gives some great advice concerning this: "Casting down imaginations, and every high thing that exalteth itself against the knowledge of God, and bringing into captivity every thought to the obedience of Christ." In other words, we must control our thoughts to avoid being distracted. The best solution for avoiding distractions is bringing every thought captive to the knowledge of Jesus Christ and His purpose in our lives.

» *What are some practical things you can do to help avoid distractions?*

III. ELIJAH PERMITTED ELISHA TO MAKE A LAST REQUEST

Elijah knew the time for his departure was near. He had also seen Elisha's faithfulness in following him. It was then Elijah made an incredible offer to Elisha, an offer that almost seemed too good to be true. Elijah said to Elisha, "Ask what I shall do for thee, before I be taken away from thee" (II Kings 2:9).

Can you imagine? It was as if Elisha had received a blank check from the great prophet Elijah. Elisha could ask for anything his heart desired. The only limitation would be what his imagination could dream up.

A. A Double Portion

Interestingly, Elisha did not ask for anything to make his life easier. He did not request financial blessings or material things. Neither did he look for anything to assure his future would be one of comfort. Instead he replied, "I pray thee, let a double portion of thy spirit be upon me" (II Kings 2:9).

Talk about reaching for the stars! Of all the things Elisha could have asked for, he asked for what most people would have never even considered. But his heart was on the things of God. Elisha knew just how much the miraculous ministry of Elijah had impacted God's people. More than anything he wanted a life that would be even more impacting.

His concern was not for the things of this world. He was not worried right then about food, shelter, or clothing. His heart was on the kingdom of God.

B. God Honors the Prayers of Those Who Follow Him

Jesus told His followers in Matthew 6:33, "But seek ye first the kingdom of God, and his righteousness; and all these things shall be added unto you." He was not ignoring the needs of daily life. He was impressing upon them that it was more important to stay focused on the things of the Kingdom than to become distracted by the things of this world. And just as He did with Elisha, the Lord will honor those who do not become distracted, but keep Him first in their lives.

Elijah told Elisha that he had asked a hard thing. But it was not an impossible request. Elijah then went on to say Elisha's request would be honored if he did not get distracted, but he kept his eyes on Elijah until he was taken up to the Lord. Elijah wanted Elisha to realize following never really ends. Elisha would have to keep looking diligently to receive the blessing God wanted to give him.

IV. ELIJAH WAS TAKEN AWAY IN A FIERY CHARIOT

Elisha had no promise of just how long he would need to keep following. For all he knew, it would be years before Elijah was taken away from him. Elisha made up in his mind that regardless of how long it would be, he would be right on Elijah's heels every day.

While continuing the journey and the conversation, out of the heavens appeared a chariot of fire being pulled by horses of fire. The moment had finally arrived in a rather dramatic way.

A. Elisha Kept His Eyes on the Mantle

The chariot separated Elijah from Elisha, but Elisha kept his eyes on his mentor. The mantle Elijah cast upon Elisha on that monumental day of his calling (I Kings 19:19) never left his sight. Though many things came his way and could have distracted him, Elisha never wavered. He ignored the temptation to simply give up, and he ignored the voices of the sons of the prophets. And he did not allow the flaming chariot and horses to cause him to lose focus.

» *What are some of the distractions you have seen turn people away from God?*

B. Where Is the Lord God of Elijah?

Elisha watched as the mantle fell to the ground. Immediately he grabbed it up in his arms and held it to his chest. He did not question where Elijah had gone. He was not left to wonder what had just happened. He knew of a certainty that this was the moment for which he had been faithfully following.

He ran to the bank of the Jordan River and cried out to the heavens, "Where is the LORD God of Elijah?" (II Kings 2:14). His appeal was no longer to Elijah; it was now to God. The mantle was resting squarely on his shoulders, and he was about to prove that the same God who had been with Elijah would also be with him.

C. God's Power Follows Those Who Follow Him

Taking an action born of great faith, Elisha struck the waters of the Jordan with the mantle that was now his. He fully expected God to respond because he knew God's power will always follow them that believe. For many long days and nights, Elisha had been faithful. He had every right to believe God would part the waters.

God honors those who faithfully follow Him. In Mark 16:17–18 Jesus told the people who had gathered around Him, "And these signs shall follow them that believe; In my name shall they cast out devils; they shall speak with new tongues; they shall take up serpents; and if they drink any deadly thing, it shall not hurt them; they shall lay hands on the sick, and they shall recover." Immediately after, Jesus was received up into Heaven in much the same way Elijah had been taken.

> *In what ways does God honor those who are faithful?*

V. NO MATTER THE DISTRACTIONS, WE MUST FOCUS ON FOLLOWING THE LORD

Starting the journey to live for the Lord is often the easiest part. The hardest part is staying faithful during the long, weary days of life. Distractions that come our way can make it difficult to continue to follow. But never forget what James declared, "Blessed is the man that endureth temptation: for when he is tried, he shall receive the crown of life, which the Lord hath promised to them that love him" (James 1:12). Those who endure the temptation to be distracted will be blessed. God will reward them. For Elisha the blessing was the mantle of the prophet who went on before him. For us, if we are faithful and avoid distractions, it will be an eternal crown of life.

⟫⟫⟫ INTERNALIZING THE MESSAGE

It is easy to follow the Lord when the road is paved and the answers are all "yes." But faithful following is not proven by being there when things are going our way. Faithful following is proven by being there when everything and everyone around is telling us to stop.

Just as Elisha had to determine that nothing would stop him from following Elijah, we must determine that nothing will stop us from following the Lord. Just like Elisha, we must silence the distractions in our lives in order to keep our eyes and ears on the Lord. We cannot afford to allow the distractions to become our primary focus.

Distracted drivers cause accidents and fatalities. Distracted spiritual drivers cause spiritual accidents and even spiritual fatalities. It is time to remove things that catch our eyes and divert our attention and our actions from focusing on God. Our focus needs to be on seeking the kingdom of God and His righteousness. He will take care of everything else.

Miraculous Multiplication

FOCUS THOUGHT

God can take what we have and miraculously multiply it to bless us.

 FOCUS VERSE

II Kings 4:7

Then she came and told the man of God. And he said, Go, sell the oil, and pay thy debt, and live thou and thy children of the rest.

 LESSON TEXT

II Kings 4:1–7

1 Now there cried a certain woman of the wives of the sons of the prophets unto Elisha, saying, Thy servant my husband is dead, and thou knowest that thy servant did fear the LORD: and the creditor is come to take unto him my two sons to be bondmen.

2 And Elisha said unto her, What shall I do for thee? tell me, what hast thou in the house? And she said, Thine handmaid hath not any thing in the house, save a pot of oil.

3 Then he said, Go, borrow thee vessels abroad of all thy neighbours, even empty vessels; borrow not a few.

4 And when thou art come in, thou shalt shut the door upon thee and upon thy sons, and shalt pour out into all those vessels, and thou shalt set aside that which is full.

5 So she went from him, and shut the door upon her and upon her sons, who brought the vessels to her; and she poured out.

6 And it came to pass, when the vessels were full, that she said unto her son, Bring me yet a vessel. And he said unto her, There is not a vessel more. And the oil stayed.

7 Then she came and told the man of God. And he said, Go, sell the oil, and pay thy debt, and live thou and thy children of the rest.

⟫⟩ CULTURE CONNECTION

MIRACULOUS HARVEST

It was time for harvest, but the rain came in torrents for an entire month. Kendall and LaVonne looked out at their fields of soybeans. Two hundred acres were completely under water and would be a total loss. Other fields were partially under water, and as the water drained, lines appeared high on the plants where the water had stayed for two weeks. This could bankrupt the entire farm.

Farms for miles around were suffering the same damage. Plants were 50 percent to 100 percent mold in the pods, which meant no one would buy them. Kendall and LaVonne had prayed and begged God to stop the rain, but it seemed there was no response. Now they had to harvest beans they knew would be worthless. Why had God not stopped the storm?

They soberly harvested the beans and sent them to the grain elevator to be evaluated. The phone rang, and Kendall braced for the news. The voice on the other end said, "Where did you get these beans? They only have 3 percent to 5 percent damage. Send us all you've got."

Other than the two hundred acres that were a total loss, all their other fields brought in a bumper crop and sold for more money than most other years.

While some of the farms did go bankrupt and others struggled terribly, God multiplied Kendall and LaVonne's crop miraculously. He did not stop the storm, but He used what they had and multiplied it in spite of the storm.

⟫⟩ OUTLINE

I. THE WIDOW WAS LEFT WITH INSURMOUNTABLE DEBT
A. Creditors Were Coming
B. The Threat of Losing Her Sons
C. At Times We Will Face Difficult Challenges

II. THE WIDOW CRIED OUT TO ELISHA
A. What Do You Have in Your House?
B. God Will Always Start with What We Have in the House

III. BORROWED VESSELS
A. They Filled All the Vessels
B. The Widow Paid Her Debts
C. God Will Multiply What We Have in the House

IV. GOD CAN USE WHATEVER WE HAVE
A. What You Have Is Enough
B. Trust God to Multiply and Bless

⟫⟩ CONTEMPLATING THE TOPIC

The woman in II Kings 4:1 is identified as one of the "wives of the sons of the prophets." She came to Elisha, apparently in great distress: "Thy servant my husband is dead; and thou knowest that thy servant did fear the LORD: and the creditor is come to take unto him my two sons to be bondmen."

The prophet Elisha responded, "Tell me, what hast thou in the house?" (II Kings 4:2). In effect the prophet was telling the widow that she already possessed the resources to meet the emergency.

All crises are not equal. Every problem needs evaluating, and the answer to everything starts from where we are. When Elisha asked what she had in her house, the woman immediately answered, "Not any thing." Then she added, "Save a pot of oil" (literally, "except for an anointing of oil"). Elisha took this one small hint of a solution—one anointing of oil—and proceeded from there.

I. THE WIDOW WAS LEFT WITH INSURMOUNTABLE DEBT

Who was this widow, and who was her deceased husband? Scripture explains that the husband was a member of the "sons of the prophets." The narrative contains several references to these groups located at various places, including Bethel (II Kings 2:3); Jericho (2:5); and Gilgal (4:38). Each group was led by the same prophet, and when he died (or was taken, as with Elijah), another guild member took his place (as did Elisha). These groups had their roots as far back as the time of Samuel, who wrote about a "company of prophets" (I Samuel 10:5, 10; 19:20), and were apparently equivalent to modern-day Bible colleges where young adults aspiring to ministry are taught and mentored by more experienced ministers.

The narrative in II Kings seems to indicate some of these men had homes, spouses, and children. Although the deceased husband is not named in the biblical text, at least two historical sources identify him as the Obadiah of I Kings 18:3–16. Josephus, a Jewish historian, stated that this Obadiah was one of King Ahab's stewards who borrowed money to buy food for the prophets, which may explain why his widow went to Elisha with the problem. She approached Elisha with language that seems to imply he had some accountability for the debt: "Thy servant is dead, and you know he did fear the Lord" (Jamieson, Fausset, and Brown, *A Commentary on the Old and New Testaments*).

The Targum, an Aramaic interpretive rendering of Hebrew Scriptures, also identifies the deceased husband as the Obadiah mentioned in I Kings 18:3–16. There is scholarly debate about these identifiers, as Scripture mentions at least twelve men named Obadiah (Charles H. Spurgeon, *The Treasury of the Bible*).

A. Creditors Were Coming

While we are not certain whose wife the widow had been, we are certain that she was the wife of a prophet who had died, leaving her strapped with debt. She sold everything of value and still lacked enough to pay the creditors. When she came to Elisha with the problem, he did not offer immediate help. Instead, he wanted to determine if the widow had any available resources.

B. The Threat of Losing Her Sons

All debt is a wager that all conditions will remain constant; therefore, all debt carries a hidden risk, because situations are subject to change at any moment. The devil is a merciless creditor; he will not settle for one son if he can get two.

The love of money smothers mercy and propagates cruelty. The creditors in our story were demanding the remaining balance of the debt be paid by the involuntary servitude of the widow's sons. What a dilemma! Money borrowed during better financial times, however righteous the reason, became an impossible responsibility to meet. The parents had no idea it would come to this.

This was all legal under Jewish law, but legality is often different than morality. Men could borrow on their personal credit, and primary security for debt was first considered to be their own persons—the value of their labor and that of their dependents.

Hebrew law stipulated two things: (1) the service rendered could not be severe (Leviticus 25:43, 46) and (2) the time of service was limited until the next year of Jubilee (Leviticus 25:40). There is nothing in our narrative to indicate the distance to the year of Jubilee, but the creditor apparently had been unable to enforce the law against the boys' father before he died, and now the law was on the creditor's side.

Strong's Exhaustive Concordance of the Bible indicates the Hebrew word ărubbâh ("surety," Proverbs 17:18) means "to take in pledge, in the sense of bargain or exchange; something given as security—a bondsman." Nâshak ("usury," Deuteronomy 23:19) was also used in financial situations. It means "to strike with a sting (as a serpent); to oppress with interest on a loan; to take a bite," which is a fitting description because debt sometimes comes back to "bite" us.

» **What are some of the consequences of debt? How can this affect us spiritually?**

C. At Times We Will Face Difficult Challenges

To calm the widow's desperation, Elisha simply asked a question that prefaced a course of action: "What do you have in the house?" In other words, he was suggesting a resource evaluation.

Panic in the face of a dilemma can skew the results of resource evaluation. *Always* and *never* (as in "it will never work out" or "everything always goes wrong") are not conducive to positive solutions. Most often we want and expect instantaneous help from the Lord from resources other than our own, and we will suggest several different solutions. How much better it is to survey our resources: What do we have to work with? Perhaps we already have in our possession the elements of our own deliverance.

The man in our story may have left his wife and sons deep in debt, but he left them something far more valuable than gold: a testimony and a legacy that he feared God and was faithful. Poverty of things can be endured if one has an anointing of oil.

The narrative of the desperate widow reveals to us that the Lord helps unnamed, ordinary, everyday people. The Bible documents numerous stories of God's deliverance of ordinary people. It shows them in their homes, in their businesses, in their joy, in their grief, at their marriage feasts, and at their funerals.

We learn lessons, both positive and negative, from kings and prophets. We also learn lessons, both positive and negative, from unidentified people like the widow in today's story. To us, she may look like a nobody, but to God, she was somebody. And her only resource was a teaspoonful of oil.

There was no mineral oil or petroleum oil in Bible times, but there was olive oil. The olives were picked before they were ripe and then pressed by foot (Micah 6:15), pestle and mortar (Exodus 27:20; 29:40), or by a stone press (Joel 2:24). One tree could yield up to a half ton of oil, which was then used for commerce, light, anointing rituals and consecrations, tithing, and, of course, cooking. Oil was not to be used for a sin offering (Leviticus 5:11), nor was it to be used as a jealousy offering (Numbers 5:15).

In the Scriptures, oil was a universal spiritual type or symbol of the Holy Spirit and was inextricably ingrained in the culture of biblical times.

» *Discuss the significance of oil in a variety of biblical events (e.g., the Tabernacle, the anointing of kings and prophets, and New Testament anointings [James 5:14–15]).*

II. THE WIDOW CRIED OUT TO ELISHA

A. What Do You Have in Your House?

A pot of oil was not much. It may have been a very small pot, and it may not have been full—it was only an "anointing" of oil. Her resources were severely limited, surely not enough to settle an insurmountable debt to save her sons from slavery. But we already know what God can do with a small amount of oil: Elijah and his benefactor were sustained throughout a famine with a small cruse of oil and a handful of meal (I Kings 17), and Elisha in today's story saved the widow's sons from slavery with even less oil. In the New Testament, Jesus miraculously multiplied five common barley loaves and two fishes. In none of these and other miraculous instances did the Lord change the substance He was multiplying; He merely replicated the original common substance into miraculous amounts. (See Matthew 14:13–21; 15:32–39.)

"Sister Obadiah" was willing to give all she had. She also was willing to obey, despite the doubts she may have had about the seemingly foolish command to gather empty pots, pans, jars, and jugs from the neighbors. Not only was she quick to seek godly counsel, but also she was quick to obey godly advice.

» *Have you had an experience in your own life when limited resources lasted far beyond what would have been expected?*

B. God Will Always Start with What We Have in the House

The Lord can multiply our ordinary commonalities into extraordinary results if we willingly put our resources into His miraculous, multiplying hands. Consider the staff in the hands of Moses, the small amount of blood on the doorposts in Egypt, a small boy with five loaves and two fish, and Paul the apostle who considered himself the least of all his peers.

III. BORROWED VESSELS

A. They Filled All the Vessels

After determining the widow had something to work with, Elisha next charged her with a curious task: "Go, borrow vessels from everywhere, from all your neighbors—empty vessels; do not gather just a few" (II Kings 4:3, NKJV). Elisha did not explain

45

how the miracle was going to be performed, so the exercise was an act of faith. The widow vigorously collected her neighbors' empty vessels—from "all" her neighbors, and not "just a few" vessels. Faith's endeavors should be pursued to utmost levels.

To some, it would make more sense for the widow to borrow full vessels, but the command was to borrow *empty* vessels and not *just a few*. The Lord will not get us out of debt by obligating us to more debt.

When the widow's house was full of empty, borrowed vessels, she "shut the door upon her and upon her sons" (II Kings 4:5). What she was about to do was not for public display. (Every widow in the neighborhood would have formed a double line in front of Elisha's door if they had witnessed the miracle.) The widow did not yet know it, but the amount of oil she received would be determined by two things: how many neighbors she had visited and how many empty vessels she had compelled them to loan her. The more neighbors she visited, the more vessels she accumulated. The more vessels she accumulated, the more oil she could pour out. The more oil she could pour out, the more money she could gain to pay off the debt, thus saving her sons from the creditors.

We can imagine the scene: empty pots, pans, jars, and jugs sitting on every surface—tables, benches, chairs, counters, and in the sink. Even the water pot was emptied out and waiting. The widow looked at the empty vessels and then at her teaspoonful of oil in the cruse; she set her doubt aside, took a deep breath, and started to pour.

The first kettle was the hardest. She tipped the little cruse of oil on its side above the kettle, and the oil began to flow—and kept on flowing. Once the first vessel was full, her faith began to build. She was afraid to tip up the little cruse lest the oil stop flowing, so her sons kept changing the containers while she held the miraculous cruse of oil on its side.

"Hurry," she admonished her son, "bring another empty vessel."

He replied, "There are no more empty vessels," and before she could react, the oil stopped—not because the oil ran out, but because the empty vessels ran out. The oil was good to the last drop. No doubt the widow at some point wished she had gone to a few more houses and begged for just a few more empty vessels. God's miraculous multiplication could have filled many more.

B. The Widow Paid Her Debts

This story ends on a positive note: the widow sold the oil, paid the debt, saved her sons from bondage, and lived day to day on the rest. It is interesting that she did not consider the abundance of oil was hers to do with as she liked; instead, she went to Elisha, told him what had happened, and obeyed his advice. We should not feel possessive of God's blessings. The men and women of God in our lives can advise us of what the Scriptures teach about good stewardship of our blessings.

C. God Will Multiply What We Have in the House

The widow's story teaches us what to do in a crisis: seek godly counsel and obey godly advice; use what resources we already have, no matter how small they may seem, and keep the faith. The Lord has unlimited resources; our task is to provide a place for His miraculous multiplication to work. Our Savior's miraculous infilling has kept the creditor from our door, delivered our children from bondage, and supplied enough left over to live day to day until Jesus comes.

> » *Jesus paid a debt He did not owe because we owed a debt we could not pay. Discuss how this well-known adage pertains to today's lesson.*

IV. GOD CAN USE WHATEVER WE HAVE

A. What You Have Is Enough

God's miraculous multiplication is equal to any need. The problem might be our lack of providing a place for Him to work. What if the widow had collected only five empty vessels? Or what if she had collected twice as many? The more empty the situation, the more space the Lord has to work.

B. Trust God to Multiply and Bless

Look at Creation: all was "without form, and void" (Genesis 1:2). But when ultimate creativity met ultimate potential, ultimate change took place. The Creator came in contact with the ultimate empty place in which to create. The more empty space we give God to work His miraculous multiplication, the more creative He can be with His solutions. Yet we tend to give God ideas and supply Him with multiple solutions as to how He could cleverly (we think) solve our dilemmas. This story of a weeping widow suggests that we should apply what oil we have to faith and let the Lord handle the "how to" part. If God's power is unlimited, why would we want to limit Him to our ideas of how He should answer the dilemma?

> » *How can we limit God?*

⟫⟫ INTERNALIZING THE MESSAGE

Is the widow's dilemma just another positive Old Testament narrative, or are there some lessons we can apply to our contemporary dilemmas? Situations sometimes develop that bring overwhelming pressure to our hearts and minds. Life sometimes seems more than we can bear, and we do not know what to do. Consider discussing the predicament with a godly counselor for possible solutions. Consider what resources you might already possess and pray about it. God may use what you already have to solve your problem, no matter how insignificant your resources may seem to you. Listen to godly wisdom and obey with faith and purpose. Trust that God will supply until all the potential for blessing is filled up . . . and do not forget to return what you borrowed.

A Humbled Leper

FOCUS THOUGHT

God delivers those who humble themselves.

 FOCUS VERSES

II Kings 5:13–14

And his servants came near, and spake unto him, and said, My father, if the prophet had bid thee do some great thing, wouldest thou not have done it? how much rather then, when he saith to thee, Wash, and be clean? Then went he down, and dipped himself seven times in Jordan, according to the saying of the man of God: and his flesh came again like unto the flesh of a little child, and he was clean.

 LESSON TEXT

II Kings 5:9–14

9 So Naaman came with his horses and with his chariot, and stood at the door of the house of Elisha.

10 And Elisha sent a messenger unto him, saying, Go and wash in Jordan seven times, and thy flesh shall come again to thee, and thou shalt be clean.

11 But Naaman was wroth, and went away, and said, Behold, I thought, He will surely come out to me, and stand, and call on the name of the LORD his God, and strike his hand over the place, and recover the leper.

12 Are not Abana and Pharpar, rivers of Damascus, better than all the waters of Israel? may I not wash in them, and be clean? So he turned and went away in a rage.

13 And his servants came near, and spake unto him, and said, My father, if the prophet had bid thee do some great thing, wouldest thou not have done it? how much rather then, when he saith to thee, Wash, and be clean?

14 Then went he down, and dipped himself seven times in Jordan, according to the saying of the man of God: and his flesh came again like unto the flesh of a little child, and he was clean.

⟫⟫ CULTURE CONNECTION

A HUMBLE PRISON PRAYER

In December of 1999, while in the Mississippi State Penitentiary in Parchman, Ron repented of his sins and was filled with the Holy Ghost.

Over time he took correspondence Bible school courses to become a minister, and he studied some law to try and get his conviction overturned. He had a stellar reputation inside the prison and earned the trust of the warden and guards. He was known for his ministry and the quality work he did all over the prison campus. Ron had family, friends, pastors, and business owners write letters to the governor. He did everything in his power to gain his release. In all of that, every door closed. Ron exhausted himself trying to find a way to be released, but nothing worked.

After eighteen years Ron finally realized that even though he was doing his best to live a life of integrity and obey the Word of God, pride still had a foothold. It took time and was one of the hardest things he had ever done, but he was finally able to pray, "God, I am guilty of my crimes, and I deserve to be here. Lord, I want You to decide what is best for me. If You decide It Is best for me to stay in prison for the rest of my life, then I am OK with that."

After that humble prayer, everything began to change. Over the next two years, doors began to open, and events happened that were unheard of in Parchman. All of this led to his miraculous release, at his first parole hearing.

Genuine humility touches the heart of God, allows our hearts to connect to His, and provides the opportunity for the miraculous.

⟫⟫ OUTLINE

I. NAAMAN
- A. A Commander of the Army Who Had Leprosy
- B. Diseases of the Body and Soul Touch All Types of People

II. A SERVANT GIRL FROM ISRAEL
- A. A Prophet Who Could Heal Him
- B. We Must Testify to Others about God's Power

III. WASH IN THE JORDAN
- A. Naaman Was Offended and Went Away Angry
- B. His Servants Convinced Him to Obey the Prophet
- C. We Must Listen to Those Who Encourage Us to Do the Right Thing

IV. NAAMAN HUMBLED HIMSELF
- A. He Was Made Clean
- B. He Testified That the Lord Is God
- C. God Delivers Those Who Humble Themselves

⟫⟫ CONTEMPLATING THE TOPIC

The entire narrative of Naaman highlights the role of servants. The story begins with Naaman, a servant of the king of Syria, being saved from his horrific diagnosis by a servant girl. His anger almost talked him out of a miracle, but his servants talked him into listening to the prophet. After his healing Naaman returned to Elisha and in humility identified himself as Elisha's servant. The narrative comes to an end as one of Elisha's servants was cursed with the disease of Naaman because of his greediness. Humbling ourselves is one of the hardest things to do. Becoming a servant of God will call us to interact with a diverse faith community. Being a servant of God will also call us to be vulnerable in this community. Admitting we have areas in our lives where we need help can be hard, but that admission allows the rest of the faith community to step up and provide care.

I. NAAMAN

A. A Commander of the Army Who Had Leprosy

Naaman was a Syrian military hero, and during this period of Israel's history, the Syrians were the greatest military threat to Israel. (See I Kings 20; 22; II Kings 6–7.) Naaman was the commander of the army of the king of Syria. It was through his many battles, probably including those against Israel, that he received praise. In this narrative the fame and valor of Naaman was referred to four times to emphasize his distinction: he was the captain of the host, he was a great man before his master, he was of high renown because of the victories he had won, and he was a mighty man of valor (August H. Konkel, *NIV Application Commentary*). However, with all this praise, the author closed out with an anticlimactic "but he was a leper." Most people would think Naaman had the ideal life. However, he found himself excluded from the "ideal life" because of his leprosy. While it is easy to look at someone else and wish for that life—because it seems that person has no problems—we do not know the struggles that person faces. Eventually we all come to understand that life is not perfect.

> » *Have you ever struggled with envy? If so, how have you worked on overcoming this struggle?*

B. Diseases of the Body and Soul Touch All Types of People

Dr. Chris Thurman found that one of the lies Christians believe is "because I am a Christian, God will protect me from pain and suffering" (*The Lies We Believe*). Somewhere in our theology, the church has mistaken Christianity to mean a life free from pain, loss, hurt, and suffering. However, the church must understand that being a Christian does not mean life will be free from issues that face non-believers. If the church is not careful, unrealistic faith in God can turn into a source of bitterness and resentment when life begins to turn bad. A Christian's ultimate hope is not that everything will go fine here on Earth, but we have an eternal hope awaiting us in Heaven. Even Jesus Christ, who should have been free from all pain and hurt, was not sheltered from struggles while He walked here on Earth. The church must accept that exemption from hurt and pain does not come with the Christian walk.

The story of Naaman brings into focus hardships for both Jew and non-Jew. The disease-stricken Naaman caused hurt and pain for the Jewish servant girl when he dragged her from her homeland. And even though Naaman received his physical healing, there is no mention of the servant girl ever receiving her freedom.

II. A SERVANT GIRL FROM ISRAEL

A. A Prophet Who Could Heal Him

A young Jewish girl, having heard the horrific stories of Syria invading her own nation of Israel, was forced to become a servant of the leader of those invading armies. While Scripture does not give us many details about her, we do see that she waited upon Naaman's wife. According to this young girl's upbringing, she was enslaved by a ritually unclean or defiled man (Leviticus 13–14), and he was under the judgment of God (II Kings 15:5; Numbers 12:1–15; II Samuel 3:28–29).

While this young girl was living a life she had never dreamed of living—inside she must have hoped that one day she would be restored to her family and people—she heard about a need within the house. Immediately she thought about the great prophet in Israel, Elisha. The prophet's reputation was widespread because of all God had done through him. He had parted the waters of Jordan (II Kings 2:14), healed the bitter waters (II Kings 2:21), called down the she bears on those who mocked him (II Kings 2:24), filled the valley with water (II Kings 3:17), deceived the Moabites into believing the water was blood (II Kings 3:22), performed the miracle of the vessels of oil (II Kings 4:4), prophesied that the Shunammite woman would have a son (II Kings 4:16), resurrected that Shunammite's son (II Kings 4:34), healed the gourds (II Kings 4:40–41), and performed the miracle of bread (II Kings 4:43). All these miracles were evidence of God's power, and this servant girl believed this same miracle power could work on Naaman. So she shared with Naaman's concerned wife about the prophet in Israel who could heal Naaman.

» *Why is it important to witness to others even while we are going through hard times?*

B. We Must Testify to Others about God's Power

The young servant girl was used to living in harsh environments. Her homeland was no longer a nation under God; the king of Israel had turned to Baal worship. Thus, coming under a household that did not worship the true God, was not necessarily something new. Still she did not let that become a hinderance to her lifestyle and witness.

God has always been a loving God. Naaman eventually learned this himself. The narrative of Naaman displays God's purpose originally spoken to Abraham: "In thee shall all families of the earth be blessed" (Genesis 12:3). No matter what situation we find ourselves in, Christians are supposed to be a blessing to all who inhabit the Earth. No gender, ethnic, or social prohibition was placed on this promise. The author emphasized that all would be blessed. We cannot be part of the church if we think we can pick and choose to whom we will be a blessing. God's Word does not place limitations on whom He can touch.

The servant was willing to put her life on the line by telling her master that their gods were not the answer and the prophet in Israel was better and could bring the answer to Naaman's situation. She was not a well-known person of influence, yet she witnessed to Naaman. No matter who we are, our testimony to one individual could change the dynamics of revival around the world.

One amazing part of this narrative is that this girl witnessed to Naaman's wife. She did not witness to the one who was sick, but she knew if she testified, God would do the rest. The testimony was then shared with Naaman through his wife. The people we testify to may not be the ones who end up coming to our church. God is faithful to use the testimony we share.

III. WASH IN THE JORDAN

A. Naaman Was Offended and Went Away Angry

Naaman arrived at Elisha's house with horses and a beautiful chariot. He was wearing some of the finest clothing in the whole world. Elisha's house must have looked insignificant as Naaman pulled up with his large caravan and riches. Naaman was a proud man and was used to receiving whatever he wanted. He was not familiar with defeat on the battlefield or being denied what he wanted. Even the king granted his wishes. But pride can become a snare if we are not careful. Proverbs warns us about pride (Proverbs 6:17; 11:2; 16:18; 29:23).

Naaman was quickly humbled out of his dignified state. Instead of meeting Naaman at the door, Elisha sent his messenger—most likely Gehazi—to speak with Naaman. Perhaps Elisha was worried Naaman was wanting a magical specialist to conduct a proper ritual that would bring healing to him. The church should not be filled with rituals or individuals seeking praise because of their works. The church should give all glory to Jesus Christ as the healer. We do not need a specific person to pray for us to see God move in our lives. I John 5:14–15 tells us those who believe and pray the will of God will have their prayers answered.

Disgusted at the thought of having to be baptized in the Jordan River, Naaman grumbled to himself about the rivers of Damascus being better than all the waters of Israel. He wondered, *Does it really matter where I get wet, as long as I get wet? Does not all water lead to the cleansing purpose? And does it really have to be that seven-step process? Really?* However, Naaman quickly learned that all waters do not lead to the same conclusion.

» **Why do you think Naaman became angry at Elisha's instructions?**

B. His Servants Convinced Him to Obey the Prophet

Naaman's frustration with the prophet came to a boil. Through his furious rage, he could have decided to gather his army and march on the man of God. As a great man, he was expecting something great to happen. However, he did not receive an audience from the prophet, and he was asked to go down into waters that were inferior to his standing.

Although the men with Naaman were his servants, they still cared about him. Their words were never disrespectful. They never said, "Finally, he gets what he deserves." Instead, they showed respect for him by using reason to convince him to obey the man of God. They knew Naaman would have been willing to do anything grand, most likely because he could turn it into a grand show. But they also recognized the simplicity of the faith that was needed. All he had to do was follow the simple instructions of the prophet. Sometimes salvation can seem like a major process; however, the hardest part is humbling ourselves before the Lord.

» **Why is it important to be surrounded by people who encourage us?**

C. We Must Listen to Those Who Encourage Us to Do the Right Thing

For some people today, Elisha would not make a good pastor. His actions could be viewed as rude, unloving, and arrogant. Church shopping has become a trend— seeking out a pastor who will please me the most and will fulfill my needs. And when Naaman got upset at the prophet, Elisha did not run after him. Elisha did not plead with him; he left Naaman in the hands of God. For us to truly succeed, we need a pastor who will speak to us as God has commanded. While the words of the preacher may seem harsh, it is important to reflect upon these words to see the change we need to facilitate. Through the way Elisha treated Naaman, Naaman found a pride issue in his life.

Naaman had to humble himself and hear the wisdom of his servants. He had to hear wisdom from those who were under him. Wisdom does not dwell only upon those who are well educated or those who seem to have it all together. God can use anyone. Naaman, the man who was used to humbling people, found wisdom from servants. Here the humbled showed they had more wisdom than the exalted.

IV. NAAMAN HUMBLED HIMSELF

A. He Was Made Clean

Once Naaman understood the only price for his miracle was humility, he found himself coming out of the water clean. His healing was not a seven-month plan. His healing was instantaneous. Naaman was not only cleansed on the outside, but something happened internally. Internal change must happen before God is able to work. The biggest obstacle to God's will being accomplished is getting ourselves out of the way.

The cleansing of Naaman did not produce a partial healing. All the skin on his body was completely restored like that of a child. No spots or marks remained. He was given a brand-new start. When we are born again, we receive a new start. Yes, people can remind us of who we once were, but that is no longer who we are. People can remind us of our past, but we are now walking as new individuals.

B. He Testified That the Lord Is God

When he returned to see the prophet, Naaman's disposition had been transformed. His pride and arrogance had been overcome with humility, and an audience with Elisha was finally granted. This man who had conquered lands turned to the prophet and said, "Behold, now I know that there is no God in all the earth, but in Israel" (II Kings 5:15). No other God can compare to the one who had granted his heart's desire. Because of God's kindness to him, Naaman was ready to make Him his Lord. Naaman was humbled, and he changed his attitude toward the land of Israel. Earlier he had not wanted to bathe in the waters of Israel, now he was willing to take that part of the land back home with him. He planned to take two mule-loads of earth back home to create an altar to his new God (Exodus 20:24–25; II Kings 5:17). He recognized God as the only true God. And his testimony would be seen by anyone who would come into his household.

C. God Delivers Those Who Humble Themselves

As we referenced at the beginning of this lesson, Naaman's story highlights the role of servants and humility. While Naaman struggled with humility, Elisha remained humble. Even though Naaman pushed for the prophet to take a reward for the part he played, Elisha refused. Instead, Elisha wanted all glory to go to the one he served.

If you are seeking for a divine solution from God, start with humility. There needs to be a check of heart, spirit, soul, and mind. Is there any place in your life where pride dwells, thus prohibiting God from moving?

» *Are there areas in your life where you struggle with humility? Explain.*

⟫⟫ INTERNALIZING THE MESSAGE

While we talk about God humbling those who are not saved, the church also needs humility. We must be honest about our true motives. Naaman's narrative is filled with prideful and humbled individuals. God is able to work through people who humble themselves.

Two true servants were mentioned in this story, Elisha's servant (Gehazi) and the captured Jewish girl. Although she was experiencing hurt and pain, the unnamed Jewish girl wanted to help those she saw in need. There was no pride in sight. However, Gehazi, the man who was learning from one of the greatest prophets, allowed pride and greed to consume him.

Gold, silver, and fine clothing will not bring complete joy. Having a famous name people would revere will not bring joy. Material things may bring fleeting happiness, but true happiness can only be found in pursuing the will of God. And that takes humility.

Unexpected Ways

FOCUS THOUGHT

God works in unexpected ways to bring His purpose to pass.

 FOCUS VERSE

II Kings 7:9

Then they said one to another, We do not well: this day is a day of good tidings, and we hold our peace: if we tarry till the morning light, some mischief will come upon us: now therefore come, that we may go and tell the king's household.

 LESSON TEXT

II Kings 7:3–9

3 And there were four leprous men at the entering in of the gate: and they said one to another, Why sit we here until we die?

4 If we say, We will enter into the city, then the famine is in the city, and we shall die there: and if we sit still here, we die also. Now therefore come, and let us fall unto the host of the Syrians: if they save us alive, we shall live; and if they kill us, we shall but die.

5 And they rose up in the twilight, to go unto the camp of the Syrians: and when they were come to the uttermost part of the camp of Syria, behold, there was no man there.

6 For the Lord had made the host of the Syrians to hear a noise of chariots, and a noise of horses, even the noise of a great host: and they said one to another, Lo, the king of Israel hath hired against us the kings of the Hittites, and the kings of the Egyptians, to come upon us.

7 Wherefore they arose and fled in the twilight, and left their tents, and their horses, and their asses, even the camp as it was, and fled for their life.

8 And when these lepers came to the uttermost part of the camp, they went into one tent, and did eat and drink, and carried thence silver, and gold, and raiment, and went and hid it; and came again, and entered into another tent, and carried thence also, and went and hid it.

9 Then they said one to another, We do not well: this day is a day of good tidings, and we hold our peace: if we tarry till the morning light, some mischief will come upon us: now therefore come, that we may go and tell the king's household.

THE PARIS AUTO PART MIRACLE

While Lugo and Valeria were stationed in Germany, they were introduced to the gospel and found a Pentecostal church. Although new Christians, the Lord directed them to go to Spain and minister to three specific people. They packed their belongings and decided to stop in Paris along the way. About two blocks from the Eiffel tower, the clutch cable on their Fiat broke and fell into the road.

Picking up the pieces off the street, they prayed for help and provision. After asking for directions and struggling with the language difference, Lugo thought he understood there was an auto parts store about six blocks away. He left Valeria and their daughter with the car and asked them to pray he could find a part.

Lugo walked a few blocks and saw a man pacing in a circle on the sidewalk in front of him. This seemed strange, but he still needed more directions. When he questioned the man, he responded in perfect English that the auto parts store was about two blocks away. The man then asked what happened, and Lugo told him about the broken clutch cable. "The same thing happened to me!" the man exclaimed. "When I went to the auto parts store, they gave me the wrong part, and I have it in my car." The man reached into his car and pulled out the exact clutch cable Lugo needed. Lugo paid the man 50 francs (about $10 U.S. at the time), and the man then offered to help install the cable.

⟫⟫ OUTLINE

I. SYRIA SURROUNDED SAMARIA

  A. Severe Famine

  B. Elisha Prophesied

  C. God's Word Will Come to Pass

II. FOUR LEPERS AT THE GATE OF THE CITY

  A. Why Stay Here Until We Die?

  B. Decided to Walk to the Syrians

  C. God Drove the Syrians Away

  D. God Responds to Hunger

III. LEPERS FOUND THE SYRIAN CAMP EMPTY

  A. Fed Themselves

  B. Did Not Keep the Good News to Themselves

  C. We Must Tell Others of the Good News We Have Heard and Believed

IV. SAMARIA PLUNDERED THE SYRIAN CAMP

  A. The Word of the Lord Came True

  B. God Works in Unexpected Ways to Bring His Purpose to Pass

⟫⟫ CONTEMPLATING THE TOPIC

Growing up in the Midwestern United States, I can remember the weather being crazy. The running joke was the speed with which the weather would change. In a word, it was unpredictable. Typically this is not a word we use to describe God. However, there is much of God that remains a mystery to us. In the words of the apostle Paul, "We know in part" (I Corinthians 13:9). This missing knowledge of God can cause us to question our faith at times.

In our journey to understand who God is and grasp His nature, we can become overwhelmed by the fact He is far beyond us. To this end, His actions are not only divinely dynamic but truly unpredictable. In our lesson text we see that God is not subject to demonstrate His power in a way we think is best. He is sovereign. Therefore, He works in the way He wants, regardless of our opinions, and in some cases, regardless of our desires.

I. SYRIA SURROUNDED SAMARIA

Sin and rebellion had once again led the people of God into a place of total loss. Surrounded, and in the midst of famine, King Jehoram (son of Ahab) was desperate. The power of God is most effective when people get desperate enough to lay down their pride and submit to His plan. It is always amazing how often people will allow pride to stop the move of God in their lives. Pride will bring division into any relationship. The first few years of marriage will teach this principle well. All newlyweds will encounter a time in their marriage when they will need to humble themselves to reduce any conflict. Most fighting in any relationship is a result of either party not being willing to let go of pride and bring the discussion to a peaceful resolution. Pride has destroyed many relationships. Any relationship that allows pride to go unchecked will end in failure. If you find yourself in a dispute or argument, make sure to check your spirit and make sure your pride is not the reason for the ongoing conflict.

» *How has pride affected relationships in your life, including your relationship with God?*

A. Severe Famine

The Scripture speaks of the economic conditions in Samaria reaching rock-bottom. The people had turned to cannibalism to satisfy their hunger. Although King Jehoram was angry with the prophet, this situation had been brought about by the king's own leadership and rebellion against the Word of God. What is beautiful to consider is the tremendous miracle God performed in the great depression of Samaria. This story should remind its readers that God's omnipotence is not limited to spiritual troubles but includes economic and financial matters as well.

B. Elisha Prophesied

In this setting, the king of Israel turned to the prophet Elisha for direction. Some believed the word of the Lord that came from the prophet; others did not. It is a picture of the gospel message that was to come. Those who believe the gospel will be partakers, but those who refuse to believe may see but not be able to partake. Here we also have the same imagery as Moses and his final days. Because of Moses' unbelief, he was not allowed to enter the Promised Land. (See Numbers 20:12.) A mistrust in God will always cause a person to miss out on the glorious things He has planned.

C. God's Word Will Come to Pass

"God can't" are not words we like to use. Nonetheless, there are some things God cannot do. The Scripture tells us God cannot lie. He is bound to His Word. The story of the lepers illustrates once again that the word of the Lord will always come to pass. The prophet wrote, "So shall my word be that goeth forth out of my mouth: it shall not return unto me void, but it shall accomplish that which I please, and it shall prosper in the thing whereto I sent it" (Isaiah 55:11). We can rest assured that God's word will always come to pass.

» *How should we respond when God has not answered a specific prayer?*

II. FOUR LEPERS AT THE GATE OF THE CITY

Banished to the outskirts of the city, the four lepers are the ones God chose to bring salvation to the Samaritans. These unlikely and unqualified outsiders changed the course of a nation and gave another chance to a king to get it right. It seems as if it is often the people no one would expect whom God chooses to use in His plan. From Abraham to Jacob, from Gideon to David, God has consistently empowered those who did not match the standard of what some would call great. This is even seen in the twelve men Jesus chose to be in His inner circle. Jesus called the disciples to have significant insight and receive unrestricted access to His ministry, yet the religious leaders were astounded. "Now when they saw the boldness of Peter and John, and perceived that they were unlearned and ignorant men, they marvelled; and they took knowledge of them, that they had been with Jesus" (Acts 4:13). It was not merely the disciples' education level the leaders were referring to, but rather the fact these were common people—fishermen and tax collectors—and yet they were well-versed in the Hebrew text and the plan of the Messiah.

A. Why Stay Here Until We Die?

The driving force of these lepers was summed up in the question they considered: "Why stay here until we die?" In other words, how can this get any worse? Their situation had gotten to the point where they no longer feared the consequence of death. The fear of death would no longer hold them back. Often people allow fear to hold them hostage. Whether it is something simple like a job or career move, fear tends to keep people in the state they are in rather than trying to reach for something greater.

Fear is something all humans share. In many ways, fear is a major factor in every life-choice a person makes. Fear can be a good thing. A healthy fear will let us know when something is wrong. It will ensure that our children and loved ones are cared for and safe. However, fear can also become unhealthy and irrational. The spirit of fear can gain strength when unchecked in our lives. (See II Timothy 1:7.) As believers, we must make up our minds that fear will not hinder the progress of the gospel, nor will it keep us from everything God has in store for our lives.

» *Have you ever had a deep, unsettling fear that seemed to paralyze you? Explain.*

B. Decided to Walk to the Syrians

Each day we will make hundreds, if not thousands, of decisions. The recipe for success is making good decisions. One study showed that the cascade of choices a person evaluates each day actually leads to what psychologists refer to as "decision fatigue." One thing rings true and is important to understand: not all decisions are created equal. For instance, choosing your spouse and choosing your toothpaste are obviously not equivalent propositions. The four lepers were faced with a decision that would determine the fate of their lives and the destiny of a nation. Understanding the gravity of our decisions is paramount in our walk with God. There may be some choices we will make today that will set us on a path of growth or lead us down a path of destruction.

C. God Drove the Syrians Away

God will always fight for His people. This story shows that God is more than just "in our corner." In fact, there are moments in life when we are too weak, too overwhelmed, and exceedingly overmatched. But it is in those situations when God steps in and fights the battle for us. Over and over stories in Scripture describe the way God defends His people.

Standing on the edge of the land promised to their fathers, the children of Israel saw an enemy of great power occupying their destiny. In the midst of their fear, two people reported the victory was within reach. The word of the Lord came to the people affirming the faith of Joshua and Caleb. This word was a consistent message to the people of Israel. The Lord said, "The LORD your God he shall fight for you" (Deuteronomy 3:22). This message of assurance was repeated multiple times throughout the journey of Israel to the Promised Land (Deuteronomy 1:30; 2:24–25, 31, 33, 36; 3:2–3; 20:4). We should never forget the battle always belongs to God.

D. God Responds to Hunger

The hungry always seem to get God's attention. Jesus, standing in the midst of more than five thousand people, said, "Blessed are they which do hunger and thirst after righteousness: for they shall be filled" (Matthew 5:6). Both spiritually and physically, it would seem God cannot resist those who hunger and thirst. This fact is deeply rooted in His character. We see His compassion for humanity scattered throughout the Bible. God Himself told Moses that His compassion is given by Himself alone. God said, "I will . . . be gracious to whom I will be gracious, and will shew mercy on whom I will shew mercy" (Exodus 33:19). This grace and compassion have been realized by the redemptive work of Calvary. The whole Bible, it would seem, is the story of how God has demonstrated His love and compassion for humanity. The redemption of humanity is the strongest evidence we have that God has shown mercy, grace, and compassion to all people.

In this story, we see a small example of what happens when people are in need. God responds to the hungry. Of course, hunger is not the only requirement to get a response from God. God is faithful to His people. David said, "I have been young, and now am old; yet have I not seen the righteous forsaken, nor his seed begging bread" (Psalms 37:25). God's people can trust Him to care for physical needs and to know that He responds to our faith for greater needs as well.

III. LEPERS FOUND THE SYRIAN CAMP EMPTY

A. Fed Themselves

When traveling in an airplane, the flight attendant will announce, "In the case of an emergency, be sure to secure your oxygen mask before assisting other passengers." Basically they are saying to help yourself first because you are no good to anyone if you are not taking care of yourself. Often those who neglect their own well-being and health (both spiritually and physically) will end up losing out on the things they have worked so hard to accomplish.

This principle is evident in the greatest commandment we find in Scripture. Jesus was asked what He considered to be the greatest commandment in the Law. His response is recorded in all three of the synoptic gospels of the New Testament. He said, "Love the Lord your God with all your heart, soul, mind, and strength." Then He gave the second greatest commandment: "Love your neighbor as yourself." It is imperative to note that we must be focused on our own salvation before focusing on the salvation of the world. These four lepers fed themselves first before turning to share their blessings with friends and family in Samaria.

B. Did Not Keep the Good News to Themselves

Think about how many problems would go away in our lives if people would just consider others more. The lepers in our story experienced the benefit of not hoarding the blessings and good news. They elected to share the news with the rest of the army. The very essence of the gospel is tied to considering others. When we consider others, we not only obey the gospel but grow even more in the image of God.

C. We Must Tell Others of the Good News We Have Heard and Believed

If the lepers had kept silent, the people would have stayed in their misery. The Samaritans were starving and the lepers had the solution. This lesson is twofold. First, the people of God have what the world needs. Hungry people are roaming the earth looking for anything to satisfy their appetite and quench their thirst. They have tried everything the world has to offer and are still empty. Like the prodigal son, they keep waking up in the pig pen wondering what went wrong. The gospel of Jesus Christ is the meat that will satisfy their hunger. The second lesson is the blessing the believer receives from sharing the good news. The lives of the people were saved, and the lepers were able to share in the victory and provision of God alongside the rest of the nation. It would seem the lepers' lives were also changed during this miracle. Without a doubt, the blessings of God will always be on those who take the Great Commission seriously.

» *Have you ever been blessed by sharing the gospel with someone? Explain.*

IV. SAMARIA PLUNDERED THE SYRIAN CAMP

Only a few changed the lives of many. The Samaritan army was able to benefit from the bravery and decision of just a few lepers. It is amazing the influence a few can have on the masses. With God, these numbers and influence is even greater. Deuteronomy 32:30 says, "How should one chase a thousand, and two put ten thousand to flight, except their Rock had sold them, and the LORD had shut them up?" With God, nothing is impossible. When God is fighting for us, one person can defeat an army.

A. The Word of the Lord Came True

Words have power. "Death and life are in the power of the tongue: and they that love it shall eat the fruit thereof" (Proverbs 18:21). We get this human attribute from our heavenly Father. The words God speaks are the most powerful force on earth. Everything He is says is true, and any predictions He makes are going to be fulfilled. Our faith is in the fact God does not make mistakes, and our trust is in the fact God is not like flawed humans. When God says something will happen, it will happen.

B. God Works in Unexpected Ways to Bring His Purpose to Pass

The prophet Isaiah wrote, "For my thoughts are not your thoughts, neither are your ways my ways, saith the LORD. For as the heavens are higher than the earth, so are my ways higher than your ways, and my thoughts than your thoughts" (Isaiah 55:8–9). It should be no surprise that God works in unexpected ways. God knows everything. We must trust that He also knows what is best for us. Often we think we know how God should act or respond. Trusting God is the ultimate test of our faith. Trust is the feet to our faith. We can say we have faith, but it is tested when we are forced to trust in God's plan.

> » *Has God ever surprised you? In what ways did God work in an unexpected way in your life?*

⟩⟩⟩ INTERNALIZING THE MESSAGE

In December each year we gather together to celebrate the birth of Jesus Christ. This one event has captured the attention of every believer, and it still stands as a sign to those who have yet to believe. It is often curious to consider the thoughts of those who were there to witness the birth of Christ. What did they think? Did they have a clue about what it meant to be the Messiah? Even with a little knowledge it seems clear that no one can know for sure what plans God has for His people. The apostle Paul said, "Now we see through a glass, darkly" (I Corinthians 13:12), meaning there are many things about which we simply do not have a clear picture. The imagery here is looking at a foggy window and trying to determine what is being reflected. In our lives, we must find the room to trust God with every decision. Like the lepers, we cannot know for certain where or when God will choose to bless, deliver, heal, or save. Our job is not to figure out the method but rather trust that God knows and will be faithful.

The Priority of God's House

FOCUS THOUGHT

We must make the house of God a priority in our lives.

 FOCUS VERSES

II Chronicles 24:10–11

And all the princes and all the people rejoiced, and brought in, and cast into the chest, until they had made an end. Now it came to pass, that at what time the chest was brought unto the king's office by the hand of the Levites, and when they saw that there was much money, the king's scribe and the high priest's officer came and emptied the chest, and took it, and carried it to his place again. Thus they did day by day, and gathered money in abundance.

 LESSON TEXT

II Chronicles 24:1–11

1 Joash was seven years old when he began to reign, and he reigned forty years in Jerusalem. His mother's name also was Zibiah of Beer-sheba.

2 And Joash did that which was right in the sight of the Lord all the days of Jehoiada the priest.

3 And Jehoiada took for him two wives; and he begat sons and daughters.

4 And it came to pass after this, that Joash was minded to repair the house of the Lord.

5 And he gathered together the priests and the Levites, and said to them, Go out unto the cities of Judah, and gather of all Israel money to repair the house of your God from year to year, and see that ye hasten the matter. Howbeit the Levites hastened it not.

6 And the king called for Jehoiada the chief, and said unto him, Why hast thou not required of the Levites to bring in out of Judah and out of Jerusalem the collection, according to the commandment of Moses the servant of the Lord, and of the congregation of Israel, for the tabernacle of witness?

7 For the sons of Athaliah, that wicked woman, had broken up the house of God; and also all the dedicated things of the house of the Lord did they bestow upon Baalim.

8 And at the king's commandment they made a chest, and set it without at the gate of the house of the Lord.

9 And they made a proclamation through Judah and Jerusalem, to bring in to the Lord the collection that Moses the servant of God laid upon Israel in the wilderness.

10 And all the princes and all the people rejoiced, and brought in, and cast into the chest, until they had made an end.

11 Now it came to pass, that at what time the chest was brought unto the king's office by the hand of the Levites, and when they saw that there was much money, the king's scribe and the high priest's officer came and emptied the chest, and took it, and carried it to his place again. Thus they did day by day, and gathered money in abundance.

TO GOD BE THE GLORY

On his twentieth birthday, Tom Marshall was drafted into the U. S. army. He trained for eight weeks and was sent to England to train for eight more months. He saw his first combat during the invasion of Northern France, better known as D-Day. He and his battalion landed on the beaches and worked their way through France. Later, following General Patton, they crossed through Belgium, Holland, and Germany. At the end of World War II, Tom watched as displaced families struggled to find food and shelter. He recalled Paul's words describing the Macedonian call: "Come over . . . and help us." From that moment on, Tom was never the same.

Tom returned home, met and married Leila, who had lost her first husband in the war. They started a family, and after a few years the weight of God's call was heavy upon him. He and Leila, in response to a call for help, left a good job and sold all they had to go pastor.

After his experiences in the war, Tom understood the importance of having a place to gather and worship—a place of safety and unity. People needed a church. Tom and Leila pastored "over forty years in five states: Texas, Arkansas, Louisiana, Mississippi and South Carolina. He built five churches, two parsonages, one large educational building and completed one church building that another minister started" (*To God Be the Glory*, Tom and Leila Marshall, 2002). They discovered people were willing to work and sacrifice alongside them to have a place that was dedicated to God and ministry.

⟫⟫ OUTLINE

I. JOASH BECAME KING AT SEVEN YEARS OF AGE

   A. He Did What Was Right in God's Eyes

   B. We Must Choose to Do What Is Right No Matter Our Heritage

II. JOASH SOUGHT TO RESTORE THE TEMPLE OF THE LORD

   A. Tasked the Priests and Levites to Collect Money

   B. The Levites Slacked in Their Work

III. THE HOUSE OF GOD AND SEXUAL PURITY

   A. Jehoram and the Moral Decay of Judah

   B. Our Worship Shows Our Priorities

   C. The Ransom Collected by Moses and Joash

   D. Our Ransom Has Been Paid by Christ

⟫⟫ CONTEMPLATING THE TOPIC

Near the beginning of the Ming Dynasty, Emperor Zhu Di of China was revered as a living god. Though he only lived from AD 1360 to 1424, he was responsible for consolidating rule over China, pushing out Mongol invaders, extending the Great Wall, and commissioning the largest naval armada in world history until World War II. However, his greatest achievement was arguably the building of the Forbidden City in Beijing.

When the Forbidden City was commissioned in A.D. 1407, it took over one million convicted criminals and conscripted slave laborers ten years to gather the proper materials for the project. It took another one hundred thousand skilled craftsmen to finish the fine details of the city. No expense was spared for the residence of the palace and the Forbidden City, and the rule of the Emperor was absolute.

Unlike the Forbidden City and its palace, the restoration of the Temple of God in Jerusalem was not a project built by forced labor or authoritarian rule. The Temple was restored by the free and cheerful giving of the faithful. The collection taken to restore the Temple was a "ransom" that had been originally required by Moses. Anyone who chose to not partake in the "ransom" of Judah would not be counted among them in the census; therefore, it was a choice to serve the Lord and contribute to the restoration of His house.

A life of faithfulness cannot be achieved without a lifestyle of sacrifice. During the reign of Joash, the kingdom of Judah would have been aware of growing foreign threats; yet they decided to put their faith in the Lord and His ability to save. Though under the direction of the king, the Temple was restored because of the collective desire of the people to honor the Lord.

The people of Judah were not giving to a fruitless cause, but they were paying a ransom required by the Law of Moses. They were giving for the restoration of the Temple of God. The Temple had been left in disorder and decay by the three rulers prior to Joash. However, Joash's mentor was Jehoiada the priest, a man of God. It was the people's willingness to be obedient to the tax of Moses and the righteousness pursued by Joash and Jehoiada that led to the restoration of the Temple, the house of God.

Since the New Testament was established, the house of God is no longer a building of brick and stone, but we as believers are His temple. When Paul admonished the church in Corinth that their bodies were the temple of the Holy Spirit, it was not just a simple metaphor. Paul's warning came in the context of sexual purity. To be sexually pure is to honor the house of God. This principle was true even during the time of Joash.

>>> SEARCHING THE SCRIPTURES

I. JOASH BECAME KING AT SEVEN YEARS OF AGE

Joash was the youngest king of Judah to ascend to the throne. In many ways, having a child on the throne was the reset the monarchy of Judah needed. Before the reign of Joash, the succession of kings from the line of Judah had been David, Solomon, Rehoboam, Abijah, Asa, Jehoshaphat, Jehoram, Ahaziah, then Athaliah, the mother of Ahaziah. Among these, Rehoboam, Jehoram, Ahaziah, and Athaliah had been unrighteous rulers because of their idol worship and self-reliance. Rulers such as Abijah (meaning "my father is Yahweh"), Asa, and Jehoshaphat were righteous.

Though Jehoshaphat was counted to be righteous, his decisions to ally with Ahab—who was wicked—set up a series of tragic circumstances that ultimately led to a seven-year-old king (I Chronicles 17:3). Jehoshaphat allied himself to the house of Ahab through marriage (I Kings 22:43–44; II Chronicles 18:1). Though Jehoshaphat trusted in God as his father and grandfather had done, his son Jehoram was raised under influences of the house of Ahab and the kingdom of Israel. Little information is given to us in Scripture about Jehoram's mother, but his wife, Athaliah, was the daughter of Ahab and Jezebel.

A. He Did What Was Right in God's Eyes

Joash did what was right in God's eyes. When Joash was made king over Israel, he knew nothing of governance; he was only a child. However, his mentor was

Jehoiada the priest. Joash was adopted by Jehoiada and Jehoshabeath. Jehoiada was instrumental to restoring the monarchy of Judah to a path of righteousness. He taught Joash to prioritize the Law of Moses. Joash's mother was also not from the house of Ahab of Israel; she was from Beersheba of Judah.

When Joash was a child, he was surrounded by godly influences who directed him to seek after and prioritize the Lord. Joash was brought up in an environment of righteousness. While Jehoiada was alive, Joash was a righteous king. It is important to surround ourselves with mentors who will encourage us to pursue righteousness. We can follow their example. No matter our age or background, we are always able to draw near to God in repentance to pursue righteousness.

» *How does repentance help us draw near to God?*

B. We Must Choose to Do What Is Right No Matter Our Heritage

Athaliah went on to raise her son, Ahaziah, to value the unrighteousness of the northern kingdom of Israel over the righteous principles of his great-grandfather (five-times), David. When Ahaziah was killed by Jehu the son of Nimshi, Athaliah ruled over Israel as Judah's first and only matriarch queen. During her reign she killed all the royal heirs of Judah (II Chronicles 22:10), with the exception of Joash. The royal coup that had begun with the marriage ended in murder and sin. Joash, a baby, was saved by Jehoshabeath, daughter of King Jehoram and wife of Jehoiada the priest. She hid Joash and his nurse in a bedchamber. He was hidden in the Temple until he reached seven years of age.

Jehoiada was a strong influence on Joash, but he was not controlling the monarchy as a priest. In II Chronicles 24:4–6, after Joash ordered the Levites to go about repairing the house of God, the Levites did not listen. Jehoiada was the chief priest and Joash held him responsible for the inaction of the Levites. In II Chronicles 24:7, Joash referenced how Athaliah had repurposed the Temple for the idols associated with the pantheon of Baal. It is difficult to imagine the chief priest being content with the Temple in a state of disarray when he had the ability to make a change with the support of the monarchy. Joash made sure the Temple was repaired by reinstituting the collection Moses required of Israel for the building of the original tabernacle during the time of the Exodus.

» *How could the drama and tragedy have been avoided in the royal household of Judah?*

II. JOASH SOUGHT TO RESTORE THE TEMPLE OF THE LORD

II Chronicles 24:4 says Joash was "minded" to repair the house of the Lord. The NKJV reads, "Joash set his heart on repairing the house of the LORD." The focus of this verse shows that prioritizing God is an issue of the heart. It would have been easy for Joash to maintain the status quo the previous three rulers before him had set. However, Joash did not let his heart go away from serving God while Jehoiada was alive.

A. Tasked the Priests and Levites to Collect Money

II Chronicles 24:5 says, "And he gathered together the priests and the Levites, and said to them, Go out unto the cities of Judah, and gather of all Israel money to repair the house of your God from year to year, and see that ye hasten the matter. Howbeit the Levites hastened it not." When the house of God was in disrepair, Joash made its repair a priority.

B. The Levites Slacked in Their Work

When the priests and Levites did not follow the command of Joash, it could have been an excuse to give up. If the priests—the ones responsible for ministering in the house of God—are not even willing to take up a collection for its repair, is there any use in repairing it at all? To Joash, the answer was yes. He had set his heart to make the house of God a priority. Joash held Jehoiada responsible for not taking up the collection (II Chronicles 24:6). Joash cited Moses' collection from Israel to create the tabernacle as a precedent for the priests to follow.

III. THE HOUSE OF GOD AND SEXUAL PURITY

To understand that the house of God is a priority is to understand the need for sexual purity. The Temple was in a state of decay long before Joash began to rule on the throne. If it had not been for the poor decisions of Jehoshaphat when he allied with the house of Ahab in marriage, the priority of the house of God would have likely remained high. However, when the daughter of Ahab and Jezebel married into the line of the kings of Judah, the gods of Israel replaced the God of Abraham, Isaac, and Jacob in priority.

A. Jehoram and the Moral Decay of Judah

The theme of unrighteous and moral decay is pervasive throughout Scripture. The righteous men who were descendants of Seth were corrupted by women who were descendants of Cain (Genesis 4:26; 6:2). Samson—whose name means "day"—was deceived by Delilah—whose name means "night"—and his last moments were spent humiliated with his eyes gouged out. Solomon, who built the Temple and was given wisdom above any other man, also fell into the trap of marrying unrighteous women (I Kings 11:1–8).

Paul made a direct reference to the pervasive theme of unequally yoked marriages in his second letter to the Corinthians:

> Be ye not unequally yoked together with unbelievers: for what fellowship hath righteousness with unrighteousness? And what communion hath light with darkness? (II Corinthians 6:14)

Jehoram, the son of Jehoshaphat, king of Judah, married Athaliah, the daughter of Ahab and Jezebel, the monarchs of Israel. Through this marriage Judah's once righteous royal family was corrupted and destroyed. When Judah began to follow after idol worship that was closely tied to adultery, the house of God went into disrepair. These events are absolutely tied together. If the kings of Judah had made God their priority, then the Temple never would have needed to be restored. Instead, because of the influences from the house of Ahab, the rulers of Judah (Jehoram, Ahaziah, and Athaliah) turned after idols and the people followed after sexual sin.

> *How is being equally yoked connected to prioritizing the house of the Lord?*

B. Our Worship Shows Our Priorities

Prostitution and adultery were a part of worship in the idolatry of ancient Israel and pagan temple cults. The narrative of II Chronicles 13–23 describes a dark descent in the monarchy of Judah from a kingdom of righteousness to a kingdom of prostitution and idol worship. The gods of the Canaanites were "worshiped" through adultery. When the prostitution of idolatry began to rise in priority in Judah, the priority of the house of God decreased. Joash was the righteous king Judah needed to both restore true worship within the kingdom and to restore the house of God.

In the Song of Moses in Deuteronomy 32:16–17, Moses addressed the root of idolatry by identifying the power behind it. He wrote, "They provoked Him to jealousy with strange gods, with abominations provoked they Him to anger. They sacrificed unto devils, not to God; to gods whom they knew not, to new gods that came newly up, whom your fathers feared not."

In ancient times, idols and false gods always carried sexual overtones. Sometimes we can be very harsh when we speak of ancient people because it is foolish to bow down to a block of chiseled stone or a statue of precious metal. On the surface, idol worship does not seem very tempting, so it is easy to criticize. However, idol worship gave ancient people an excuse to justify sinful sexual acts. Sinful sexual temptations are still present in today's world, but they manifest themselves differently. Instead of using an image or precious metal to justify sin, people choose to boldly deny God without shame. Just as devils were behind the worship of idols, there are spiritual forces behind our culture's obsession with sexual sin.

> *How is adultery and sexual sin connected to idol worship?*

C. The Ransom Collected by Moses and Joash

The reference Joash made in II Chronicles 24:6, 9 to the collection Moses placed on the people for the building of the Tabernacle is found in Exodus 30:11–16. In Exodus, the money that was used for the Tabernacle was not simply a "collection" or a "tax," but it was called a "ransom." Moses began by taking a census of the people. Then all the males twenty years of age and older, despite economic status, were commanded to "ransom" themselves to God for the price of a half shekel. By calling this collection of funds a "ransom," Moses was telling Israel that without fulfilling the contribution of half a shekel, they would not be represented as being among the people of Israel. The ransom Moses instituted was to be given every time a census was taken in Israel.

D. Our Ransom Has Been Paid by Christ

Paul mirrored the theme of "Ransom" when he spoke against fornication and idols in I Corinthians 6. Verse 20 clearly connects the idea of being "ransomed" to Christ's work on the cross. By taking the punishment for our sins, Jesus Christ has paid the ransom of death that sin held against us. Paul's answer to sexual immorality associated with idol worship is rooted in the concept of ransom. Jesus said, "For even the Son of Man came not to be ministered unto, but to minister, and to give his life a ransom for many" (Mark 10:45). If Jesus Christ has paid the ransom for the sins of every believer and the temple is no longer a building of stone, or a tent, but the human body, then all worship from the body belongs to God. If we identify with Christ, then we are more than His people; we are also His temple. Paul's teaching is not directed to the individual, but to the corporate church. Sexual impurity by one member of the body has far-reaching impact throughout the corporate worship of the entire church.

» *How do we apply to our lives the ransom paid by Christ?*

〉〉〉 INTERNALIZING THE MESSAGE

Just as sexual temptation was a part of the culture surrounding Judah, it surrounds our culture today. Joash made an intentional and conscious decision to repair the house of the Lord. Likewise, we need to be intentional about living in purity. To live in purity is to show God His sacrifice is a priority to us and that we will not allow His house to fall into disrepair.

Purity in relationships includes setting boundaries before marriage and staying committed to only your spouse in marriage. If you are unmarried and looking to become married, then you should also be sure to find someone with whom you can be equally yoked. Because we are the temple of the Lord, we should abstain from sexual sin because it disgraces Jesus Christ's sacrifice.

It is also important to remember that Paul wrote to the Corinthian church, "And such were some of you: but ye are washed, but ye are sanctified, but ye are justified in the name of the Lord Jesus, and by the Spirit of our God" (I Corinthians 6:11). Our past is in the past when we repent of our sins, are baptized in the name of Jesus, and receive His Holy Spirit. Jesus Christ paid our ransom on the Cross and that good news is still true. Our past mistakes do not define the relationship Jesus wants to have with us now; He has made us free to be sanctified temples and living sacrifices.

The Puzzle of King Uzziah

FOCUS THOUGHT

God calls us to live a faithful life that ends as it began.

 FOCUS VERSE

II Chronicles 26:5

And he sought God in the days of Zechariah, who had understanding in the visions of God: and as long as he sought the LORD, God made him to prosper.

 LESSON TEXT

II Kings 15:1–7

1 In the twenty and seventh year of Jeroboam king of Israel began Azariah son of Amaziah king of Judah to reign.

2 Sixteen years old was he when he began to reign, and he reigned two and fifty years in Jerusalem. And his mother's name was Jecholiah of Jerusalem.

3 And he did that which was right in the sight of the LORD, according to all that his father Amaziah had done;

4 Save that the high places were not removed: the people sacrificed and burnt incense still on the high places.

5 And the LORD smote the king, so that he was a leper unto the day of his death, and dwelt in a several house. And Jotham the king's son was over the house, judging the people of the land.

6 And the rest of the acts of Azariah, and all that he did, are they not written in the book of the chronicles of the kings of Judah?

7 So Azariah slept with his fathers; and they buried him with his fathers in the city of David: and Jotham his son reigned in his stead.

II Chronicles 26:3–5

3 Sixteen years old was Uzziah when he began to reign, and he reigned fifty and two years in Jerusalem. His mother's name also was Jecoliah of Jerusalem.

4 And he did that which was right in the sight of the LORD, according to all that his father Amaziah did.

5 And he sought God in the days of Zechariah, who had understanding in the visions of God: and as long as he sought the LORD, God made him to prosper.

⟩⟩⟩ CULTURE CONNECTION

REFILLED WHILE IN A COMA

Dr. Joey Peyton received a call to visit an elderly couple in the hospital. According to the doctors, something rather strange was happening while the man lay in a coma. With his wife in visible distress, the hospital thought Dr. Peyton, being a Pentecostal chaplain, might be the best to handle the situation.

Upon entering the room, Dr. Peyton instantly realized the man, though in a coma, was speaking in tongues. He told the wife that her husband was fine, he was just praying. "He doesn't pray and hasn't even attended church in years!" she responded. She became quite angry and said she was no longer interested in any more discussion.

The next day when Dr. Peyton arrived in the room, the man was sitting up in a chair. When asked if he remembered anything from the previous day, he talked of a dream he remembered having. In his dream, he was back at an old brush arbor with his parents and had been refilled with the Holy Ghost.

This man had left his Pentecostal faith when he and his wife decided to get married. He had been raised Pentecostal and she was Catholic. They both walked away from their faiths and decided to attend a different church. She was faithful with the kids, but he could not bring himself to attend.

While on his deathbed and in a coma, he had returned to God and had been refilled with the Holy Ghost. He spent the last few days of his life testifying of what God had done and declaring there was only one way to God.

⟩⟩⟩ OUTLINE

I. THE RISE AND FALL OF AZARIAH

   A. Early Success

   B. Final Demise

   C. Almost Succeeding Is the Worst Tragedy

II. PUZZLING PERSPECTIVES

   A. The Reign of Azariah/Uzziah in II Kings

   B. The Reign of Azariah/Uzziah in II Chronicles

   C. Self-Reflection Is Vitally Important

III. FALLEN HEROES—A CALL TO REFLECTION

   A. Humans Not Heroes

   B. Re-Envisioned History

   C. We Must Begin and End Well

⟩⟩⟩ CONTEMPLATING THE TOPIC

One sobering reality of our social-media saturated world is that one moment of weakness or one indiscretion can literally ruin a person's life forever. In its own brutal way, our society is learning that being a good person "most of the time" really does not count for all that much in the end. It is absolutely vital, in this social era where we are daily rocked by scandals from the most unimaginable places, that we as the people of God learn again the importance of faithfulness.

That is the real topic of today's lesson. How do we ensure that our lives are truly consistent and faithful to God? By looking at the telling and the retelling of the life of King Uzziah in the books of II Kings and II Chronicles, we will explore the scriptural call to faithfulness and the path to developing it.

I. THE RISE AND FALL OF AZARIAH

A. Early Success

Just before the fall of the northern kingdom of Israel to Assyria, the divided nation enjoyed an extended period of surprising prosperity with Jeroboam II reigning in the north and Uzziah/Azariah (essentially variant spellings of the same name) reigning in the south. During this period, Assyria was occupied with internal issues. The more proximate Syrian power, centered in Damascus, had been broken to the point that it never fully recovered. This relative peace and quiet, it seems, reignited both Judah's and Israel's expansionist tendencies. For example, of Jeroboam II's reign, II Kings 14:25 (see also v. 28) declared: "He restored the coast of Israel from the entering of Hamath unto the sea of the plain."

The Chronicler, who presents an expanded account of Uzziah's reign, points out that he largely followed Jeroboam II's example: "And God helped him against the Philistines, and against the Arabians that dwelt in Gurbaal, and the Mehunims. And the Ammonites gave gifts to Uzziah: and his name spread abroad even to the entering in of Egypt" (II Chronicles 26:7–8). With these newly expanded borders, the divided kingdoms' extent nearly matched the extent of the united kingdom under Solomon, which is the acknowledged apex of biblical history, Israel's own "Golden Age." The Chronicler added another clue to the greatness of the era by noting that Uzziah's fame had spread southward to the border of Egypt. This is language similar to that used to describe King David's successes in I Chronicles 14:16–17. For all intents and purposes, it appeared that the "glory days" had returned despite the division of the kingdom.

The Chronicler's expanded recounting divides the description of Uzziah's successes into two sections, dealing with foreign and domestic affairs respectively. Uzziah's foreign expansions represented success in that they served to subjugate long-standing enemies of Judah (e.g., Philistia, Ammon, Arabia). Uzziah's domestic successes include rebuilding and fortifying the city of Jerusalem; abundance of flocks, herds, and crops; and equipping a mighty standing army.

The note in the text about the creation of "engines" (II Chronicles 2:15) that stood upon the towers has intrigued generations of scholars. Many have suggested these may have been a type of catapult; however, catapults appear to have been a later invention and, furthermore, there is no known type of catapult designed for use with both stones and arrows. J. Barton Payne suggests they are better understood as defensive mechanism, a kind of shield "used to cover defending troops as they repelled enemies seeking to scale the walls" (*Expositor's Bible Commentary*).

These two sections are united by the use of the catchword *strong* (Hebrew *hazaq*) in verses 8 and 15. Furthermore, the term appears in close proximity to the word *help* (Hebrew *azar*), referring explicitly here to divine aid and support. Thus, the story of

Uzziah's stunning success, as told by the Chronicler, is a story of divine blessing rather than simply personal achievement.

» *Why is it important for us to recognize our blessings as being from God instead of the result of our intellect and ability alone?*

B. Final Demise

In the Chronicler's record, II Chronicles 26:16 essentially reverses the entire story of Uzziah: "But when he was strong, his heart was lifted up to his destruction." This is the third appearance of the catchword, but this time Uzziah's strength is not the strength of divine favor and blessing; it is the strength of human hubris and pride! Uzziah had perverted the very blessings of God. Instead of acknowledging God as his help—as the One who made Uzziah's success possible—he claimed these blessings as markers of his own personal prowess and ability.

What makes Uzziah's usurpation of divine blessing as personal accomplishment even more brazen is that the Book of Psalms, with its undeniable linkage to the great King David, frequently uses "Help" as a divine title, similar to "Rock" or "Shield" or "Refuge." In fact, the celebratory psalm that inspired Martin Luther's hymn, "A Mighty Fortress Is Our God," is built around this metaphor of God as our help. (See Psalm 46:1–3, 5, 10–11.)

Because of Uzziah's pride, he assumed responsibilities forbidden to the king since the establishment of the Israelite monarchy and was struck down as a leper in the Temple of God. Because of his leprosy, he was driven not only out of the Temple precincts but also out of Judean society altogether. He lived the rest of his days in an isolated house ("several house"—KJV). Steven McKenzie points out that this phrase, literally translated "house of separation," has been found in Ugaritic texts, where it is used as a description of the underworld, the abode of the dead (*I–II Chronicles*). In other words, because of his pride, Uzziah became a "walking dead man"!

» *Why do you think it is easy for people to abuse or misuse God's blessings?*

C. Almost Succeeding Is the Worst Tragedy

Uzziah's auspicious beginnings only serve to heighten the sense of tragedy at his dishonorable end. Uzziah had an opportunity to be the "next David," to restore the former glory of the kingdom of Israel. He had everything he needed to be successful: an extended period of international peace, agricultural abundance, renewed access to international trade, and—most important—the blessing and favor of God. Yet, the tagline of Uzziah's life would have to be: "He *almost* succeeded." Even with all those secular benefits and spiritual advantages, Uzziah's life ended in dramatic failure.

72

II. PUZZLING PERSPECTIVES

A. The Reign of Azariah/Uzziah in II Kings

We may tend to overlook the differences in how the story of King Uzziah's reign is related in the books of II Kings and II Chronicles. As can be seen from this lesson's Scripture text, the Kings account of Uzziah's life is only a brief outline, following the familiar pattern of the so-called "regnal formula." The use of this formula has several important effects on the narrative of Kings. First of all, the regnal formula is introduced after the kingdom is divided into northern and southern realms; by constantly synchronizing the royal history of both kingdoms, the book was subtly emphasizing that, even though Judah and Israel were divided politically, they were still considered together as God's one chosen people. This approach held out hope that one day the divided Kingdom would be reunited.

The most crucial element of the formula is the evaluation of the king's reign, usually given in comparison to King David (for Judean kings) or in comparison to King Jeroboam (for Israelite kings). There is only one criterion for success: faithfulness to God's covenant. Furthermore, there is only one test for such faithfulness: worship of God alone. The writer of Kings positively evaluated Uzziah, saying, "He did that which was right in the sight of the Lord" (II Kings 15:3). But he added a qualification: "Save that the high places were not removed: the people sacrificed and burnt incense still on the high places" (II Kings 15:4). Therefore, the reader is led to understand that though Uzziah was a good king overall, he did not measure up to the faithfulness of the ideal King David.

The only other information provided about the reign of Uzziah is found in verse 5: "And the LORD smote the king, so that he was a leper unto the day of his death." Coming as it does on the heels of what appears to a be positive evaluation of Uzziah's reign, this statement has a shocking effect, especially since there is no explanation offered. Clearly, Uzziah did something that brought about divine displeasure and a judgment of leprosy, but the writer said nothing more.

» *Why is it such a tragic thing to see leaders make such dire mistakes?*

B. The Reign of Azariah/Uzziah in II Chronicles

The writer of Chronicles took a much greater interest in the reign of King Uzziah. In fact, the Chronicler added key pieces of additional information. First, the Chronicler included the fact that Uzziah recovered the port city of Elath, which would have reopened Judah's access to international trade. According to Steven McKenzie, this would have invited the readers to think of Uzziah as a new Solomon (*I–II Chronicles*). Second, the Chronicler acknowledged that Uzziah "sought God," but then immediately qualified that statement to a specific time period "in the days of Zechariah." The statement concludes ominously: "As long as he sought the Lord, God made him to prosper." This recalls the story of King Joash, who, like

73

Uzziah, also followed God as long as the priest Jehoiada was present to guide him. However, as soon as Jehoiada died, Joash ceased to follow the Lord with all of his heart. (See II Chronicles 24:2, 15–18.)

The final addition is the significant expansion that detailed the sin that caused King Uzziah's leprosy. In fact, the Chronicler's preference for the name "Uzziah" (rather than the variant "Azariah") probably arose from the inclusion of this story, in order to avoid confusion of the king with the high priest, who was also named Azariah (II Chronicles 26:17). Uzziah's specific infraction was his entering the sacred precincts of the Temple intending to offer incense as a priest. First of all, the list of royal duties given in the Mosaic Covenant (Deuteronomy 17:14–20) granted the king no such priestly right or privilege. Furthermore, Uzziah's actions here recall both the sins of Saul (II Samuel 13:2–5) and Jeroboam I (I Kings 12:33; 13:1)! However, Uzziah was not judged for offering incense (which he never actually did); he was judged instead because of his prideful spirit.

C. Self-Reflection Is Vitally Important

What is most noticeable in the Chronicler's story of Uzziah are all the allusions and connections to the stories of other kings who began well but ended badly— Solomon, Saul, Jeroboam I, Joash. In every case, the root problem was a false sense of accomplishment that gave birth to pride and arrogance.

There is a reason Scripture often calls us to seasons of remembrance and reflection, and it certainly is not to bolster our flagging sense of self-worth with a rehearsal of our greatest accomplishments. No, any honest review of our lives would reveal how much we have been undeservedly blessed; our accomplishments are rarely our own. We have often had others help us in crucial ways at key moments and, most certainly, we have been strengthened by the hand of God. The real tragedy of Uzziah's life is that he simply became another king who "forgot where he came from," as the old saying has it.

» *What do you do personally to maintain a thankful heart?*

III. FALLEN HEROES—A CALL TO REFLECTION

A. Humans Not Heroes

As this lesson draws to a close, we can draw some key truths from the sobering example of King Uzziah. First, we can be thankful that the story of Uzziah is in the Bible. Perhaps one of the most wonderful things about Scripture is its realism about human nature. The kings of Israel and Judah are no comic-book superheroes or Hollywood movie stars with near-magical superpowers or unbelievable good looks and charm. No, the kings of Israel were real flesh and blood. There is no attempt in either Kings or Chronicles to cover for Uzziah's sin, but neither do the books ignore the good he accomplished. Both his successes and his failures are there for all to see.

Such honesty lets this story serve as both encouragement and warning. Like Uzziah, if we are faithful to God, we know God will bless us and prosper us in our work for the kingdom of God. If, however, we let our hearts be lifted up with pride—if we ever confuse our blessings as our accomplishments—then we run the risk of a ruinous fall.

B. Re-Envisioned History

The story of Uzziah also demonstrates the importance of revisiting our past, over and over again. Though we cannot date the composition of the books with absolute precision, it is clear that Kings presents to us an "exilic" perspective on Israel's monarchical history, focused largely on explaining the national tragedy of the Exile. Chronicles comes from a later generation and utilizes a "post-exilic" perspective, focused more on finding patterns of hope and warning in Israel's national story to inspire and exhort those who are trying to rebuild a fallen nation.

Chronicles, however, is not "revisionist" history; rather it is "re-envisioned" history. As was noted above, the Chronicler did not simply focus on Uzziah's successes; in fact, he offered a more detailed record of Uzziah's sin! Clearly, the Chronicler wanted to emphasize the importance of treating the newly-rebuilt Temple with reverence, but it seems he wanted to do something greater. If Israel was to succeed in rebuilding herself as a nation, she must address this nationalized pattern of early success followed by pride and apostasy.

» *What is one thing you wish you could tell your younger self about what it means to live for God successfully?*

C. We Must Begin and End Well

The lessons of faithfulness from the life of Uzziah still apply to us. First of all, the biblical metric for the "good life" is not success but faithfulness. By most external measures that we utilize today, Uzziah's reign was successful. It was a period of peace and prosperity, there was a strong military, and international trade and commerce revived. It is not enough to simply begin well; we must also end well, maintaining our faithfulness to God.

▶▶▶ INTERNALIZING THE MESSAGE

Beryl Markham, the first person to fly the Atlantic solo from east to west, said in her memoir, *West with the Night*: "If a man has any greatness in him, it comes to light, not in one flamboyant hour, but in the ledger of his daily work." If there is anything to be learned from the life of Uzziah, it is that a lifetime of faithfulness to God always comes down to today's decisions. The question that faces us is not "Will you be faithful to God *for the rest of your life*?" but "Will be you faithful to God *today*?"

Josiah and the Power of Obedience

FOCUS THOUGHT

God expects us to obey His Word.

 FOCUS VERSE

II Kings 22:13

Go ye, inquire of the LORD for me, and for the people, and for all Judah, concerning the words of this book that is found: for great is the wrath of the LORD that is kindled against us, because our fathers have not hearkened unto the words of this book, to do according unto all that which is written concerning us.

 LESSON TEXT

II Kings 22:8–13, 18–20

8 And Hilkiah the high priest said unto Shaphan the scribe, I have found the book of the law in the house of the LORD. And Hilkiah gave the book to Shaphan, and he read it.

9 And Shaphan the scribe came to the king, and brought the king word again, and said, Thy servants have gathered the money that was found in the house, and have delivered it into the hand of them that do the work, that have the oversight of the house of the LORD.

10 And Shaphan the scribe shewed the king, saying, Hilkiah the priest hath delivered me a book. And Shaphan read it before the king.

11 And it came to pass, when the king had heard the words of the book of the law, that he rent his clothes.

12 And the king commanded Hilkiah the priest, and Ahikam the son of Shaphan, and Achbor the son of Michaiah, and Shaphan the scribe, and Asahiah a servant of the king's, saying,

13 Go ye, inquire of the LORD for me, and for the people, and for all Judah, concerning the words of this book that is found: for great is the wrath of the LORD that is kindled against us, because our fathers have not hearkened unto the words of this book, to do according unto all that which is written concerning us.

. . . . .

18 But to the king of Judah which sent you to inquire of the LORD, thus shall ye say to him, Thus saith the LORD God of Israel, As touching the words which thou hast heard;

19 Because thine heart was tender, and thou hast humbled thyself before the LORD, when thou heardest what I spake against this place, and against the inhabitants thereof, that they should become a desolation and a curse, and hast rent thy clothes, and wept before me; I also have heard thee, saith the LORD.

20 Behold therefore, I will gather thee unto thy fathers, and thou shalt be gathered into thy grave in peace; and thine eyes shall not see all the evil which I will bring upon this place. And they brought the king word again.

ADVICE FROM AN ELDER

Wayne and Gayle Ellard had been pastoring in Greenville, Mississippi, for around twenty years when the district superintendent, G. R. Travis, came to discuss retirement. He was traveling and encouraging the Mississippi ministers and their churches to invest in a retirement plan with the UPCI. Pastor Ellard had believed in pouring as much as possible back into the church and did not in any way want to be a burden or take advantage of the people he served. Due to the insistence of a trusted church official and the desire of the church to start retirement for their pastor, Wayne Ellard agreed to obey the advice of his elder.

Around age fifty-five it became apparent that Pastor Ellard was suffering from an illness the doctors in Mississippi could not diagnose. After suffering for close to ten years, and at the recommendation of his doctors, the Ellards moved to Colorado to be with two of their daughters and receive better medical attention.

He was diagnosed with Primary Progressive Aphasia, and God opened the door for him to be able to live in a new, beautiful care center with medical personnel who understood this illness. The time he was there was completely paid for by his retirement fund. He and his family were treated with respect and honor as he finished his life on this earth. The month the retirement fund ran out was the month God took Pastor Ellard home. God knew what would be needed years in advance and worked through His people's obedience to bring it to pass.

▶▶▶ OUTLINE

I. AN ERA OF REVIVAL

A. The Disastrous Reign of Manasseh

B. The Dawning of Hope

C. God Can Intervene in My Worst Circumstances

II. A NATIONAL TRAGEDY

A. The Death of Josiah

B. The Dissipation of the Revival

C. Sometimes Good People Face Tragedy

III. THE MANY FACES OF FAITHFUL OBEDIENCE

A. To Obey Is Better Than to Succeed

B. The Aftereffects of Josiah's Revival

C. We Must Remain Faithful in the Face of Failure

▶▶▶ CONTEMPLATING THE TOPIC

Thomas Edison, Steve Jobs, and Henry Ford. These names are all quickly recognized as three of the world's greatest twentieth-century inventors. However, not many would recognize the names Spencer Silver and Art Fry. Yet it is no stretch to say their invention is even more ubiquitous than the iPhone.

Spencer Silver was an engineer working at 3M in 1968, trying to create super-strong adhesives for the aerospace industry. He discovered a type of adhesive called acrylate copolymer microspheres (ACMs). Unfortunately, instead of being incredibly strong, ACMs were incredibly weak. However, they did have two unique features. First, when removed from a surface, they left no residue. Second, even after being adhered to a surface, they retained their stickiness and were effectively reusable multiple times.

Five years later, in 1973, Silver approached Geoff Nicholson, 3M's products laboratory manager, with an idea for a product—an ACM-coated bulletin board. Papers could be stuck to it without using thumbtacks or staples and could be removed without getting any "sticky stuff" on the displayed items.

Enter Art Fry, a 3M product development engineer. He was already familiar with Silver's ACM adhesives and his proposed bulletin board. However, Fry sang in a church choir and constantly dealt with the problem of his paper song-page markers falling out of the hymnal. Then he had an idea: Why not use some of Silver's ACM adhesive on the page markers to keep them in place? Fry then suggested to Silver and Nicholson that they put the adhesive "on a piece of paper and then we can stick it to anything." And, just like that, the Post-It Note was born.

From one perspective, Spencer Silver's work could be considered a total failure; from another point of view, though, it could be considered a stunning success. In today's lesson, we will explore the life of a Judean king whose own story can be read in two very different ways. And it reminds us, just like the lowly Post-It Note, that not every so-called "failure" is quite as disastrous as it first may seem.

⟫⟫⟫ SEARCHING THE SCRIPTURES

I. AN ERA OF REVIVAL

A. The Disastrous Reign of Manasseh

His fifty-five-year reign in Jerusalem was the longest of all the kings of Israel or Judah (II Kings 21:1). Usually, in Scripture, long reigns (like long lives) are symbolic of divine blessing on righteous living. However, in the case of Manasseh, quite the opposite is true. He not only was Judah's longest-reigning king but also its most wicked ruler. The author of Kings catalogued many of Manasseh's offenses, comparing them to the prior occupants of the land (II Kings 21:2, 9).

In other words, under the reign of Manasseh, Judah became more wicked than the Canaanites whom the Lord had destroyed when Israel conquered the Promised Land! This is a key part of the reason that during the reign of Manasseh God first proclaimed His intention to destroy the city of Jerusalem and send the people into exile (II Kings 21:11–15). Manasseh set in motion the disaster that brought the destruction of Judah's capital and Yahweh's holy Temple.

» *Why do you think God's judgment so often takes years to come fully to pass?*

B. The Dawning of Hope

Against that extremely foreboding background, the reign of Manasseh's grandson Josiah burst onto the scene with the light of hope. Josiah was the last and greatest of the reformist kings of Judah, in the tradition of Asa (I Kings 15:11–15) and Hezekiah (II Kings 18:1–8), both of whom walked in faithfulness to God. In fact, in offering an evaluation of the quality of Josiah's reign, the author of Kings reported: "And he did that which was right in the sight of the LORD, and walked in all the way of David his father, and turned not aside to the right hand or to the left" (II Kings 22:2). Josiah's faithfulness was unmatched, even by the "man after God's own heart," David! As great a king as David was, even his life was marred by his sin with Bathsheba and the murder of her lawful husband, Uriah. (See II Samuel 11.) There was no such blot on Josiah's recorded reign.

Josiah's religious reforms were more extensive than any other. First, the catalog of King Josiah's reforms exceeded the description of Manasseh's sins (II Kings 23:2–25). Second, Josiah's reforms included the destruction of the high places, especially the false altar of the Northern Kingdom erected at Bethel, an altar that had stood since the time of Jeroboam I and had become the iconic symbol of Israel's apostasy. (See I Kings 12:28–33; II Kings 17:9–12.)

This second action was vitally important because King Josiah was used by God to fulfill a prophecy given by an unnamed prophet from Judah at the time of the altar's construction (I Kings 13:2).

Josiah fulfilled this centuries-old word of judgment to the letter, even disinterring bones from nearby sepulchers to burn upon the altar (II Kings 23:16). In so doing, Josiah's reform reversed the apostasy of both Jeroboam and Solomon.

Josiah's final reforming action was to observe a national Passover at Jerusalem (II Kings 23:21). The only other recorded Passover celebration of this scope is found in Joshua 5:10–12, just before the children of Israel crossed the Jordan River into the Promised Land.

C. God Can Intervene in My Worst Circumstances

It is important to pause here and contemplate the spiritual distance between the reigns of Manasseh and Josiah. No one who lived during Manasseh's reign, with its rampant idolatry and immorality, could ever have imagined a revival quite like Josiah's. It would have seemed to the average onlooker as if all hope for national restoration and a return to God was dead. Yet Josiah's revival was greater than any the nation had previously seen. Speaking through the prophet Isaiah, God commanded His people:

> Remember ye not the former things, neither consider the things of old. Behold, I will do a new thing; now it shall spring forth; shall ye not know it? I will even make a way in the wilderness, and rivers in the desert. (Isaiah 43:18–19)

One of the most fascinating and pivotal figures of modern history is British Prime Minister Winston Churchill. When he came to power in May 1940, the nation teetered on the brink of total collapse. Churchill, however, with that bulldog glower and growling voice, was able to inspire the nation to continue resisting. In his book about Churchill, *Darkest Hour: How Churchill Brought England Back from the Brink*, author Andrew McCarten points out a key reason why Churchill's words were so inspiring: "In stark contrast to Hitler's egomaniacal speeches—which emphasized the word 'I'—Churchill . . . knew the power of 'We' when exhorting the British public to take up such a fearful struggle." Churchill's words, like the words of the rediscovered Book of the Law in Josiah's day, were able to inspire hope and courage. And yet today, the Word of God should continue to inspire us to never give up hope, even when all appears to be hopeless.

» *What passage of Scripture do you often turn to when you need inspiration?*

II. A NATIONAL TRAGEDY

A. The Death of Josiah

It is fun to speculate about the national feeling in the weeks following Josiah's celebration of the first national Passover since Joshua's day. The atmosphere could only be described as euphoric. True change had come at last; the sins of past generations had finally been dealt with. In the midst of this revival, the conclusion of the story of Josiah's reign comes like a thunderclap. In one brief verse, the author of Kings tells us Josiah went to war and was killed (II Kings 23:29). Scholars today are still puzzled by Josiah's actions in this matter. It does not appear Pharaoh Necho was threatening Judah, so why did Josiah go out to meet him in battle? Josiah's actions are not presented as foolishly provocative nor as rebellious against God's Word. It appears Josiah was simply doing what he felt was right to protect his kingdom, and he died for his efforts.

B. The Dissipation of the Revival

Unfortunately, Josiah's untimely and unexplained death quickly killed the revival's momentum. Jehoahaz, his son, was quickly deposed as the Judean king, and his brother Jehoiakim was set up as a pro-Egyptian "puppet-king" of Judah. As the memoirs of the prophet Jeremiah testify, Jehoiakim was nothing like his righteous father. He plundered the newly restored Temple to pay tribute to Egypt and imposed a heavy and oppressive tax on the people of God (II Kings 23:35). The concluding evaluation of Jehoiakim's reign by the author of Kings is made more tragic in its brevity: "And he did that which was evil in the sight of the LORD, according to all that his fathers had done" (II Kings 23:37). All the good Josiah had accomplished was undone by Jehoiakim.

C. Sometimes Good People Face Tragedy

The difficult reality is that bad things do happen to good people for no apparent reason. Even though we know such suffering is ultimately the result of sin's corruption of God's perfect world, such an understanding does not assuage our grief when we see those we love caught in the throes of pain and heartache. These are the moments that can push our faith to its breaking point. If we are honest, we all, at one point or another, have wrestled with what C. S. Lewis called "the problem of pain."

Yet if we are to persist in our honesty, we would also be forced to admit the truth of Lewis's further observation about the reality of pain: "I have seen great beauty of spirit in some who were great sufferers. I have seen men . . . grow better not worse with advancing years, and I have seen the last illness produce treasures of fortitude and meekness from most unpromising subjects" (*The Problem of Pain*). The deepest mystery of pain's reality lies not in the suffering, but in the wondrous beauty only pain's endurance can produce.

> » *Consider for a moment one of the most difficult or painful times in your life. Would you say it made you a better person? If so, in what ways has suffering and pain actually benefited you? How can you use the lessons you have learned to help others cope with their pain?*

III. THE MANY FACES OF FAITHFUL OBEDIENCE

A. To Obey Is Better Than to Succeed

Josiah's death, even today, calls into question the value of his reform. Certainly, he was the greatest reformer the nation had ever known, restoring the rule of God among the people of God to an extent unmatched by any before or after him. So what? When he died, his sons went right back to following the evil ways of their great-grandfather Manasseh. In fact, Josiah's reforms lasted so short a time, it is difficult to even describe them as a "success." Honestly, Josiah's reign would appear to be better categorized as a failure.

This becomes even more certain when we consider the prophecy of Huldah to Josiah, given before Josiah ever launched his reform program:

> *Thus saith the Lord, Behold, I will bring evil upon this place, and upon the inhabitants thereof, even all the words of the book which the king of Judah hath read: because they have forsaken me, and have burned incense unto other gods, that they might provoke me to anger with all the works of their hands; therefore my wrath shall be kindled against this place, and shall not be quenched. (II Kings 22:16–17)*

Josiah's reforms were not enough to reverse God's decision to destroy Jerusalem and send Judah into exile! Then why would Josiah exert so much energy on a reform that was useless? Quite simply, because doing the right thing is more important than being successful. Once Josiah learned from God's Word what obedience to the covenant required, the outcome no longer mattered.

> » *Why is it so easy for us to fall into the trap of serving God in order to get something from Him?*

B. The Aftereffects of Josiah's Revival

Before we assign Josiah's reform to the category of "Abject Failure," we should consider briefly a story from the Book of Jeremiah, taken from the time after the city had fallen to the Babylonians. As would be expected, it was a time of tremendous upheaval. Within just a few weeks or months of his appointment, the Babylonian governor Gedaliah was assassinated by Ishmael ben Nethaniah (Jeremiah 41:1–3).

The day after, a group of eighty pilgrims arrived in Jerusalem to mourn the loss of the Temple. Ishmael, fearing discovery of his crime, murdered all of them in cold blood and buried them in a mass grave (Jeremiah 41:4–7). However, what gets lost in the horror of all this senseless bloodshed is the brief aside that these pilgrims came "from Shechem, from Shiloh, and from Samaria" (verse 5), cities located in the region of the long-overthrown Northern Kingdom.

Ever since the days of Jeroboam, Israel had been rife with idolatry and false worship. There were no righteous northern kings; every one of them was wicked and evil. Yet Josiah's brief foray decades before into the territory of the Northern Kingdom to destroy the shrine at Bethel seems to have brought something of a revival to the remnant of the people left there. Though Josiah's reforms did not last in Jerusalem, they had a lasting effect in these northern cities!

C. We Must Remain Faithful in the Face of Failure

Was Josiah's reform a failure? The answer, it seems, is not clear-cut. Certainly, Josiah's reforms did not rescue the city of Jerusalem from destruction, but they did revive the worship of God in northern territories long overrun by idolatrous worship. Josiah's reforms may not have had the lasting effect he hoped for, but they did have a lasting effect!

This points us again to the importance of faithfulness, even in the face of apparent failure. Just because we do not achieve our purposes or goals does not mean our obedience and faithfulness do not achieve any purpose or goal. In fact, obedience to God is never about achieving our purposes, but should always be focused on achieving His purpose.

» *Have you ever faced a situation where you had to obey God without understanding why? Was it difficult? Why? What thoughts and feelings did you battle? In the end, what was the result of your obedience?*

▶▶▶ INTERNALIZING THE MESSAGE

It is important that we understand Josiah did not simply obey God because He hoped to get God to bring him success and prosperity. Josiah obeyed God because God is to be obeyed. Too often, we treat obedience and faithfulness as a means to an end—success, happiness, fulfillment, contentment—when, in reality, obedience and faithfulness must be seen as ends in and of themselves. Otherwise, obedience sImply becomes another tool in the sinful human quest to control God and make Him do what we want. The fundamental principle of Scripture is that God is God . . . and we are not: "We are His people, and the sheep of His pasture" (Psalm 100:3, NKJV).

The Righteous Judge

FOCUS THOUGHT
God loves us enough to judge our rebellion.

 FOCUS VERSES

II Chronicles 36:15–16
And the LORD God of their fathers sent to them by his messengers, rising up betimes, and sending; because he had compassion on his people, and on his dwelling place: but they mocked the messengers of God, and despised his words, and misused his prophets, until the wrath of the LORD arose against his people, till there was no remedy.

LESSON TEXT

II Chronicles 36:11–21
11 Zedekiah was one and twenty years old when he began to reign, and reigned eleven years in Jerusalem.

12 And he did that which was evil in the sight of the LORD his God, and humbled not himself before Jeremiah the prophet speaking from the mouth of the LORD.

13 And he also rebelled against king Nebuchadnezzar, who had made him swear by God: but he stiffened his neck, and hardened his heart from turning unto the LORD God of Israel.

14 Moreover all the chief of the priests, and the people, transgressed very much after all the abominations of the heathen; and polluted the house of the LORD which he had hallowed in Jerusalem.

15 And the LORD God of their fathers sent to them by his messengers, rising up betimes, and sending; because he had compassion on his people, and on his dwelling place:

16 But they mocked the messengers of God, and despised his words, and misused his prophets, until the wrath of the LORD arose against his people, till there was no remedy.

17 Therefore he brought upon them the king of the Chaldees, who slew their young men with the sword in the house of their sanctuary, and had no compassion upon young man or maiden, old man, or him that stooped for age: he gave them all into his hand.

18 And all the vessels of the house of God, great and small, and the treasures of the house of the LORD, and the treasures of the king, and of his princes; all these he brought to Babylon.

19 And they burnt the house of God, and brake down the wall of Jerusalem, and burnt all the palaces thereof with fire, and destroyed all the goodly vessels thereof.

20 And them that had escaped from the sword carried he away to Babylon; where they were servants to him and his sons until the reign of the kingdom of Persia:

21 To fulfil the word of the LORD by the mouth of Jeremiah, until the land had enjoyed her sabbaths: for as long as she lay desolate she kept sabbath, to fulfil threescore and ten years.

CULTURE CONNECTION

THE DANGER OF NO DISCIPLINE

Doctors and nurses scurried around the emergency cubical as a young mother attempted to calm her toddler. The child sobbed uncontrollably as nurses carefully removed the first-aid bandage from her charred and blistered hand. The damage was so severe, amputation would have to be considered. At best there would be permanent nerve damage that would be a reminder of the incident for as long as she lived.

As the staff wheeled the frightened child off to the operating room, the responding officer began asking the mother for additional information. The mother said her daughter had been electrocuted when she inserted a metal rod into the electrical junction box on the side of the warehouse where her husband worked. The mother and daughter were waiting for the father to get off work when the toddler found the piece of metal and began trying to pry the electrical cover open.

"Do you mean you just watched your daughter playing around the high-voltage box?" asked the officer.

"Yes," answered the mother defensively, "I had warned her twice, but she was being stubborn. I don't believe in nagging or spanking, so all I did was watch."

OUTLINE

I. Zedekiah Became King of Judah
- A. He Did Evil in the Eyes of the Lord and His Heart Was Hardened
- B. He Defiled the Temple of the Lord
- C. Hardened Hearts Lead to Rebellion

II. THE LORD SENT MESSENGERS
- A. The People Mocked God's Messengers
- B. The People Despised God's Word
- C. God Will Compassionately Reach for Those Who Have Rebelled against Him

III. GOD JUDGED JUDAH'S REBELLION
- A. The Lord Sent the Babylonians
- B. The Babylonians Destroyed the Temple and Broke Down Jerusalem's Wall
- C. God Will Judge Those Who Rebel against Him

IV. THOUGH GOD WILL JUDGE, HE ALSO WANTS TO PARDON
- A. He Loves Us Enough to Judge Us
- B. He Desires for Us to Turn from Our Rebellion and Receive His Pardon

CONTEMPLATING THE TOPIC

We tend to criticize the rebellious attitude or actions of others while brushing off our own sin as a mistake or a moment of weakness. Our sinful nature leads us along the path of sin, justification of certain behaviors, and the internal delineating of our value of the sin versus its consequences. The desire to do things our own way and the belief that we know best is a result of sin. Realizing this tendency is an important step in identifying the rebellious nature that resides in each of us. God "calls out" our sin not to shame us or punish us, but to bring us to repentance so we can be restored to Him.

I. ZEDEKIAH BECAME KING OF JUDAH

Second Chronicles 36 contains the account of the heartbreaking demise of a nation. It is an iconic warning to humanity, the story of a nation and a king who disregarded God and blundered into oblivion. The king was twenty-year-old Zedekiah. While his tender age and inexperience may have contributed to his ultimate destruction, the Bible clearly delineates the core reasons for this king's failure. The account also explains why God felt the need to respond with righteous judgment. He would not stand by as His people disobeyed.

A. He Did Evil in the Eyes of the Lord and His Heart Was Hardened

Second Chronicles 36:12 tells us that Zedekiah "did that which was evil in the sight of the LORD his God, and humbled not himself." One translation says "he was a stubborn man." The hardening of a heart is a frightening thing. It is like the deadening of nerve endings. People who begin down that path actually convince themselves to believe their own lies. This does almost irreparable damage. According to Proverbs 29:1, "He, that being often reproved hardeneth his neck, shall suddenly be destroyed, and that without remedy."

Zedekiah's "stiffened neck" and hard heart (II Chronicles 36:13) caused him to resist the prophet Jeremiah and even King Nebuchadnezzar. The result was complete chaos among all of the nation's leaders.

> *How do God's rules serve as a protection against evil?*

B. He Defiled the Temple of the Lord

As can often be observed not only in Bible stories, but also in contemporary life, evil always takes people beyond innocent mistakes to an in-your-face kind of bad behavior. It was not enough to do what he wanted; Zedekiah had to do it in a way that showed disrespect toward God and His Word. Once the evil was set in motion, it eventually polluted the most important things in their lives. "All the chief of the priests, and the people, transgressed very much after all the abominations of the heathen; and polluted the house of the LORD which he had hallowed in Jerusalem" (II Chronicles 36:14).

C. Hardened Hearts Lead to Rebellion

Satan, flesh, and sin are never content to simply do wrong; they are intent on being in charge. Thus, rebellion always follows unrepentance. Rebellion has often been glamorized, but when one rebels against benevolent leaders, the result is never good for the rebel. Like the toddler in our opening story, those who rebel will experience dire outcomes. But unlike the parent in our opening story, God will do something to salvage His people.

The above is a predictable pattern: (1) people do evil, (2) harden their heart, (3) disrespect spiritual authority, and (4) eventually rebel against God. Since the end of this pattern is self-deception and destruction, every believer would be wise to notice the early signs of unrepentant sin and then pay special attention when they begin to feel a rift between them and their local church or someone in leadership. These are red flags that, if ignored, mark the point at which the enemy begins to gain the upper hand and soon separates the sheep from the flock.

> *What are some safety nets to help us avoid developing a hard heart?*

II. THE LORD SENT MESSENGERS

A. The People Mocked God's Messengers

Since God is loving and merciful, He continually reaches for people who are caught in this downward spiral. His primary means of saving them is through words of warning sent through willing vessels. Second Chronicles 36:15–16 points out that "the LORD God of their fathers sent to them . . . messengers . . . but they mocked the messengers of God, and despised his words, and misused his prophets, until the wrath of the LORD arose against his people, till there was no remedy." God sends messages until people stop listening. When people stop listening, there is no remedy. The only remedy is to heed God's warnings. This point underscores the importance of preaching and of having a teachable spirit.

Scripture is replete with stories that expose the arrogance and stubbornness of human nature. Noah's contemporaries laughed at the idea of judgment. David was ridiculed when he offered to kill Goliath. Children made fun of Elijah. Paul evidently had full-time detractors who followed him all over the world opposing him. And Jesus' ministry was plagued with accusers, questioners, and mockers. Ultimately, God in flesh was mocked while He was in the process of saving the world.

B. The People Despised God's Word

Mocking messengers quickly leads to a disrespect for higher authority, and Judah was no exception; they "despised His words." Just as a parent must help a child who despises their words to learn the value of respect, God had to do something to teach His people respect for His Word.

The United States has been "Exhibit A" in this arena. America was founded on biblical principles and has enjoyed incredible prosperity as a result. Many of those principles are etched into the stone on federal and state buildings. However, as culture began to reject biblical morals and values, educators, politicians, and courts began to systematically attack the Word of God. It has been challenged in the Pledge of Allegiance, on US currency, and on federal buildings. Many have even demanded that the Ten Commandments be removed from all public buildings. The Bible has been banned from being taught in public schools and even barred from some public venues.

And it is plain to those with any discernment that the results have been devastating. America is experiencing the rise of rebellion. The rule of law is diminishing. Flesh is running wild. Truth has been defined as relative, and our culture has been weakened on every level, all because a nation despised the Word of God.

The good news is that our churches and our personal lives need not follow the same deadly path. We can preserve our personal integrity and the integrity of our families and churches by maintaining high respect for the Word of God. Disregard for His Word will bring righteous judgment in a very organic way even if God does not choose to send specific judgment.

» **Can you think of a contemporary example of someone who demonstrated a high regard for God's Word both in word and in deed?**

C. God Will Compassionately Reach for Those Who Have Rebelled against Him

Hebrews 12:6 (NLT) declares, "For the LORD disciplines those he loves, and he punishes each one he accepts as his child." In the case of Zedekiah and Judah, we see how God used prophets, kings, and circumstances to reach for them. But as their stubbornness escalated, so did God's response. God is often trashed for taking action, but according to stories like this one, He is merciful and patient. In this case, He loved them and reached for them for over a decade.

A single mother was struggling to make ends meet and live a holy life. She had been baptized, filled with the Holy Ghost, and delivered from a number of destructive habits. From time to time this woman allowed her church attendance to lag, and before long she found herself re-captured by one or more of the things from which she had been delivered. In one of those vulnerable times, she became involved with an unsaved man and allowed him to move into her apartment. She knew this was wrong and soon began to reap the fruit of her choices. The man began mistreating her, became very demanding, and refused to move out.

One day she encountered her pastor in a grocery store parking lot. She confessed her situation and expressed her regrets, and they prayed together that God would forgive her and provide a solution. Upon her return to her apartment, she found the man for whom she had prayed very angry. He proceeded to chide her and then informed her that he was leaving and would not be persuaded otherwise. God had provided a way of escape even though it was her poor choices that put her in that situation. God is longsuffering and forgiving, always ready to forgive and restore those who approach Him with repentant hearts.

III. GOD JUDGED JUDAH'S REBELLION

Because of Zedekiah's stubbornness, God used a heathen nation to discipline the nation of Judah. Their rebellion had to be dealt with. They had to be saved from themselves. It was a merciful God who reluctantly used Babylon to bring His own people back to their senses.

A. The Lord Sent the Babylonians

It is always sad to watch the disciplinary action of God. When the Babylonian soldiers descended on Jerusalem, Zedekiah and his family tried to escape, but they were captured near Jericho. That is when the king witnessed the fulfillment of Jeremiah's prophecy: he was brought before Nebuchadnezzar at Riblah and sentenced to exile in Babylon. But before having his own eyes gouged out, he was forced to watch as his sons were executed. Their execution was the last thing he would ever see.

It would have been better if King Zedekiah would have listened when God tried to correct him through the prophets. We would do well to pay close attention to this cautionary tale. How much easier our lives will be if we are the first to respond to conviction and visit an altar of repentance when the Word of God goes forth. Paul asked, "Do you not know that the goodness of God leads to repentance?" (See Romans 2:4.)

» *Can you remember a story or sermon God used to redirect your life? Explain.*

B. The Babylonians Destroyed the Temple and Broke Down Jerusalem's Wall

Not only was the king's family judged, but the Babylonians removed all the valuables from the Temple in Jerusalem. They broke down the walls and set fire to it all. The holy city lay in ruins. The sacred Temple was desecrated, and the nation ceased to be a nation because God's people insisted on doing things their way. Such is the nature of unrestrained flesh.

C. God Will Judge Those Who Rebel against Him

This story stands as a testament to the righteousness of God. He will not cheat, even for His own people. Many other Bible stories attest to this character trait, such as the judgment that came to Samson, the people of Noah's day, and the cities of Sodom and Gomorrah. God will judge those who rebel against Him because His righteousness demands it. Sometimes His judgment is delayed. Sometimes it is not recognized. Sometimes it is reserved for eternity. But judgment is inevitable. Although this may be a sobering thought to some, it is also a reassurance to those who believe in a just God.

If God did not judge, how could we be confident that He will eventually be fair in His treatment of Satan and those who stand before Him in judgment?

IV. THOUGH GOD WILL JUDGE, HE ALSO WANTS TO PARDON

A. He Loves Us Enough to Judge Us

Although God will judge us, His ultimate goal is to lead us to repentance and restoration. His discipline is meant to teach us a lesson. A pre-teen boy experienced this same kind of loving correction from a favorite uncle. The uncle was welding in the shop on his small farm. Although the boy had been instructed to wear welding glasses, his uncle caught him peeking, so he put down his welding rod and proceeded to scold the boy for his indiscretion. The correction was not all that painful, but the boy cried, devastated that he had disappointed his uncle. The uncle was protecting his nephew from potential blisters on his eyes. He loved his nephew enough to discipline him. And the boy never looked at a welding arc again without eye protection.

B. He Desires for Us to Turn from Our Rebellion and Receive His Pardon

God's judgment is discipline, not retribution. He is not getting even or settling a score when He judges. His goal is always pardon and restoration. He is a loving, forgiving, and righteous heavenly Father.

> » *Can you think of some biblical characters who were pardoned and restored because they responded properly to God's judgment?*

▶▶▶ INTERNALIZING THE MESSAGE

He lived a Huck Finn existence, coming and going as he pleased. The rest of us kids in the neighborhood considered him lucky. His parents did not nag him or set boundaries. Every time our mothers called us in for dinner, we secretly wished we had his life. He was roaming the streets late at night, going home to eat whenever he felt like it, and experimenting with whatever he wished. How lucky could a young man be?

From where I stood, my friend lived an exotic life. Once he showed up at our house with an owl on his arm. I mean, how many kids get to have a pet owl? Admittedly, he did a few excessively adventurous things, such as putting a water snake In his mouth, so when he opened his mouth it would stick its head out and flash its tongue. Of course, his unsupervised escapades led to more devious deeds, such as tying cats' tails together and hanging them over a clothesline to watch them fight.

As we grew up and entered high school our paths diverged, and I was aware that he was experimenting with drugs and alcohol. He was still doing whatever he wanted without anyone standing in his way. It was a few years later, while away at college, that someone gave me the tragic update. My lucky friend had been shot and killed in a drug deal gone bad. He did not even make it into his mid-twenties. He never knew the joys of marriage or parenthood. He never even got to grow up.

Suppose someone had cared enough to discipline my friend. Suppose they had loved him enough to teach him to discipline himself. Observing the end of a life that had been lived without anyone caring enough to hold him accountable gave me a fresh appreciation for our heavenly Father who loves us enough to judge us and hold us accountable.

To embrace God is to embrace His discipline. If we trust His character, we will eagerly count on His discipline and be grateful that He loves us enough to save us from ourselves.

God Is Faithful

FOCUS THOUGHT

God is faithful to those who turn to Him in humility and prayer.

 FOCUS VERSE

II Chronicles 7:14

If my people, which are called by my name, shall humble themselves, and pray, and seek my face, and turn from their wicked ways; then will I hear from heaven, and will forgive their sin, and will heal their land.

 LESSON TEXT

II Chronicles 12:5–7

5 Then came Shemaiah the prophet to Rehoboam, and to the princes of Judah, that were gathered together to Jerusalem because of Shishak, and said unto them, Thus saith the Lord, Ye have forsaken me, and therefore have I also left you in the hand of Shishak.

6 Whereupon the princes of Israel and the king humbled themselves; and they said, The Lord is righteous.

7 And when the Lord saw that they humbled themselves, the word of the Lord came to Shemaiah, saying, They have humbled themselves; therefore I will not destroy them, but I will grant them some deliverance; and my wrath shall not be poured out upon Jerusalem by the hand of Shishak.

II Chronicles 13:10–16

10 But as for us, the Lord is our God, and we have not forsaken him; and the priests, which minister unto the Lord, are the sons of Aaron, and the Levites wait upon their business:

11 And they burn unto the Lord every morning and every evening burnt sacrifices and sweet incense: the shewbread also set they in order upon the pure table; and the candlestick of gold with the lamps thereof, to burn every evening: for we keep the charge of the Lord our God; but ye have forsaken him.

12 And, behold, God himself is with us for our captain, and his priests with sounding trumpets to cry alarm against you. O children of Israel, fight ye not against the Lord God of your fathers; for ye shall not prosper.

13 But Jeroboam caused an ambushment to come about behind them: so they were before Judah, and the ambushment was behind them.

14 And when Judah looked back, behold, the battle was before and behind: and they cried unto the Lord, and the priests sounded with the trumpets.

15 Then the men of Judah gave a shout: and as the men of Judah shouted, it came to pass, that God smote Jeroboam and all Israel before Abijah and Judah.

16 And the children of Israel fled before Judah: and God delivered them into their hand.

SISTER PARKER

Minnie Weems Parker was in her forties when she heard about the Holy Ghost. She desperately wanted to receive this gift from God. It was during the Great Depression, and she was working long hours on the family dairy farm as well as battling a serious snuff habit. God delivered her from snuff and many other bad habits even before filling her with the Holy Ghost two years later.

The railroad track ran in front of her house, and she fed many "hoboes" with a warm meal and the gospel message. Her front porch was known as a preaching spot for traveling ministers, and many people received the Holy Ghost on or near her porch. As a result, she became known for miles around as Sister Parker. One particular night, men from other churches came to burn down her house. As they stood there with flaming torches, Minnie came out and began to pray. A white dove landed on the roof of the porch, and one by one the men left.

One night a man knocked on her door needing prayer for his dying baby. Minnie was sick in bed with a gallbladder attack, and her husband told the man there was no way she would be able to travel in her condition. Yet she got up and rode the man's mule out to his house and prayed. The baby was healed, and so was she! From that moment forward, she never had another gallbladder attack.

Minnie faithfully shared the gospel and was a light to her community until she died in her early nineties.

OUTLINE

I. THE KING OF EGYPT ATTACKED JERUSALEM
- A. Shemaiah Prophesied to Rehoboam
- B. The King and Leaders of Israel Humbled Themselves
- C. The Lord Responded to Their Humility
- D. God Will Deliver Those Who Humble Themselves

II. ISRAEL WENT TO BATTLE AGAINST JUDAH
- A. Abijah Confirmed Judah's Reliance upon the Lord
- B. Judah Cried Out to the Lord and God Gave Them Victory
- C. God Will Give Victory to Those Who Rely on Him

III. GOD'S PROMISE TO SOLOMON
- A. If My People
- B. Humble Themselves and Pray
- C. God Is Faithful to Those Who Turn to Him in Humility and Prayer

CONTEMPLATING THE TOPIC

One of the greatest struggles a person has in his own flesh is the struggle with pride. Ego is inherent in each of us. It is always lurking beneath the surface, eager to be recognized, flattered, and lifted up. Pride drives us to succeed at any cost, living life on our own terms. We want to be self-made and we want everyone to recognize just how great we really are.

Deep in the heart of a Spirit-filled believer is the quest to live a life of true humility, but it cannot be achieved until the struggle against pride is won. It is astonishing how much effort it takes for humility to overcome pride to the extent it can flow outward in our conversations and actions. In the struggle between pride and humility we find truth in the saying "The spirit is willing, but the flesh is weak."

I. THE KING OF EGYPT ATTACKED JERUSALEM

Throughout Old Testament history, God's people found themselves at war with heathen nations. Most often, the cause of each conflict was rooted in the pride that had worked its way into their hearts and lives. The cycle repeated itself over and over: God would bless, the people would become proud of their blessing, their pride would lead to worldliness, God would bring an enemy army to do battle with them, and finally His people would humble themselves and pray, returning to a right relationship with God.

This is where we find Israel in II Chronicles 12. After Rehoboam had become king of Judah, he forsook the law of the Lord and led the people into sin. In the fifth year of his leadership, Shishak, king of Egypt, attacked Israel. The Bible tells us Israel was attacked because they had transgressed against the Lord (II Chronicles 12:2). Rehoboam had strengthened himself as king and was convinced he no longer needed to follow after the Lord.

> » *Can you think of a time when you allowed the blessings of God to cause you to become arrogant, thinking that you had arrived? Explain.*

A. Shemaiah Prophesied to Rehoboam

God is a God of great mercy. He does not simply wait for people to rebel against Him so He can judge them. Instead, He will send a warning before He ever sends judgment. It was not the Lord's intent for His people to be destroyed by Shishak without first giving them an opportunity to humble themselves.

Before God turned them over to Shishak for retribution, He sent the prophet Shemaiah to speak with Rehoboam. The best way to deal with the actions and attitudes resulting from foolish pride is to address the problem head-on, and that is exactly what Shemaiah did. He told the king, "Thus saith the LORD, Ye have forsaken me, and therefore have I also left you in the hand of Shishak."

> » *In reflecting on your life, can you recall a time when God sent you a warning and extended mercy to you before bringing judgment to the situation? Explain.*

B. The King and Leaders of Israel Humbled Themselves

This warning struck terror into the heart of the king as well as the princes of Israel. They knew Shishak was a vicious warrior-king. They knew he was capable of destroying them and decimating their land. So their swift and humble response before the Lord was no surprise.

When our pride is confronted, a response is demanded. We can humble ourselves before God and fall on His mercy, or we can continue in stubborn pride and ultimately be destroyed. Like Rehoboam, we need to be quick to respond in humility and bow our faces before Him.

C. The Lord Responded to Their Humility

In their humble response, they declared, "The Lord is righteous." There is more depth in that simple statement than we may realize. It was both an admission that their proud actions had been unrighteous, and an acknowledgment that God was righteous in punishing them for their pride. They found the right response when confronted with brutal honesty in the presence of God. It drove them back to a place of humility where they could realign their perspective and put God back in His proper place in their lives.

The Lord told Shemaiah that because the people had humbled themselves, He would show mercy to them. He would not allow Shishak to completely destroy them. Instead, the Egyptian king would only be allowed to take the treasures of the house of the Lord and of the king's house.

D. God Will Deliver Those Who Humble Themselves

Shishak could easily have taken the life of Rehoboam and held all of Israel captive. But because of Judah's act of humility before the Lord, the king's hand was stayed from doing so. God proved to His people once again that He will deliver those who humble themselves.

They not only found out that "pride goeth before destruction, and an haughty spirit before a fall" (Proverbs 16:18), but if people will humble themselves, God will deliver them from pending destruction.

It is wise to remember that even though God delivered them, they still suffered the loss of their treasures. There may be times when God will spare you while still allowing you to feel the pain of what your pride can cause you to lose. He does this so that your loss can serve as a future reminder of the danger of allowing pride to overtake you.

» *Can you recall someone else in Scripture whom God delivered after they humbled themselves and prayed? Give a brief account of the circumstances.*

II. ISRAEL WENT TO BATTLE AGAINST JUDAH

Soon after this, Abijah, the son of Rehoboam and the grandson of Solomon, ascended to the throne of the southern kingdom of Judah. At the same time, Jeroboam, an evil king, was ruling over the northern kingdom of Israel. Second Chronicles 13:2 lets us know there was war between the two nations.

Abijah had assembled an army of four hundred thousand proven men, but Jeroboam had amassed an elite fighting force of eight hundred thousand men. The numbers alone seemed to indicate an easy victory for Israel.

Before a sword was ever drawn or an arrow ever flew, Abijah stood on the edge of the battlefield and called out to Jeroboam. He reminded him that God had made a covenant giving the kingdom to David forever.

A. Abijah Confirmed Judah's Reliance upon the Lord

Abijah continued his speech by telling Jeroboam that he had rebelled against the Lord. Jeroboam had gathered children of Bellal unto himself to give him ungodly counsel. He and his people were worshiping false idols of golden calves, and the Levitical priesthood had been dismissed and replaced with worldly priests.

After letting Jeroboam know just how far his pride had taken him away from God, Abijah declared, "But as for us, the LORD is our God, and we have not forsaken him" (II Chronicles 13:10). He went on to say the priesthood was still doing service in the house of the Lord and that God Himself was with them as their captain.

B. Judah Cried Out to the Lord and God Gave Them Victory

Judah did not allow pride to make them think they could win the battle. Neither did they allow arrogance to drive them into a war they could not win. The words of Abijah were not offered from the vantage point of pride, but rather from a strong confidence that God was with them and would fight for them. He boldly warned Jeroboam not to fight against the Lord God of his fathers because he surely would be defeated (II Chronicles 13:12).

Jeroboam disregarded Abijah's words, and the battle began in earnest. He sent troops along Judah's flanks in an attempt to surround them and attack from all sides. No doubt Jeroboam was confident this strategy would win the victory.

When Judah discovered they were surrounded, they responded quickly. Interestingly, they did not reposition their troops. They did not fight back-to-back. They did not attempt to breach the battle lines. Instead, they cried out to the Lord, and the priests blew the trumpets. Then, as one voice, the men of Judah shouted a blood-curdling battle cry. God violently smote Jeroboam and all Israel (II Chronicles 13:15). They turned to flee, but were caught by the armies of Judah. Jeroboam lost five hundred thousand warriors that day—more than half of his fighting force.

» *How have you learned to depend on the Lord during difficult situations?*

C. God Will Give Victory to Those Who Rely on Him

Being humble before the Lord will pave the way for Him to bring you victory in the battles you face. Second Chronicles 13:18 gives the following insight: "Thus the children of Israel were brought under at that time, and the children of Judah prevailed, because they relied upon the LORD God of their fathers."

Relying on God tells Him you do not trust yourself to fight your battles. It is letting Him know you are humbling yourself in His presence and need Him to be at work in your life. You are leaning on Him and not on yourself.

III. GOD'S PROMISE TO SOLOMON

Several years before the biblical account of this lesson, God spoke to Solomon while he was the king of Israel. His instructions to Solomon contain a timeless formula for us concerning living our lives in such a way that God will fight for us and deliver us.

In II Chronicles 7:14, the Lord told Solomon, "If my people, which are called by my name, shall humble themselves, and pray, and seek my face, and turn from their wicked ways; then will I hear from heaven, and will forgive their sin, and will heal their land."

A. If My People

We need to realize identity matters to God. He created us to be in relationship with Him. His desire is for us to be His people and for Him to be our God. In a world where the term *Christian* has become so broadly defined, we need to be sure we are truly His by being born again and having His name applied to our lives.

B. Humble Themselves and Pray

We cannot expect identity alone to be some magical formula for victory in our lives. The battle with ego and pride will constantly be with us. These two enemies will give us ideas for how to wage war; they will speak words of false bravado into our ears that can cause us to be destroyed.

The Lord told Solomon that His people needed to "humble themselves and pray." In other words, He was calling them to go beyond the flesh and walk in the Spirit. We must not wait for life to humble us. We must not wait for circumstances to humble us. We must not wait for God to humble us. It is far better to learn to humble ourselves and pray, choosing to rely completely upon the Lord.

» *How can we humble ourselves?*

C. God Is Faithful to Those Who Turn to Him in Humility and Prayer

When you turn to the Lord in humility and prayer, you can have full confidence that God will respond. As He informed Solomon, humbling yourself and praying will get the attention of Heaven: "Then will I hear from heaven, and will forgive their sin, and will heal their land" (II Chronicles 7:14).

God could choose to move at any moment on your behalf. In fact, He could keep the battle from ever coming your way. However, He often chooses not to do so. Instead, He waits to see what your response will be when the struggle comes. He waits to see what role pride will play when you are confronted with the blessings He sends your way.

He will resist you if you allow pride and arrogance to lead you. But if you willingly choose to humble yourself and pray, He will be faithful to you and deliver you.

⟫⟫ INTERNALIZING THE MESSAGE

The outcome of our life is determined by how we live moment by moment. The Word instructs us on every aspect of our lives. Yet some instructions serve as foundational principles on which to build our lives.

First Peter 5:5 says, "Likewise, ye younger, submit yourselves unto the elder. Yea, all of you be subject one to another, and be clothed with humility: for God resisteth the proud, and giveth grace to the humble." Take a moment and pay particular attention to the words "and be clothed with humility."

Every morning, we look in our closet to decide what we are going to wear for the day. Often, our mood can determine which garment we choose. Sometimes the activities of the day will dictate the decision for us. Regardless, we choose our outfit for the day and then display it for everyone to see.

We also have a spiritual closet we enter into at the beginning of each day. The choices are laid out before us, and we decide how we will adorn our spirits for that day. James tells us we should be clothed with humility. Let it be the humility of mind, heart, and spirit that is put on display for all the world to see. By doing so, we are ensuring that God is on our side and will faithfully fight our battles for us.